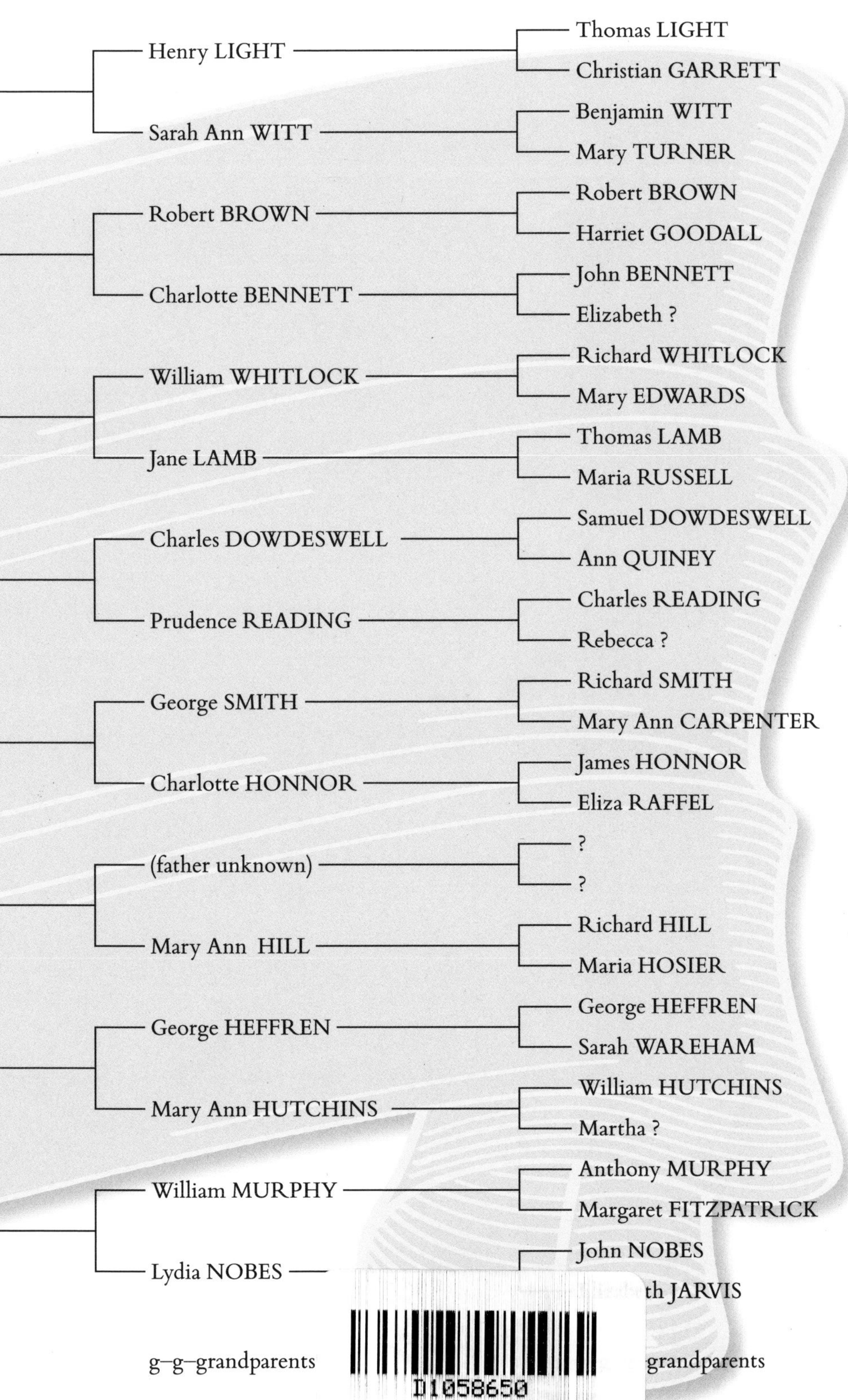

- Henry LIGHT
  - Thomas LIGHT
  - Christian GARRETT
- Sarah Ann WITT
  - Benjamin WITT
  - Mary TURNER
- Robert BROWN
  - Robert BROWN
  - Harriet GOODALL
- Charlotte BENNETT
  - John BENNETT
  - Elizabeth ?
- William WHITLOCK
  - Richard WHITLOCK
  - Mary EDWARDS
- Jane LAMB
  - Thomas LAMB
  - Maria RUSSELL
- Charles DOWDESWELL
  - Samuel DOWDESWELL
  - Ann QUINEY
- Prudence READING
  - Charles READING
  - Rebecca ?
- George SMITH
  - Richard SMITH
  - Mary Ann CARPENTER
- Charlotte HONNOR
  - James HONNOR
  - Eliza RAFFEL
- (father unknown)
  - ?
  - ?
- Mary Ann HILL
  - Richard HILL
  - Maria HOSIER
- George HEFFREN
  - George HEFFREN
  - Sarah WAREHAM
- Mary Ann HUTCHINS
  - William HUTCHINS
  - Martha ?
- William MURPHY
  - Anthony MURPHY
  - Margaret FITZPATRICK
- Lydia NOBES
  - John NOBES
  - Elizabeth JARVIS

g–g–grandparents

grandparents

Common People

Alison Light is a writer and critic who is also currently a Visiting Professor of Modern English Literature and Culture at Newcastle University and at Sheffield Hallam University. She was born in Portsmouth, read English at Churchill College, Cambridge, and was awarded a D.Phil. from Sussex University. She has worked at the BBC, in adult education, and also lectured at Royal Holloway College and University College London. She spent several years helping to establish the Raphael Samuel History Centre and Archive in London. She writes regularly for the press, and also frequently broadcasts on radio and television. Her last book was the much-acclaimed *Mrs Woolf and the Servants*, which is published by Penguin.

By the same author

Forever England: Femininity, Literature and Conservatism between the Wars

Mrs Woolf and the Servants

Common People

The History of an English Family

ALISON LIGHT

FIG TREE
an imprint of
PENGUIN BOOKS

FIG TREE

Published by the Penguin Group
Penguin Books Ltd, 80 Strand, London WC2R 0RL, England
Penguin Group (USA) Inc., 375 Hudson Street, New York, New York 10014, USA
Penguin Group (Canada), 90 Eglinton Avenue East, Suite 700, Toronto, Ontario, Canada M4P 2Y3
(a division of Pearson Penguin Canada Inc.)
Penguin Ireland, 25 St Stephen's Green, Dublin 2, Ireland (a division of Penguin Books Ltd)
Penguin Group (Australia), 707 Collins Street, Melbourne, Victoria 3008, Australia
(a division of Pearson Australia Group Pty Ltd)
Penguin Books India Pvt Ltd, 11 Community Centre, Panchsheel Park, New Delhi – 110 017, India
Penguin Group (NZ), 67 Apollo Drive, Rosedale, Auckland 0632, New Zealand
(a division of Pearson New Zealand Ltd)
Penguin Books (South Africa) (Pty) Ltd, Block D, Rosebank Office Park,
181 Jan Smuts Avenue, Parktown North, Gauteng 2193, South Africa

Penguin Books Ltd, Registered Offices: 80 Strand, London WC2R 0RL, England

www.penguin.com

First published 2014
002

Set in Bembo Book MT Std 12/14.75pt
Typeset by Palimpsest Book Production Limited, Falkirk, Stirlingshire
Printed in Great Britain by Clays Ltd, St Ives plc

A CIP catalogue record for this book is available from the British Library

ISBN: 978-1-905-49038-7

www.greenpenguin.co.uk

Penguin Books is committed to a sustainable future for our business, our readers and our planet. This book is made from Forest Stewardship Council™ certified paper.

For my mother, Barbara Light, with love and gratitude, and in memory of my father, Rob (Sid) Light, who first taught me that

'No man is an island'

Contents

List of Illustrations and Credits

Every effort has been made to trace copyright holders. The publishers will be glad to rectify in future editions any errors or omissions brought to their attention.

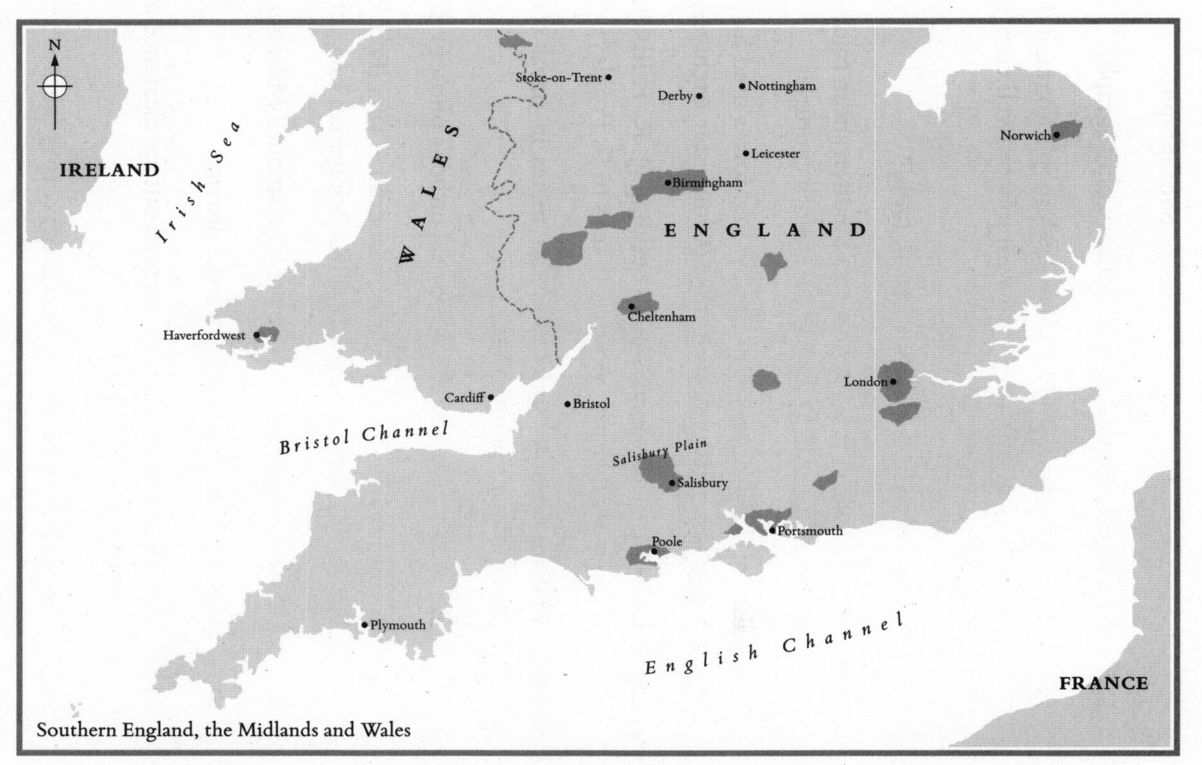

Southern England, the Midlands and Wales

WHITLOCK

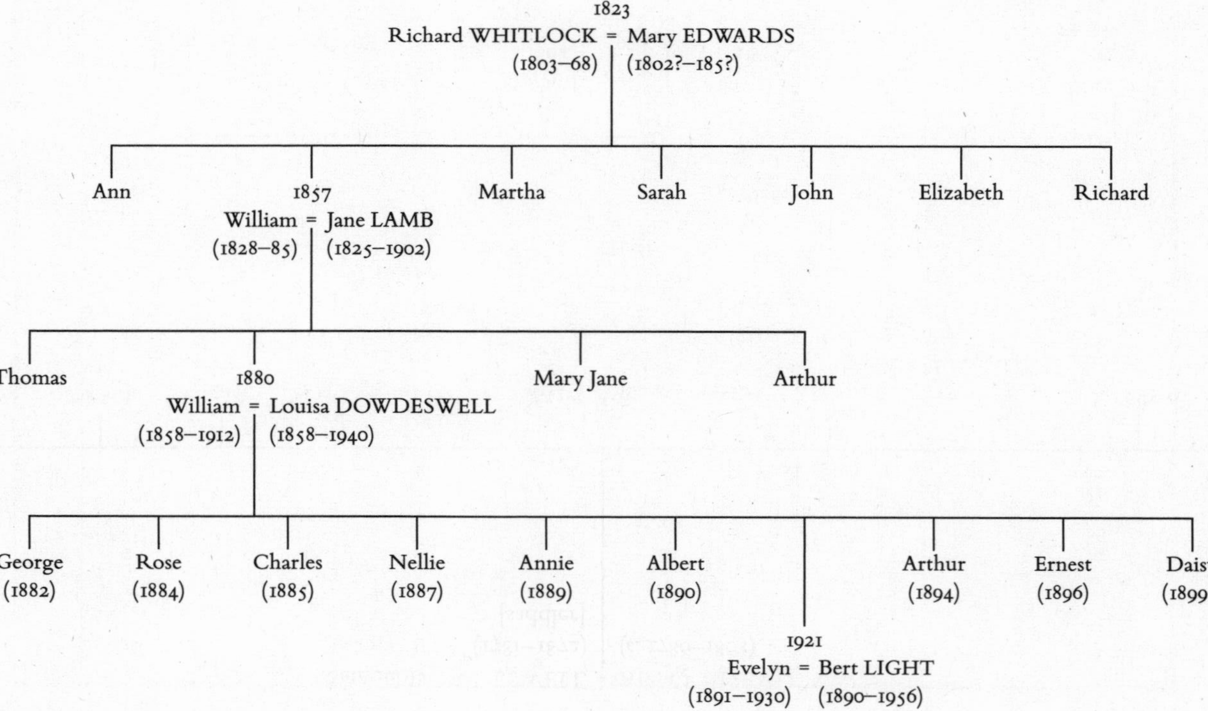

Note to reader: *I have simplified these family trees for the purpose of identifying the people mentioned in the chapters. Dates before 1832 are generally those of baptism not birth.*

DOWDESWELL

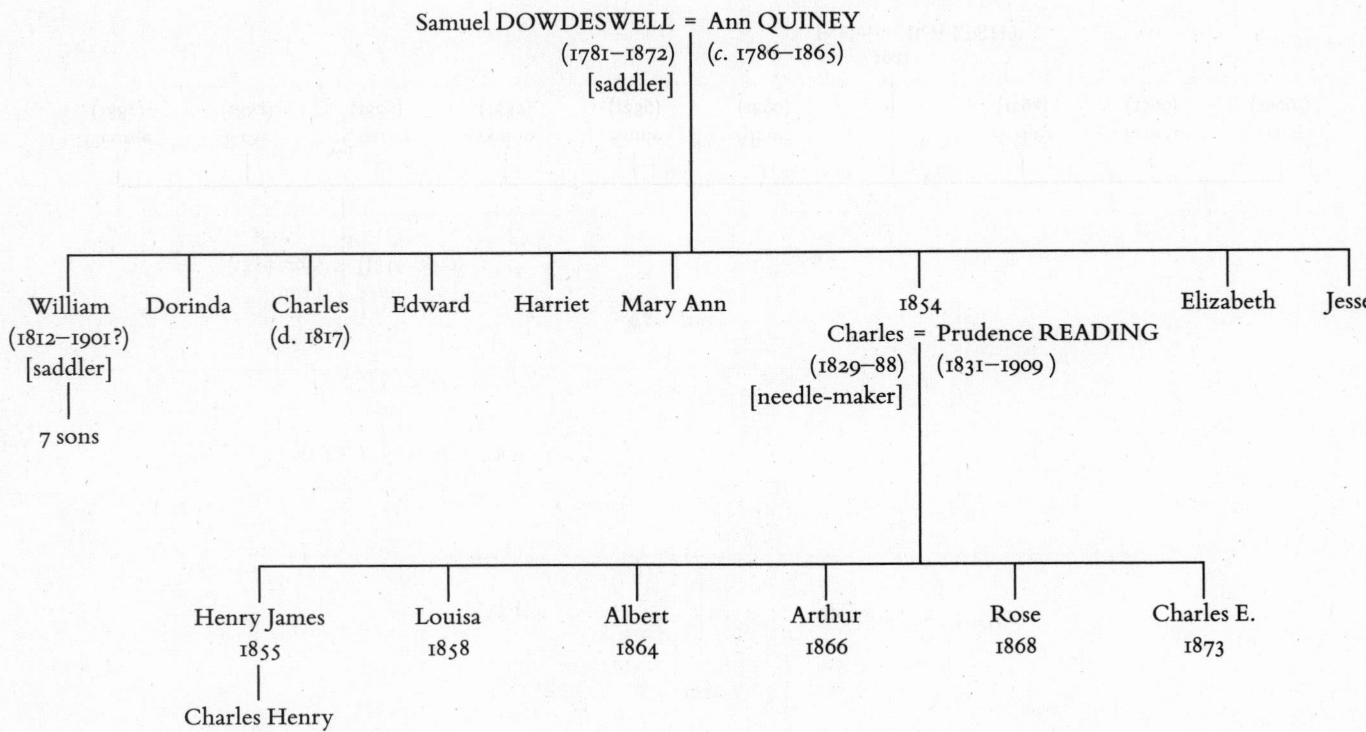

Samuel DOWDESWELL = Ann QUINEY
(1781–1872) (c. 1786–1865)
[saddler]
William
(1812–1901?)
[saddler]
7 sons
Dorinda
Charles
(d. 1817)
Edward
Harriet
Mary Ann
1854
Charles = Prudence READING
(1829–88) (1831–1909)
[needle-maker]
Elizabeth
Jesse
Henry James
1855
Charles Henry
Louisa
1858
Albert
1864
Arthur
1866
Rose
1868
Charles E.
1873

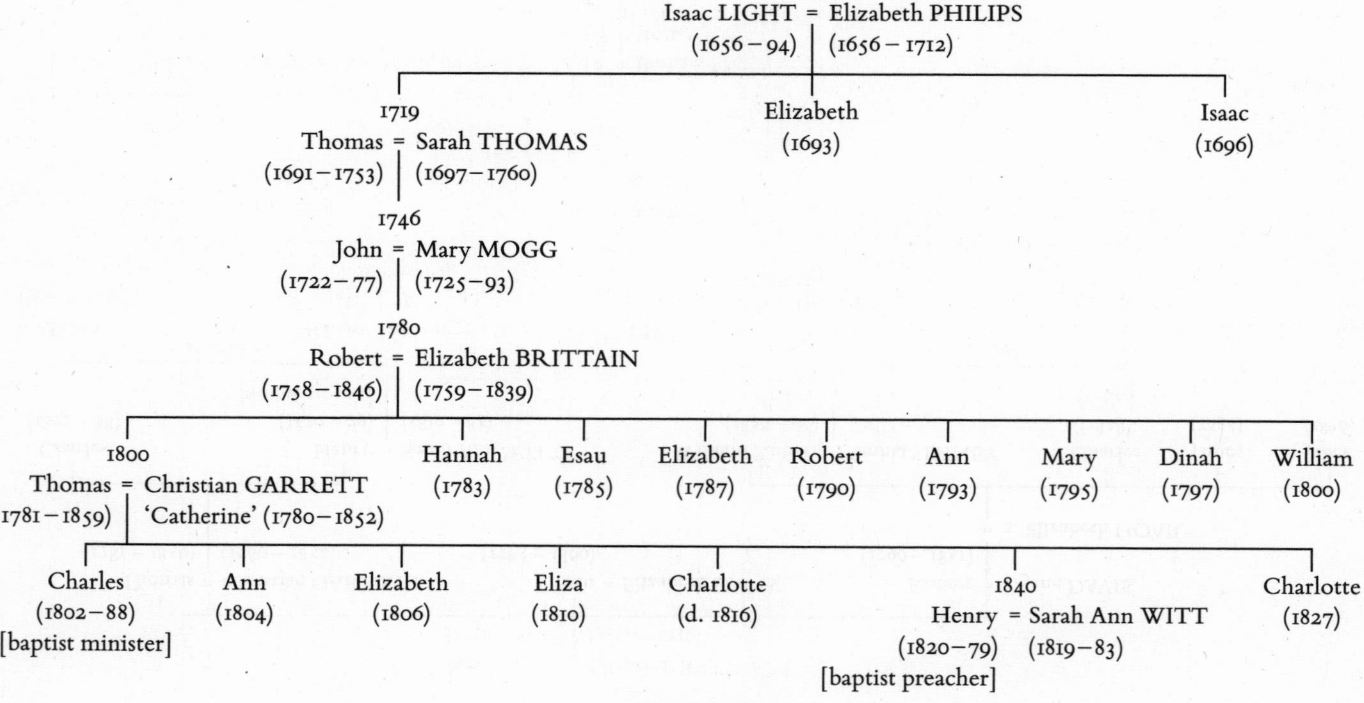
LIGHTS OF SHREWTON
1688
Isaac LIGHT = Elizabeth PHILIPS
(1656 – 94) (1656 – 1712)
1719
Thomas = Sarah THOMAS
(1691 – 1753) (1697 – 1760)
Elizabeth
(1693)
Isaac
(1696)
1746
John = Mary MOGG
(1722 – 77) (1725 – 93)
1780
Robert = Elizabeth BRITTAIN
(1758 – 1846) (1759 – 1839)
1800
Thomas = Christian GARRETT
(1781 – 1859) 'Catherine' (1780 – 1852)
Hannah
(1783)
Esau
(1785)
Elizabeth
(1787)
Robert
(1790)
Ann
(1793)
Mary
(1795)
Dinah
(1797)
William
(1800)
Charles
(1802 – 88)
[baptist minister]
Ann
(1804)
Elizabeth
(1806)
Eliza
(1810)
Charlotte
(d. 1816)
1840
Henry = Sarah Ann WITT
(1820 – 79) (1819 – 83)
[baptist preacher]
Charlotte
(1827)

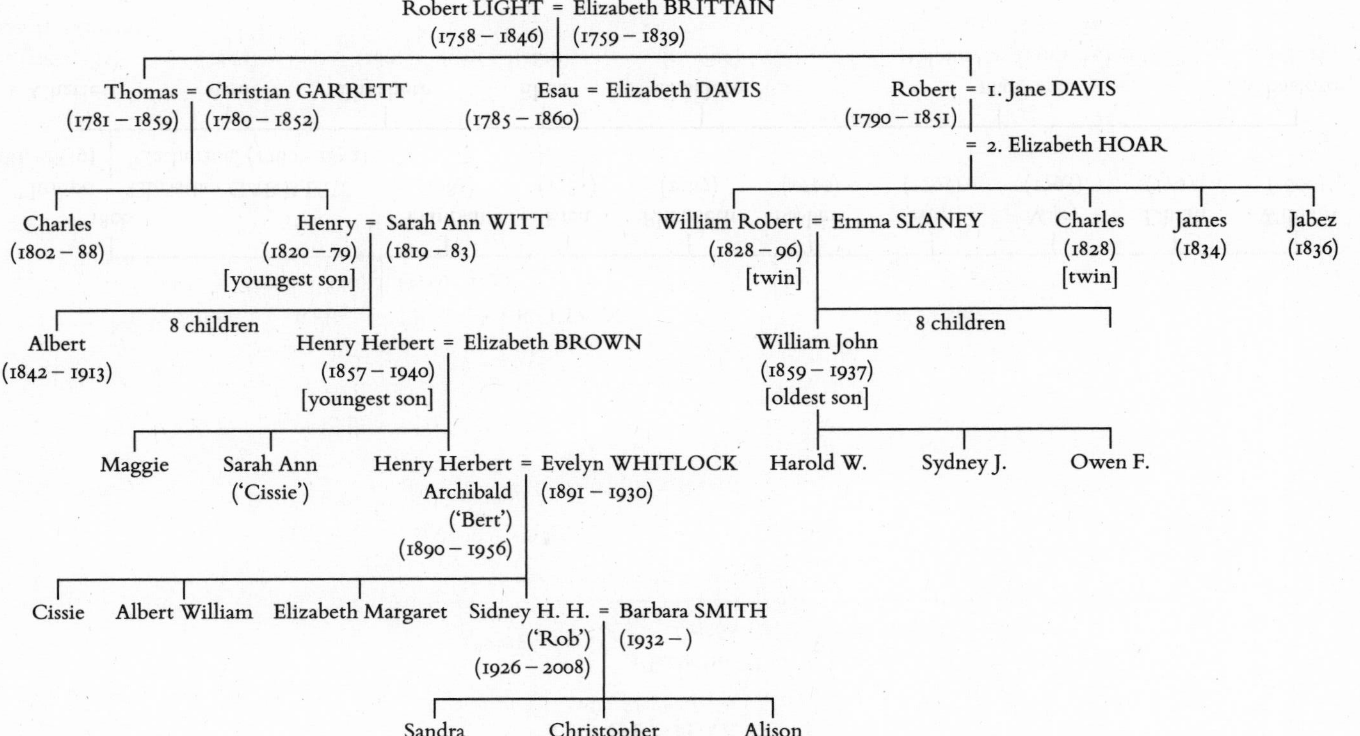

Two branches of the paternal line

HOSIER/HILL

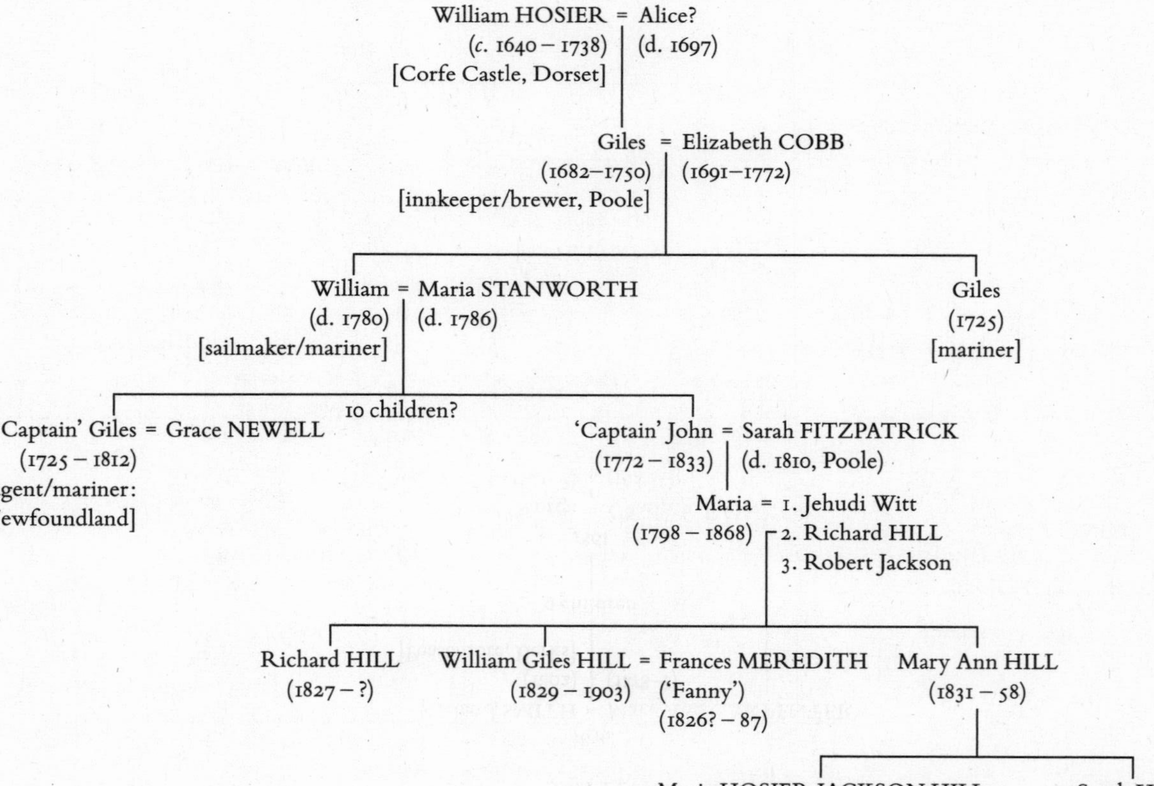

William HOSIER = Alice?
(c. 1640 – 1738)
(d. 1697)
[Corfe Castle, Dorset]
Giles = Elizabeth COBB
(1682–1750)
(1691–1772)
[innkeeper/brewer, Poole]
William = Maria STANWORTH
(d. 1780)
(d. 1786)
[sailmaker/mariner]
Giles
(1725)
[mariner]
10 children?
'Captain' Giles = Grace NEWELL
(1725 – 1812)
[agent/mariner: Newfoundland]
'Captain' John = Sarah FITZPATRICK
(1772 – 1833)
(d. 1810, Poole)
Maria = 1. Jehudi Witt
(1798 – 1868)
2. Richard HILL
3. Robert Jackson
Richard HILL
(1827 – ?)
William Giles HILL = Frances MEREDITH
(1829 – 1903)
('Fanny')
(1826? – 87)
Mary Ann HILL
(1831 – 58)
Maria HOSIER JACKSON HILL
(1851 – 78)
Sarah HILL
(1858 – 1911)

SMITH

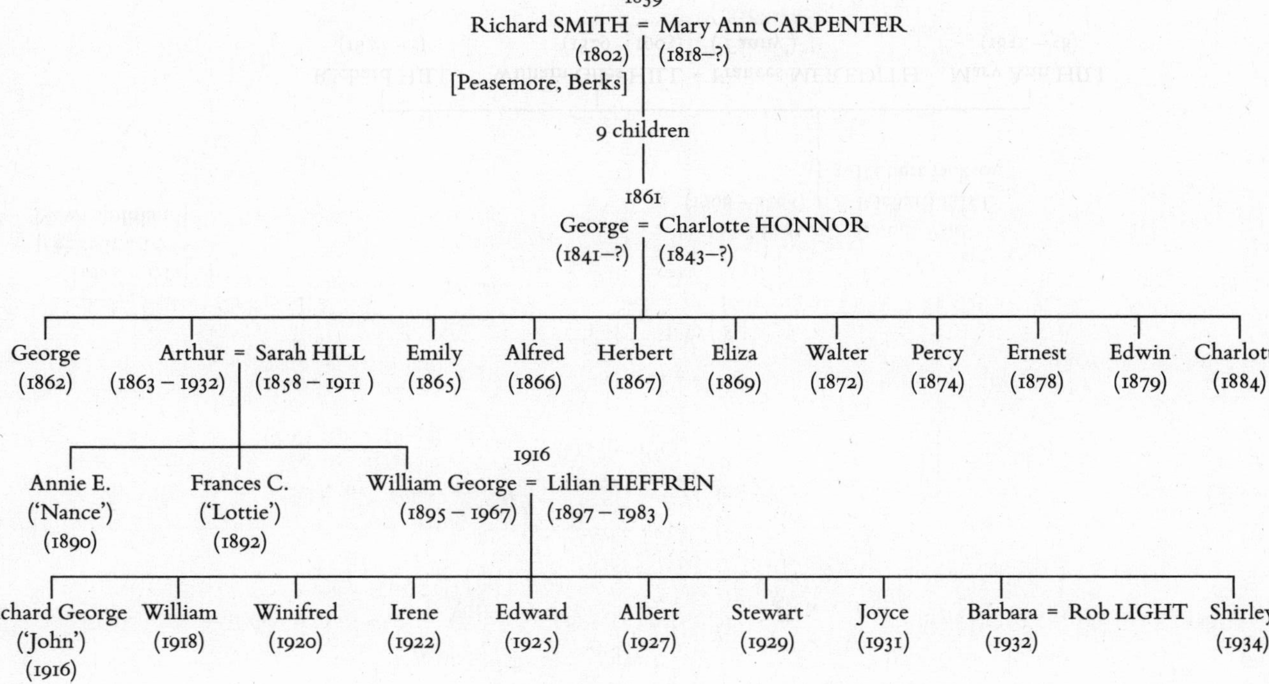
1839
Richard SMITH = Mary Ann CARPENTER
(1802) (1818–?)
[Peasemore, Berks]
9 children
1861
George = Charlotte HONNOR
(1841–?) (1843–?)
George (1862)
Arthur = Sarah HILL
(1863 – 1932) (1858 – 1911)
Emily (1865)
Alfred (1866)
Herbert (1867)
Eliza (1869)
Walter (1872)
Percy (1874)
Ernest (1878)
Edwin (1879)
Charlotte (1884)
Annie E. ('Nance') (1890)
Frances C. ('Lottie') (1892)
1916
William George = Lilian HEFFREN
(1895 – 1967) (1897 – 1983)
Richard George ('John') (1916)
William (1918)
Winifred (1920)
Irene (1922)
Edward (1925)
Albert (1927)
Stewart (1929)
Joyce (1931)
Barbara = Rob LIGHT
(1932)
Shirley (1934)

MURPHY/MILLER

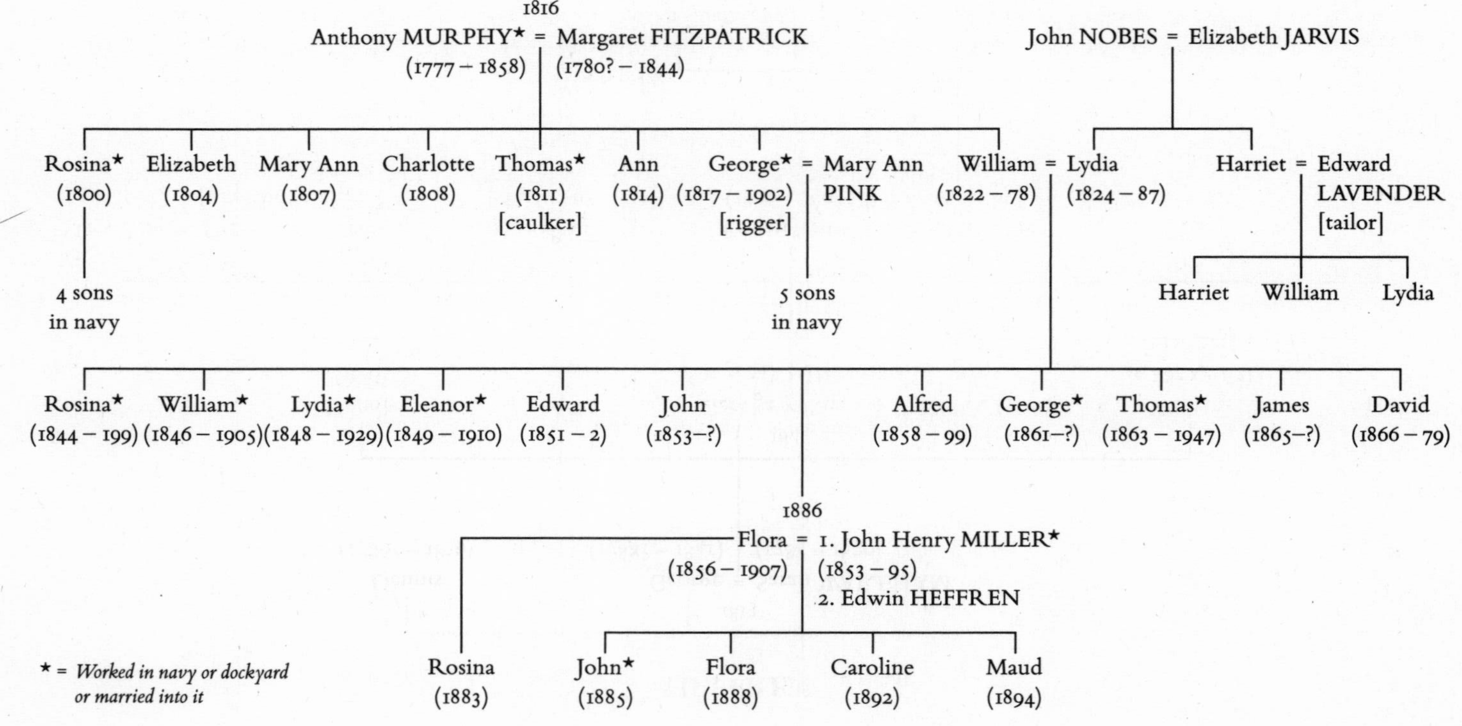

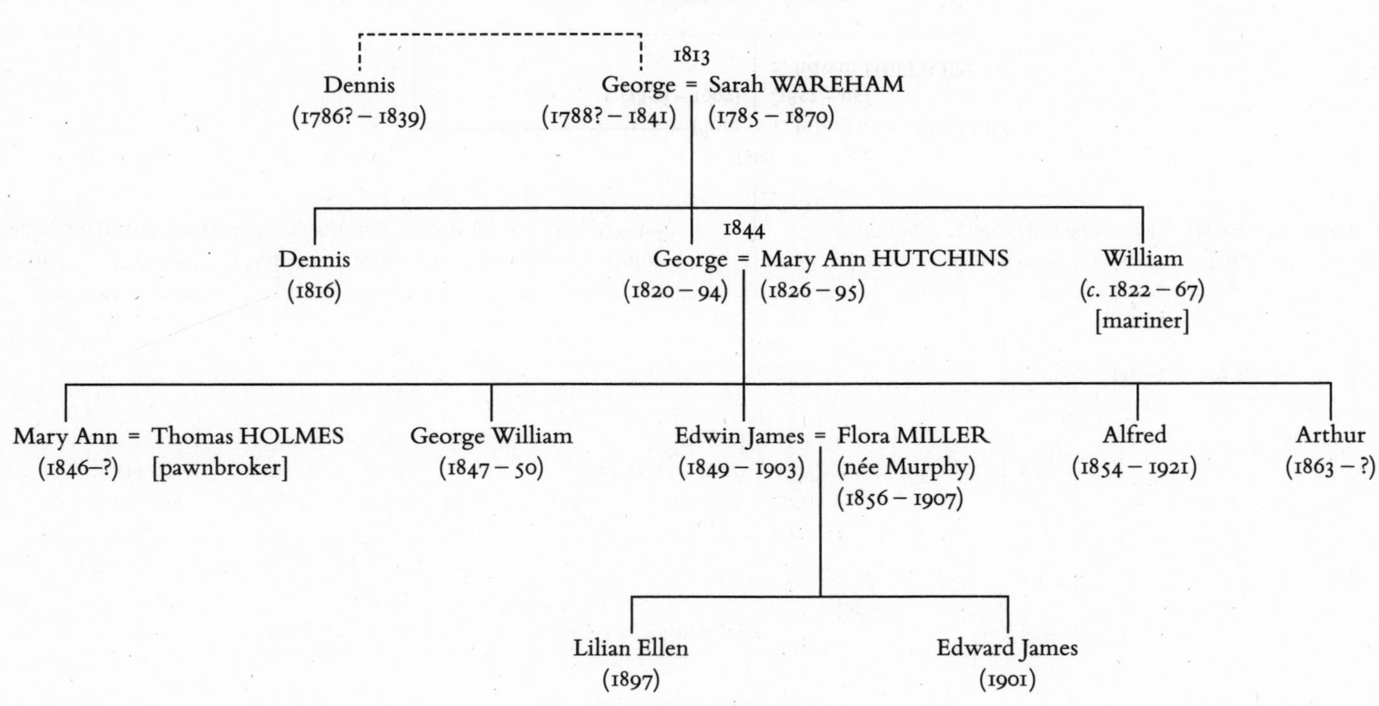
HEFFREN
1813
Dennis
(1786? – 1839)
George = Sarah WAREHAM
(1788? – 1841)
(1785 – 1870)
1844
Dennis
(1816)
George = Mary Ann HUTCHINS
(1820 – 94)
(1826 – 95)
William
(c. 1822 – 67)
[mariner]
Mary Ann = Thomas HOLMES
(1846–?)
[pawnbroker]
George William
(1847 – 50)
Edwin James = Flora MILLER
(1849 – 1903)
(née Murphy)
(1856 – 1907)
Alfred
(1854 – 1921)
Arthur
(1863 – ?)
Lilian Ellen
(1897)
Edward James
(1901)

Preface

I began this book because I realized I had no idea where my family came from. Of course I knew things about my parents, and some stories about my grandparents. But I knew very little, and what I did know was not part of a bigger picture. Our family history was especially truncated. My mother's mother was an orphan; my mother's father left his family behind when he joined the navy. The Smiths, my mother's family, ten brothers and sisters, were a universe unto themselves; they had no roots, it seemed, except in the immediate past. On my father's side, things were equally amputated: his mother died when he was four and nothing much was known about her. His family had then moved across Britain, and lost touch with any cousins or aunts and uncles, had they ever existed. My grandfather Light had died when I was still a baby. I had dabbled in checking births and marriages for my last book, when I researched the women who worked for the writer Virginia Woolf, and had begun an embryonic family tree for my father's seventieth birthday. I hoped that a family history would bridge the gap between the official records and the felt loss of the person who had really lived, a man or woman who had once been known and cared for.

Everyone does family history nowadays. Genealogy used to belong only to the wealthy; once upon a time only they owned a past and laid claim to a history based on land and property. Now everyone who can use a computer or go to a local records office has a stake in the past. Since the 1970s, family history has boomed; it's now the third most popular activity on the Internet in Britain after shopping and porn – and equally addictive, some would say. Once forbidding and hushed, Britain's records offices have become welcoming, embracing family history. Once squeezed into the corners of town museums or town halls, or even, as in Pembrokeshire, taking up the corner of a castle, they have moved into large purpose-built archive centres; local and international societies are mushrooming; magazines and television programmes (like the BBC's hugely successful *Who Do You Think You Are?*) give advice, and an endlessly proliferating variety of websites and software make it possible to turn any home computer into a public search room. What was formerly an eccentric hobby for a handful of antiquarians, or the territory of *Burke's Peerage* and the Herald's Office, is now ancestry.co.uk or findmypast.co.uk. Everyone feels entitled to trace their pedigree or sketch a family tree. But family detectives in search of lost ancestors need to be democrats: their forebears are far more likely to be dustmen than noblemen, labourers rather than landowners. At the beginning of the twentieth century about 85 per cent of the British could be deemed working class.

That, though, is not the point. Poverty homogenizes, whereas family history humanizes. Despite decades of 'history from below', and the immense popularity of historical novels, of rags-to-riches autobiographies, film, TV and heritage re-enactment, there are still few histories of the working poor and even fewer in which they have names and faces, and stories to tell. Family history can individualize what otherwise seems an anonymous crowd. And yet even that may not be what people are after. If they are not searching for a story to tell, a unique person who 'bettered' themselves or one who went to the dogs in a grand manner, most people, it seems, are looking for a place. They want to know where they 'come from', an origin. They want that plot of land which will give *them* a plot, a story of their lives. They want to feel connected, where formerly they felt cut off.

When I began investigating my family's past I soon found I had little to go on. There was scant evidence of the lives of earlier generations. I had a handful of official certificates pertaining to our immediate family (though my parents' birth certificates, like my own, were cheap replacements showing only place and date of birth), but almost no 'ego-documents', as historians now call them – letters, diaries, memoirs – which might give the flavour and attachments of a life. Nothing had survived: school reports, farm or shop accounts, passports, certificates from work or Sunday school, union or political party membership cards, character references, mortgage documents or deeds to land or graves, not even shopping lists or cheque stubs. Had such evidence ever existed? I did not know. The ancestors were silent, unattached, and also invisible. While I was growing up, I never saw wedding photographs of my grandparents on either side, no pictures of chubby Edwardian babies on leopard-skin rugs, no school or college photographs, studio portraits of budding beauties or earnest young men in uniform. There were no visits to family graves where a nineteenth-century epitaph or two might have sketched in an outline; no portraits hung on walls. Our own photo album stretched only as far back as army photographs of the 1940s, my father in shorts in Egypt. There were none of him as a child with his parents or siblings. My mother appeared briefly in button boots, but she too had no prehistory.

We were city creatures for at least a couple of generations, that much I knew. We rented Victorian terraced housing, like the vast majority of Britons. There was no family pile or seat to return to, an attic in a farm or manor house to investigate, where the relics of our past were stored. I was not going to be able to track my family through a treasury of biographical objects which might stand in for their lives. Nor were there heirlooms, if an heirloom, unlike a bequest, comes to you from those unknown in your lifetime, a sign of continuity and care, and, usually, of respectability. No family Bible with its litany of marriages and baptisms on the flyleaf; no oil paintings, *objets d'art*, silverware or porcelain, cultured pearls or diamond rings passed down through the generations; no grandfather clock or dresser, fur coat or fob-watch, nor the lace tablecloths or pillowcases of a trousseau, no christening robes or apostle spoons; not even a souvenir mug or trinket, a plate to mark Victoria's Diamond Jubilee or a medal from a child's sports day. No battered toys cherished from nursery days or books inscribed from doting relations. My parents began married life with a couple of relics from wartime. A scratchy grey-brown army blanket that did the rounds of our beds; and my father's khaki, sausage-shaped kitbag, which served to take the washing to the new launderette in the fifties, my brother and sister, each clutching a leather loop, swinging me as I sat astride. Our hand-me-downs were not heirlooms to look forward to but cast-offs. Such ornaments as we acquired were modern, like the pottery Spanish donkey that graced our sitting-room mantelpiece. A holiday memento from a family friend, his panniers sometimes held a shilling or two for the electricity meter (forty years later I salvaged it when my parents moved, and now use it for paper clips).

Wherever my forebears had come from, they had travelled lightly through time, without baggage. Who had these travellers been? Was their lack of belongings a sign of deprivation or of mobility (or both)? Had they been desperate or enterprising, both or neither? The paucity of letters and papers suggested little schooling, but an absence is not a proof. Any treasures that my mother's mother had inherited might have gone in the Blitz of 1941 when their house was bombed. What did a lack of belongings mean? Were belongings and belonging related? I knew, or thought I did, that they had been poor, these working people from the past, but who were 'the poor'? And why had they been poor? Every historian, like every biographer, wonders how much is chance, how much is choice, how much people's lives are shaped and limited by forces far bigger than themselves.

★

I did not know what I would find when I started digging into the past behind the figures of my four grandparents. This book follows that archaeology. It begins with the woman I knew least about and who had died longest ago, Evelyn Whitlock, my father's mother, and with my search for her grave; it ends with my mother's mother, Lilian Heffren, who was a part of my childhood, and with a return to my home town where she had also grown up. Each pair of grandparents is necessarily linked together and, as each section of the book became the back-history to a grandparent's life, each was framed by a sense of what I could remember of my relation to them, or what I knew about them from my parents. This grounding in time allowed me to take the leap into the past and gave me a place to go back to. I also hoped that my speaking voice would anchor the reader as we moved through time. Family history is a special form of group biography since the writer is ineluctably one of the group. But this was not to be a memoir of my own life, nor of my parents' – that would be another story.

Some part of me assumed that I would find an ancestral village or home, but what I immediately learnt was that my ancestors had long been on the move: servants, sailors, watermen, farm carters, for instance, and artisans in the building trade. My grandmother Evelyn's grave opened up a road for me, taking me into the territory that historians call 'the Industrial Revolution', a world made by rural migrants who had come from all over Britain and beyond. My father's forebears, the Lights, chose to leave their Wiltshire village, in deepest England, to work in a growing city, and my mother's antecedents had crossed both land and sea to arrive finally in Portsmouth, the premier naval base on the south coast. Their nineteenth century had been one of motion: Britain's industries, and the navy which was the mainstay of its empire, needed the migrants who had left home and hearth to create the nation's wealth. But those who left had different stories to tell. As I learnt to 'do' family history, first as an armchair traveller on the Internet, and then in the regional history centres scattered across the country where the older records are kept, I found myself making a series of actual journeys across county boundaries, mimicking in a small way the journeys my forebears had made to find work. I was getting to know different localities in Britain, mainly across the south of England, and realizing too that family history, with its spiralling lists of names, can be very claustrophobic. I decided to ventilate the stories I was telling with some reflection on the process, now and then, just to let the texture breathe a little, and to capture, if I could, something of the emotional see-saw which accompanies archive visits and historical discoveries.

My first instinct in writing *Common People* was to find the people who had been missing from my past. I wanted not so much to rescue them from 'the condescension of posterity' – Edward Thompson's marvellous phrase in *The Making of the English Working Class* (1963) – but from sheer oblivion. The word 'common' has a long history in English, but my choice of *Common People*, not *The Common People*, for a title was deliberate. I did not want to heroize the working people I wrote about, nor treat them as a collective noun. Nor did I want to avoid the derogatory overtones associated with the word, of the sort I frequently heard in my girlhood: 'It's common to eat in the street,' I was told, or 'Pierced ears are common' – meaning, *not* that everyone could be seen sandwich in hand, or that ear-piercing was now all the rage, but that it was lower class, and all the worse for that. Class consciousness of this kind is a way of policing each other but also of generating who we are, and its effects go deep. In *Great Expectations* (1860), that painful anatomy of becoming a snob, Charles Dickens has his anti-hero, Pip, discover he is just a 'common labouring boy' when he visits the home of Miss Havisham and is taunted by her proud niece, Estella. Squirming with shame and misery from this 'smart without a name', he is reduced to kicking a wall and twisting his hair, as he swallows down his tears. But Dickens – as ever – is an acute psychologist. When Pip goes home to the blacksmith's forge, he tells his expectant relations the most tremendous lies about the superior lives he has encountered, inflating them and puffing himself up by proxy. Nothing stays the same after this exposure to the judgement of others; he remains forever insecure and unsettled. Every family has its tall stories – the inheritance that mysteriously disappeared, the wealthy connections lost to time, the exploits exaggerated or invented. I wanted to take seriously the family legends and romances I heard as a child and ponder their psychological truth. Such fabrications seem to be – as Dickens knew – at the heart of class feelings, part and parcel of a divided society.

The people in this book are nearly all nineteenth-century people. Like many others who are moved to write their life stories, James Dawson Burn, in his *Autobiography of a Beggar Boy*, published in 1855, used writing to secure a sense of who he was. Often he felt 'like a feather on the stream . . . continually whirled along from one eddy to another', adding that 'amid the universal transformations of things in the moral and physical world, my own condition has been like a dissolving view, and I have been so tossed in the rough blanket of fate, that my identity, if at any time a reality, must have been one which few could venture to swear to'. But there is a wider, historical dimension to Burn's feelings of being adrift and rudderless. The period of 'universal transformations' he refers to was the making of Britain as the first industrial nation, which depended on a migrant workforce vulnerable to the vagaries of the market, economic depression and boom, and the rise and fall of wages. Versions of Burn's story are now retold across the globe, and although the stories I tell here are very

British, I hope they resonate with those of others who start from elsewhere and whose home turf is very different.

★

Ancestor worship is common to all human cultures and as old as the hills. Those existential questions – 'Where do I come from and what has shaped me?' – are hardly recent. People have always wondered whom they 'take after' and what they have inherited from their forebears – the tendency to melancholy as well as the receding hairline – and what room they have to make something of themselves. Like all historians, family historians are resurrectionists, repopulating the past, trying to put flesh to bones and bring past eras to life. But they are also salvagers. More than any others, perhaps, they are motivated by the search for lost objects. If family history is for some an extended mourning, they hope to recover and reuse the past, which otherwise seems like wreckage. The central moral or ethical questions of historical inquiry are unavoidable and immediate in family history: why does the past matter? How much and what do we owe the dead? I returned in my mind many times, while writing this book, to a line from the great Russian lyric poet Joseph Brodsky: 'What's the point of forgetting/ if it ends in dying?'

Professional historians have generally given family history short shrift. It's 'history lite' or 'comfort-zone history'; solipsistic and myopic. Its practitioners, critics say, are only interested in themselves. The family history we choose to write, the past we believe in, is always a selection of stories from the many at our disposal in the past. Family history individualizes but it can also privatize, make us feel more singular. I have wanted to resist that way of 'finding my past'; to pay my respects but to look for wider perspectives on what too easily is seen as a chapter of accidents, hapless human tragedy in the lives of those struggling to find decent housing and steady work. I have no doubt that some of my ancestors were vicious, stupid and cruel. I wouldn't have liked them much if I had met them. But why were their lives so hard and what were their 'options', if they had them? Family history worth its salt asks these big questions about economic forces, political decisions, local government, urban history, social policy, as well as the character of individuals and the fate of their families. It moves us from a sense of the past to an idea of history, where we are no longer its centre, and where arguments must be had. It entails loss too, not least in seeing ourselves as representative, rather than simply unique.

'Doing' family history has flourished in Britain at just the time when mobility is the norm, when fewer families live within a stone's throw of each other, when fewer families actually live as families. Discovering shared family members from the past also creates links between the living, though usually at a distance, and I met many remote relations online with whom I had a forebear in common. Long-lost ancestors can, of course, be infinitely preferable to the families in which we live: grander or more victimized, apparently more interesting, more appealing, morally more worthy. 'We all have half a dozen possible ancestries to choose from, and fantasy and projections can furnish us with a dozen more,' the historian Raphael Samuel wrote in *Island Stories* (1998), wondering if people turn to make-believe identities in the past because they can no longer find a home for their ideal selves in the future. Family history might be a sign of the morbidity of our culture, the frantic search for origins a measure of the deathliness of a post-industrial society where museums open every week. Or is it rather a sign of the vitality of the historical imagination, evidence of the huge appetite and curiosity about past lives that flourishes well beyond the purlieus of the university?

At its best, as I suggest in this book, family history is a trespasser, disregarding the boundaries between local and national, private and public, and ignoring the hedges around fields of academic study; taking us by surprise into unknown worlds. None of that makes it automatically democratic or radical in outlook. It can be profoundly conservative, upholding the idea that blood must always be thicker than the more fluid bonds of a civil society where strangers work out how to live together. It has its own preferred versions of the national past and its often unspoken assumptions about who belongs there. Like all history, family history, once it is more than a list of names and family trees, is never neutral in what it wants to say about the past. This, of course, makes it more interesting as well as politically volatile.

As I have written this book, many questions have weighed on my mind but one more than any other: why do we need these stories of people we can never know? What is it we are after and why do we so regret not talking (or not listening) to our elders when they were alive? Partly, of course, it is about ourselves, about our need to make reparation to the dead, to apologize to them for not realizing that they too had lives like ourselves – fallible, well intentioned, incomplete – and to understand how mistakes were made that resulted in our lives; how much was accident, how much choice. We think we are asking to be forgiven, but perhaps we want to offer forgiveness too, to see our parents as children again, full of possible futures, not yet thwarted or humdrum. But how much historical freight is enough and how much weighs us down? As culture becomes more 'globalized', and migration becomes the norm, as more of us than ever live in cities, what do we want from those stories which both anchor us and tie us down, evoking lost ancestral places to which we can never return? Can there be a family history for a floating world?

Prologue

A Child's Sense of the Past

When I recall how I first knew about the past, I hear a medley of grown-up voices telling stories, weaving in and out, like the soundtrack to some lost film, until one or other suddenly breaks through the hubbub to regale the audience, and the cacophony subsides into a chorus of 'Well, of all the . . .' or 'Some people, I ask you!', or 'Hang on a minute, and another thing . . .', on and on, each vying for their turn like soloists in an unending improvisation. (Another fainter noise is heard in the background: the clatter of trays and teaspoons, cups settling in their saucers.) Stories weren't so much told as staged. My mother, for instance, eyebrows raised, would mimic accents or strike attitudes, her hands slicing the air for punctuation, gesticulating for effect. Timing had to be nicely judged, since the aim was to embroider a tale without making too much of a palaver. The point of a good story was in how you told it. But the past, when I first heard of it, had no dates. There was 'when you were just a toddler' or 'not even a twinkle in your father's eye' or 'when your dad's dad was alive'. Time was measured in people, by their length and breadth, as it were, like hands for a horse, a physical spanning in which the listener's size was also gauged. (Recently, asking my mother which year my father's father died, she thought and said, 'That was when you were still in the pram, sitting up,' calculating my age at the time.) Time flew backwards in generations, like a kite, leaving you a tiny figure, holding on, tethered.

The past was an enormous, seamless stretch without horizon, as daunting as Southsea Common on our Sunday promenade, all that grass, reaching from the main road across to the beach, much too far for a small child to manage. Portsmouth, the city where we lived, was saturated with the past, but the different stories about different times had been plunged into one big wash in my mind, swirling round indiscriminately. The sailor biting on his rum-soaked handkerchief as the surgeon hacked off his leg with a handsaw (as told on a trip to Nelson's Victory *in the local dockyard) was as recent, and as remote, to me as the bedbugs which my mother said she used to pick off her bedroom wall with a bar of soap or singe off with a candle when she was a kid. One of the terrifying* 'dares' of a Saturday morning, when I was being minded by my brother and sister, was edging our way across the glass-strewn windowsills of a bombed-out house; yet my sense of that war was confused with the litany of names on the stone anchors and obelisks along the seafront: Trafalgar, Alma, Aboukir, and on the white bulk of the cenotaph listing the dead of both wars. My father's stories of close shaves during the Blitz – his mates sneaking to the better seats at the Prince's when the lights went down while those who stayed in the front stalls were blown to smithereens – mingled with what he told me on family outings, bluebelling or 'wooding' high up on Portsdown Hill, overlooking the town. There were the forts out at sea, shimmering in the distance, and here was Fort Widley, nearby on the Hill – all of them 'Palmerston's Follies', erected as a bulwark against a French invasion. I had no idea who – or when – Palmerston was.

Before I went to the grammar school I played in the street and made up my own stories for my gang of friends to enact, tales from the past which were added to our store of dressing-up clothes, as we cut off each other's heads or escaped from concentration camps. We raided the past like a props department to supply us with imaginary sets, borrowing from whatever we had seen at the Gaumont Picture Club on a Saturday morning – Kenneth More in Reach for the Sky or Virginia McKenna as Violette Szabo in Carve Her Name with Pride furnished a few wartime scenarios, I remember – and the BBC children's serials at Sunday teatime, Kenilworth and The Three Musketeers also come to mind. When Doctor Who came on the television, I loved the idea of time-travelling, the Doctor collecting companions by chance from the centuries: the wild, kilted Jamie from the killing fields of Culloden and Victoria, a prissy, crinolined miss from her stuffy, upholstered home. This was the past of outings and trips, to be dropped in on, like a series of wishes granted by the genie; they were spots of time without causation or consequence.

When I began to borrow books from the Carnegie Public Library on Fratton Road I revelled in a more, not less, porous present into which I could expand. My mother, who was the reader in the family at that time, never touched non-fiction and neither did I. The Arabian Nights, Grimm and Andersen, fairy tales and the myths of ancient Greece and Rome, took up where my weekly comics or Children's Hour on TV, peopled by talking animals and toys, left off. Here was another shape-changing world in which a person became a star or a flower, or at worst a spider. I loved to be transported: 'Up the wooden hill to the

Land of Nod,' I'd repeat, holding on to the banister, as I went upstairs to bed.

A child's world is perhaps always amorphous, searching for shapes to contain it, drifting between parallel universes, overlapping with, but not matching, where the adults live, full of multiple, shifting dimensions, more like a kaleidoscope of patterns than a stable view. This inner world is protean, can make infinite space of a nutshell; its walls are thin and airy, yet they can also stretch and insulate. This is the boundlessness of boredom, of fear and of play; the place where the child is perhaps most itself and most inaccessible, and where even at the bleakest of times, when all the colour is drained and the walls begin to buckle rather than bend, something which is isolated is also preserved. If this world exists in time then it is the time of dream and nightmare, of fugue rather than narrative. The past may be part of its material, its stuff for a burgeoning ego, for the reverie and wool-gathering which makes up the fabric of a self. Historical thinking, perhaps, involves separation, distinction and discrimination, a boundary, however temporary, between the self and others.

When I was small I liked to stretch my hand behind the wardrobe in my brother's bedroom. I discovered there a gas tap from the days when we lived upstairs in three rooms and this was our kitchen. I couldn't remember those times, but that tap was evidence, cold and decisive, and I liked to touch it. It was a part of history, an anchor, where personal experience, as relayed to me by the adults, remained vague and misty. Their past was not real to me, or rather it was as real as all the other make-believe in my life. I knew from an early age that my grandmother had been an orphan, dumped in the local institution with her baby brother, and shunted into domestic service as a teenager. I don't think I was at all harrowed by the stories of getting up at five to skivvy, carrying cans of water, 'blacking the ranges' (whatever they were). I found it thrilling, as fabulous and glamorous as Cinderella covered in ash. Her stories added lustre to her because they gave her a past and she had lived to tell the tale. It was many years before I could think of it as history. I only had her word for it, after all. To be history it had to become bigger, more peopled, and, like the gas tap, held at arm's length.

I absorbed the adults' stories, as perhaps all children do, like a sponge. What strikes me now is not that it was hard to know about the past as a child but how uncomfortably close, how awfully intimate it could be, rubbing shoulders with the present, fraying its edge. No distance between then and now, only a hairline fracture. The past was just around the corner, left over from yesterday like the spent fireworks we collected from the pavement and gutters the morning after Guy Fawkes, a faint whiff of gunpowder still in the air. The past lurked and lingered and could easily be surprised. It particularly favoured the dark and the dangerous – the dank corners in the Round Tower at Old Portsmouth, for instance, where you could imagine, my mother said, all the people who had been imprisoned there, or the soldiers who had worn out the steps, trudging to and fro. I was troubled by ghosts (ghost stories ran in the family); ghosts were where the past leaked into the present like dye. I certainly learnt that the past was perilous, stalked by legendary illnesses – whooping cough, scarlet fever, rickets, polio – which had ravaged my relatives; people in the past, they said, had to live in pigstyes and they died like flies. Women were its walking wounded. In fact their legs, clotted with veins, seemed especially to have borne the brunt of the long march into the present. I was a sickly child and I may have been especially alert to physical frailty, but I think we were all brought up with a dizzying sense of mortality, of time rushing, a whirling dervish, or a wind spinning you headlong from past to present to the graveyard. Among the lines of poetry my father was wont to recite were those relentless ones from FitzGerald's translation of The Rubáiyát of Omar Khayyám*:*

The Moving Finger writes; and, having writ,
Moves on: nor all thy Piety nor Wit
Shall lure it back to cancel half a Line,
Nor all thy Tears wash out a Word of it.

They surface in my memory, tied to another of my father's favourite tags, more mirthful but more doom-laden, 'Eat, drink and be merry, for tomorrow we die.' The past was always blowing up a gale. It was important to wrap up warm.

Everything the grown-ups said about their own childhood and the past, the vehemence with which they animated it, made it seem stronger, smellier, dirtier, louder and brighter than the present. It was a lot for the children to take in. We fidgeted on laps, or made the tea and passed round the biscuits. We weren't encouraged to be raconteurs. I think everyone craved the limelight, yet at the same time dreaded showing off or making an exhibition of themselves. Naturally the adults took up the most room since they were making up for lost time. A great many of the stories that I heard as a child dealt in extremity of one sort or another – poverty, cruelty, suffering – but they were told for their entertain-

ment value and shared theatre, always for a laugh. The hilarity made it safe, temporarily at least, to venture across a minefield of undetonated memories. On the other hand it was their being stories, the very making of a narrative, which protected against any random flak. A story gave durability and duration to what had been broken or fleeting. Perhaps the main reason that I couldn't distinguish between my family's past and that of our city was because the grown-ups couldn't either: they didn't seem to have enough of a continuous past to separate from it. The past was inchoate, embryonic, pressing on the membrane of the present; stories helped bring it to birth.

This was why the sing-song became such an important ritual in our life, as it did in so many other families. It gave us the continuity, or the illusion of it, which allowed us to see ourselves as a group with a past. When my mother's family got together and sang, they overflowed with strong feeling, heady stuff, often nostalgic in the original sense of painfully longing for home and for the peace of a perfect union: 'A garden of Eden,' we'd sing, 'just made for two, and nothing to spoil the view.' But the songs also celebrated the unattached, spontaneous and casual – strolling, roaming, tramping, being of no fixed abode. Needs were declared minimal – 'All I want is a room somewhere,/ Far away from the cold night air' – and the best things in life were free: 'I'd rather have Shanks's pony!' The sing-song was a makeshift, eclectic form: 'What shall we have now?' someone would ask, and bystanders in the pub would chip in with their own requests. It was robust, inventive and compensatory, drawing at random on a repertoire of melodies and music-hall renditions, going back to my grandmother's childhood and forward to the Beatles ('Yesterday' was an inevitable favourite, relished for its melancholy) or the show-stoppers from Rodgers and Hammerstein. These weren't 'traditional'. In fact we borrowed shamelessly from the Irish or the cockneys ('Maybe it's because I'm a Londoner,' we'd sing gaily). I didn't learn any English folk songs until I was at school, when Ewan MacColl and others introduced them on the radio.

Our sing-song, in other words, was an invented tradition. My parents were fond of a drink, and had as rich a vocabulary for the shades and nuances of inebriation as the Inuit do for snow, but the sing-song depended on domesticating an older drinking culture. Men, women and children (if the landlord was lenient) all sat together on plush velvet seats in the 'lounge', quite unlike the spit-and-sawdust public bars in which my grandfathers had drowned their sorrows or had to be fetched from before they drank the housekeeping money. Of course, the sing-song was a fabrication. That was its point. It wrought a harmonious present out of rows and rivalries, and it mended a past full of rents and tears. (I was a keen performer, but whenever I remember my solos I see my sister's face, clouded with resentment.) Sing-songs were also one of the few times when children were on equal terms with the adults and could join in without the usual put-downs that peppered grown-up conversation – 'What do you know about it?' or 'Who asked for your opinion?' The sing-song defied the old adage that children 'should be seen but not heard'.

I think now that we were fashioning a shared past from something as yet only imminent in the history books, which hadn't yet turned into history, let alone 'history from below': the lives of the vast majority of city-dwellers, the great unwashed, the itinerants and unrecruitables, the 'unskilled', the people whose tenancies were always precarious and whose footholds on the social ladder were slippery, like our own. Though I didn't know it then, what I took to be a tradition of song was evidence of our lack of tradition, of our migrations and relocations and flittings, of people who found themselves marooned in the tenements and slums, or bombed out and rehoused. Our songs and our stories were a safe harbour; in singing, we found a settlement in the past, if only for a while. We thought we had always been there, but we had only just arrived.

PART ONE

Missing Persons

1 Evelyn's Grave

When my father was very ill with cancer, I went in search of his mother's grave. It was an odd, possibly morbid thing to do. Family history begins with missing persons – missed in both senses of the word. But when do we register an absence as a loss? The absence, not of mothers and fathers, brothers or sisters, close and intimate relations whose deaths or disappearances are felt on the pulses, but of older connections – grandparents, great-grandparents – 'ancestors', who might only linger in the memory and conversation of one's elders. One obvious answer is when mortality is borne in on us, comes home to us in the form of a generation dying, or when, Janus-faced in our own middle age, every disconnection reminds us of our own future. Faced with the death of a parent, only then can we begin to understand what our parents themselves have been through. In my mid-fifties, I was appalled by the prospect of my father dying, despite his being a man in his eighties. But *his* mother had died of tuberculosis when he was an infant. Now I began to wonder what he had lost and what I, through him, had missed. I thought that by visiting the grave I could make it up to him somehow – an absurdly grandiose but understandable desire.

Of course my father's mother, Evelyn Light, had been a comfortable absence long before I decided she was missing. Like most children, I looked into the past for my own reflection, and my father's story only mattered to me because it explained why I was born so far from his own birthplace in Birmingham, Britain's second-largest city. As a child I looked for inheritance by reading faces and finding shared traits – the shape of a nose, colour of hair and eyes, the roundness of a face. With my broad nose and the pouches under my eyes, I 'took after' the Lights. This suited me. Evelyn was a romantic figure, the good mother who had died young, part of a lost childhood. My other grandmother, my mother's mother, was anything but mysterious; she was 'Nan', a constant presence if not a known quantity. But for most of my life I was happy not to know anything more about this missing person.

After his wife Evelyn's death, my grandfather had brought his four children to Portsmouth on the south coast. My father had never returned to Birmingham, a place we thought as remote and exotic as Timbuctoo. We knew no one from that side of the family – the Whitlocks. Dad could not remember his mother; she was called 'Evie' by his father, he thought, in later years. There were only a couple of photos of her, undated, but no letters or keepsakes, bits of jewellery, souvenirs or household goods; my sister Sandra had inherited 'Evelyn' as a middle name, but she thought it horribly old-fashioned. Dad had not been taken to his mother's funeral but a tiny remembrance card had survived, bordered in silver and black, with 'In Memoriam' and a spray of snowdrops draped over a cross on its cover. Inside it gave notice that she was interred at Brandwood End Cemetery, the funeral 'furnished' by N. Wheatley and Sons of Station Street, Birmingham. This was my lead.

I suppose I imagined a quest of sorts, and saw myself in a foggy graveyard, searching alone among the tombs, until I came across a weather-beaten stone with a barely legible inscription: name and dates – 'Evelyn Prudence Light, 1891–1930' – and perhaps a flourish or two. I would photograph the memorial and take it to show my father; there might be a few tears. This pilgrimage would end in reunion. Dad had been cut off from his early childhood, his mother and his antecedents, and I hoped to give him pleasure by restoring some of that – a tall order, and one I could have followed at any time in the previous thirty years. What was I thinking of? But I was in the grip of grief and I didn't see that it was my own need that drove me, not his. Perhaps it was a way of staving off death: I couldn't save my father but I could resurrect his mother. Perhaps I wanted to give him something my mother couldn't, she who was looking after him every day as he grew weaker. I was living at the other end of the country, and this was a way of 'mothering' him and of relieving my guilt too for not being there more often. My father was fond of John Donne's much-quoted meditation on the tolling of the bell for the dead: 'Any man's death diminishes me'. With his dying, memory and history seemed to be ebbing away; like all sorrow, mine contained the loss of many things, not least the fading of my own childhood, which is kept fresh and green as long as parents and siblings are living.

Whatever my fantasies, there was to be no solitary quest. It was a bright, sunny day when I arrived at Brandwood End. My friend Erica drove us both to the cemetery and accompanied me, so there was to be no lonely catharsis. Thanks to the cemetery's staff and the Internet, there was no anxious searching either. I had the location of the burial plot, I knew exactly where we were going, and what we would find there. Which was precisely nothing. Evelyn was buried in a common grave. Her family had not been able to purchase a grave plot, so the local authorities had buried her. There was no epitaph or memorial, nothing much for me to photograph. We walked briskly down the tree-lined central avenue and found the place in a matter of minutes.

★

C.1. F/C is a large grassy area, worn and mossy in patches, scattered with branches and twigs. There are no headstones, no monuments or even burial mounds. The rough, scruffy ground looks like a bizarrely misplaced picnic spot or an area awaiting development. Off to one side an old, abandoned concrete slab designates it 'Unconsecrated ground'. Two newish-looking boulders, part of the restoration work of the 'Friends of Brandwood End', are more forthcoming: 'Public Graves: Grave Numbers 1A–527', but what is public about them is not clear. Evelyn's grave is recorded in the cemetery's register as number 227, but it's anyone's guess which patch of earth contains her bones. There is another identical zone on the other side of the avenue, 'Grave Numbers 1–502. One thousand and twenty-nine unnamed dead in one cemetery in one city in Britain.

Though I knew what to expect I was shocked, though mostly by my own ignorance. Evelyn died in 1930. I had imagined common graves were a feature of Victorian Britain, not of a modern city like Birmingham. This was not a pauper's grave, where the body was taken from a public institution to be buried without ceremony 'on the parish'. Nor was it a mass grave, where bodies were mingled indiscriminately. These graves, the Assistant Bereavement Officer told me, were unlikely to hold more than five people buried on top of one another in a depth of at least thirteen feet, though this sounds pretty snug; more often three bodies shared a nine-foot grave. The grave would usually – but not always – be filled in between occupants rather than left open, before other, unrelated people of either sex and any age were buried in a 'second-hand' grave. Certainly the cost of lying six feet under, alone, was beyond the pocket of many people, and some of the occupants would have come from public institutions and been interred at the expense of the local authorities. Others, like Evelyn's family, did not purchase the burial right for an individual plot and could not therefore put up a headstone. Whoever owns the cemetery owns her grave and that of the other 1,028. The term 'public' graves, though seemingly less derogatory than 'common', shields us from the fact that they are shared with strangers while reminding us whose property they are.

Brandwood End Cemetery opened in 1899 as a public burial

ground. Anglicans, Catholics, Dissenters and Jews (and, more recently, Muslims) would be buried in strictly symmetrical plots following a grid pattern laid out behind the matching mortuary chapels (western chapel for Anglicans; eastern for Catholics and Nonconformists). The 'Free Church' area, like 'unconsecrated ground', was meant to reassure Dissenters that the land had not been blessed by the Established Church and that those without affiliations or whose religion was not known would receive the same treatment. Though no one was refused, the fine gradations in grave plots, their size and placement, and the furnishings of a funeral, betrayed rank and status. As elsewhere in Britain's Victorian cemeteries, the more affluent purchased plots nearer the entrance and the chapels, and put up costly and imposing monuments; the cheapest plots might be on the lowest ground, and therefore liable to flooding, or further from the chapels. The cemetery was a meritocracy, not a democracy. In Leeds at the Beckett Street Cemetery the deserving poor could purchase 'guinea graves', which included the humane novelty of writing names on each headstone, though they were set so close together they resemble the terraced rows of housing from which their occupants had come. Parish paupers, the unwanted or unclaimed, were stowed away in 'Free Church' areas amid common graves. But even these were divided by caste and on a sliding scale of costs; the most expensive were the first and deepest dug; lowest of the low were the shallowest and nearest to the surface.

The stark stretch of bare grass over the common graves is the only spot not landscaped among the carefully designed avenues and paths. Brandwood End was influenced by the 'gardenesque' style of John Claudius Loudon, himself a disciple of the great landscape gardener of the eighteenth century Humphrey Repton. Entering the gates, passing under the bell tower which unites the Gothic mortuary chapels, the bereaved crossed the threshold into another world, the city of the dead, their procession repeating the idea of the journey, as if death to which the soul has 'departed' was truly a destination. Wandering down shady walks, or pausing to grieve under the luxuriant foliage of redwoods, cedars and pines, they would be comforted by nature, evergreen, while the stone angels pointing heavenwards with their wings outspread would elevate their thoughts. But the common graves have no sense of place. No wonder I feel dislocated: I do not know where to put my feet; I might be standing on someone's remains.

Brandwood End Cemetery

Near the public graves the Friends have erected a noticeboard where relatives can leave a temporary memorial of some kind. A couple of dog-eared postcards were pinned there, when I visited, edged with black; one tree had a ribbon tied to it; another had a withered bouquet at its roots. I felt it would be presumptuous, theatrical, to leave a note. I never knew my grandmother, so who was I to claim ownership? I could not mourn someone I knew nothing about. Apart from feeling a weak, generalized pity for my grandfather as I imagined him leaving his wife there, I was more concerned that I might try to trump up an emotion; feeling blank in this non-place seemed a more appropriate response.

So much for my pilgrimage. My first foray into family history was literally a dead end. It had yielded nothing. No echo came back from Evelyn's grave. It was as if I had thrown a stone into a bottomless well, or, worse, that her grave was a pit into which the past had poured, a black hole which swallowed up people like her, flattened out their lives and personalities so that they became faceless, charmless wraiths; undistinguished. She was a nobody, just like millions of others, her death banal. I should have realized, I thought angrily, that people like us, common people, would be in common graves. Far from resurrecting her or paying her the tribute of an epitaph, I had sent her back to the underworld to be lost among the anonymous shades crowding the Styx.

A week after my visit my father died. When, eventually, I told my mother what I'd found, she was more pragmatic. It was sad, she said, but perhaps the family were grateful that the corporation had taken care of the body; such burials were two a penny and the funeral might have been a relief, and not a matter of shame. At least Evelyn had been properly buried and in a proper cemetery. There were plenty who were worse off. This was a different perspective. I could not imagine this level of gratitude or of poverty: to be that beholden. The poor, I knew, went to enormous lengths to avoid a pauper funeral, saving up their pennies to pay weekly contributions to funeral clubs. My grandfather had mustered enough for a funeral cortège and service, and to print a funeral card, but not for an individual grave which would entitle his wife to a headstone. Were they just keeping up appearances? And for whose sake? Evelyn's non-existent grave cast a long shadow and the visit nagged at me. I wanted a context for her life; for her to be more than someone missing, one of history's disappeared.

Time-travelling

Family historians are history's speed-freaks. Other historians usually begin their stories from a point in the past, advancing gradually forward, covering a few decades, perhaps half a century at most. Some are content with covering even less ground, inching their way into the future, month by month, slowly accumulating a chronology like moss. Family historians, by contrast, work backwards, accelerating wildly across the generations, cutting a swathe through time, like the Grim Reaper himself. In the course of an hour's research, surfing the

Web at home or scanning the records in a local Family History Centre, they watch individuals die, marry and be born in series, a dizzying sequence of families falling away and rising up, eras going and coming, wars fizzling out and flaring, cities turning back to fields. The past looks like a hectic, crowded business. At the very least, following a person over time as the censuses unroll soon dispels the sense of isolation that hangs over the grave. With its listing of the inhabitants of house after house, street after street, farm after farm, the census is a record of connection and kinship, both deep and temporary; of who lived next to whom, who lodged and who took in lodgers, who cared for elderly family members, who shared with whom. Even the solitary is a neighbour, a life in the midst of social relations.

Evelyn's early life thronged with family. At the end of March 1911, the last census available, she was nineteen and living at home in King's Norton, a district about five miles south of Birmingham's centre. Trelliswork Place, Lifford Lane, sounds pleasantly rural, but Evelyn's father, William, is a 'metal scraper' and her brother Albert is a labourer at the metal works. 'Eveline' – as her name is spelt sometimes, like the purple flowering shrub – is a paper sorter in a local paper mill; another brother, Arthur, at seventeen, works at a rubber mill, as does Ernie, his junior by two years, employed in the mysterious occupation of 'tube turner'; the youngest, Daisy, is still a schoolgirl. William and Louisa have been married thirty years; ten children have survived. This is the family, my father's uncles and aunts, whose children would be his cousins, who were left behind when his own father left Birmingham.

Roll back another decade and Evie is a little girl surrounded by her full complement of nine siblings, living at number 64 Frances Road, still in King's Norton, in an area called Cotteridge. Like King's Norton, it's unknown territory to me, but at first sight looks disappointingly familiar. I grew up in a mesh of similar streets, close to the railway line, and ran errands to corner shops like the one in Frances Road. This is an urban environment made instantly recognizable from the memoirs of growing up poor, especially of life in the East End of London, from black-and-white photography like that of Bill Brandt or Bert Hardy, and those random images of poverty now blurred into the timeless features of 'the classic slum':

peeling wallpaper, newspapers for a tablecloth, dirty children without shoes, half an uncut loaf on the table, the 'God Bless Our Home' print framed over the mantelpiece – the generic landscape of a 'traditional' working class, replete with its pub and pawnshop. But I am disoriented by the industrial occupations of Evelyn's other siblings: George, a 'metal roller', Rose, a 'press worker' at a needle works; metal works, needle-making, rubber mills – this is a world unlike any I knew in the south of England.

Nor is the family settled. Following Evelyn's family through time I find that her people had long been on the move. William and Louisa make a new home at least once every ten years. At the turn of the century William Whitlock is not a metal scraper but a railway policeman, his life bound up with the traffic of people and goods. In 1891 they are in Stirchley, just north of Frances Road (Evelyn will be born in August later that year) and as they move backwards in time, they journey further away from Birmingham, south and east, into the neighbouring county of Warwickshire. In 1881 the Whitlocks, both in their early twenties, are in the village of Binton, a few miles from Stratford-upon-Avon, 'Shakespeare country', not far from Anne Hathaway's cottage, in fact. William is a young village constable, with a steady income, uniform and a house provided. The Internet obligingly furnishes a photograph, the 'station' from a few years later, looking like any other cottage. Next door is the curate, and a farmer is just up the lane. They stay long enough in Binton to have their first two children, but any image of a bumbling local Dogberry is dispelled because I can see the future: I know that William will join the railway police, a vote for modernity, the track which leads to the metal factory at Lifford Lane.

I need a larger-scale atlas as William travels back into his childhood, away from Stratford-upon-Avon, away from Binton, westwards over the county border into Worcestershire, to rejoin the mother and father he left. It is 1871 now and he is a boy of thirteen again. The Whitlocks are in deep country, in the village of Cotheridge, a name confusingly close to that district in King's Norton, but whose rural life would not revolve around Birmingham but Worcester, the ancient market town with its medieval cathedral. William's father, William senior, is a farm

Binton police station, 1890 (Shakespeare Birthplace Trust)

labourer and young William is listed as 'farm servant'. He has a younger sister, Mary Jane, and a little brother, Arthur, too young as yet to work. The family live in one of five cottages near Hill Top Farm where John Clift, a dairy farmer, employs four labourers and two boys, apart from the cowman, dairymaid, carters and servants who live in on the farm. One more leap back over another decade, and there is 'my' William (my father's grandfather, I remind myself, so the connection still feels live), a three-year-old with his parents, William senior and Jane, and now an older brother, Thomas, still in the parish of Cotheridge, still farm workers, but at a place called 'Black Fields'.

Is this then where the Whitlock family came from, their roots? I can't resist a couple more shots at the census and go back another generation, finding William senior as a boy. I start to draw a family tree to keep track as names repeat. We're in the mid-nineteenth century now and his parents, Richard and Mary Whitlock, are living next to Hill Top Farm; Richard is a gamekeeper, Mary makes lace. By the time William senior has grown up to marry Jane, his old father, Richard, will be widowed. Richard is working as a gamekeeper and lives in nearby 'Moat Cottage' on the estate of 'Cotheridge Court'. The manor house belongs to William Berkeley, 'Landed Proprietor', and his wife, Lucy, now in their seventies, their son William Comyns, who is the curate of Cotheridge, his wife, Harriet, and their boy of ten; and to serve these four adults and a child are the footman, John Lyons; John Bridges, a stable boy of sixteen; and a lady's maid, kitchen maid, nurse, cook, housemaid. The staff are all Worcestershire-born except for the nurse, Grace Mar, who is a long way from her home in Devonshire. Cotheridge is a textbook example of the three-tiered world of mid-nineteenth-century agriculture – farm labourers, tenant-farmers and the landowners – with the Whitlocks especially dependent on the family up at the 'big house'. William senior's younger sister Elizabeth works as a dressmaker, and the local gentry, their likely employers, are next door. No surprise then that the gamekeeper's grandson, Evelyn's father, becomes a policeman, protecting property, though this is not a particularly welcome lineage. Gamekeepers were much hated by village people, as the lackeys of landowners, betraying their own kind; village constables weren't always popular either.

One last turn of the wheel. In 1841, the earliest census available to the armchair traveller, Richard and Mary are in a hamlet called 'Down Norton', west of Cotheridge, in Herefordshire, a county which borders on Wales. Richard must have turned gamekeeper in the 'hungry forties' because here he is listed as an agricultural labourer. Mary and her daughters, Ann and Martha (the younger is only ten), are all lacemakers. They have come from Syresham, Northamptonshire, but by now I'm travel-sick: so many journeys, too much strange country – did these people never stay still? Not long after the end of another century, the eighteenth, Richard and Mary were born in a county more than fifty miles away to the south, another world, another local economy, a bridge too far for me. In a sweep of three generations the family have crossed four counties and around 100 miles. Evelyn's father has gone from farm boy to village policeman, to work on the railways and then in the factory, and from the black fields of Worcestershire to city streets. I need to stop the clock, to step outside the machine, and take a look around.

Cake-town

In 1880 my grandmother Evelyn's parents, William Whitlock and Louisa Dowdeswell, were married in the parish church of St Nicholas in Alcester. A small town, in the south-west of Warwickshire, in the centre of England, it borders Worcestershire on the west and lies about halfway between Hill Top Farm, which William has left, and the ever-growing Birmingham. Their fathers are their witnesses to the marriage. William Whitlock senior is recorded merely as a 'labourer'; Charles Dowdeswell is a 'needlestamper'. Both of the married couple can sign the register. When I find that Louisa Whitlock grew up in a needle factory, I imagine 'dark Satanic mills' and hundreds, perhaps even thousands, of workers (in shawls and clogs) congregating outside the great textile factories of the north of England, 'operatives' in the cotton and woollen industries of, say, Manchester or Leeds. They live in rows of blackened two-room back-to-backs, in densely packed tenements and courts, or are crowded into filthy and damp cellar dwellings. I see an indistinct vision of the 'Black Country', with its belching furnaces, towering smelting works, slag heaps and coal slurries – the lurid nightmare world of Dickens's 'Coketown' in his novel *Hard Times*. Behind the factory and the works are the mines, displaced in my imagination much further north or to the west. These are to me the landscapes of industrialization.

Alcester hardly fits the bills. A small town, its total population in the nineteenth century is never more than 2,500. It is the centre of a farming district, and has looked after itself for centuries, providing its own corn, brewing its beer, growing flax for linen, tanning hides for leather. A weekly cattle fair is held in the square in front of the old Market Hall, butter and cheese sold on Tuesdays in winding Butter Street, so narrow that it rarely sees the sun and keeps the goods cool, and once a year the 'Mop' is held, a hiring fair begun in Shakespeare's time, one of many celebrations of which the town is fond. Alcester is so full of bakers that, in Louisa's day, it is known locally as 'Cake-town'. The brick facades of shops on the High Street hide seventeenth-century interiors, but there are still plenty of sloping

Alcester High Street, 1860

black-and-white frontages on cottages and inns, though the picturesque chequerboard painting of timbers is a Victorian innovation. The jettied top storey of Malt Mill House has overhung Malt Mill Lane since Tudor times. A short ride or walk across the town's bridges and along its two rivers, the Arrow and the Alne, which join to flow south into the River Avon, past the cows and sheep grazing peacefully in the meadows, there are quiet hamlets apparently unchanged since medieval times. Yet Alcester, and the villages surrounding it, are also at the heart of the 'Industrial Revolution' fuelling Britain's turbo-capitalism.

In Bleachfield Street, where Evelyn's grandfather Charles Dowdeswell establishes his works, farm labourers and needle-makers live side by side. 'Dowdeswell's', like many of the other needle works in Alcester, was, to begin with at least, not much more than an extended shed in the yard, an outbuilding tacked on to a home, not a grand enterprise with hundreds of 'hands'. Only a dozen men and ten women worked at Dowdeswell's in the 1870s. Needle-making involved very many processes or stages of work, including the cutting of the wire for the needles, the straightening, punching or stamping, pointing and eyeing, filing, scouring, hardening, polishing and finishing, not to mention the final packaging. Much of the work could be performed by women and children. Alcester's needle factories were often small-scale, domestic businesses; alongside the larger works, individual families, or just two or three people, laboured at particular processes in their back kitchens and outhouses, before passing the needles on for the next stage of the operation. Dowdeswell's specialized in stamping, eyeing and filing – the former usually a man's job, but the latter open to all.

Who knows when someone first used a thorn and then a splinter of bone to pierce an animal skin? There are needles surviving from the Palaeolithic Age, and the needle could surely vie with the hammer in claiming to be the first human tool. The earliest needles had no eyes but a groove for holding firm a leather tong; flint boring tools made holes for fibre or sinew, to make skins and furs more robust and better-fitting; Siberian needles made from antlers, dating from 1500 BC, could still be used for heavy-duty work today. Without needles, civilization was impossible, and the basic shape of a needle hardly changed as those civilizations came and went. The Midlands in Britain, with its plentiful iron ore, had been making needles since Roman times; even earlier Iron Age needles had, of course, long rusted away. Medieval needle-makers were probably the local blacksmiths and whitesmiths, or tin workers, but needle-making in England was never a purely English trade. Spanish and German craftsmen were the first to produce a fine steel wire, and stronger, more flexible needles. Families of Spanish needle-makers, called 'Moors' by the locals, settled close to Alcester, near Redditch, from the 1530s (in Thomas Colwell's play of 1575 the whole village is agitated when Gammer Gurton loses her 'goodly sprior', or prized Spanish needle). In 1565 twenty-two German craftsmen and their families were brought to Tintern in Worcestershire to help establish the drawing of wire for needles by use of water-powered mills rather than by hand. Queen Elizabeth I 'encouraged her nobles to install foreign craftsmen' on their estates away from London, and away from the interference of spies and ambassadors, to improve native workmanship. Her agent at the French court, Nicholas Throckmorton, set up a number of Norman needle-making families on his estate in Coughton, near Alcester. By the mid-eighteenth century there were watermills in the Arrow valley and Alcester rapidly became the centre of the industry. Some 600 needle-workers lived in Alcester by the 1820s, between a third and a quarter of its inhabitants.

Needle-making began as a cottage industry, and Charles Dowdeswell married into a needle-making family which went back at least two or three generations. His wife, Prudence Reading, was a needle-maker, as was her mother, Rebecca, from the village of Great Alne, close to Alcester. Prudence's own father, Charles Reading, was a farm worker born in nearby Coughton. In the seventeenth century specially designed two-roomed cottages were built in Coughton with interconnecting hatches near the fireplaces to allow a kind of needle-making production line between neighbours: wire, usually procured ready-drawn, came in at one end of the row of cottages, 'dabs', or batches of unfinished needles, were passed along for each of the processes, and a finished needle came out at the other. It was hard and often dangerous work. Needle-pointing by hand had a particularly fearsome reputation for shortening lives. Needle-makers breathed in a perpetual cloud of stone and steel dust from the grindstone beneath their noses; they had to rinse their mouths about once an hour and frequently developed 'grinder's asthma'. Before the days of protective visors, they were in danger of being blinded by the sparks and shards of metal which flew off into their faces. Home workers were dependent on the middlemen or dealers, who brought them the raw material and collected the finished product. Only the entrepreneur – when trade was good – could turn a profit. But money and goods were not the only, or even the main, priorities for the men and women of the day, whose work at home kept them from dependence on the parish. Needle-workers smashed the first machines when they appeared; they were obstinately attached to the crafts that destroyed their eyes and lungs, because this was their source of pride and self-respect, and a life at least partially within their own control. As the work became more mechanized and centralized, they had to look for employment elsewhere, uprooted from a way of life, from neighbours, friends and family, the lie of the land.

In the 1790s the vicar of Coughton, one John Chambers, carefully put a large 'P' alongside the names of the children baptized and all the inhabitants buried in his parish if they were paupers. Among them were John and Ann 'Redding', Charles's parents, and all their children. Charles Reading, Prudence's father, grew up at a time when farms were getting larger and jobs in farm service were declining. By 1841 he and Rebecca had left the village to try their luck in Alcester, joining the squatters on the open fields at the north end of the town, an area known as the 'Moors' (*mor* is Old English for 'waste'), where the new arrivals lived in hovels and makeshift homes. Eight of their children made needles at home here. Only one, Henry, plied the needle as a tailor; he went to Redditch, which by mid-century was overtaking Alcester as the centre of needle-making, thanks to its superior mills and water power. Henry's daughters were needle-makers too.

On the Dowdeswell side of Evelyn's family, the women had been workers for generations. Outworkers like the needle-makers were not tangential but central to Britain's Industrial Revolution. Most of the metal trades and hardware industries began as indoor work, in villages surrounding Birmingham, in the cottages of Staffordshire, Warwickshire and Worcestershire. Those smelting works and furnaces of Dickens's imagination, the crucible of the iron and steel industries of the West Midlands, spawned thousands of outworkers, among them the screw- and washer-makers, chain-makers, pin- and needle-makers, those who forged and hammered and filed the myriad tools and parts, literally the nuts and bolts, which made the machines that made industrialization possible. The great Victorian boom of the building trade, for instance, needed nails, and nail-making was the largest employer of women in the district. In their lean-to workshops, often dirty, low outbuildings tacked on to their cottages, women and girls worked at a hammer and anvil amid atrocious filth and in continuous heat and smoke. Unlike their more respectable sisters, for these women home and workplace were cheek by jowl. Government investigators into the employment of women and children were outraged not only by the squalid conditions and long hours but by women who did not conform to their feminine or domesticated ideal. 'The effects of early work, particularly in forges,' wrote one shocked commissioner in 1843, 'render these girls perfectly independent. They often enter the beer shops, call for their pints, and smoke their pipes like men.' Many outworkers married young, carrying on work with their children around them, or, like Prudence Reading, Louisa's mother, hoped to become the wives of 'little masters' and make some money out of their fellow workers.

The new textile industries demanded a surge in the production of needles. Aside from the making of clothes and household linens, cloth was a ubiquitous wrapping material, used in packing or as sacking; cloth tarpaulins were stitched for transporting loads on carts and barges; sailcloth was sewn. There were needles with eyes and points for every material: wool and hemp, silk and cotton, chenille for tablecloths, straw for hats, and for threading beads or sequins. Everything from saddles to wounds, canvases to books, required needles of the right thickness, length and sharpness. A glover's needle had a triangular point so as to cut, not tear, the leather, carpet needles were short and thick, surgical needles were flattened; the poor-sighted could buy needles with double eyes, needles with extra-large eyes for embroidery like crewel work on curtains and bed-hangings, bodkins for darning, or for upholstery and tablecloths and all the new furnishings increasingly enjoyed by the middling sort in the nineteenth-century home. By the 1860s 'Needle-land', as the area around Redditch and Alcester was called, was producing over 50 million needles *a week*, and by the end of the century, as the factories grew into ever-larger concerns, 1,000 million a year from the country as a whole. Packets of needles stuck into cloth or black paper found their way across the globe.

My grandmother Evelyn's grandfather Charles came from a family who had also worked with needles for hundreds of years, but as saddlers and harness-makers. Those cattle calmly grazing in the Midlands fields were a source of leather and leather-working. Tanning and currying (softening the leather), dressing and stitching were all done by hand in small workshops. Samuel Dowdeswell, Charles's father, hailed from Gloucestershire, inheriting the trade. In the 1830s he acquired a piece of freehold land in the village of Bidford through his wife, Ann Quiney, patrimony for his business and his sons. Saddler was one step up from the hard manual labour of the blacksmith, though a saddlery was often combined with or run alongside a forge. Samuel set up a small shop of harnesses and tackle in Bidford-on-Avon, four miles to the south-east of Alcester, where Louisa's father, Charles, was born. Charles's older sister Dorinda (a splendidly eighteenth-century name; I liked to think of Louisa with an Aunt Dorinda) was a 'gloveress'. Like needle-making, that too meant piecework rather than finishing the entire article. Charles grew up watching his father stitch saddles, saddlebags, harnesses and reins, but the business in Bidford went to his older brother William.

Samuel and his wife moved with their son Charles to Bleachfield Steet in Alcester. Charles would have needed capital for the purchase of a steam-driven stamping machine which flattened the ends of the wire before putting in the eyes of the needle; workers paid for all their tools, and for any use of scouring mills. Evelyn's grandfather Charles Dowdeswell became a petty capitalist, making small-scale profits: Bleachfield Street, where the needle-workers lived, mostly in cramped seventeenth-century cottages, was not a salubrious area. Originally the place where linen bleached in the sunshine in the days of the medieval trade, it led away from the town, and with some of Alcester's poorest inhabitants, it became a community unto itself, hard-working and hard-drinking. This is where 'Dowdeswell's' grew into a small 'factory', though one still reliant on the old division of labour and not on an assembly line. A new stamping machine could strike needles at a rate of about 5,000 an hour. There was a colony of family help on the doorstep, among them the relatives of Charles's wife, Prudence, including her brother who lived on Bleachfield Street, and his daughters, who were all needle-eyers. Three of Charles and Prudence's own boys became needle-stampers at the factory. Only the youngest Dowdeswell, Charles Ernest, escaped the factory; he became a confectioner, catering to Alcester's sweet tooth.

Dowdeswell's flourished. By the time of his daughter Louisa's wedding in 1880, Charles's workforce had doubled to around sixty, including fourteen children. On the census he was now a 'needle manufacturer'. The family still lived on the premises, but Charles and Prudence had money to spare for a second business, as licensed victuallers, running the Rose and Crown, a small pub, on Evesham Street in the centre of the town. Brewing was another family business in Alcester and there were already connections in Prudence's family, while Dorinda Dowdeswell, now Mrs William Russen, was landlady of the Turk's Head, one of the eight or nine hostelries on the High Street (her ninety-year-old father, Samuel, was living with them). Alcester, with its twenty or so pubs and beer shops, was a boozy town. The local *Alcester Chronicle* reported the doings of the innumerable friendly societies, professional groups and drinking clubs that met in the pubs, like the 'Old Bear Society' whose members were distinguished by the fact that they liked to go to church before they retired to the Turk's Head for dinner. Perhaps they also played skittles: the seventy-foot saloon bar did service as a bowling alley for which Russen supplied special brass tokens. Louisa's wedding was likely to have been a beery affair, but drink soon divided the family. Since the 1860s the Methodist Band of Hope and Temperance Society had been active in the town, holding monthly meetings and tea assemblies. The Russens took the pledge and turned teetotal in the 1880s, left the Turk's Head and tried to convert another public house, the Apollo, to the 'Lord Alcester Temperance Hotel'. It didn't go down well with Alcestrians and they soon sold up. (In 1897 the hostelry was born again as Bowen's drapery stores.)

When Charles died in 1888 he left his wife nearly £700, worth about six times as much today and with far more spending power back then. Prudence carried on the pub with her oldest son, Henry James; running the needle works fell to his younger brothers Albert and Arthur. As publicans, Louisa's parents may have been hedging their bets, investing sensibly for the future. The rest of the Dowdeswell story is familiar enough in the history of industrial capitalism: those who can invest in more plants and machines do; bigger works buy out the smaller, who slowly go to the wall; work concentrates in one area. Overshadowed by Redditch, by the 1900s Alcester needle-making was struggling. One of the oldest needle-making families, the Allwoods, was confident enough to expand into new premises in the 1880s, which became the grand 'Minerva Works'. William Allwood went bankrupt in 1912 and sold it off. Other businesses in Alcester adapted to the times. Harrison's needle works turned to making bicycles in the 1890s, then pins; Henry Wilkes, an Alcester needle-maker on the Redditch road, made fishing rods. Though only twenty or so were working in 'the Yard' at Dowdeswell's in the early 1900s, Albert kept it going for another twenty years but capital must have been leaching away. Some of the Dowdeswell inheritance must have gone on cakes and ale. Louisa's brother Henry James had been the guiding light and captain of the local cricket team for twenty-five years (at the Ragley Park ground a batsman was declared out if a ball rebounded from a large tree standing within the boundary). His youngest son, my grandmother Evelyn's cousin, Charles Henry, a keen player too, took over the running of the Rose and Crown and was no doubt also a liberal supplier for the beer tents. The Rose and Crown left the family and in 1926 Charles Henry became a postman.

Like the other older needle shops, with their outbuildings and backyards, Dowdeswell's was eventually demolished and the needle-makers themselves left few traces. The timbered cottages on Bleachfield Street were destroyed along with a number of seventeenth-century buildings in a rash of town planning in the 1950s; the barrack-like building of the Minerva Works is now a business centre. Only one firm in Britain – in nearby Studley – manufactures needles now, while at Redditch the Forge Mill is a museum, dedicated to the history of needle-making (and sports a fine example of a Redditch surgical needle produced for the stitching of the thermal barrier tiles on the space shuttle *Columbia*). Back in Alcester I found one Dowdeswell relic. H. J. Dowdeswell, who had had a good innings, died in 1929 at the age of seventy-five. In 'affectionate remembrance' his family and friends commissioned a gravestone incorporating a cricket bat, cricket stumps and bails flying off. Henry had finally been bowled out, but the grave stands as a whimsical memorial to Caketown's love of fun and games, and testament to the cash put into the pockets of the Dowdeswells by generations of needle-workers.

Longitude and Latitude

Unless it is to be simply a catalogue of names, the history of a family is impossible to fathom without coming up for air and scanning the wider horizon. Once the branches proliferate, families become neighbourhoods and groups, and groups take shape around the work they do and where they find themselves doing it. Without local history to anchor it, family history is adrift in time. The armchair traveller surfing the Internet has to take to the road to locate the geography of a family's past, to go beyond the census to the parish registers of the village church or to find those accounts of a district which only exist in the local record offices and centres. Already the path from Evelyn's grave in Birmingham had taken me to Worcestershire and Warwickshire, criss-crossing those boundaries as her own antecedents had.

But the local is always connected to a wider world; the apparently parochial to the national; the national to the international. Without these connections and inflections, the moves people make are often meaningless. I can see the rise and fall of cottage industries and crafts writ differently on Evelyn's paternal Whitlock side too: in Northamptonshire in 1823 Mary Edwards married Richard Whitlock, who was to become a gamekeeper. Like the needle-maker Rebecca Reading, her contemporary, Mary was a homeworker, a lacemaker in an area renowned for its lace made by women, sitting in their doorways, crouched over their pillows and bobbins, from daybreak to dusk. She left the county at just the time when hand-lacemaking was in decline; changes in fashion, the decision to allow French lace back into the country after the Napoleonic wars, together with the new machines, all put paid to the old lacemaking and threw thousands of women on the poor rates.

And what of those who had stayed put? I had left behind Evelyn's other grandparents, William Whitlock and his wife, Jane, who remained in Worcestershire during the mid-century peak of Victorian 'high farming'. The engrossing of land in enclosures, the investment in machinery and new forms of cultivation, increased the yield but bigger and wealthier farms also meant less work for live-in farm servants. Many, like Charles Reading, became day labourers driven out on to the road. Those who were in jobs like Jane's husband, William, were less likely to move, especially in the later years of the first agricultural depression during the 1870s. Women's lives, like Jane's, a labourer's wife tied to domestic work, were surely the most static of all. Jane Whitlock lived at Hill Top in the tiny village of Cotheridge for more than forty years of her life. Yet nothing in a woman's life, I soon found, can be taken for granted. Pregnancy, marriage and widowhood might all mean drastic changes. These wives and daughters had no private income to cushion or to save them from disaster, no servants to look after them; they could not afford to 'suffer and be still'. And every life, even glimpsed through the chinks of the census, has its surprises and secrets.

When Jane was twenty-three she had an illegitimate child, Thomas, baptized on 24 July 1848 in Broadwas, about fifteen miles from Hartlebury, where Jane was born. The vicar of St Mary Magdalene did not write pointedly on the baptism register, as his successor was to, 'single woman' or 'illegitimate son' but simply gave Jane's occupation, 'servant', and left the column for father blank. Jane's parents, Edward, a wheelwright and carpenter, and Maria Lamb, were from Worcestershire villages too, and Jane, their youngest, at fifteen, had gone as a farm servant to work for a Hartlebury farmer, Samuel Taylor, and his wife, Ann. There were two sons her own age and two sisters, ladies of independent means, Miss Hannah and Miss Mary Glasbrook, who lived with them. Perhaps one of the Taylor men was responsible. It is impossible to know, but in her home village of only 400 souls her pregnancy, if not the paternity, would be public knowledge since the parish would have to maintain her and her bastard if the family could not. Jane left Hartlebury for Broadwas, as did her parents, who took on the care of Thomas while she went back to work. For another eight years she was a domestic servant in the family of Reverend Ellis Palmer, a chaplain for the Welsh church, living half a dozen miles away in Claines, to the north of Worcester, until she married William Whitlock in 1857. Women took on the settlement of their husbands when they married, so the Whitlocks went back to his home of Cotheridge to marry in the parish church there. She called herself a 'spinster' on the register (like many servants Jane had learnt to write her name but her husband could not). The Reverend William Comyns Berkeley, the vicar, and heir to Cotheridge Court, who presided over the marriage, could have no idea about her eight-year-old child. Baby William, Evelyn's father, and the grandfather my father never knew, was born just inside wedlock, six months or so later. In due course Thomas joined the family and became a Whitlock.

Nineteenth-century village people are often said not to have travelled much more than five or six miles beyond their parish, but women's lives could be marked by upheaval. After their children had grown up and left, Jane was dependent on her husband working. In 1885, when William died, she left – or was evicted from – the tied cottage at Hill Top and moved to live alone at Cheketts cottage, next to Cotheridge church. She was in her early sixties. Her options were few and outlook grim. Without work she might find herself in the Worcester workhouse (perhaps this was the fate of John Handley, an agricultural labourer, nearing fifty, who slept in a nearby shed on the night of the 1891 census and did not know his own birthplace). Jane certainly had some gumption. She travelled 300 miles out of her own 'country' to work as a caretaker for George Lionel Dashwood JP, of Wilton House, Shenley, Barnet, a village on the outskirts of London. Her daughter, Mary Jane, had married a Cotheridge lad, Charles Maylett, who was now the Dashwood's coachman and here was another life in motion. The Dashwoods had a town house near Regent's Park, London, and the Mayletts spent twenty years moving between the cramped quarters of their stables accommodation at Bryanston Mews, where they lived among the colony of grooms, maids and footmen, and Shenley. As caretaker, Jane lived alone in Shenley for much of the time when the family was in town; the gardener and his family lived next door. I imagine her wandering the shuttered rooms with their shrouded furniture. Wilton House was – and is – a substantial property, with 'considerable pleasure grounds', almost a park. Now a private nursing home for the elderly, its fifty-one single bedrooms give an idea of its size. Jane died in her daughter's lodgings at the Wilton House stables in 1902. She was seventy-seven. Not such a predictable life after all.

Tracking all the members of a family over time unsettles assumptions. When Charles Dowdeswell's older brother, William, inherited the saddlery in Bidford-on-Avon, it was to stay in the family for almost another century. He must have thought the future of the business secure with three of his seven sons apprenticed to the trade, but that continuity was very shaky. His son Tom set up elsewhere, William Edgar joined the police, and Charles lit out for Kensington, London, lodging in Portobello Road, making harnesses next to the coachmen and grooms catering to the fashionable carriage folk of Hyde Park and Bayswater. William senior and his wife, Mary, were to outlive six of their nine children, including John, who had left the village well behind, gradually climbing the rungs of the Midland Railway company. First a porter at Bradford station in Yorkshire, on sixteen shillings a week, then promoted to passenger guard, he was killed at Skipton at the age of twenty-five, in one of the many fatal accidents in the early days of the railway. William carried on the saddlery himself until his death at nearly ninety.

Rather than following a 'line', I find myself drawn to all the people I encounter, including those who, only by the most obtuse reckoning, can be thought of as relatives. Every life deserves telling; none is without drama and change. Without following the byways the mere facts of the census deceive. After William Dowdeswell's death in 1901, Charles, his youngest son who had gone to Kensington and was now a 'master harnessmaker', returned from London with his wife, Mary, to run the saddler's shop in Bidford. His history had been fraught. In 1876 he had first married Fanny Temple, whose brief life connects the worlds of the needle-makers, the seamstresses and the textile workers. At seventeen she was a draper's assistant, one of seven at James Kirby's shop in Norfolk Terrace in Kensington, more migrants seeking a better life: their families came from all over the country, from Scotland to Sussex (Fanny's own father a Yorkshire builder). In the 1870s Fanny and her fellows lived over the shop, sharing beds and working all hours, as many did, for the sake of more respectable employment – 'a sacrifice to their own notions of self-respect and the throng of thoughtless purchasers to whom they are often less than nothing', according to the *Daily Chronicle* in an exposure of shop life. None of the protective laws governing factory employment applied to shops. The autumn of 1881 was a terrible time for Charles and Fanny; in September, within a fortnight, they lost their five-month-old, Arthur, and Gertie, who was eighteen months, to tuberculosis; then in November Fanny herself died of the disease. She was thirty. One in six people died of tuberculosis in Victorian Britain, and Fanny Dowdeswell, living in their crowded accommodation in the Kensington slums, was likely to have passed it on to her children. In the late nineteenth and early twentieth centuries there were almost no hospital beds for poorer patients: the big general hospitals rejected them as 'incurables'; the medical profession, like the government, saw the problem as 'vast and hopeless'. Most of the poorer victims lingered at home to be nursed by their families until they were removed to the workhouse infirmary to die. There would be no one to inherit the Dowdeswell saddlery after Charles had returned to Bidford. His only surviving son from his marriage with Fanny, Frank, had died of acute rheumatism and a weak heart at the age of twelve. The Portobello Road was a very unhealthy place.

Thinking in generations rather than epochs or 'periods', each family becomes a saga, a novel in miniature as it spirals across the years, but family history gives us latitude as well as longitude. Tracing the lives of siblings and cousins, as history is played out at home, a group emerges with its hopes and disappointments, its random tragedies, its enormous efforts to make a living within the bounds of what is possible. In 1873, while his father, William, ran the saddlery, John Dowdeswell's fellow railwaymen travelled down from Bradford to put up a large memorial to him in the churchyard of St Laurence's in Bidford-on-Avon as 'a mark of their esteem and respect', the gravestone records. In their smart company uniforms and caps, they might seem a tribe apart from the farm labourers of Warwickshire and Worcestershire, with their broken teeth, and clay pipes, their smocks and white beards. But ploughmen and dairymen alike had brothers and sons who 'went over the fence', as they called it, from the neighbouring farms as the railways were cut into the countryside, leaving the land with its seasonal rhythms for a new life of rigid discipline and meticulous timekeeping on the railway. In 1824 there was not a single railwayman in Britain, but by 1847 there were 47,000 permanent staff; by the 1870s, 275,000.

The police also offered country boys like Evelyn's father, William Whitlock, pay that was regular and graduated and a job that, most of all, was permanent and might offer a home. Kin and the constabulary conspired to bring Louisa and William together: Louisa's cousin, William Edgar Dowdeswell, one of the saddlery boys who had left the workshop, had also joined the service, and Binton, the tiny village where William Whitlock was village policeman, was barely three miles on from Bidford, where the Dowdeswell saddlery was. All the constables reported to Alcester, which was the centre of the local division, and they all knew each other. William Whitlock's younger brother, Arthur, went into white-collar work too, suggesting both were properly literate. Arthur first tried the railways as a booking clerk, finding himself in Deptford, one of the poorest districts of London, lodging with an aunt who had herself married a railway inspector. He can't have liked the life much because ten years later he is delivering the post back in Worcestershire. (Here were a further five cousins for Evelyn by the time she was ten.) The postal service was another respectable form of employment, secure, pensioned and with 'clean hands'.

A conservative streak runs through these two families of ancestors – Dowdeswells and Whitlocks. There are no signs of any radical spirits among them. Saddlers had often to oblige the carriage folk, who were their wealthiest customers; gamekeepers depended on the local farmers or landowners for their jobs and homes; and the Whitlocks, who lived in the shadow of the Berkeley family and the manor house, were unlikely to join Joseph Arch's National Agricultural Labourers Union, which originated among farm workers in Warwickshire in the 1870s. Policemen and publicans, and especially brewers, were usually Tory to a man, as were small capitalists like Charles Dowdeswell, who paid his workers a pittance. The hierarchical structure of the railway was modelled on the army, demanding total commitment to the job, a 'loyal servitude' from those who took the company's livery. Railwaymen had to be prepared to be sent, at the company behest, all over the country; drivers were fined for being unpunctual; guards had their wages docked for any thefts of luggage. Hours were long and discipline severe; their turnout had to be immaculate and any misdemeanours, from drinking to pilfering, meant instant dismissal. Railway policemen like Evelyn's father, William Whitlock, kept an eye not only on goods traffic but on their fellows too. Like the postal service, they became part of a deferential, newly uniformed working class before the days of union organization and strikes.

But I am reminded too how often a life, a job and a sense of belonging hang on a chance or have to be reinvented; how often people weighed their attachment to home or to kin against their desperation or the hope for a better life. And not for the last time in writing this book, I see that an individual can only do so much. Louisa's father, Charles Dowdeswell, the needle-maker, and his brother William, the saddler, depended ultimately on the small inheritance of land from their father and his business. Without that start in life, the possibilities for ambitious lads, let alone dreamy girls, with next to no schooling, were very limited. Nor does a feeling for one's country mean staying there. Louisa's uncle, John Reading, Prudence's older brother, another needle-maker, had married into the Fourts who ran the Fox Inn in Alcester. In the 1860s when his wife, Hannah, died, he went to farm in Guelph, Ontario, one of many persuaded by the government emigration agents to try their luck in the colonies. John left his ten-year-old son, William, to the care of his parents and, seemingly, put behind him any sentiment about England or home. In Canada he married again, named his new baby daughter Hannah and ended his life a 'gentleman'. I could find no evidence in the census that his son ever joined him.

A century later, my own father, fed up with casual work, some of it back-breaking, failed to persuade my mother to emigrate. I faintly remember, or think I do, the talk of New Zealand, of its lush scenery and its temperate climate 'being like England'. My father appears in my mind as middle-aged but I realize now that he was in his mid-thirties. Without much education, the opportunities for a steady income and respectable jobs for an unskilled man were still few: he also thought of the police and of the prison service, but he was not tall enough – which I found funny as a child, not thinking of what he could see ahead, perhaps another thirty years of manual labour in jobs he sometimes loathed. Every family has these stories: the roads taken and not taken and the parallel lives that might so easily have been led in another country by someone else.

Settlers

My grandmother Evelyn was the daughter of rural migrants who were drawn in stages towards Birmingham as the city reached out to meet them; they were often on the fringes of old communities, places where the differences between country and city were blurred. A rural or an urban way of life did not exist in sealed compartments. Evelyn had brothers and sisters in the factories and mills, Dowdeswell relations at the saddlery, family who worked in the heat and noise of the needle works, her Whitlock cousins working on a farm, still others who moved with the police or on the railway. One grandmother ran the Rose and Crown in Alcester; the other was a live-in servant for a baronet in a country house close to London. This is the reach of a family in time. And far from being a long-established urban world, the place where she herself grew up was only recently settled.

Cotteridge, where Evelyn was a girl, was part of King's Norton, the largest parish in Worcestershire and in the 1890s predominantly agricultural. In medieval times the land had probably belonged to someone from the Worcestershire village of Cotheridge, hence the confusion of names. Evelyn's family lived north of King's Norton's old village green, flanked by the handsome thirteenth-century church and timbered buildings, the Saracen's Head, once a prosperous wool merchant's house, and the fifteenth-century grammar school. Her universe, by contrast, was thoroughly forward-facing. In 1892, the year after her birth, Cotteridge was still Cotteridge Farm, with a sprinkling of perhaps twenty houses and no more than 100 people. By the turn of the century there were getting on for 900 houses, mostly in rows of tunnel-backed terraces, and over 4,500 people. This was just the beginning of a staggering transformation.

Birmingham grew at a phenomenal rate during the nineteenth century, from a town of nearly 74,000 in 1801 to over 522,000 a hundred years later. Prosperous merchants and industrialists had long given up living 'over the shop', moving out from their businesses or works in the cramped central wards to live in the leafy purlieus of the periphery, escaping the city's tentacles. Men like Thomas Lane, a bullion dealer, or the jeweller Benjamin Goode, who pulled down King's Norton's old farmhouses or built grand extensions, encasing Jacobean timbers in brick and upgrading them from 'farm' to 'hall', to make them suitable gentlemen's residences. Once a new, improved railway station opened in King's Norton in 1868 with a large ticket hall, urinals, and waiting rooms for ladies and gentlemen, commuting up to town was possible; spacious villas appeared with names like 'Hill Crest', 'Fair View', or 'The Dell', the latter erected in 1870 on fourteen acres, replete with ten resident staff, greenhouses and 'farmery', and belonging to George Belliss, partner in a firm of steam engines and boiler-makers. Manufacturers and factory owners as well as a tranche of the old professions migrated to genteel villadom. They were soon complaining about the rowdiness of the old village, especially the vulgarity of King's Norton's annual 'Mop', no longer a hiring fair but a hugely popular event, lasting several days, that took over the village green with its ox roast, sideshows, swings and rides.

But the movement of workers created far more social division. In the late nineteenth century Birmingham's manufacturers also wanted more space for their bigger factories and conglomerated works; larger sites meant a larger turnover and bigger profits. They too looked to the outer ring of villages and growing suburbs beyond the inner wards. In 1879 Richard and George Cadbury moved their cocoa and chocolate business out to Stirchley, eventually building a model village estate – Bournville – for their employees. The nearby area was where the old turnpike roads met a network of canals and railways, and the river was crossed by Lifford ('la ford') Lane. In the late eighteenth century Lifford had already supported some industry, including an 'aqua fortis' (nitric acid) chemical works, shut down once farmers claimed compensation for crop pollution. A reservoir made in the 1850s supplied the copious water needed for paper-making at James Baldwin's steam-driven paper mill; Nettlefold and Chamberlain's screw factory re-established itself close to Cadbury's. But further industrial development in the late nineteenth century, beginning with the arrival of the King's Norton Metal Works in 1889, and the doubling in size of Nettlefolds, wrought more lasting change. Once there was employment in these outlying districts, new workers poured in to live in the area. And to die there. King's Norton district council bought some farmland at Brandwood End and the new municipal cemetery, where Evelyn was to be buried, opened in 1899.

My nine-year-old grandmother saw in the twentieth century at number 64 Frances Road, Cotteridge, a terraced street with two rows of sixty-odd houses opposite each other, tucked into a corner below the main Pershore Road, a loop of railways, and the junction of the

Stratford-upon-Avon and the Worcester and Birmingham canals. The Whitlocks were living in a heavily built-up industrial area but surrounded by tracts of open countryside. Not an island exactly, since its boundaries were expanding, but a community in the process of emerging, one which was seen by many as an unwanted invasion. Other residents in King's Norton observed the advance of the 'thin red line' of houses with horror, 'the outposts of the enemy' as John Bridges, a gentleman farmer and local churchwarden, put it. Hostilities increased. According to local historians, by the turn of the century industrial Cotteridge and King's Norton village faced each other across the valley of the River Rea 'like two opposing armies holding high ground'. The sense of difference encouraged the new inhabitants to create a distinctive identity for their area and to feel a strong allegiance and affection for what they called 'the Cotteridge'. In Frances Road descendants of the first families were to stay for generations, but what I thought at first glance was a 'traditional' working-class neighbourhood had only just been made.

Frances Road at the turn of the century was newly built, a street of new arrivals. Like the Whitlocks, the majority of the incomers had made their way from the adjacent counties and nearby villages. A few families had moved out from Birmingham but many had come looking for work after travelling hundreds of miles. The new factories depended on the railway, canal and roads to bring in raw materials and shift finished products, but they also brought the men who had built the transport system or continued to work on it. William Taylor (at number 3) from Worcester is among several navvies, or 'navigators', on Frances Road, the men who first cut the canals, literally moving mountains of earth with pick and shovel. Ernest Hamblin and his younger brother, Charles (at number 115), from Gloucestershire are canal boatmen; they have to negotiate Lifford's 'guillotine' lock, a contraption designed to prevent water, jealously guarded by private companies, flowing from one canal to the other. Frances Road has its share of railwaymen: porters, trolleymen, and paviours, like Tom Archer at number 63, who work on the tracks. Michael Kenny (at number 119), an engine driver, is a long way from Ireland; Fred Fairhead (number 61) drives a 'dray', delivering to and collecting from stations. He and his wife, Eliza, are Norfolk-bred. Children have been born en route. The Fairheads have a son from their Sheffield days; their daughter was born in York. Like the boatmen and draymen, the carters working in the factory, railway and builders' yards, or for long-distance hauliers, rely on horses to pull their loads (in the midst of all this industry there is a blacksmith at 99 Frances Road, Edward Mullard, originally from Surrey). The horse and cart of William Smith, living at number 69, has taken him hundreds of miles from his tiny woodland village of Little Dewchurch in Herefordshire, to the seaside resort of St Leonards in Sussex on the south coast, where he and Fanny had their son Thomas, then back to Llanwarne, in his home country on the Welsh borders, where seven years ago little Beatrice was born, before moving on. This is what the Industrial Revolution has meant: generations of people on the road.

Most of Birmingham's poorest inhabitants, stuck in casual or irregular jobs, could not afford to move to these new industrial suburbs where the rents were beyond their reach. They remained in the increasingly decrepit tenements in the centre. The houses in Frances Road were hardly palatial but were generous by comparison: upstairs were two bedrooms and a box room, downstairs was the front room kept as a parlour 'for best'. The family lived mostly in the back room, where the cooking range was, and a small scullery; outside would be the lavatory and coal shed; cold water was laid on but no one had a bathroom. Many of the new houses were built by the local firm of Grants, who kept a timber yard in the road. The building trade brings men like Sam Germans, a house painter at number 39, and Fred Thorn, a bricklayer (number 116), the only two men from Exeter in Devon, and a typical team of workmates. Charles Clarke at number 123, who hails from the opposite direction – Boston, Lincolnshire, on the east coast – is a carpenter and joiner, as is Alfred Watkins, at number 74, from Cardiff in Wales, while Ben Gilliam (number 91) is a Lancashire lad, one of the many builders' labourers in the road. Henry Williams (number 65) makes the roads and pavements which are being laid down in the district; he comes from Shropshire and operates a 'road steam roller', flattening out the new tarmacadam surfaces. I allow myself a detour and discover that his father was a coal miner in Shropshire: how many here, I wonder, are from farming families like William Whitlock, how many the second generation to be swept along by the industrial juggernaut?

In the Midlands the local industries are in full swing. Evelyn grows up on a road where every man and all the young adults are in employment. This one census for one road affords a glimpse of that thriving world of work from the highly skilled mechanical engineers and toolmakers to the labourers who are also all in jobs. Metalworkers – rollers and annealers, who heat and cool the metal to get it ready for cutting, sheet turners and finishers, filers and stampers – all manner of fitters and machine cleaners; workers in the ammunitions factories making guns and cartridges and in a myriad other hardware trades, screw-making, brass-working, button-making, enamelling, lacquering: the list goes on right down to young Thomas Glover (aged twenty) who lives at number 98, precisely recorded as a 'Sacking Washer/ Paper Mill'. Their labour produces a mini-inventory of Edwardian things, from the brass fenders which Llewellyn Porter (at number 86) polishes for a living, to the shiny new bicycles Sarah Holbeche (at number 14) sends out gleaming, and which will soon take them all to work or on jaunts into the countryside. In the age of steel pens for the masses, Llewellyn's wife, Mary (an Essex girl, born in Colchester), is a pen grinder. But she is an exception. Hardly any married women with children are working, unlike the poor and desperate in the city wards who grub up a pittance from the 'sweated trades' at home, wrapping hairpins into packets, varnishing pen holders or sewing buttons on to cards. Those women in Frances Road who do work after marriage are generally coping alone or among the hardest-up. Annie Daley at number 31, a gun-cartridge maker: married, in her mid-twenties, but with no sign of a husband; and Harriet Bunyan (at number 108), whose husband, George, is a navvy, and who works as a char. Emma Webster, a widow nearing fifty, also goes out charring; her lodger, Emily Cox, helps with the rent for the two of them at number 35 by filling 'Lyddite' shells, dangerous and potentially toxic work. Euphemistically named after their first trials at Lydd on the marshes of Kent, these contain the explosive picric acid used by the British artillery to rip through the Boers. Such women will be much in demand after 1914.

It is a street astonishingly full of children: at a rough count, 192 babies and children under the age of twelve from 100 inhabited houses. Opposite Evelyn, the Perks and Harrises have fifteen children between them – plenty of playmates for her. In 1897 the council built Cotteridge school for 600 pupils, a short distance away from Frances Road on the main Pershore Road, but no registers survive to tell me if Evelyn went there. Out of school, much of her time, like that of other older siblings, would be spent minding the little ones or running errands. Boys and girls start to pull their weight by the age of thirteen, often following their brothers and sisters into particular factories or mills. With seven younger siblings at home, Alfred Harris (at number 55) does his bit as a paper cutter, and Archie Tilling (at number 131), also thirteen, is the street's youngest 'house painter'. The Cadbury's Bournville factory offered all kinds of jobs to juveniles, and its perks must have made it especially appealing as they worked their way up the ranks. Youngsters help make the boxes or cover (wrap) the chocolate; at sixteen, they might be chocolate makers or mixers, or work on the packaging, as Agnes Tilling, Archie's sister, does. Nineteen-year-old Frank Penrice, the Petfords' boarder at number 117, has graduated. He has the more skilled position of moulder, pouring liquid chocolate into the shapes for bars.

In Frances Road every household has their own house; we are a long way from the crowded slums. Even so, despite their constant hard work, big families like the Whitlocks can only survive with their children earning or if they rely on lodgers to make ends meet. Countrymen lodge with countrymen; kin with kin; lodgers are often workmates. The Irish Kennys at number 119 have a month-old son; their three male boarders, Thomas Welch, William Madden and Patrick Lawly, are all single, all early twenties, all Irish, all bricklayers' labourers; next door are the Carrolls (Patrick and Bridget), the only other Irish in the street. The Fairheads' boarder, Charlie Gooch, is Eliza's brother from her home of Bedingham in Norfolk. Tom and Louisa Haigh at number 79 have sixteen-year-old Llewlyn King, a saddler, from Tom's Yorkshire village of Melsham. The Holbeches let a room to Alice Burrage, an unmarried mother with a three-month-old baby girl, and the only woman in the road to work as a domestic servant. There are many kinds of arrangement: the three Breeze siblings at number 85 are managing without their parents; their lodger delivers coal. Equally unusual, Edward Mullard, the blacksmith, is the street's only employer; he and his wife live alone. Louisa Minton at number 104 is a different kind of rarity: a single woman in her mid-forties who sells groceries and is bringing up her niece, Jessie Gwilliam. The house is shared with a middle-aged widower, Walter Williams, 'living on his own means', a long way from his home town of Kingston in Surrey. Did the neighbours talk?

Every census detail starts a story. Not for the first time I feel the urge to fictionalize these people, these Edwardians. How did John Ashford, a 'metal sheet turner (finisher)' born in Birmingham, about as far from the sea as it is possible to get in England, come to marry Nellie from Newcastle upon Tyne on the furthest edge of England's north-east coast? Did they meet in Wolverhampton, where their oldest child was born? Was Jessie Gwilliam really Louisa Minton's daughter? Did Louisa marry her mysterious lodger? Yet ultimately I prefer the frustration of not knowing to the omniscience of a novelist. Whenever a reverie begins, chance encounters with other searchers on family history websites pull me up short; they remind me that each person, a name on the page, was somebody's ancestor, great-grandfather, grandmother. There are limits to the liberties I can take.

It's a tough world for Evelyn to grow up in. Her family are not among the worst off but they are not secure either. About a fifth of the houses in the road are uninhabited: for all those who stay, others, like the Whitlocks, will have to move on. Everyone in the street works but no one has a servant: families rely utterly on their mothers to keep these homes clean and warm, provide meals, look after infants, do the washing, provisioning, and a thousand other chores besides. Only the fittest survive. An accident at work, pregnancy, sickness or the breadwinner's death can spell disaster. Those in seasonal employment, like coalmen or bricklayers, are particularly hard-pressed, but with an average wage of eighteen shillings (90p) a week and rents at five shillings (25p) married men with large families will have little spare to go round. In 1907 Cotteridge's new Anglican church, St Agnes, found it necessary to provide a soup kitchen in its parish hall. Nor is it a world for the elderly or frail. In Frances Road few are over sixty. The Lockers, Sam and Florence at number 113, have Sam's father, James, a widower, living with them; at sixty-two he is still working as a bricklayer's labourer. Those who can't work or have no family to support them have only the workhouse to fall back on. At seventy-four, Jacob Levinsky is the only septuagenarian and the only foreigner in Frances Road. A dealer in old clothes at number 58, he originates from Poland; the word 'Jew' is baldly written in by the census enumerator. Mr Levinsky – what was *his* story? – lives with two elderly widows, Mrs Ainsworth and Mrs Bunn, one his housekeeper and the other a laundress.

For all its rich display and suggestive detail the census remains a still life, frozen in time, giving the illusion of a settled world, in place at that moment, for that date at the end of March or beginning of April, once every ten years. We never learn what happened the next day, the next week or month, or the day before. Between the census columns, dividing private and public into its categories of home and work, lies the street which it cannot register and where much of life goes on. The girl indoors at the corner of the kitchen table, eating her tea, asks to get down from the table and runs out to play; women scrub steps; neighbours stand and talk in doorways, calling out to children; shoppers bustle; traders put out their wares or stop to chat; passers-by accost the milkman or joke with the coalmen on their rounds; boys loaf and flirt on corners; men congregate outside pubs: all the sounds and the smells of a way of life that escape the census and its enumerator in his stiff white collar and his sober frockcoat. Like the social investigators of the period, the census upholds an image of respectability, everyone in his or her place, dogs on leashes and front doors closed.

My grandmother was soon among the gaggles of young women walking and laughing together on the way to the factory. At thirteen or fourteen she followed her sister Rose to work as a paper sorter. Rag sorters did the worst work, shifting through piles of old rags and clothes, a proportion of which went into the paper; paper sorters were engaged in another kind of recycling, going through mounds of waste paper by hand, or else sorting the finished paper. Long hours on one's feet (a fifty-eight-hour week was usual, slightly less on a night shift), which were thought excessive even at the time, helping to turn out tons of box-board and brown wrapping paper, gun wadding, or blue paper for grocery bags, much of it demanded by the growing number of other industries in the area. But in an age when the majority of young women went into domestic service, factory girls were only too glad not to be skivvying, or wearing the hated white cap, the maid's badge of servitude. However deadening the work, they preferred the camaraderie, the adult sense of responsibility and independence, which the factory gave them. Handing over a few shillings for the housekeeping, with perhaps a bit of cash left over to put in a clothing club or towards a new pair of shoes, they tasted freedom. It was even possible to leave home and rent rooms, like Rose Godfrey, aged twenty-one, who was boarding with the Sears family at number 127 Frances Road, a 'chocolate confectioner'. Where critics saw the factory worker as coarse or common, the girls themselves often pitied their sheltered contemporaries, those 'daughters of educated men', immured at home, unable to fend for themselves and constantly chaperoned.

Evelyn's family, however, were struggling. By 1911 they had moved down the road to Trelliswork Place, off Lifford Lane, amid the din of the Lifford mills. This was the crowded house where I first found them: the Whitlocks senior, Evelyn, three of her brothers and little sister, Daisy, plus Evelyn's older sister Nellie Reeves and husband, Fred, with their one-year-old. Ten people in five rooms, plus kitchen – a bit of a squeeze, though not impossible. A bedroom for both married couples (the baby in a cot in a corner?), and one for the girls, would leave the boys sleeping downstairs in the front room. Fred Reeves must have been finding life hard as a domestic gardener, but the household had four young people working. Evelyn's father was no longer in the railway police but working as a metal scraper, and then, finally, as a labourer. Perhaps he left the police to avoid being moved on again or was finding the work too hard as he aged; perhaps he was dismissed – there are no records surviving. Either way, there was no pension. Most likely William Whitlock's health was failing, for he dies, aged fifty-five, the following winter of tuberculosis. Lifford was bad for the health. William's older brother, Tom, Jane Lamb's bastard, still working with carthorses on a farm in the Worcestershire countryside, outlived him.

After all this time-travelling I realize that there is no ancestral place for me to attach myself to, no settled landscape to serve as a backdrop for family memories or fantasies about my ancestors. In 1911 Birmingham extended its boundaries and swallowed a number of its outer suburbs and rural districts, of which King's Norton was the largest. This 'annexation', as local historians still call it, added an area three times the size of Glasgow and twice that of Manchester, Liverpool or Leeds, and made Birmingham a city second only in size to London. Evelyn could now say she came 'from Birmingham', but her loyalties were surely to 'the Cotteridge'. In her lifetime, though, country and city were cheek by jowl and both were in easy reach: her pleasures could be taken by the River Rea, or strolling the dusty, leafy lanes of King's Norton; a tuppence halfpenny ticket from the tram depot, 'the nerve centre' of Cotteridge, would transport her to Navigation Street to admire the municipal grandeur, the wide Parisian boulevards of Joseph Chamberlain's redesigned city, or join the bustle of the markets in the Bull Ring. She could watch horses bring in the harvest in the fields or gaze at the latest fashions through the plate-glass windows of the smart shops in Stirchley. There were even newer sights closer to home. In 1913 the Cotteridge Picturedrome opened, the heavy curtain lifted by the winding of a large iron handle, and the film, often liable to break down, 'ably accompanied' by Mrs Macdonald on piano or the blind Mr Taft on harmonium. Adult performances would invariably feature Sergeant Dawns, a veteran of the Crimea, reciting 'The Charge of the Light Brigade' 'to the patrons' delight'. Perhaps it was on one such evening that Evelyn, a week before her twenty-third birthday, heard that war with Germany had been declared.

Happy Valley

My family had long known that Evelyn did 'something' during the First World War. A photograph of her in uniform, serene and relaxed, with the hint of a smile on her lips, looks like the kind of studio portrait taken after joining up and given to proud members of the family. The initials on her cap – 'PC' or 'FC'? – are indistinct, but neither the police nor the Forestry Commission tally with her uniform. A second portrait of the same vintage was equally baffling. Flanked by a horse, she holds the bridle, crop under her arm, boots just visible beneath her smartly buttoned skirt. She looks worried – or is it determined? – glowering at the camera in an unladylike way from under her wide-brimmed hat. Because we imagined her growing up in the slums of Birmingham the horse seemed an anomaly, but it turned out to be the clue to her war.

The 'family detective' in television programmes like the BBC's immensely popular *Who Do You Think You Are?* has the resources instantly at her command: a budget from the TV company to pay professional genealogists or to ferry her across the country or even continents to pursue branches of her family; immediate access to librarians and archivists, who drop whatever they are doing for the

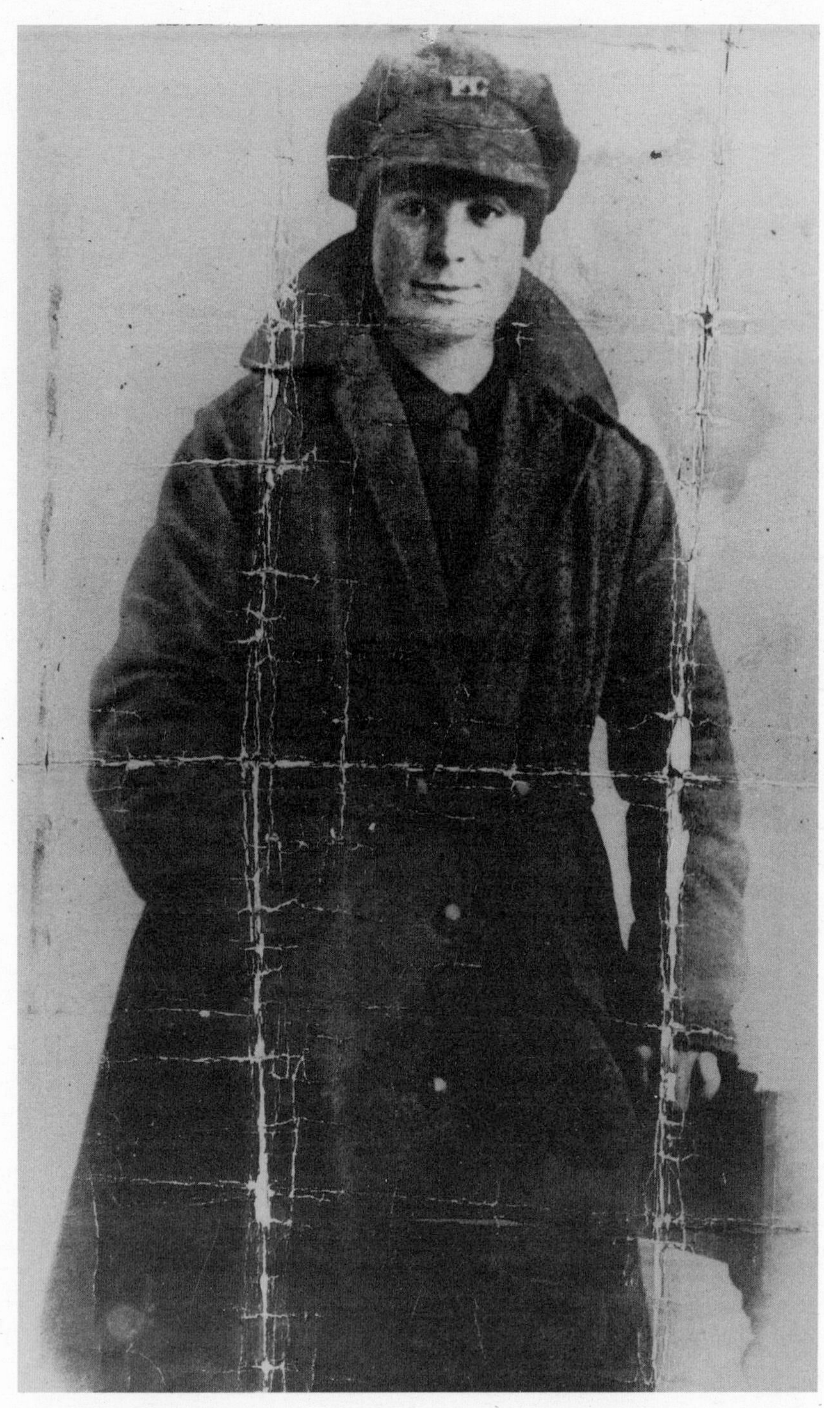

The photograph was carefully folded to show her face

film crews and put a finger straight away on the right document (the team of researchers fresh from university, who have already done the legwork, disappear from view); academic experts and local historians on call, who explain the context. In order to shape a story several possible 'leads' will have been discarded; months of searching concertinaed into a finely honed hour on air. But as most viewers know, family history, like all historical work, is messy and loose-ended, full of false starts, red herrings and wild goose chases, discoveries which are sheer serendipity and might so easily have been missed.

Far from being dead ends or time-wasters, these detours are part of historical work. They reveal our misconceptions and dislodge our assumptions about the past. In search of Evelyn's war, I scoured the archive of Studley agricultural college because it was close to her home and taught women how to breed, work with and even break in horses. The warden of Studley, Dr Lillias Hamilton, led a contingent of Red Cross nurses in Serbia in 1914 and during the war the college, which deserves a proper study, was 'exceptionally full with students'. But the registers showed the girls were mostly from private schools like Cheltenham or Roedean: Studley was for ladies. It was a sharp reminder that women's war work was largely determined by their social class. Far less prestigious, and largely forgotten, was the job of supplying feed for the horses. Then, by chance, I came across a photograph of sixteen-year-old Annie Webb wearing what looked like Evelyn's cap and coat, the uniform of the Women's Forage Corps. Annie had been in service in London since the age of eleven and the Forage Corps was for girls like her.

Formed in 1915 the Forage Corps was the first attempt ever to organize women volunteers to work on the land. Its success led to the establishing in 1917 of the much larger Women's Land Army (WLA), but it has been overshadowed by its later sister; it also sits awkwardly within women's history. Women like Evelyn joined as civilians but came under the joint control of the Royal Army Service Corps and a woman superintendent, Mrs Athole Stewart; they were not in the Women's Army Auxiliary Corps (the WAACS), and although later recruited and organized by the WLA, they remained part of the army. Their work was peripatetic. They were not stationed on farms, and unlike those women who were so noticeable and frequently photographed, taking the place of men in civilian life, driving buses or heaving coal, the Forage Corps were rarely seen in town. Being on the move also meant they did not appear in recruitment drive displays or demonstrations at county shows as the Land Girls did, proving to farmers that they could plough a furrow or use a hoe. Unlike the Forestry Commission, which carried on after the war, they faded away with the coming of peace. There was not much glamour attached to the manual work they did and perhaps that too made them easier to forget, like the battalions of male labourers sent out to dig the trenches before their fellows died in them. But their work was crucial: the British Expeditionary Forces depended on their horses and the horses needed fodder. These women baled, stacked and forwarded the hay. By March 1918 the Forage Department had enrolled over 5,000 women workers.

War is always about provisioning, about feeding not only the troops but also the animals. Vast numbers of horses and mules were requisitioned by the army from farms and blacksmiths to transport weapons and supplies; even when motorized transport appeared, horses remained the primary means of transport. Estimates vary, but more than 600,000 horses were ultimately 'on active service' at the war's peak. The demand for hay and fodder was enormous. On the Eastern Front especially, horses were on the front line, in action as cavalry mounts, or as draught animals, pulling artillery guns, ambulances or wagons, lifting and hauling in and out of the mud. Amid the carnage, at least 250,000 horses were destroyed in the fighting: a different, and terrible, slaughter of innocents.

Earning money and working for a living was not a novelty to factory girls like Evelyn, and there was plenty of wartime employment in Cotteridge. She could easily have worked in munitions, but my grandmother had no father to object to her leaving, no husband or children to worry about. If her future had followed the usual path, she would have left the factory for marriage and most likely several children, till she became one of those harassed and worn-out women, prematurely aged, for whom the youthful good times vanished with the youthful good looks. The war gave her a different kind of freedom, extending her young womanhood for a few years more. Perhaps thanks to her Whitlock relatives on the farm or the Dowdeswell saddlery, Evelyn was familiar with horses. Joining the Forage Corps was still a bold step. It meant leaving home and the factory for a life on the road.

'OUR SOLDIERS' HORSES MUST HAVE HAY,' announced the recruiting leaflet for the Forage Corps, adding that every girl instinctively loves a horse – 'the patient, hard-working, four-footed friend of man'. The girls were part of a gang of eight, including three soldiers, with a woman 'corporal' in charge. They travelled from farm to farm with the steam baling machine, or worked at a 'Chaffing Depot', chopping the hay or straw into short lengths for the horses' fodder. They stacked and loaded the hay and the 'conductress' would accompany it to the railway station, where 'the forwarding supervisor' dispatched it. Girls like Evelyn formed the rank and file in the hierarchy; girls with clerical experience did the paperwork as section clerks; the more genteel could aspire to the role of supervisor, area inspector or assistant superintendent. No training was required but the commitment was for the minimum of a year, twice the length of time asked by the other sections of the Land Army, no doubt because of the complex organization needed. The pay was better than in the other sections of the WLA, between twenty-six and thirty shillings a week, with bonuses if a gang's baler produced extra bales. There were tedious times, mending sacks and heavy sheet tarpaulins (a job that in pre-war times had been deemed essentially man's work) or guarding forage dumps all night in the freezing cold in case of non-existent enemy attacks. Some women were based at the army camps, tending to the animals' needs, and some travelled with the animals to France. The bulk of the work was not bucolic, despite the pastoral imagery the recruiters were fond of promoting. War photographer Horace Nicholls captured women doing the hot, dusty work on the hay baler, engulfed by the filthy smoke belching from the steam engine.

Members of the Women's Forage Corps in Middlesex, 1918
(Imperial War Museum)

It was a 'gipsy life'. Moving from village to village was not for the delicate but it was fun and different from the other war work, not least because the women mixed with the Tommies. I like to think this was Evelyn's 'heyday' in every sense. The women were billeted in local cottages, often in the most remote countryside, though sometimes the authorities provided a caravan for the girls to 'mess' in, cooking up stews and soups communally. They were very careful to stress in their reports that the girls *never* slept there. Inevitably all the women working on the land were given stern advice, constantly exhorted to behave themselves and to dress modestly: no jewellery, no lace, and their dark green corduroy breeches always to be covered by an overall if worn in public so that legs were not shown:

> You are doing a man's work and so you are dressed rather like a man but remember that just because you wear a smock and breeches you should take care to behave like an English girl who expects chivalry and respect from everyone she meets.

Evelyn had been working in a factory for several years, so one wonders how all this gentility struck her. How could they possibly manage to be ladylike while forking hay or loading it into a truck? The local villagers who encountered these trouser-wearing women could be hostile: 'It isn't decent to come out dressed like that,' was one typical comment; there were stories of misbehaviour and 'indiscipline'. The women themselves enjoyed new masculine freedoms: one woman with the Forage Department in Gloucestershire especially relished being saluted and treated with respect by the eight soldiers under her as she went 'out all day in all weathers on my motor cycle'.

Class distinctions, though, were not as easily overturned. The women in the ranks were the 'Industrial Members' of the Corps, 'most of whom were drawn from the domestic servant class', as one overview put it in 1919. The improvement of their health was much remarked upon. Gladys Wiles, enthusiastically describing 'life on a hay baler', noted 'the strong free movement of the girls . . . as . . . they toss the hay into the mouth of the hungry engine. How different from the cramped positions of floor-scrubbing or dish-washing.' Wiles was eager to scotch any rumour of fraternizing or 'the giggles of flirtation'. The 'girls', she maintained, working with men 'as comrades and equals', were exemplars of a new breed of Englishwoman: 'It is not tinsel and jewellery that will attract the man now, but energy and stability that will awaken his admiration.' This inspiringly classless vision was short-lived, however. After the war, girls were expected to return to domestic service, women in factories encouraged to make way for the men, while their 'superiors' found managerial or supervisory posts or took up the reins again as mistresses at home.

The Forage Corps was disbanded at the end of 1919, having recruited over 8,000 women. Evelyn went back to Cotteridge and to the paper factory. She was working there in July 1921 when she got married to Bert Light. Signing the marriage register, Bert carefully distinguished between his occupation as 'journeyman bricklayer' and his father's as 'master bricklayer', a man at the top of his skills. Bert was part of a gang and would be paid by the day ('journeyman' is from the French *journée*, meaning 'day'), going wherever the work was. Evelyn put the age twenty-eight on the register, but she was three weeks short of her thirtieth birthday and she was five months pregnant. They started married life in a rented cottage on the canal wharf at Breedon Cross, next to the Lifford industrial area, but soon moved to King's Heath, not far from Cotteridge, where Cissie Evelyn, my auntie Cis, was born. There were to be three more children in five years, all in different locations: Albert William, my uncle 'Bob', born 150 miles away, down south in Fareham, Hampshire; Elizabeth Margaret, my auntie 'Marg', eighteen months later, back in Worcestershire, in Wythall; and finally in 1926 my father, Sidney, in Birmingham. These places had one thing in common. They were all on the edge of building sites.

*

This kind of family history, with its scraps of information, is not conventional biography; the second half of Evelyn's life is truncated. She died nine years after her marriage, and beyond a copy of the usual certificates I could find no other documentation of her life. My father had no memories of her and always spoke as if she were a distant relation, as indeed, in one sense, she was; he was not yet four when she died. 'She looks a nice person,' he would say, 'from her photograph.' No chance now to flesh her out: my uncle and aunts were dead and I had never thought to ask them what she was like. For the family historian the feeling of belatedness is an occupational hazard, if not a chronic condition. Questions that should have been asked when relatives were alive; answers, when they do come, that have no one to receive them. So why do we go on asking? My father would have been interested in hearing about his mother's family and her war. Now I was talking to his ghost.

Since the trip to Evelyn's grave I had been on a rollercoaster, lurching from excitement to disappointment and back again. Historians are familiar with the queasy switchback of working in archives, happily absorbed in the material one minute, suddenly overwhelmed by what they might be missing the next, frantically ordering up a new batch of documents before last orders are called. The Internet produces its own version of 'archive fever', as more and more documents are available online, and its own addiction to the hit and the discovery-high. But family history has special lows. Most of the people I was tracking would have little more than a name, age and perhaps an occupation. They were history's losers, the non-achievers; they had not made names for themselves. Who would care what happened to them? In such a disheartened mood I trudged uphill to the Warwick record office one January in heavy snow, the locality as unfamiliar as a foreign country, the accents alien and abrasive, only to find more paupers like the Readings in Coughton, more nobodies. Yet the thrill of a discovery, the random detail, say, of William Russen's bowling alley in the Turk's Head in Alcester, would buoy me up for days.

I was trying, I realized, to put my grandmother back into history, a history where she would not feature, as she did in our stories, only as the lost mother. But I wanted more than that. I wanted the family's past not to be limited by the facts, which seem to rigidify so many lives into victimhood. I didn't want to elevate them into heroes and saints, projecting my own desires, fancying they were all likeable or loveable, acceptable objects of pity or of admiration. I didn't want a 'history from below', though I might be writing one, so much as to gesture towards a history 'from inside', which took for granted their capacity for happiness as well as suffering; a life that could surprise. I could prove nothing about Evelyn's character, but even a few details, as the psychoanalyst Christopher Bollas puts it, 'recovered from ordinary oblivion' and set against the 'dumb effect of events' could gather a force to them, a life force. As she became more human and less of an image, she was becoming more, not less, of a mystery. The questions I was asking, whether I answered them or not, were freeing her memory from the burden of the few facts about her life. The cramped space of the past was opening out. Historical work meant giving it breathing room.

*

My father did not know how his father came to be in Birmingham or how his parents met. If Bert was looking for work, there was plenty of it for a bricklayer willing to travel in the years after the First World War. House construction had ceased during the war, and the rising population, including thousands returned from the services, plus the ever-deteriorating state of much of the Victorian housing stock, had led to a dire housing shortage. Birmingham, with its desperately congested slums in the central wards of the city, embarked on a massive and ambitious building programme. The Housing and Town Planning Act of 1919 had ushered in a new national policy for housing reform – 'Homes for Heroes' – whereby local councils were offered financial aid for building houses. Reformers were moved by a complex mix of motives: humanitarian concern for the miserable conditions in which the poor lived, mingled with a fear of social unrest, a belief that the lower orders needed moral improvement, and a wish to cultivate a national stock of contented, healthy workers. By 1926 Birmingham council had built more municipal houses than any other local authority in Britain. The boom in council-house building took place between 1924 and 1931, before the economic depression led to entrenchment, but in total between the wars over 50,000 council or corporation houses were built. The figure for private building was about the same. It was, for a while, a bricklayer's paradise.

I was now crossing over into the territory of my father's memories. Always begin with memories, family historians are told, but memories cannot be trusted; and as they are passed on through the generations, they accrete new details or are subtly changed with each repetition like the game of 'Chinese whispers' we played as children. We misremember the memories we inherit; their fabric is coloured by our own desires. My father's memories of his early childhood were very few. He knew his address, Cleeve Road, and in his mind's eye could see himself playing on a green in front of the house, Acock's Green, perhaps, the district given on the abbreviated copy of his birth certificate. His recollections were wholly benign: his father bringing home ginger pop in stone bottles; a 'happy valley' by a river where the family went; the neighbours making a fuss of him, a motherless child, and a sweet one at that, with his golden hair and his sailor suit, the brass buttons shining in his memory because they must have delighted him as a child. I had heard, and half listened to, these fragmentary stories many times and merged them seamlessly into tales of his later years in the slums of Portsmouth. I saw them all against a backdrop of terraced streets, the urban landscape of my own childhood.

Dad was always proud of being born a 'Brummie'. My chest swelled with a little of that municipal pride as I walked from New Street station into Chamberlain Square on the way to the Central Library. I wondered if he had also marvelled at the monumental town hall, built in the 1830s in the style of a Roman temple, when radicalism and republicanism were the order of the day. I was soon deflated. My father, it turned out, was not a townie at all. His full birth certificate gave 'Billesley Common', a sub-district of Acock's Green, but Bartholomew's *Pocket Atlas Guide* to the city for 1924 showed Billesley as an area of scattered farms, commons and woods with few main roads. In 1926 the council register of private applications for new buildings had Cleeve Road slowly spawning a cycle-repair shop, a milliner's and 'motor houses' (garages). It was Cotteridge all over again. My father was born not long after the houses in Cleeve Road were built. But this was not an industrial development. Billesley Common was dominated by a council estate. The Billesley Farm estate in 1924–5 was one of the first council housing developments in Birmingham. Thanks to the recommendations of the revolutionary Tudor-Waters report the new houses were no longer to be channelled into back-to-back terraces with parlours, like Frances Road, but were to be brighter and more spacious, with proper amenities, built in different styles, and with space between the small blocks of six or eight, no more than twelve houses per acre in a town. By 1926 between fifteen and twenty families were moving in a week. Bert Light could have easily been employed by the council, or by private contractors like Howells, who built most of the estate.

I was pleased to think of my grandparents settled and secure for a few years at least in a brand-new council house. But I was aiming too high. I had again forgotten that poverty was so often not a matter of unemployment but of low and irregular wages. Further investigation produced more disillusionment. While Bert may have been building council houses, he would not have qualified to live in one. In the early 1920s he might have taken home as much as eighteen shillings (90p) for a nine-hour day (well over double the going rate before the war), over £4 a week, but that was on a good week and in the years when there was a shortage of bricklayers. Much depended on the employer; there were stoppages in bad weather, for 'short time', sometimes for weeks in winter. Bricklaying was unreliable contract-work without sick pay and no guarantee where the next job was coming from. Council houses were only for the respectable working class in steady jobs who could guarantee their weekly payments of rent. In fact Cleeve Road was in neighbouring Warstock, not Billesley, whatever the registrar had written, south of the Chinn brook which formed the boundary of the council estate. Bert and Evelyn probably got a house at a reduced rent through the builders. It was common practice for employers to help their workers temporarily.

105 Cleeve Road, my father's birthplace

I made my pilgrimage to Cleeve Road, sitting in the taxi with mounting excitement but also a guilty feeling of committing mild sacrilege: I would see my father's birthplace, which he had largely forgotten. Cleeve Road is a wide, sweeping crescent upon high ground. The houses have front and back gardens, and there are views across treetops. What I had taken for hazy sentiment was a clear memory: the house *was* set back from the road with a grass verge, a green in front of it for children to play on. Nor was 'Happy Valley' the fantasy of an old man 'babbling of green fields', like Shakespeare's Falstaff. I found a book of postcards of the spot where the Stratford-upon-Avon canal crossed nearby Yardley Wood Road, a popular haunt for picnickers, with a bandstand and boats for hire: 'Happy Valley', it was called locally. Every image I had of my father's early childhood was now changed for the better: he'd been a baby and a toddler in a new house, a light and airy place surrounded by woods. But like Cassandra I could spoil it all. I knew his mother's death loomed. My father was fond of quoting from A. E. Housman's *A Shropshire Lad*, whose 'blue remembered hills' were just as poignant for us city-dwellers, since they are the contours of the country of childhood which everyone leaves behind. They evoke nostalgia in its purest form, a longing for home and mother. Thinking of what was to come, I stood on the pavement at Cleeve Road, feeling that I had given with one hand, only to take away with the other, until some inner prompter – the ego's comforter, no doubt – offered me another favourite tag. Better, I could almost hear my father saying, to have loved and lost, than never to have loved at all.

⋆

Pulmonary tuberculosis, an infection of the lungs, develops slowly, the symptoms only showing themselves when the disease is advanced, while the final 'decline' usually takes between three and five years. It is a disease that has been long associated with silicosis, fibrosis of the lungs caused by breathing in metallic particles or dust and fluff from industrial processes – 'consumption', asthma and chronic hoarseness among women textile workers was noted as early as the 1840s. Living conditions in the cottages in Lifford Lane, near the canal, were damp and cramped; Evelyn's work at the paper mills may have taken its toll, just as scraping metal may have injured her father's lungs. She would have been examined for the Forage Corps and found fit and healthy, but by the time she moved to Cleeve Road Evelyn – 'Evie' – was likely to be suffering. Poorly for most of my father's infancy, losing weight, tired out by a short hacking cough and night sweats, pale but with that rosy flush which comes from spasmodic fevers, spitting up phlegm and eventually blood, she was unlikely to have held her new baby, my father, very much. She would eventually be isolated in hospital. Even so, she was lucky, comparatively speaking. She might have died at home in wretchedness in front of her children or in the workhouse infirmary, but she died a modern death, in a clean, comfortable bed of her own. Treatment cost her nothing and none of her children were infected. Thanks to its proximity to the Lickey Hills and its healthful air, the West Heath Hospital, not far from Cleeve Road, opened as a sanatorium in 1919, devoted entirely to tuberculosis; pavilions with outdoor beds for advanced female cases were also available in nearby Yardley Road. Nonetheless, the barracks-like building of West Heath frightened the locals, who, it was said, covered their mouths when they walked by.

Though it has always been a disease to afflict both rich and poor, tuberculosis thrives above all on undernourished bodies in overcrowded districts. In Birmingham in the 1930s it killed twice as many people in the central wards of the city than in the leafy suburbs. Slowly an improved standard of living and better housing was bringing down the death rate, but for working people the National Insurance Act of 1911, a contributory system which insured workers and gave them some unemployment benefit and sick pay, was crucial. The first step towards a welfare provision which moved away from stigmatizing the poor under the old Poor Law, it included free treatment for tuberculosis and access to a 'panel' doctor when they were taken sick. Medical science had long proved that tuberculosis was infectious, a 'family disease', frequently passed between parents and children, and local authority services were being directed towards its control by setting up special clinics and sanatoria where patients, especially from over-crowded homes, could be isolated. It was not a cure, but it did much to save other lives. The right combination of drugs to combat the disease was not developed until 1952. On the upper part of my left arm is the half-inch white circle left by the 'BCG' vaccination (named for the dual creators of the drugs, 'Bacillus Calmette-Guérin'), the free immunization given to generations of British schoolchildren. Such scars are historical documents.

Evelyn died in West Heath, but she was well cared for and her children were not abandoned: the electoral roll for May 1929 lists Louisa Whitlock, Evelyn's mother, at Cleeve Road nearly a year before her daughter died. The doctor in charge of overseeing tuberculosis treatment in Birmingham urged that 'voluntary segregation' be 'practised benevolently' and patients who were clearly in the advanced stages of the illness be 'granted concessions', including visitors. Evelyn may have chosen isolation to protect her children, but TB patients often remain lucid until the end; death would certainly be anticipated and my grandparents had time to talk about money and the future. A headstone would be very expensive and was only an option if my grandfather also bought the burial rights to the grave. I could even imagine a scenario in which this saving was Evelyn's idea. I would never know, but it no longer mattered. It mattered to family and friends that Evelyn had a 'decent' funeral, a public occasion to be shared. The unmarked grave might be an affront to human dignity, but it said more about the costs of dying in a class society than it did about a person's life. I would have to learn to sacrifice the thrill of melodrama, with its intense emotions and its tendency towards the Gothic, as I followed the lives – and deaths – of the working poor. Graves, even non-existent ones, were historical evidence to be sifted and interpreted. Anonymity has a history.

I was wrong to think that Evelyn was not memorialized. I'd passed quickly over the verse on the remembrance card because I found it trite and conventional, no doubt one of several on offer in the funeral parlour. Now I could hear in the flat lines and predictable rhymes some echo of the feelings to which they once had spoken:

A life linked with my own,
Sadly I miss her footsteps as I wander all alone;
But God is good. He gives me strength.
To bear my heavy cross.
He is the only one who knows
How bitter is my loss.

A bleak little verse, very personal, offering no hope of reunion or of redemption, no meeting in a better place. Like Christ with his cross, my grandfather claimed Evelyn's death for himself; his loss and his alone (but perhaps he could not bear the idea of his children's suffering). It sounds lonely but dogged, with that touch of self-pity so indistinguishable from grief. Under the verse he had put, 'Evelyn Prudence, Beloved Wife of Henry Herbert Light, who fell asleep Feb 14th 1930 aged 38': so it was also a Valentine. Why care about headstones? This funeral token had been carefully kept by her husband, passed on to his children and now to me. It had survived more than eighty years. I looked at it again. The preservation of a flimsy piece of cardboard said as much as any monument in stone.

*

My father's family hung on in Birmingham for a few years while a series of housekeepers came and went. The country was heading into an economic depression and the work may have dried up in the area, or the house rent proved too expensive, or more likely both. Either way, my grandfather needed to leave. By the autumn of 1934 Bert had taken his children to Portsmouth, 200-odd miles away. He rented a basement and three rooms for them in Hope Place, a courtyard of crowded tenements in what was one of the most run-down parts of the dockyard town, a place as bad as any of the Birmingham slums. It was a far cry from the green fields of Billesley Common or the peace of Brandwood End. My grandfather was back home and was to stay there for the rest of his life, but I knew little about his forebears. Evelyn Whitlock was the daughter of generations of rural migrants caught up in the whirlwind of the Industrial Revolution, but had the Lights also taken to the road, or would I find somewhere settled and rooted in their past?

2 Hope Place

It could be any time in history; any country; any story where a young man seeks his fortune and sets out to find the place where the streets are paved with gold, or at least paved, or at least where there are jobs paving them. The decision to leave is easy in the end. No work and less and less to eat. It is time to leave the village, home and family, and head for the town.

When shall we say it was? And where? Sometime in the 1800s, and two brothers are walking a track which runs, pitted and rutted, across the smooth slopes of the chalk downland. It is a raw morning, the mists lifting. This is Wiltshire, a large county to the west of England, 200 miles from London, and they are high on Salisbury Plain, heading south-east to the coast fifty miles on. A carter will take them part of the way, but they have no money to squander and will walk if they have to. The chalk is their country but they have seldom been further than Salisbury, a stretch of fifteen miles. Sheep shuffle off as the strangers approach, their wool glistening with damp. Across the Plain there are hundreds of sheep, closely cropping the grass; corn will be planted where the flock has been folded, making the most of the manure. To the north, though, the soil turns dark and clayey, good for cattle and dairy. Wiltshire is two different countries: chalk and cheese.

England is at war, but it has been at war – on and off – for the whole of their lives. War has driven the brothers on to the road, not to join in the fight against the French, but to get a living. Four miles from their home they pass the stone circle. They know all the stories: how wild men from Wales dragged them overland, how foreigners ferried them over the water, or Merlin's magic flew them through the air. But to the brothers it seemed that men like themselves must have hoisted each stone, resting one atop two others, like the lintel for a door. 'Grey wethers' the locals call those other stones that lie scattered around like hunched sheep, and sometimes 'sarsens', after 'saracens', the sign of the outlandish.

The true subject of these stories is the road. It runs through their lives and it must ever be borne in mind. Never imagine, not for one minute, a country of peasants, or labourers, preserved in their postures, miniaturized and quaint, like figures in a tapestry, or solitary and still, like the stone menhirs that stand exposed to all-comers. Imagine instead the road and all the people on it. People on the move, men and women and children, by choice or by necessity, or because there is no difference, because wayfaring is their living or because begging is their last resort. All across Britain they travel, out of their own country, out from the villages, with their brains and bodies to sell.

There they are, then, the brothers on the road. No longer the bustard or the wheatear overhead but the incessant gulls and the salt air stinging their cheeks. Whistling and singing, well wadded against the wind (what they own is what they stand up in), one with a cloth bag, one with a basket. They hold a loaf and cheese, some ale, a neckcloth or two, and their tools of the trade, without which they might starve: a trowel and axe, plumb line and square. The future, they are certain, will be built in brick.

★

When my father talked about his childhood, it was as if the five of them were adrift on a raft on a stormy sea. They had to cling together because there was no one else, no other family. There was an old man with a pipe, it's true, living in the north of the city, who visited once or twice. He was my father's grandfather. One afternoon he took the little boy outside to the garden to see the orchids he grew there. The flowers were as wondrous as the cucumber sandwiches he was given for tea, but the old man was less memorable. At home the family huddled together in Hope Place, the children learning to keep the front door shut when their father was at work, lest 'the authorities' come to take them away, a threat which left my father shy of answering the door even as a young man. I grew up with my father's stories and they took on, as such tales do, all the power and unreality of fable. Why were there no relatives in my father's childhood except for the old man with his orchids? What was the spell that had been cast over the family, keeping them apart from others?

My father's father, Bert Light, was a wanderer, that much I knew. Evelyn Whitlock had married a man whose work took for granted a series of fresh starts. They spent most of their lives close to building sites, and had she lived who knows where the family might have ended up. Apprenticed as a bricklayer to his father, Bert gave it up to join the navy. He left home, my father always said, because his parents were 'Salvationists' and 'he couldn't stand it'. Nobody knew what this meant, though my father half hoped they were Salvation Army, recalling with admiration the 'Hallelujah lasses', selling their magazines in the smoky pubs of his youth, 'shaming men into giving them money', holding out their hats, like flowerpots, for the coins. 'They had some guts, those girls.' After Evelyn died, so the story went, Bert came back to Portsmouth 'with his tail between his legs' and had to ask for work from his righteous father. There were other Lights in the building trade in Portsmouth, a Sid and a Ben, with a yard near Hope Place, who also gave him some work, my father thought, but they were only faintly connected.

Evelyn Whitlock's people were movers-on but their lives and skills were transformed by mechanization. Her father, one of those thousands of rural migrants who came off the land, adapted his labour to suit a new environment. He began life as a farm boy and ended it working in a metal factory. Bert Light, on the other hand, took his work with him and the skills he had never changed. Masons and bricklayers have always travelled – even Egypt's slave labourers had to be moved to build the pyramids. In feudal times masons were among the first 'free labourers', hired to build cathedrals or palaces, though they might travel together in gangs under the same master. In later centuries tramping artisans would call at inns to learn about the work on offer in an area. The Bricklayers' Arms, like the Bakers' Arms, were unofficial labour exchanges and this tradition became a mechanism for coping with unemployment. Conditions of work varied but laying bricks did not. Metal cranes and scaffolding replaced rope pulleys and wood, bricks might be made by machine and not by hand, but a medieval mason could have borrowed my grandfather's tools and built a wall or an arch with them.

In 1996 – without the Internet – I sketched a preliminary family tree for my father's seventieth birthday. Most family historians start by tracking the paternal surname across time, bumping up against the repeated first names that characterize a branch or act as a clan-marker between several sons. It is easy to think that the poorer sort sometimes had nothing to leave except their names, but they often had a precious legacy to pass on: their skills and knowledge, and the chance to make a living. I soon found that my dad's forefathers had all been masons and bricklayers as far back, at least, as one Thomas Light born in the late eighteenth century. An apprenticeship to one's father might be informal, as was my grandfather's; there were no indentures or seven-year commitments on paper. Not much more than a boy, an apprentice would join the other labourers, carrying loads of bricks on hods, moving earth or rubble, digging trenches or 'footings' for the buildings, as he learnt bricklaying. Once a journeyman with his labour to sell, and with enough experience behind him, he could progress to being master and take on his own apprentice. As one of the oldest crafts, bricklaying offered what a working man wanted most of all: the opportunity to become independent.

Bricklaying makes no one's pulse race but it seemed that I had also found my father's ancestral village, a prospect to lift the spirits of any family historian. Thomas Light had been born and died in Shrewton in Wiltshire, on the south-eastern edge of Salisbury Plain, 300 square miles of bleak chalk plateau, much of which is now given over to the Ministry of Defence for army exercises and manoeuvres. Wiltshire is an ancient part of the country, once the centre of King Alfred's Saxon kingdom of Wessex, and Shrewton lies close to the most famous of all England's prehistoric sites, Stonehenge. We had never heard of the village, but my parents made a summer excursion there. It was the usual story: no graves in the churchyard, no sign of the existence of Lights. I kept the postcard of St Mary's, a handsome flint-built church, and put it away in a file, and there matters rested until after my father died.

*

In the wake of my father's death, I took to tinkering about in the Portsmouth Record Office. It was a way of carrying on my conversations with him. Leafing idly through old trade directories, I came across an Esau and a Robert Light of 'Lake Lane', builders and bricklayers from the 1820s. W. R. and C. Light, A. C. Light and Sons, other building firms, were also listed. They meant nothing to me. I say 'idly', but the urge to memorialize is far from idle and I was desperate to find something more than a mere litany of dates – baptisms, marriages and deaths – something to give substance to my father's family past. It wasn't enough to have lived and died: we all did that. I wanted some distinguishing features. I didn't need more bricklayers. I wanted some sign of an inner life, of hopes and dreams, of loves and hatreds, not this endless flitting past of lives like aimless moths, seen in the light for a matter of seconds. Too many lives were being shrunk to fit inside a pair of dates in brackets, just as my father's now was. I was depressed by the levelling effects of death, by a feeling of having seen it all before. There was nothing new under the sun.

Whether my father's story of 'Salvationists' had lodged in the back of my mind, I don't know, but something made me turn to the lists of 'Dissenters', those who worshipped outside the Church of England. I found a 'Jane Light, died 1824, Lake Lane Baptist' and her husband, Robert the bricklayer of Lake Lane. Robert and his second wife, Elizabeth Hoar, had the births of all their children registered at Meeting House Alley, the oldest of the Baptist chapels in Portsmouth, and soon, like dragon's teeth, Baptist Lights were springing up everywhere. The connections between Portsmouth and Shrewton began to knit together. Robert had been born in Shrewton; Jane in the next village. Robert and Esau were the younger brothers of 'my' Thomas Light, my father's direct ancestor. Were there Baptists in Shrewton too? According to *The Victoria County History of Wiltshire*, the local historian's first port of call, about 350 people attended worship at Shrewton's Baptist Zion chapel for morning, afternoon and evening services, when the religious census was taken in 1851. This was surely an astonishing number in a village of barely 500. Hardly a minority sect. In the Wiltshire censuses the Baptist world suddenly lurched closer still. The minister of Zion chapel was one Charles Light, Thomas's oldest son. In 1871 the Baptist chapel was itself the residence of Thomas's youngest son, Henry, and his family. The family name on my side of the family began to repeat. Thomas's grandson, Henry's son, was Henry Herbert and he grew up living in the chapel. This man, born in 1857, was my father's grandfather, from whose fierce piety Bert (Henry Herbert Archibald) Light had fled. The direct line in Shrewton ran through the Baptist church from Thomas to the man with the pipe and orchids.

My father's story ought to have alerted us, but we mistook the past for a mirror reflecting back our own preoccupations. Because they shared the same name and the same trade, we imagined the Lights were kindred spirits. In my childhood, religion barely impinged on our home life; the pub and not the church was the place where we congregated. Churches were for weddings and occasional christenings, and as a family we went in for cremations, not burials. Both my parents had a strict sense of right and wrong, believed in discipline and punishment, but there was no talk of sin or hellfire at home – or indeed of the life to come. We might take turns to say 'grace' before Sunday dinner – 'For what we are about to receive, may the Lord make us truly thankful' – or to say our prayers before bedtime when we were infants, but these were rituals as much to instil calm and order as godliness. No parish priest ever came to our house and none was ever known by name. My father, who had a smattering of the Bible and a wedge of hymns from school, considered himself an agnostic. He was a great believer in what he called 'the fifth dimension': a mix of moral philosophy, humility in the face of the unknown, Wellsian science and hedging his bets. My mother, a resolute atheist, was vehemently opposed to interfering or patronizing clergy, 'do-gooders' with their superstitious 'mumbo-jumbo'. She thought my grandfather Bert Light 'well out of it'. A Baptist minister in the family was at best an exotic species, at worst a kind of black sheep.

Empathy can take the historian only so far. Our forebears are also strangers whose deepest concerns are often alien to us. Religious faith, and especially Nonconformity, was crucial to so many working people in the nineteenth century, the foundation of their lives. It made all the difference to them: to their labours and to their household, their treatment of their neighbours, their values and aspirations. I knew that the Baptists were 'Dissenters', refusing to show allegiance to the Church of England, but the nature of their beliefs, the internecine differences – between, say, 'General' or 'Strict and Particular' – were thoroughly obscure to me. The Baptists ran their churches themselves. After a dearth of evidence proving the existence of any ancestors, now I was inundated with documents spanning more than 100 years: church books or minutes of the meetings of church members, the 'messengers' and deacons, account books, lists of Sunday-school teachers, baptism tickets and notices, and a plethora of magazines and other ephemera for youth study groups, the Band of Hope, anniversary or jubilee pamphlets. Here was a feast after famine but one I could hardly digest. As a non-believer I did not find it palatable.

I had always sympathized with the account of my grandfather's life, seeing him as a modern individual, leaving home and moving on, no doubt because my own life followed something of that pattern. This was what people did, it was the norm. But if the Baptist Lights travelled for work, they would take their God with them. Their new community could take precedence over a feeling for place or neighbours; it could cut through the bonds of parish, village or town, and be re-formed elsewhere. Like John Bunyan's Christian, they were prepared to leave family behind in order to seek salvation. Blood-relatives, like my grandfather, could become outsiders, even pariahs. Yet this community of faith, both in the flesh and in the spirit, offered sustenance at home, comfort and support, and an inner scaffolding for a labouring life. To understand my grandfather's wanderings and his return, I needed to follow the path back from Portsmouth to Shrewton. I wanted to discover why the Lights had uprooted themselves in order to take the straight and narrow road to the New Jerusalem.

Sheriffs and Maidens

Shrewton has no obvious centre, no village green or duck pond duly flanked by church and pub. The houses straggle along the busy road which is now its High Street in a ribbon development, merging with the neighbouring village of Maddington. Most of the thatched cottages, where the majority of the villagers lived, have long since disappeared. Some were little more than huts, too temporary or too humble to survive, their 'cob' walls, made from mud mixed with straw or lime, or from 'daub', which added dung and cow hair to the mix, supported by a network of split wood or 'wattle'. But the brick-built Zion chapel where Charles Light was minister is firmly there. It faces proudly up Shrewton's High Street, aslant the junction with the Salisbury road. Now 'Zion House', a private residence, there are no memorials to the Baptists on its walls. A few hundred yards further on is 'Chapel Lane', at right angles to the High Street, which once referred to the existence of a second meeting house. It houses the doctor's surgery and, ironically enough, the vicarage for St Mary's. As I discovered on my pilgrimage, a visitor to Shrewton would never know that more than half of its villagers once walked away from the Church of England or that Nonconformity galvanized the villages on the Plain.

Zion chapel

A 'village' is only a rough-and-ready shorthand for varieties of settlement on the ground, from budding townships to a couple of farmsteads surrounded by fields. Initially Shrewton was one of several tiny hamlets, nestling close together in the valley of the Till. In Domesday they were called 'Winterbourne', a reference to the fact that the river dries out in summer. Shrewton first surfaced distinctly in the thirteenth century as 'the Sheriff's farm' (the Anglo-Saxon *tun* had often signified land cleared for an estate), the manor held by Edward of Salisbury and his successors, who were sheriffs of Wiltshire. Shrewton's dwellings were hard by the manor of Maddington – 'the Maidens' farm' – where the nuns of Amesbury were housed until the priory was dissolved in 1539 during Henry VIII's land-grab. The neighbouring hamlets eventually met on either side of the Till and coalesced. I found that the Lights had lived in both places, blurring their allegiances and frustrating mine. Now I had two parish churches and a double set of parish registers for baptisms, marriages and deaths; not one ancestral village but two. At least seven generations of Lights had lived and worked in Shrewton or Maddington, from one Isaac Light who married Elizabeth Philips, a Shrewton girl, in 1688, to Henry Herbert Light, born in the mid-nineteenth century, my father's grandfather, and the last link with their rural past.

The myth of the harmonious village, watched over for centuries by the kindly vicar of the parish, is hard to budge from the English imagination. But in the late eighteenth century, when the Baptist cause revived in Wiltshire, St Mary's, Shrewton, and St Mary's, Maddington, like many other rural parishes, barely saw a priest from one year to the next. After centuries of religious strife both the Church of England and Dissent were in the doldrums. During the English Civil War, Thomas Worthen – 'The Intruder', as later Anglicans like to call Puritan divines – preached twice on Sundays; in 1652 John Hillman, Shrewton's minister, brought the world vividly into their midst when he made a collection 'towards the instructing and relieving of the Indians in New England', chipping in his own five shillings. But these outbursts of clerical activity were rare. During the Restoration the village lapsed into a religious vacuum. Richard Bygge, the vicar for thirty years from 1669, absented himself and left any pastoral care to his curate. Throughout Wiltshire, Dissenters were being fiercely persecuted under the Clarendon Code and hounded out of the country. At the close of the seventeenth century, when Isaac Light arrived, there were still Nonconformists in Shrewton, and even a Baptist meeting house, but this too fell into desuetude.

Population was sparse on the chalk. When Isaac's grandson John married Mary Mogg in July 1746, theirs was one of very few weddings at St Mary's, Shrewton. The curate noted woefully in the register for 1737, 'Marriage None: Poor Times.' In 1758 he editorialized a little more: 'Marriages: None; very poor doings indeed.' Life in the village gathered pace a little after the old London to Warminster road, which ran north of the village and past the gibbet tree, was turnpiked in 1761. A new road was made to the south, drawing Shrewton and Maddington even closer together and ensuring that a new inn, the Catherine Wheel, would receive some custom. Carters stopped to buy or deliver goods; Shrewton got more than the usual share of tradesmen and was no longer solely dependent on an economy based on sheep. It was also a convenient spot for lodging prisoners on their way from the Assize Courts in Devizes to Salisbury's Fisherton Gaol. Wrongdoers were housed overnight in the tiny pepper pot of a lock-up at the junction of Maddington and Shrewton by the river. Windowless, and no doubt airless too, 'the Blind House' was what the villagers called it. The road across the Plain could lead to the gallows or to the hulks moored in the English Solent, and on to Australia or Van Diemen's Land.

The Lights may have left no traces in the parish graveyard, but they frequently left their mark on the stones of the church. The first sign of their trade comes in the churchwardens' accounts, whose collection of pew rents reminds us that villages always had their pecking order. In the 1750s John Light had a pew in the second 'seat' at St Mary's, Shrewton, usually the preserve of tradespeople, behind the gentry or the local farmers (the poorest villagers had to stand at the back). Pew rents went towards the expenses for the running of the church, from the purchasing of wine and bread for the sacrament to the upkeep of the building. In 1793 the churchwardens noted that John's son Robert repaired the church walls with lime and bricks carted from Amesbury; Robert and *his* son Thomas also did regular work for the wardens and sent in their bills. Thomas Light sometimes called himself a 'mason', as did his son Henry, though that generally meant working in stone, not brick. In Wiltshire there was little of either available locally, only flint and chalk. Bricks were expensive and used only for grander houses. The distinction between occupations was negligible in the small village, especially as bricklayers, like masons, cut and shaped their bricks by hand late into the nineteenth century. Men worked with whatever materials were available, with the aid of an apprentice or a labourer or two, alongside the carpenters who erected the wooden scaffolding and made timbers for ceilings, doors and windows. Each craftsman was paid individually. Francis Garrett, the local carpenter, sent in his bills to the churchwardens at the same time as the Lights, and in 1800 his daughter Christian married Thomas Light, uniting the trades.

Despite being artisans, the Lights also 'applied to the parish' for aid. Bricklaying was out of the question in bad weather or in winter, when damp and frost made it impossible for the mortar to set and bond the masonry. At other times they found agricultural work. Though he had been paid for repairing the church walls, Robert Light could not find the money to bury his mother, Mary, nor the three shillings for her shroud and her coffin costing eight. The parish covered the costs. Deaths 'on the parish' in Shrewton were not anonymous nor necessarily unneighbourly but a joint responsibility, from the sewing of a shroud to the making of the coffin by Francis Garrett. Nor did the absence of headstones always mean a person was forgotten. The novelist Thomas Hardy recalled that for much of the nineteenth century in the villages he knew in nearby Dorset, 'the places of burial, even of the poor and tombless, were all remembered'.

Shrewton has only one surviving volume of accounts kept by the 'overseers of the poor', men elected from the ratepayers in the parish, who administered the poor rate and gave out 'relief' in cash or kind to the needy of the village. It spans the thirty-odd years between 1785 and 1817, when the numbers of people applying to the parish rocketed sky-high. Wiltshire was a largely agricultural county 'poor in infrastructure'. With few mineral sources and no ports, it had little industry, and with less than a quarter of the land unenclosed by 1811 there was not much chance of speculation or of investment. Life for farm workers on the chalk was especially hard. Work was often seasonal and insecure; there was little alternative employment and few villagers had any grazing rights. A rising population and the effects of engrossing and amalgamating farms meant that more and more of Wiltshire's working men were landless labourers reliant solely on their intermittent wages. During the French wars the escalating prices took a further toll. By 1803 nearly a quarter of Wiltshire's population were in receipt of parish relief. Of course 'top-down' documents like the overseers' accounts hardly give a full picture of village life. They tell us more about its woes than its pleasures, and even the picture of poverty is slewed, for there were always far more in need than were ever on relief – a 'penumbral poor' – who did not qualify for aid or make it into the records. Shrewton's account book reveals the coping mechanisms the overseers found to deal with increasing deprivation, but it also shows the human scale of the provision and the pains they took to look after their fellow villagers. It was in these years, as more and more villagers began to suffer want, that the Baptist preachers arrived in Shrewton.

In Shrewton the overseers were not remote officials but men like Thomas Munday, a village tailor, from whom Robert Light rented a cottage. In 1785 they needed only half a page to list the 'weekly poor', nineteen regulars who received a shilling or two, for the year, mostly the elderly or sick who could not work. The overseers also listed 'the extraordinary expences [*sic*]' for the year, parish business, such as the cost of a warrant and a trip to the local magistrate at Westbury when Henry Snook served Thomas Smith a summons 'on account of Martha Snooks bastard'; a mad dog that needed to be destroyed; or the fees which were owed the sexton and the coffin-maker. Rent was paid for a handful of families; fuel – the Plain had few trees – handed out to others. 'One bushel of coal and three faggots' were given to the ailing Mary Netton 'to keep her warm in her final illness', while Mary Bacon got a shilling a week 'for her trouble' in looking after her neighbour until she died. Invalids like Mary Light were given the odd 'bottle of stuff' costing two shillings, or sixpence for 'bleeding', though 'Best's wife' did rather better with half a pint of port wine at nine pence 'ordered by the Doctor'. Some were so poor as to need bedding. Shoes and breeches were supplied for those being apprenticed; stays, caps, hat and handkerchief for Sarah Hawkens, obviously going into service. Betty South earned a few pence from the parish, sewing smocks for the poor from 'dowlas', or linen supplied by a local clothier. But even regular doles ('gifts') of a shilling or two a week were not enough to live on. They were a supplement in a world where the villagers had to rely on 'an economy of makeshifts', on kin and neighbours, on kindliness and cadging, and on other ways of making ends meet. Picking up stones and flints to be used in building and road construction was one such sideline, mostly the work of women and older children. When Thomas Light was thirteen the parish paid him six shillings and sixpence – sixpence a load (5p) – for thirteen loads.

Shrewton's overseers seem compassionate by the standards of the day, paying out ever-larger sums, raising the rates ever higher. But it was not a fair or equitable welfare system. Each parish raised its own money, so distribution was uneven between villages and payments were inconsistent. Much depended on goodwill and on the character of those in charge, particularly when it came to 'casual' or occasional doles (not everyone got bread, cheese and seven quarts of beer, as Francis Garrett did, for the burying of his wife). There was no 'flat rate' for unemployment: different sums were paid to different people in deference to their position or the overseers' view of their moral worth. Out of employ for a week in January 1800, Robert Light was given fifteen shillings; others, also with several children, got half as much. In a small village of not much more than 250 people, the overseers knew who they were dealing with and this knowledge was double-edged. Applications were made face to face, and suitable displays of gratitude were expected (the usual habit was for 'collectioners' of a regular pension to assemble in the porch of the church). The records do not show how many applied to the parish and were turned down. Even at their most generous, the overseers were caught in a cleft stick, as ratepayers duty-bound to save the ratepayers – viz. themselves – money. In Wiltshire most of the rateable property belonged to farmers, who rapidly found it cheaper to economize on wages, hire and discharge men as they needed them, then keep them in reserve on minimum poor relief, rather than offer them full-time work. 'The fox had access to the hen house at will,' as one local historian puts it.

By the end of the eighteenth century Wiltshire was at the bottom of any national table of wage scales, and the villagers on the chalk downlands, in their mud-walled, earth-floored huts, were at the bottom of the bottom. On 24 July 1795 Shrewton's vestry and the villagers gathered together in the parish church to agree emergency measures: 'that is to pay to every grown person being poor people and belonging to the parish one gallon loaf per week for 14d [pence] and to each child a three quarter loaf' (the overseers also ordered 'a change of linen for each child of Stephen Blake and a bed for Jane Kemble'). Sometimes the men received subsidized wheat in return for their labours. The local farmers were never out of pocket, since the parish paid them what they were owed; occasionally the baker was given cash so that the poor could buy at reduced prices. These allowances were a version of what became known as the 'Speenhamland' system, named after the village in Berkshire which tried it first. Such subsidies led to bitter criticism and even outrage as the rates grew ever higher and the number without work rose. Indignant voices were raised, like those of the Reverend Thomas Malthus, complaining that the doles encouraged the labouring poor to be idle, dependent and inclined to over-breed. The term 'labouring poor' was itself controversial and seen by many as a contradiction in terms. It acknowledged that a man could work and still be poor; that wages were kept too low and that many living in poverty were not workless or shiftless but underemployed. Such arguments could lead to Jacobinism and revolution.

In Shrewton attempts were made to ramp up patriotic feeling during the wars with France. Invasion fears reached the Plain, and the vestry paid for the printing of 100 handbills 'for getting a man to serve in the army of defence' (the news of Nelson's death at Trafalgar took three weeks to reach the village on 11 November 1805; the ringers earned five shillings tolling the church bell). There was rioting in Wiltshire when a lottery for service in the local militia was first proposed, not least because the wealthy could always buy their way out. Shrewton's vestry paid £2 to the parish of Headington for a substitute when Thomas Harper, its blacksmith, was drawn. They travelled back and forth to the Sun Inn at Fisherton to do swaps with other overseers and negotiate with the regulating officer. Thomas Light, with four children to feed, volunteered for two weeks' local duty, for which his wife received £1 3s 4d. At times the roads across the Plain were dotted with exhausted and often emaciated casualties: soldiers and their families with permission to ask a shilling from the overseers before they moved on; homeless mothers and children desperate for a few pence; figures like the 'Female Vagrant', in the young Wordsworth's 'Salisbury Plain' (1793–4), written in protest against the corruption and tyranny of Pitt's government: 'Oh! what can war but endless war still breed?' 'Gave sixpence: a poor woman on the road' runs like a threnody through the overseers' accounts, with occasional variations on the theme: a shilling to 'two sailors in distress on the road' and 'buried a poor woman on the road'.

Sometime in the 1800s Thomas's younger brothers Esau and Robert left Shrewton for Portsmouth, a flourishing dockyard town. Their father, Robert, was a long-liver and a competitor for work. There was also Thomas, and his son Charles, who was learning the trade. Leaving the parish meant losing the chance of relief elsewhere if they fell on hard times or, if they looked like being 'chargeable' to the new parish, finding themselves sent back to where they came from. Settlement laws, as the saying went, 'tied a man by the leg' but they did not hobble him completely. They existed to protect local communities rather than to regulate the labour market, and the new industries in burgeoning towns and cities could not have managed without the flow of migrants or the pool of labour they provided. The brothers may have gone ahead to make homes for their sweethearts, as migrants often do. Each came back to marry a girl from Maddington. In 1809 'Esau Light of Portsmouth', thus distinguished as a foreigner, married Elizabeth Davis; three years later his brother, similarly described, married her sister Jane.

With only the overseers' book to go by, the prospects for the Lights who stayed in Shrewton looked grim. The village had grown

– nearly 400 inhabitants by 1811 – and by the end of the war occasional doles had become a regular system of relief. Accounts, now kept half-yearly, stretched to a dozen pages or more. There were simply too many 'weekly poor' to list by name. The category of 'extraordinaries' was abandoned altogether in this time of extraordinary measures, and large sums of up to £9 or £10, relief for several men, were entered merely as 'two weeks' pay' or 'four weeks' pay', without names attached. Any available jobs were shared out for minimal wages; the Lights were among those 'on the stem', as it was called locally. Thomas Light and his fourteen-year-old boy, Charles, sometimes worked on the 'yard lands', or strips and fields owned by the Church. Thomas was frequently ill and his wife, Christian, like other women in childbirth, got £1 to tide her over every pregnancy. Thomas's father, Robert, had lost his cottage when Thomas Munday died; the family often needed coal and were one of several who had their rent paid. Thomas's spinster sisters, Elizabeth and Dinah, were also in need and got a few shillings now and then. Without religion, what would have become of them?

Where was the parish priest while his parishioners endured such suffering? In Shrewton and Maddington, as usual, the vicar was absent. John Skinner DD preferred to reside in Salisbury where he was master of the cathedral choristers, leaving his underling to serve three parishes for a combined income of less than the £150 a year which the Church considered a proper wage. The hard-pressed curate only celebrated Communion at Christmas, Easter and Whitsun, and was lucky to get three dozen turning up. He could barely have known his flock, since he had no time to catechize them. By the 1830s half the parishes in the county would be without an incumbent. The returns to bishops' visitations in Wiltshire noted a general fall-off in church attendance throughout the county. 'Careless indolence' was mooted as the cause, though John Elderton, the vicar of Aldbourne, had the grace to observe that some 'Sabbath breakers' refrained from attendance 'from want of raiment'. In Shrewton the overseers dispatched a hapless 'Mr Swayne of Wilton' to petition for charity monies owed the parish. He came back empty-handed and was asked, more than once, to 'persevere'.

In Wiltshire, as elsewhere, the rifts between the village and the Established Church were growing wider. Indifference to an institution which expected farm workers to go up last for Communion, and be buried in the worst corner of the churchyard, was curdling into hostility. Enclosures of land had enlarged the standing and lined the pockets of many clergy, making them important landowners or absentee landlords; the numbers of clerics who were gentlemen farmers – 'squarsons', or squire-parsons – was on the up, associating them more firmly with the gentry and alienating them further from their parishioners. The poorer sort were now more likely to encounter a clergyman magistrate on the bench, criminalizing what many felt to be their right to gather sticks for a fire or kill a rabbit for the pot, and issuing severe sentences – up to seven years' transportation – under the proliferating laws that served the landed classes. Tithes were also widely resented, since finding the Church's portion from his produce was often the farmer's justification for lowering his workers' wages. The flip side of the pleasant image of a bucolic and latitudinarian parson was the fat cleric, clutching his tithe pig, a favourite butt of cartoons in the period. This was the moment for a revival of religious dissent. As many in the Church of England washed their hands of their grubby parishioners, who, in Bunyan's phrase, could not, with Pontius Pilate, speak Hebrew, Greek and Latin, a new generation of evangelists came travelling across Wiltshire and made their way to the villages on the Plain.

Building Zion

The first Baptist meeting house in Shrewton was a do-it-yourself affair. It was put up in 1796 in the garden of William Hewett, a tinker who had sinned but been born again in the Lord. A mud-walled, thatched-roof house like those in which the villagers lived, it was made with local materials: homely, recognizable and vernacular. The money for its erection came from a loan of £25 and subscriptions contributed by other local Baptists. In the Wiltshire archives, tiny pocket-size leather-bound books testify to the meticulous managing of the money: every debt tabled, every item of expenditure noted, including 10 quarters of lime (£1 12s); flints, chalk stones and the costs of wheeling the dirt for the walls (£1 2s); 1,000 lathes with nails (1s); 500 bricks and their carriage from Warminster and Salisbury (16s); 23 bushels of hair, presumably cow or horse for packing the clay walls (13s 5d); and 1,700 pantiles for the roof (£4 16s 4d). It was a job opportunity for several villagers, male and female: two women, who worked for over three weeks digging and drawing earth, earned twelve shillings each. Their names are not recorded. But a 'Mr Light', most likely Robert, was paid the substantial sum of £17 14s 6d for building the walls of the Meeting House, tiling and plastering.

The Baptist cause was established in Shrewton – 'amidst great opposition' – by two of the most indefatigable itinerant preachers, Thomas Wastfield and John Saffery. Influenced by the Methodist John Wesley's phenomenally successful proselytizing tours of the country, the Western Association of Baptist Churches set up a fund to encourage evangelizing. The Baptist Missionary Society, formed in 1792, sent its emissaries to convert the heathen, whether they be in India or Jamaica, in the darkest corners of Cornwall or the isolated villages of Salisbury Plain. Wesley had mostly toured the urban districts of Wiltshire, but the Baptists rode or walked across the remotest parts of the county. Wastfield was a schoolmaster from nearby Imber, sent out from the Particular Baptists at Brown Street in Salisbury, where Saffery was the dynamic pastor. Preachers needed to be robust. Wastfield's journal has him all but permanently in the saddle, starting at 6 a.m., riding thirty miles a day, preaching half a dozen times to crowds of up to 100, putting in a fifteen-hour day on the road. Farmers kicked preachers off their land; eggs were flung while heckling, abuse and the threat of arrest kept them on the move. Sympathizers were vulnerable too and the authorities could be vindictive. One 'poor Tommas' in Netheravon, scraping a living from stone picking, was 'turned out of his common work on the gospels account', and in nearby Entford, Ann Carter, a widow who offered Wastfield her house, was then denied her two shillings and sixpence from the parish. She appealed to the justices 'but they did nothing but ridicule', offering to increase her dole if she shut her doors to Wastfield. He gave her money himself. Circuit preaching also raised collections for new 'mission stations'. Richard Parsons walked about forty miles a day on a begging tour to build a chapel in Corsley.

Nonconformity spread across the county with astounding speed. Between 1800 and 1850 nearly 1,200 premises were registered in Wiltshire for dissenting worship, averaging about one a fortnight (innumerable other meetings were held unofficially). Licences were issued for cottage gatherings, others took place in sheds and barns, workshops and inns; meetings out of doors or in tents could be certified, even in an orchard or a garden. Buildings did not matter. The Established Church, the preachers said, had gone astray and lost sight of the Christian message. Ornament, costly plate, like all church property, encouraged greed; the altar was a relic of ritualistic sacrifice; 'a man in black clothes' set above the congregation was divisive; there was no need for bishops or college-trained clergy on paid stipends fixed to 'their' places. Each gathering that made a covenant to worship together was independent, running itself. Labouring men and women chose their pastors and paid them from their own collections. Nor was the ministry a sinecure. Pastors could be dismissed if unpopular, and whole congregations might vote with their feet. In these early days there was much moving between denominations and blurring of lines between Baptists and Congregationalists, Methodists and 'Independents'. Choosing a chapel was itself an element of the self-esteem which Nonconformity bestowed on a person. The local Anglican vicar was unlikely to ask the farm workers in his congregation what they thought of his sermon.

Kneeling down to pray in the little mud-walled house, in your own home, or in that of a neighbour, among a small group of friends and family; hearing the beautiful language of the Bible read with feeling in a dialect or accent like your own; and receiving the sacrament from a plain deal table, without having to wait to traipse up, last of the village, touching your forelock or bobbing a curtsey to the squire and his family: how must that have felt? Nonconformity invited labourers and their wives to an unheard-of 'speech- and thought-sharing'. They found the confidence to air their views and manage their own affairs. Relying on each other was essential to a village community, and these early village gatherings were based on that sense of a life in common. Other believers were not fancy folk but had known hardship and insecurity like oneself. They knew what it was to go hungry or to walk through the valley of the shadow of death. Help with the rent or with clothing could be offered through the church without social condescension but, most of all, believers felt they mattered to each other and to God. The comfort offered by religion, the assurance of a better life beyond present misery, were not empty words but deeply sustaining. Cottage meetings, where people were converted and knew they were saved, were often intensely emotional, overwhelming experiences, punctuated by cries of abjection, tears and shouts of joy.

Protestant Dissent had long been embraced in Wiltshire, despite the often appalling consequences, fertile soil both for Puritanism and the later chapel movement. In the fifteenth century the Lollards, followers of John Wycliffe, were extremely active, secretly reading his English translation of the Bible, attacking the corruption of the Catholic Church and already emphasizing a direct approach to God without the need for ritual, a church building or a specially costumed priest. Villagers in Tilshead, the hamlet next to Shrewton, were among those protesting against Catholicism in 1450 when a plot to murder the Bishop of Salisbury failed. By the 1620s there were Baptists in Salisbury corresponding with those in Amsterdam: their opponents called them 'Anabaptists' –'re-baptizers'. Rejecting infant baptism, the Baptists held that only conscious believers, or 'professors', should be 'dipped' (rather than 'sprinkled'), immersed as Jesus was by John the Baptist. In the eighteenth century the dissenting Baptists of the Revival tended to be more Calvinist in outlook. Baptism was only for those who by grace, the workings of the Holy Spirit, knew they were among the saved or the 'Elect'. Unlike the 'General' Baptists of old Dissent, 'Strict and Particular' Baptists restricted Communion to believers and church members only.

Believers' baptism was much more than a doctrinal difference. From the seventeenth century it meant 'absolute separation from the Church of England and therefore alienation from their natural communities'. Dissenters had their own collective sense of identity. They were outside the parish, the administrative unit of the church and state. Until 1837 they were nonetheless obliged to christen, marry and be buried by the Established Church. In May 1798 one of the six men to sign the application for the licence of Shrewton's first meeting house, Thomas Shergold, a carpenter, travelled all the way to Saffery's chapel, Brown Street in Salisbury, to register the birth of his son Thomas. He also had to baptize him at St Mary's, Maddington. In 1829 Thomas Shergold junior married Elizabeth Light, Thomas Light's daughter. In January 1837 Thomas Light and his wife retrospectively registered the births of their last children, Henry and Charlotte, at Brown Street, though both were teenagers; their oldest son, Charles, and his wife, Elizabeth, followed suit a month later. Around this time Thomas's wife changed her name to 'Catherine' from 'Christian', a name that now perhaps was deemed too male and inappropriate, especially given Bunyan's protagonist.

Those who had their doubts about the new proselytizing could not deny its results. In 1798 there were sixteen Baptist chapels in Wiltshire. This number had all but doubled by 1830 and was to reach nearly eighty in the heyday still to come (with twenty-eight village 'stations', not yet settled churches). Shrewton's Baptist church began its official, settled life in 1812 with thirty-seven members and a new chapel, completed four years later, a sturdy and simple brick-built building which bore witness that the Baptists were here to stay. In his letter of 'dismission', cutting the umbilical cord to Brown Street, John Saffery exhorted them to 'love one another with pure hearts fervently' and to maintain both the internal vigilance of their community and their evangelical zeal. The Baptist presence soon grew. Thomas's son Charles Light, who became pastor of Zion for thirty-four years, had begun 'from a very early age to evangelise'. In 1838 he had his own house licensed for prayer and he also became a member of what grew into a large second meeting in Shrewton, with its own chapel, 'Bethesda' on Chapel Lane, built in 1831. There was some prejudice against 'itinerants' and village lay preachers, who were frequently tradesmen and might work up too much emotion rather than a 'healthy enthusiasm'. Ministers, it was felt, ought to be 'called out' by a congregation and ideally be educated men, rather than freelance like

Charles. The more liberal reminded their brethren of the example of Christ's disciples and the powerful work of the Holy Spirit: 'By his Almighty operations, he has made fishermen, tent-makers and other mechanics, lively, bold, spiritual, faithful, laborious and successful preachers of the gospel, and he can do the same still, and sometimes does.' Charles Light was one such 'mechanic preacher'.

According to his obituary in the *Baptist Union Handbook*, Charles transformed village life as much through teaching as preaching. 'Being of an energetic character', he gathered children together for a school, but 'feeling the need of something more being done for the youth of the place', he also ran evening study groups for young adults in the village. Unlike the private efforts at schooling in Shrewton, which lasted a year or two and never catered for more than two dozen children, the Sunday school, under Charles's superintendence, had a roll averaging about 200 pupils. It was immensely popular, and above all it was free. Left to the tender mercies of their betters, village children would have to wait another half a century for any free schooling from the state. In Shrewton, his obituarist maintained, 'many owed all the education they possessed to these schools'. Yet the school does not appear in the only official record of the village, *The Victoria County History*.

From the late eighteenth century the Sunday School movement, interdenominational at first, attracted thousands of students, largely and purposively drawn from the poor. As a bricklayer, Charles Light was typical of those self-employed craftsmen who took it upon themselves to set up schools, teaching the basic skills of reading and writing. There were Sunday-school teachers who could read but not write, teachers who could not make out words of more than two syllables but whose fervour carried them on. Debates raged about the schools. Some thought that only reading, as opposed to writing, should be taught on the Sabbath (writing could be taught during the week if need be) and there were those, especially among the Anglican bishops and upper classes, who would rather not have the field workers' children taught at all, and especially not by their own sort. Before the 1830s there was very little literature available for children, and village teachers relied on their Bible, a prayer book and their imaginations.

Children learnt to spell from sentences such as 'Amen – Allelujah – Aaron held his peace', graduating to 'Abstain from all appearances of Evil'. The most popular publication was Isaac Watts's hymn book, *Divine and Moral Songs for the Use of Children*, which went into hundreds of editions, though its language, 'flowing with cheerfulness' – 'How doth the little busy Bee/ Improve each shining hour' – was the source of much later parody. Watts, like the Sunday schools, assumed that even if the child was a miserable sinner in need of redemption, he or she was a rational being, capable of moral growth. By 1850 at least 2 million children were enrolled nationally. Learning the Bible would inculcate good habits of discipline and obedience, but religious instruction was not merely a kind of indoctrination. To judge by the figures for baptisms and the many warm testimonials left by pupils, Sunday school was more likely to foster the ethic of self-improvement and self-respect than to produce converts. Put simply, at a time when most poor children were merely cheap labour, the Sunday schools offered them knowledge and hope.

The Baptists did not preach revolution. They wanted to bring about an inner change of heart which might in turn improve society. Much of their literature assumed that people should not be educated 'out of their station' but Dissent could lean in more radical directions, especially for those who combined their scripture with the writings of William Cobbett or Richard Carlile. Among other village preachers, particularly the Primitive Methodists, there was often fighting talk, those who spoke 'familiarly about Jesus Christ, as if he were a labourer keeping a family on one shilling a week' and whose citing of the text 'Cursed be he that removeth his neighbour's landmark' (Deuteronomy 27:17) was greeted 'with hearty amens' in the wake of local enclosures. Shrewton, like other villages on the Plain, was among those in Wiltshire not immediately affected by rioting and the farm workers' attacks on the hated threshing machines which threatened to rob men of their winter wages. But protest was very near at hand. The Luddites had put Ezekiel 21 – 'I shall overturn, overturn, overturn' – into practice, and when the Chartists later met in Wiltshire, they too called each other 'brother' and 'sister', and marched singing hymns. In the years to come, those who became the leaders of new trade unions and the nascent Labour movement also acknowledged their debt to the Sunday schools, where they had picked up the rudiments of an education. If Shrewton settled down to respectability, elsewhere in the county religion became, for a while, a liberation theology and did not necessarily mean quiescence.

In 1846 the two Shrewton meetings combined and Charles Light was chosen to be the first pastor for the united congregation. Zion chapel was extended to seat up to 500 people, big enough for the whole village. In the years that followed 'Brother Light' became thoroughly conversant with the Baptist love of 'connectedness', attending the annual or biannual regional Association Meetings, the highlight of the church's year, leading his brethren in prayer, reading aloud in Zion from the circular letters which listed new churches, statistics of membership, the state of subscriptions and collections, and gave advice on the issues of the day. Zion would have heard the letter from Bristol in 1849 which 'affectionately' pressed its members to 'the support of such publications as supply a cheap and intelligent advocacy of the political and religious rights of all classes'. Charles was apparently 'naturally gifted as a public speaker', though his obituarist felt obliged to add, 'he lacked the advantages of the college training'.

Shrewton's 'Bethesda' was named after the pool in Jerusalem where Jesus healed the sick – and there were plenty in the village who needed succour. The names of other nearby chapels were less consoling (at some point in the 1820s or thereabouts, the older term of 'meeting house' was replaced by 'chapel'). The names suggest how thoroughly these rural congregations were steeped in biblical metaphor and allusion, and shine a light on their Calvinist outlook. Upavon's 'Cave of Adullam', the stronghold where David sought refuge from Saul's armies (1 Samuel 22ff.), is a reminder of the persecution suffered by Dissenters. 'Little Zoar', near Calne, refers to the place where Lot took shelter, the only city of the plain to be spared by God before the destruction of Sodom and Gomorrah (Genesis 19:22ff.). Strict Calvinists among the Baptists believed that only the Elect would be redeemed. Those who were saved were deemed among the exclusive company of the 'saints', but salvation was recognized not by study or intellect, or even good works, but by signs of their 'election'. Church members examined their souls, and those of their neighbours, for assurance of their salvation or anguished evidence of backsliding and sin. From John Bunyan to James Hogg, these often tormented heart-searchings fuelled the need for self-expression, prompting an outpouring of spiritual autobiographies. As Marjorie Reeves affirmed, charting the Baptist tradition within her own family in the villages on the Plain, 'non-conformity loosened tongues and touched off pens'.

Zion chapel apparently had little of the fortress mentality. Large numbers of villagers gave notice to marry there during Charles's pastorate (including several Lights), in part because they could do so more speedily without the longer residence and the process of banns required by the Church of England. Their attendance at chapel might be opportunistic and their religion skin-deep but such would also be true of a proportion of all British worshippers. In the middle of the nineteenth century half of the nation now chose chapel over church, and in parts of Wiltshire Anglicans were in a minority. On Census Sunday in March 1851, among those 300-odd people who walked up Shrewton's long, straggling High Street, turning their backs on the Anglican St Mary's, where their employers gathered, were labourers, washerwomen, thatchers, hedgers, carters, carpenters and servants. Some surely went to hear Charles Light preach because of his message and because the language in which it was couched spoke to them. It was 'the people's Church', said William Doel, another Wiltshire pastor, and not 'the State Church'.

Mid-century Shrewton, now rebuilt in brick, became a small centre of commerce on the Plain. How much this prosperity owed to the ethic of self-improvement encouraged within Zion, or to the increase of literacy and 'ciphering', as arithmetic was called, cannot be judged but business was booming at the chapel and for its pastor. Charles had moved up the social scale and was now a grocer 'with a somewhat extensive business' on the High Street. His wife, Elizabeth, served in the shop. His thriftiness seems to have got the better of him. In 1854 he was fined £3 for keeping 'unjust scales', as was his neighbour, Jane

Miles (the alternative was a month in prison). He benefited too as trustee and executor for the sale of the land and seven cottages attached to Bethesda. The conveyancing took nearly ten years and ended up in Chancery. Meanwhile, he acted as landlord while his elderly parents, his aunt Mary and her husband lived in a couple of the cottages. In the early 1860s a schism broke off from Zion to set up the Wesleyan Methodist church on the High Street, but Charles, widowed and married again, weathered any storms. He was now known as 'Reverend', and his 'neat dissenting chapel' found its way quite happily into the 1865 Harrods directory. Chapel life was sociable and the Baptists' mild amusements and treats, from Sunday-school outings to races and evenings of songs and recitations, were now part of the everyday rhythm of life in the villages on the Plain.

Despite – or perhaps because of? – their close connections to Zion, the Lights went on leaving the village. Charles's daughter Sarah had married a carpenter, George Wickham, in Zion chapel and in the 1870s the Wickhams joined the stream of rural emigrants to the USA. Family legend has it that George made walnut chests for their belongings on the trip and later turned them into furniture for their home, apt metaphors for accommodating the past. Sarah's younger sister, Susanna, stayed with her parents and was, for a while, a schoolmistress in Shrewton. Then she joined the Wickhams and is buried near Sarah in an Iowa City grave. By the time Charles retired in 1878, his sister Charlotte and most of his brother Henry's family had all migrated to Portsmouth. Charles had no son to follow in his footsteps.

Henry Light, my grandfather's grandfather, took to the road early but kept his religion close. Younger than Charles by nearly twenty years, he was also a lay preacher but an itinerant. Still plying his trade as a bricklayer, on Sundays he would 'work the cause' at a 'mission station' in Chitterne, five miles away. The story of the man from Shrewton who walked over the wild Plain in all weathers to take morning service, then home for dinner, then repeated the journey to take the evening service – a twenty-mile stretch – entered village lore. Jacob Smith, who came to Chitterne in the 1860s with sixteen shillings in his pocket and a basket of wheelwright's tools, was so impressed by the preacher's dedication that he threw in his lot, and that of his family, with the Baptists: 'If that's the sort of people who go to the chapel, that's where I'm a-going.' Henry Light's ministry began in the late 1850s, and in 1862 twenty-seven people were 'dismissed', that is, with blessings, from Zion to form a congregation at Chitterne. He was still preaching in the 1870s when he and his wife, Sarah, were living as caretakers in Zion chapel itself with their youngest son, Henry Herbert (my great-grandfather, the man with the pipe and orchids). A mechanic preacher in an age when ministers were increasingly college-educated, he was not called upon to minister to Zion once Charles retired, nor at the settled church of Chitterne. Henry and Sarah could no longer go on living in the chapel. They left the village on the Plain to join their children in Portsmouth. Soon there would be no more Lights – Baptists or bricklayers – in Shrewton.

The memory of Charles Light's thirty-four-year pastorate, the old dispensation, lax and friendly, was far from cherished by the next generation. In 1883, when Zion's membership had shrunk to fifty, revisionists drafted a 'correct epitome' of their history in a new volume of the church book. Revd Light had baptized 140 people and done much good work, but discipline needed to be tightened. Too many principles had been violated. Zion's record, they wrote, contained 'much to sadden': 'unscriptural marriages of members with the ungodly; slander; immorality; drunkenness; bad language; neglect of the means of Grace . . . and members of the Church carrying their children to the Establishment to have them christened'. Charles was alive, though ill, in Shrewton, when this was written. It looks like a palace coup, but the church members were also protecting their church and him from the prying eyes of posterity (that funny business with the scales comes to mind). Nonetheless, a historian can only blench at the words, 'the new book was accepted and it was resolved that the old one be destroyed'.

Light and Son

'Family' is never one organism but fissiparous, endlessly dividing itself. In a family tree everyone seems connected, but in life families fragment or are not 'in touch' with other branches. Feuds and enmities, snobberies and social inequalities, rows over religious beliefs, political avocations, sexual preferences and marital choices: all can splinter the family or cause lasting estrangement. Even without these conflicts the passage of time itself pushes family members asunder. In large Victorian families, where there may be twenty years between the first and last born, such differences are exaggerated. Family history constantly goes back to the future, mapping the distances that grow between the branches, asking why some flourish and others wither – historical questions which are always more than a matter of individual character. People want to know where they came from but they also want to know where they could have gone and why their branch of the family did not go there.

In families, as in love, timing is crucial, especially the timing of a migration. When my father's direct ancestors, Henry and his wife, Sarah, went to Portsmouth in the late 1870s, they followed the road first taken by Esau and Robert, Thomas's brothers and Henry's uncles, who had left Wiltshire at the turn of the century. That first generation had arrived on Portsea Island as the townships close to the naval base were expanding and the evangelical revival planted new churches among a growing population. By the time Henry and Sarah arrived, more than half a century later, history had moved on and they were out of sync with their own generation. Henry's cousins, Portsmouth born and bred, had an established business and an honourable lineage in the Baptist movement. In the next two generations the differences between branches would become even more pronounced.

Esau and Robert arrived in the midst of a building spree. During the French wars few places in Britain were more bustling than the southern coastal town of Portsmouth. 'What with sailors out for prize money and dockyard hands, flocking in from the surrounding countryside', there was, as one contemporary excitedly put it, 'a greater circulation of cash than is to be found in most parts of the kingdom'. As Portsmouth was Britain's key naval base at the turn of the nineteenth century, the population there had mushroomed, expanding far beyond the original garrison town. No one quite knew what to call the marshy spot where Esau and Robert settled. At first it was 'Halfway Houses', after a nearby inn, being midway between Portsea, where the docks were, and the church of St Mary's, Kingston, where Esau's children were baptized in the 1810s; then, briefly, 'Southport', until finally 'Landport', the name that stuck. Nearly 4,000 dwellings were erected in the town in the first fifteen years of the century, dwellings 'generally taken', the *Hampshire Telegraph* commented, 'as soon as the foundations are laid'. Developers were snatching up individual strips of land that had belonged to the old town fields. These were small parcels in the hands of a variety of owners, rarely more than an acre and usually sold freehold. The island had no large landowner or local peer to do battle with, and anyone with £100 to risk, or the nerve to borrow it, could purchase enough to knock up a house or two. After paying costs, an individual builder-cum-developer might net three or four times his expenditure, sometimes more. On Portsea Island were scores of small-time speculators and builders: naval men, the best-paid dockyard hands, and especially craftsmen, in particular bricklayers and carpenters, who combined skills and went into partnership as land promoters or bought individual plots. Few developers put up more than a house or two at a time, but with all the rest of the island to build on, building regulations as yet unheard of and migrant labour flooding in, there was a killing to be made. The Lights set up in Lake Lane, named for the old pond nearby, among the dockyard hands and farm labourers, the old sea salts and the market gardeners, whose single heads of 'the brocoli', very popular with Portsmuthians, could weigh in at over twenty pounds.

Lake Lane became a home for the Baptist church. Robert Light's family, though not Esau's, were involved from its very beginnings there, suggesting that he and his wife, Jane, brought their religion with them. The links between the Baptists of Shrewton and of Portsea Island were strong and intimate. Before he was minister at Brown Street, Salisbury, John Saffery, the dynamic preacher who fostered the meeting at Shrewton, had married the daughter of

Joseph Horsey, the pastor at Portsea's 'mother church' at Meeting House Alley. Saffery and the current pastor, Daniel Miall, were both stewards of the Western Association of Baptist churches to which Shrewton and Portsea belonged. In 1813 'missionaries' with ties back to Meeting House Alley hired a large schoolroom in Lake Lane and began teaching. Jane Light was one of the first four people to be baptized there when a new church was properly formed seven years later. Robert was among the first of the Sunday-school teachers, helping with the choir and with setting up a library. The church gave support and an instant community to newcomers and, as in Shrewton, mattered not only for its teaching of the gospel but for its 'outreach' and the services it offered: Sunday-school classes in literacy, a sick fund – a collection of £1 12s given to a classmate with a gangrenous leg – clothing for the ragged and shoeless, as well as adult mentorship in a town where many children were scavenging on the streets.

In these early days of the town's development, Lake Lane was a propitious place to settle. Portsmouth had very little industry or manufacturing outside the dockyard and the naval areas, which were hemmed in behind the old fortifications. New arrivals made their way to Landport as those older districts became over-crowded. 'Neat little new private houses, inhabited chiefly by artisans, nautical men, and mechanics,' wrote one surveyor of Landport, 'spring up as if by magic' and 'streets diverge in all directions'. As first the canal and then the railway station opened in Landport, the district became the hub for business and trading. Lake Lane was transformed into the bustling Lake Road, debouching into Commercial Road, the main thoroughfare that connected the dockyard district of Portsea with the London Road and now united the town. The Lights began as small tradesmen, building maybe half a dozen houses a year (Esau, the older brother, is listed in *Pigot and Co's Hampshire Directory* of 1828). They still had only a dozen men between them when the census of 1851 lists Robert as a master bricklayer and Esau a master builder. But they were ideally situated for expansion.

In Shrewton a jobbing craftsman like Thomas Light took on work and put in his individual bill. On a large building the eighteenth-century investor usually contracted with each small master, who would then hire men in his own speciality, such as bricklaying or carpentry, to do the work. By the early nineteenth century the building industry was opening up on an unprecedented scale and a new species of being had appeared: the builder turned contractor, assimilating and overseeing all the building trades on a project, and taking on large developments for estates of houses over many hundreds of acres. In the 1820s in London that 'leviathan' of builders, Thomas Cubitt, creator of Belgravia and Pimlico, and of Cubitt's Town in the East End, had up to 2,000 on his payroll, while Smith and Taylor, contractors for the Foreign Office and the India Office, might take on 500 bricklayers of a Monday morning. By mid-Victorian times building and construction employed the fourth-largest number of workers and was one of the fastest-growing sectors of the economy. Men were putting nearly twice as much money into bricks as cotton. Most builders operated far more modestly than Cubitt, and in London 80 per cent of them employed fewer than fifty men. As the big firms won the big money, the smaller fry became increasingly dependent on providing them with a variety of subcontracting services. Competition was rife and conditions for working men were up for grabs. In what has been called 'this most anarchic of industries', the bricklayer was rapidly becoming less a craftsman working towards his independence than a waged worker at the mercy of his employers.

Though none of their account books survive, in mid-century the Lights begin to appear in the borough records, competing for contracts and doing house repairs for the council. Like many builders, they were also landlords, ploughing rents back into the business: after Robert's death, his second wife, Elizabeth, is noted as 'a proprietor of houses'. While Esau's descendants died young or drifted towards the sea, Robert and Elizabeth's twin boys, William Robert and Charles, bricklayers in their late twenties, inherited the business in the 1860s. As 'W. R. and C. Light', with a yard and further premises on Commercial Road, they took on more substantial public projects, eventually building the Gas Company offices, a number of large banks and the extensions to the town post office. By the 1870s they had joined the ranks of 'builders and contractors'; a decade later they had over 100 men on their books. Unlike Esau's branch of the family they were also 'chapel' and they married women from Nonconformist churches. The family business and the family religion went hand in hand.

In 1865 a new chapel was erected in Lake Road, replacing the old schoolroom premises. It was the largest in the south of England, costing £6,000 and seating 1,800 people. Its foundation stone was laid by the Reverend Charles Haddon Spurgeon, 'the greatest preacher of the Victorian age'. Nonconformity spoke to the new urban populations like no other religion. Its emphasis on making one's own way in the world, according to conviction and individual conscience, appealed to the entrepreneurial and the aspirant alike. The Baptists in Portsmouth found a ready congregation among the skilled and semi-skilled workers in the dockyard town where the genteel were thin on the ground and chapel-going provided the experience of self-organization, a route to respectability and an extensive social network. For working men, chapel was the virile alternative: they were on equal terms with the minister and could take the initiative discussing church business, proposing or seconding resolutions, electing executive committees and officers, attending conferences and, not least, policing the membership. These practices had already made their way into the trade unions and early Labour movement, while trade union men who were chapel-goers were reckoned to make sober, industrious and reliable workmen. They would also be literate. A chapel like that at Lake Road served as a labour exchange too, a place 'where diligent young men could catch the eye of an employer'. Within a generation it had paid dividends in terms of social advancement for Robert and Elizabeth. Although their oldest boys, William Robert and Charles, were bricklayers like their father, their brother Jabez, eight years their junior, was trained as a clerk and was never to be a manual worker. Fast-tracked into the middle classes, he rose to be a manager in the railways, with a villa in Croydon, south of London, three servants, and a son destined for the medical profession.

Lake Road Baptist chapel with Sunday school built by W. R. Light next to it on right (Portsmouth Museums)

The sumptuous interior of the chapel (Portsmouth Museums)

Baptized in the new chapel in 1866 at the age of thirty-eight, William Robert was a deacon of the church for twenty-seven years and involved in every aspect of chapel life. He helped manage church affairs, opened meetings with prayers, and as a 'messenger' kept 'a loving and watchful oversight' on members, placing widows on the relief list (about four shillings a month), or proposing 'with much sorrow and regret' the names of those to be 'erased' or 'excluded' from membership for 'disorderly walk' – a term from Paul's epistle to the early churches (2 Thessalonians 3:6), which covered all manner of misdemeanour from absenteeism to drink, fornication and gambling. His firm was also called in whenever work was needed, repairing the roof or a leaking skylight. W. R. and C. Light built the new Sunday school for infants to the rear of the chapel, in line with a national shift aimed at delivering children 'from the thraldom of the family pew'. In 1873 the renovation of the chapel brought the firm around £400, no mean sum.

Chapel, like the firm, was patriarchal. Women could not be deacons, although this had been allowed in the previous century. Nonetheless, Emma, William Robert's wife, and later their daughters were extremely busy, collecting for charities, presiding over the tea urn for the endless fund-raisers, teaching in the junior Bible class, playing piano at the Band of Hope or the Youth's Temperance Institute. Emma was treasurer for the Maternal and Dorcas Societies, visiting the sick and elderly, though only those who were known to be 'sober, industrious and necessitous'. The worthy recipients were given religious instruction and also the perhaps more welcome 'Maternal Boxes': a 'free gift of soap, tea, sugar and oatmeal' and baby clothes. Chapel was intensely sociable: families met each other, children made friends and young people began their courting. In an age before the music hall and football, sermons provided much entertainment and were a popular form of reading, relished or criticized for their different approaches and styles; visiting preachers were eagerly anticipated. This was the high summer of Victorian Nonconformity, and at Lake Road, under the pastorate of Reverend T. W. Medhurst (1869–88), 948 people were baptized. Special gowns were made, and letters reminded female candidates to bring 'a white cap, white cotton gloves, black boots or shoes, one sheet, two towels, stays, and a complete change of linen' (to be needed after total immersion). Pastel-coloured yearbooks were printed, recording a dizzying social whirl: concerts given by the orphanage boys, amateur drama, the pastor's Bible class, anniversary tea meetings (Mrs Light received £1 10s for the tray she sold). There were lectures every Wednesday evening, prayer meetings, public meetings. Collections were held at every event, as members and adherents stumped up for the Southern Baptists or the Foreign Missionary Society, or put their hard-earned pence into a burial club, or the penny bank, which rewarded teetotallers. Every activity had its own committee, and 'the Ways and Means Committee', the committee to organize the committees, had as its treasurer W. R. Light, now resident of Priory House, a genteel villa on a crescent, replete with general servant. The William Lights no longer lived 'over the shop'.

I try to imagine my direct ancestors Henry and Sarah Light arriving from Shrewton in the late 1870s, and I wonder what they would have made of this thriving urban chapel. Henry may have been welcomed in Lake Road as an honoured elder, the link back to the village forebears who built the mud-walled house of worship, but he would surely have found it hard to fit in. At Lake Road college men dominated the pulpit and carefully prepared sermons were delivered to a mass congregation. Henry was an itinerant preacher, a Wiltshire countryman with a West Country burr, used to speaking extempore by the roadside or to a tiny, sometimes candle-lit, gathering of familiar faces, reading the Bible out loud together. With its sumptuous fittings of brass, mahogany galleries, fluted iron pillars and balconies, and a magnificent organ, Lake Road chapel was almost as worldly as the Anglican St Mary's, Shrewton. Would they have turned to one of the stricter tin tabernacles in the town, Reheboth or Salem, where such trappings were deprecated and services more spontaneous and uninhibited? There is no sign of either of them on the membership rolls at Lake Road chapel.

Henry and Sarah lived with their widowed daughter, Mary, at 25 Paradise Street, Landport, not far from Lake Road, close to their other children: Albert, the oldest, and John, both bricklayers; and Annie and Emily, who, like Mary, had married tradesmen. Unlike the women on William Robert's side of the family, the girls had also worked before they got married, mostly in domestic service. The youngest, my great-grandfather Henry Herbert, also arriving in the late 1870s, married a local girl whose father was a foreman among the dockyard labourers. The family were barely on the first rung of respectability and Paradise Street was far from heavenly, a backstreet in a jumble of narrow courts and sublet tenements. Shortly before his parents came, John, aged only thirty-five, died of 'phthisis', or consumption. Within a year, Henry senior was dead from bronchitis. Perhaps all the years of walking across the Plain to spread the Word had worn him out. More likely, the move from the village to damp housing amid dirty, crowded streets took its toll. Mary witnessed her mother's death from the same disease in the same house four years later.

Like their cousin Henry, William Robert and his brother Charles had trained as bricklayers, but as heads of a firm their loyalties increasingly lay as much with other builders as with 'the hands'. Their sons, trained as clerks and foremen, not bricklayers, would be even further away from the men. As the century wore on the large contractors were effectively casualizing labour, engaging and dismissing their workers at will, paying them hourly not daily rates, imposing their own discipline while undermining their employees' skills (there were violent clashes over the introduction of machine-made bricks). Demands for regular, stable conditions and a nine-hour day, spreading the work between the men and across the year – as was the case in other industries – were voiced by trade unionists in the building trades in the 1860s, with bricklayers and carpenters 'incontestably' the strongest branches. The builders in Portsmouth felt their interests threatened and formed a Master Builders Association in 1872, arguing for the freedom of the capitalist to run the business how he saw fit: the standard rate for work was opposed longer in the building trade than elsewhere and opposition to unionism could be fierce. During one dispute locally, William Robert, now chairman of the Master Builders Association, wrote to the editor of the local paper. He sounds baffled and affronted, arguing that the men should have acted 'less independently and not have entirely ignored their employers' interests'. At the Association annual dinner he took the position that 'Every man had a perfect right to take his labour to any market he pleased but he had no right to coerce his fellow men.' A laissez-faire view of the market, which assumed that 'individuals might be at liberty to forge their own future', chimed perfectly with William Robert's Nonconformist conscience. He also trusted to the goodwill of the employer and to the paternalism of the family firm, where the head looked after 'his' body of men.

Builders, like Baptists, were a close-knit group, if not a cabal, putting work each other's way. Seconding William Robert Light's motions at the Master Builders' dinners was T. B. Hayter, contractor, a Shrewton carpenter who had married Charlotte, another of William Robert's cousins, Charles and Henry's youngest sister. Hayter's son became a clerk of works, supervising public works. In the navy-dominated town, the firms with the biggest Admiralty contracts became part of a new commercial elite subcontracting down the line. In 1866 the Hampshire and Landport Permanent Building Society was set up to ease the load for builders and developers with offers of loans and mortgages: William Robert Light was a director, then its chairman. Such connections would also have helped Henry's oldest son, Albert, set up a small business in the 1900s, round the corner from the other Light premises. W. R. and C. Light, and then, after Charles's death, 'W. R. Light and Son', were seemingly untouched by the boom and bust of the industry. In the last decades of the century they built grand churches: a Baptist chapel at Elm Grove, Southsea, in the Gothic style some Baptists had formerly denounced as 'Romish-Priest architecture', with seats for nearly 1,000; the Presbyterian St Andrews; and with startling ecumenicalism, and the aid of £4,000 from the Duke of Norfolk, the first Roman Catholic cathedral in the town, in the striking red bricks from the local Fareham brickfields which also graced the Royal Albert Hall in London. The Lights were well known in the town's municipal affairs. Both brothers were guardians of the Portsea Union Workhouse and chairmen of the Board. In the 1890s William Robert was elected a town councillor for the Liberals in Landport, and eventually made his way on to the magistrate's bench.

William Robert's final project, the most spectacular of all, was a tribute to the social campaigning which cut across denominational boundaries in Portsmouth at the end of the century. Lake Road's new minister, the outspoken Reverend Charles Joseph, had forged a strong alliance with a crusading Anglo-Catholic priest, Father Robert Dolling, a controversial Irishman whose mission hall was next door to the Baptists. Both leant towards Christian Socialism, favoured trade unions as producing a more educated and more civilized workforce, and joined forces against drunkenness, slum landlords and 'moral impurity' in the town. (If only, Dolling wrote, the Anglicans could be more like the Nonconformists with their 'perfect equality' and active social conscience.) Meetings at Dolling's hall were packed with 'men who meant business, strenuous, keen-faced, level-headed men' (ladies were not allowed): trade unionists, labour leaders among them, who decided which abuse to 'go for'. They were spoilt for choice in a run-down naval district with a pub on every corner, where the brewers were a powerful political faction, the brothel-keepers included magistrates as absentee landlords, and shopkeepers worked their assistants round the clock seven days a week. Dolling deemed William Robert 'one of the most useful, honoured, and respected of [Portsmouth's] citizens' and engaged him to build his parish church of St Agatha's in Landport, a huge Italianate basilica amid the slum streets. Decorated with colourful mosaics and sgraffito murals by Heywood Summer, a follower of William Morris, and with its interior of granite, alabaster and oak, St Agatha's was 'a touch of Venice on Portsea Island'. Too much so for William Robert's men, all trade unionists, who downed tools when London Italians were brought in at cheaper rates to do the marble work and the inlaid wood floor. An Italian was stabbed in the hand and the dispute delayed the opening. In the event Dolling resigned and left Portsmouth rather than abandon saying Mass for the dead as his bishop wished. The firm was still owed £1,200 when William Light died.

St Agatha's, Portsmouth

A House of Many Mansions

It is often said by family historians that you cannot choose your ancestors. Of course this is not true. It may be a shock to discover that your forebears were dustmen, not dukes, but they can easily be disowned. Family historians are always selective. Some branches simply cannot be followed; others are deliberately preferred. Those ancestors we lay claim to tell us as much about ourselves and our own desires – or fears – as they do about any historical influence or connection. Encountering a good act, I was tempted to bask in borrowed glory as if the lives of these long-dead people whom I had never known somehow reflected well on me. Perhaps it is impossible to relinquish these identifications, especially when they embody ideals or models to emulate. Since I was brought up to respect education and revere books, the Lights appealed to me far more than the Dowdeswells with their needles and cricket. I found myself cherry-picking among the attributes I liked best, composing an idealized portrait that was partly a homage to my father and compensated for his absence. Ancestors have long played the role of mediators between the living and the dead, acting as spectral parents, less fallible and human than the elders we know in flesh and blood.

Who would not want William Robert Light for an ancestor? The great and the good of Portsmouth swelled the ranks at his funeral alongside a crowd of the firm's workmen. Lake Road Baptist chapel was full to capacity for his memorial. 'A most courteous man extremely anxious to temper justice with mercy,' said his fellow magistrates; 'he abhorred sanctimoniousness', wrote the Baptist press, though adding somewhat nervously, 'there was no sinful levity or wrongful purpose in Mr Light's bright fun'. A Poor Law guardian for twenty-five years, he was 'greatly beloved by the aged and the poor'; a councillor who lost his seat for arguing against corruption, he had been made a JP without knowing it, so that when honour came, 'he neither bought it, nor sought it, nor thought it'. Even allowing for the reluctance of obituarists to speak ill of the dead, he sounds a good man. But history interferes with the clear stream of empathy and muddies the waters. For William Robert Light, goodness and godliness were inseparable. His civic spirit was fuelled by his faith in the Christian God, his sense of mission at one with the belief – shared with millions of others – that those who were not saved would burn in hell. His values were not my father's, or mine.

In 1891, five years before William Robert died, the *Hampshire Telegraph* painted a jolly portrait of 'Builders in the Country', the twentieth annual excursion of 'the artisans employed by Messrs W. R. and C. Light, the well-known local firm of builders'. A suitably warm glow is cast over what must have been a thoroughly enjoyable works outing in 'delightful weather' as seventy men in 'three well-horsed brakes' sally forth to play cricket and quaff beer. At the 'well-spread tables', regaled by 'an admirable programme of vocal and instrumental music', they drink to the continued prosperity of the firm and to its head, who presides over 'the festive board' (the toast to Mr Fred Light, William's youngest son, 'who has settled in North America', far from his Baptist father, hints at another story).

The notice reads nostalgically, like a swansong, as if full knowing that the days of the paternalist family firm were over. Only two years later 600 bricklayers and their labourers in Portsmouth joined a general strike called by the Operative Bricklayers' Society and the General Labourers' Amalgamated Union, and paraded peacefully through the main streets of Landport. They wanted an increase in pay from seven to eight pence an hour and a code of rules which would standardize and stabilize their working conditions. They got the rules and a halfpenny, but the battles over working conditions went on.

In the twentieth century the big builders were pressured to be hard men, driven by the need to undercut each other and put in the cheapest tender for the work. The biggest bosses were prepared to 'command' their men and 'if necessary, endure their hatred', while the smaller firms, always a majority, angling to be subcontractors, were dependent on what the bigger men did. This free-for-all was compounded, as anyone with 'a £5 note and plenty of cheek' might set himself up as a 'capitalist', farming bits of work out to slaters or glaziers, hiring scaffolding, and borrowing to pay for materials, though he might not manage to break even. The carpenter and bricklayer were no longer, as *Punch* liked to portray them in the 1870s, formally and affectionately, 'Mr Chips and Mr Hod'. They were 'chippies' and 'brickies', too often working all hours, unpaid during bad weather, without proper overtime payment, in unorganized firms. This is the building trade in the 1900s depicted with such savage fury by Robert Tressell in his novel *The Ragged-Trousered Philanthropists*, 'a *Pilgrim's Progress* of our time', if not a bible for many trade unionists. The painters and decorators in 'Mugsborough' (a version of nearby Hastings), working for the firm of Rushton and Co, 'scamp' the work and slosh on the paint, and live in fear of dismissal. 'Crass', the foreman, fawns on the works manager, 'Nimrod', or Mr Hunter, a chapel-goer, whose aim is to shave a few pence off every job in order to collect more of the profits. Meanwhile, the embattled loner, Frank Owen, hopes to convert the men to socialism.

In the next generation of the Lights, William Robert's son, William John, expanded the firm: W. R. Light and Son, 'builder, brick maker and contractor'. On my side of the family, the other side of the tracks, my father's grandfather, Henry Herbert Light, remained a bricklayer all his life. William John was still a Baptist and a trustee of Lake Road chapel, following his father into the local council, elected an alderman (Tressell dubs the equivalent body in his novel 'the Forty Thieves'). Henry Herbert, according to family stories, became a 'Salvationist'. He was named for membership at Lake Road Baptist chapel in 1889 when two 'messengers' were sent to watch him and report on his conduct, but he was never baptized there. He was 'restored' to them a year later, and the record suggests his attendance had waned or he was worshipping elsewhere. He did not need to wander far. In 1876, at the time Henry Herbert first came to Portsmouth, William and Catherine Booth, founders of the Salvation Army, established their Portsmouth No. 1 'Corps Barracks', or mission station, in the old school hall that had once belonged to the Baptists on Lake Road. Thereafter Lake Road was home to their 'Citadel', a few doors down from the Baptists. In the 1890s the Baptists' minister, Reverend Charles Joseph, presided over a huge meeting and welcomed Mrs Bramwell Booth, lauding the work of her cadres. About 90 per cent of the Army's members – or 'soldiers' – had come from Nonconformist churches and it looks as if my great-grandfather was one of them. 'Salvationist', as my father suspected, was not a generic term but the precise denominational label adopted by those who joined the Salvation Army or went to their meetings. The *Salvationist* was the title of one of their major publications, and 'Salvationists' is what they called themselves.

It made sense. Henry Herbert had grown up in Zion; both his father and uncle were lay preachers of the old school. The Salvation Army was a revivalist organization which sought 'expressly to oppose the staid complacency' of some Nonconformist chapels and their drift towards a flabby Anglicanism. Part of a new 'holiness movement', the Army returned to the old values of Dissent – sobriety, frugality and discipline – but gave them new and strikingly dramatic form. Evangelizing in the open air, as Henry's father had once done, but on the streets, outside pubs, theatres and music halls, wherever new converts could be reached, its preachers offered 'entire sanctification', namely, full delivery from all sin, to those who saw the light. No longer needing to wait for a sign or to be tormented by endless soul-searching, the newly saved began to evangelize straight away, much as in the old days of the itinerant preachers in Shrewton. Unlike the more prosperous Nonconformist chapels, the Army was overwhelmingly working class in membership, and women played an equal part (one version of the family past had my grandfather leaving home because 'his parents', not only his father, were Salvationists). The Army was the church militant in militaristic times. With their brass bands and uniforms, their flag and motto – 'Blood and Fire' – 'soldiers' made their neighbourhood their particular 'battlefield', inviting drunks, prostitutes, thieves and onlookers to wrestle Satan to the ground. Attacking the vices of urban culture, they exploited its attractions. They advertised their meetings via bold, circus-style posters, entertained their heckling audiences like street vendors, and sang religious hymns to well-known music-hall tunes, with boisterous accompaniment on tambourine and drum. Their aim, like so many philanthropic, and indeed socialist, plans for the poor, was 'rescue work', a social mission among the down and outs and 'undesirables', lifting them out of their 'dens of iniquity'. In Portsmouth, as elsewhere, they set up shelters and soup kitchens, taking in the homeless; as my father recalled, the 'Sally Army' were fearless and much respected in the city, selling the *War Cry* in the spit-and-sawdust pubs, crowded with labourers and sailors. I can imagine that my great-grandfather, wavering in his attachment to Lake Road, and looking for an invigorated religion, less dominated by his affluent relatives, would turn here. But Portsmouth's Salvation Army records were destroyed in the Blitz. The census shows only that his family left the Lake Road area and moved to the north of the town where the Army established another Corps.

Like the Church, family history is a house of many mansions, but it is the same house, and in the new century the Lights took up residence in many of its rooms. In the largest, most spacious and airy apartments lived William John Light, well away from Landport at a superior address in Southsea, the only genteel suburb of Portsmouth. When he died in 1937, the estate of £10,000 left by his father had turned into

£98,000, a large fortune. His cousin, Robert James, Charles's son, left the business to become a registrar of births and deaths. Their sons in turn, 'Owen Fuller Light' and 'Dudley Oakshott', architect and solicitor, were far removed from manual labour and no longer lumbered with the Victorian inheritance of family names. In the same generation, my dad's father, Henry Herbert Archibald, inherited two of his, a sign of how backward-looking and tribal his father was (though 'Archibald' may have been a reckless concession to modernity). Henry Herbert – 'Bert' – was the first to benefit from state education until the age of twelve, but his future as a bricklayer was mapped out. His trade tied him to the past as much as his father's religion.

In the next grade of accommodation was the Shrewton migrant who had arrived in the city in the 1860s and caught the tail end of prosperity. Henry and Sarah's oldest son, Albert, came early enough to make the right connections and was blessed with five sons, all bricklayers (his grandchildren were attending Lake Road in the 1900s). Less lucrative than W. R. and C. Light, but still doing well, A. C. Light and Sons took on substantial contracts, among them the enormous new reservoirs at Farlington, outside the city. Albert too was a landlord and left his widow, a 'proprietor of houses', with about £1,200. Three of his sons carried on the business, Sidney, Benjamin and Robert Witt Light, names that kept the ghost of old Benjamin Witt from Maddington, their grandmother's father, flickering. In the 1930s they were 'Light Bros Ltd' of Craswell Street in Landport, round the corner from Paradise Street. When my grandfather Bert, a jobbing bricklayer of the lowliest sort, surely destined for lodgings in the basement, reappeared in Portsmouth with four children in tow, he went to them, asking for work. Not distant relations at all, as my father had thought, but his cousins.

And on one of the upper floors where the rooms are stuffy and cramped but nearer to heaven, I see my great-grandfather Henry Herbert Light, a respectable, conscientious tradesman, who soldiered on, a master bricklayer with a surname which must have been a calling card in the tight-knit world of Portsmouth builders. I imagine him a skilled artisan, a hot-gospeller, and a union man of a conservative temperament. He did the same job and lived in the same place for fifty years and tried to live righteously. Salvationists were committed to total abstinence from gambling, drink and tobacco, and to chastity and purity. He must often have prayed for his son in the years to come.

Bricks and Mortar

Every son is his father's apprentice and that apprenticeship is also a burden of expectation, a limit on the chance of being one's own man. My grandfather's turn against religion was a rejection of the family tradition but it was also typical of his generation of working-class young men for whom the Nonconformist chapels had less to offer. Board schools, technical schools and public libraries gradually made their educational provision redundant and there were other ways of spending Sunday than in church – cycling or football among them. The Labour movement offered many young people its own version of visionary idealism: 'I claim for socialism,' said Keir Hardie, the chairman of the Independent Labour Party, 'that it is the embodiment of Christianity in our industrial system.' With fewer fresh recruits from rural migration, inner-city congregations were especially prone to thinning; and as the more prosperous families, like the William Lights, moved out to the suburbs, their children joined the comfortable classes in the parish church. Still, my grandfather seems to have turned on religion with a vengeance.

Bert had few opportunities and little money but in Portsmouth there was always a way of escaping home and family. In 1910 he joined the Royal Navy. Both his sisters were married to men in the services and the navy provided comradeship, food, regular pay and a place to live. Bert signed on for twelve years as a 'cook's mate'. At nineteen he was fresh-faced, with grey eyes and brown hair, short and stocky like all the Lights, only five foot three and a quarter of an inch, the navy recorded punctiliously. Cook's mate was a lowly position in the hierarchy on board ship, and low in status, doing essentially women's work. Even fully fledged cooks might be disparaged as merely officers' servants. A 'slushy' needed to be tough with 'a strong sense of self-worth', according to one naval historian, not to find himself browbeaten by the seamen. Bert's record suggests that the life did not suit him: 'acting cook's mate' soaring to the heights of 'leading cook's mate', then demoted back again, his conduct went slowly downhill from 'very good' to 'good' to 'fair' and 'satisfactory'. Perhaps this was where he first discovered strong drink. Though the navy would never admit to a problem with alcoholism among the men, drunkenness was widespread. It would be hard for any young man, let alone one breaking free from a religious upbringing, not to go 'on the batter'. There are other blots on his copybook: two spells of thirty and thirty-five days' detention for bunking off – this during wartime. Navy discipline was at least as strict as his pious father. He had gone from the frying pan into the fire.

Bert spent the early years of the war with the Dover patrol, but on 7 September 1915 his ship, HMS *Attentive*, was one of the first to be bombed from the air; two men were killed and several wounded. It was a different kind of Blighty that got him home. Venereal disease was declared a national emergency at the beginning of 1917, but the British navy, unlike the Germans, discouraged any handing out of 'dreadnought packages' containing useful swabs – calomel for syphilis, and potassium permanganate for gonorrhoea – for fear of encouraging 'the ignorant class' to 'assume that sexual indulgence is a necessity'. The ignorant class got infected instead. Although no navy would issue condoms on moral grounds, eventually 'skilled disinfection' was available at 'ablution chambers' set up on shore advertised by a blue light. After a night on the town a sailor was expected to call in at a 'Blue Lamp depot' for the pleasure of having his penis painfully irrigated with the chemical Protargol, and ointment briskly rubbed on his genitals. After seven years' service, in September 1917 Bert was invalided out with gonorrhoea and a war gratuity. Where he went next is a mystery, but by 1921 he was bricklaying in the Midlands and after nine years of marriage found himself a widower with four children.

I heard the story of Bert's return to Portsmouth, 'with his tail between his legs', begging work from his father, many times. It was a story about the necessity of sacrifice for one's children. Here was a man who gave up his pride to feed his children. No father could do more. But it was also mortifying, for what is a working man without his pride? All the memories of my grandfather which my father passed on to me were a legacy of bittersweet emotions, distilled into the portrait of a man who worked hard and managed to keep the family together against all the odds, and who also drank. 'Drink never came first; he always put something in the cupboard for us when we were kids,' my father told me, and I believed him. Being a cook came in handy: he made huge fry-ups for his children's tea at a time when few men would ever be seen in the kitchen. But the family's survival was often precarious, with wages low and work intermittent. No sheets on the bed, they slept under an old overcoat and a blanket, warmed by milk bottles full of hot water. 'The Portsmouth Brotherhood' in Landport ladled out soup for them (free boots from the Brotherhood were marked to stop parents pawning them). There was the occasional visit to Bert's father, the man with the pipe and orchids. Bert's mother was dead and in 1919 his sister Sarah Ann, known as Cissie, had died of septicaemia and 'puerperal fever' after giving birth to twin girls. Bert and Evie had named their two girls after Bert's sisters – Cissie and Maggie – but their daughters never knew their cousins, the motherless twins, who also had the same names. They were, according to family tales, too 'snooty' to mix with them. In 1940 it was Bert who registered his father's death. Aged eighty-four, Henry Herbert Light left a respectable £66 to another Portsmouth builder, John Croad, perhaps paying off a debt. He was buried with his wife, Elizabeth, in the plot they had purchased for Cissie. I could not find it when I went looking.

Eventually my grandfather Bert became a master bricklayer, in charge of his own gang but subject to the bosses and their snooping foremen with their unannounced inspections. He worked all round the city on those buildings that ushered in a new phase of British social life between the wars; on pubs like the Coach and Horses in Copnor, in the north of the town, one of the many roadhouses in the mock-Tudor style, preferred by the sherry-on-Sunday drinkers, and especially on the cinemas. In the 1930s seven new picture-houses opened in Portsmouth, making a total of thirty by 1939 for a population of around a quarter of a million. Among them was the Odeon in Southsea, built (in the words of one rather lofty architect) in 'a peculiar, crudely festive version of the International Modern style', and most sumptuous of all, the Regent, with plush seats for nearly 2,000 people, a tea room and its own small orchestra – a new kind of congregation. Bert was in the middle of building the Classic when the Luftwaffe filled the sky. My father, bringing the soup and sandwiches for the midday break, looked up as they strafed the area with bullets to see 'the old man' waving his fists from the scaffolding, shouting at the Germans, 'You buggers, don't you ruin my brickwork!' In this story of bravado put on to reassure his son, humour camouflaged terror. Was I wrong to hear a note of forgiveness too in so many of my father's affectionate remembrances, as he passed them on to me, exonerating 'the old man' for the family's unsteady foothold in life?

After the war, when his children were all married, my grandfather was living in another run-down tenement, 19 Arundel Place, in the middle of bombed-out streets. Fortunately, the Cobden Arms, his favourite watering hole, was still standing across the road. Alone in digs, Bert declined the invitation to live with his oldest daughter, preferring to soak in the company of his shabby pals (the pub was still an unofficial labour exchange). His work, his drink, his smokes, his independence. The building trade was on the up again. In the photograph I have of him, he is – inevitably – on a building site. A man in his fifties or sixties, he is dressed for work in full rig-out: cap and tweed jacket, V-neck pullover, shirt and tie. He faces the camera with a cryptic smile, the tips of his fingers resting lightly, perhaps in a mildly proprietorial way, on a pile of bricks. Behind him are what look like suburban houses, and this is probably sometime in the 1950s, not long before his death. Cameras were unknown in my family before then. I do not know who took it.

Memories become epitaphs. In my last conversations with my father, he fleshed out his father a little more. 'He was near to being a drunkard,' he admitted, and he 'couldn't have him' at his wedding in case he made a fool of himself. He was embarrassed when his father came round in case the children – my brother and sister – saw him the worse for wear. Turning up with sweets for the kiddies, flat cap pulled down, 'his ciggie in the corner of his mouth', Granddad never came in. But, my father maintained, 'the old man' never drank on the job since it would mean instant dismissal, and he was proud that his dad always made up the men's wages himself – a sign of his competent arithmetic and, like the pocket dictionary he kept, a measure of his schooling. 'I admired him,' my mother commented, never one to pull her punches. 'He was a lovely man, a very obstinate man, but always gentle, very mellow when he was in his cups.' It was possible, then, to be a good father and a heavy drinker, and not to be a brute.

Like Evie, Bert left little behind. Along with the pocket dictionary and the memorial card for her funeral were the two notes he had scribbled from hospital, written when he was dying of lung cancer (all those smokes were indeed his 'coffin-nails'). He writes as if he is in detention in the navy, longing to be let out. The doctor 'has stopped all leave at Whitsun, so there is plenty of moaning going on here'. He was fed up and had had enough. Always the longing for independence – did he ever feel his freedom had cost him dear? Was the drink his protest as well as his solace? I think of that element of self-pity in Evelyn's memorial, his 'wandering all alone'; the half-maudlin catch in the throat; the cap pulled down and the front door closed. And yet, 'a lovely man'. A sinner and a reprobate, a fornicator and a drunkard, he finally got leave to die at his daughter's house in Sussex. The family gave him a Christian burial, with a proper headstone, and he lies in the churchyard in Sutton.

My father kept the pocket dictionary. He wrote his own name inside it and repaired it over the years with masking tape, the kind painters use to save windowpanes from splashes, carefully inking 'H. H. Light', his father's name, in large capitals on the spine. My dad should have been a bricklayer, the last of the Lights to follow the family trade, but he had never fancied it. He looked at his father's hands, all blue and gnarled, and thought, 'That's not for me.' He wanted to stay on at school – 'I loved school, I *loved* it,' he told me – but there was no money and 'we couldn't think of it'. He left, just thirteen, in the month that war with Germany was declared, and started working for his father as a 'tea-boy apprentice'. In the end war saved him from bricklaying. He liked to see the old man, though, flip a brick in the air and 'tap it in half with his trowel exactly in the middle of the frog'.

★

In January 1941, as Lake Road was heavily bombed, my grandfather and my father stood watching the flames from the backyard at Hope Place. Inside the Baptist chapel, the memorial reading desk given by William Robert Light's daughters went up in smoke, though they knew nothing of this. Other 'Free Churches' were destroyed, including the oldest Baptist church, Kent Street, the successor to Meeting House Alley, whose first congregation had met in a barn on Portsea Common in 1698. Elm Grove, which the Lights had built, the Unitarian chapel and the Salvation Army Citadel were all burning. To Baptists, as to bricklayers, however, buildings come and go. Baptists 'did not believe in the special sacredness of places', Charles Spurgeon had preached, laying the foundation stone for Lake Road chapel, citing Jesus as his authority. 'Neither in this mountain nor yet at Jerusalem shall ye worship the Father,' Christ told the woman of Samaria (John 4:21), for 'God is a spirit' and can be worshipped anywhere. A religion tied to place became mere tradition and had no life or future.

This was the view, despite her 'twinge of sadness', of one of four remaining elderly members at Shrewton's Zion when it was about to be sold in 1997. She had 'borne witness' for forty years. Writing to thank the minister after the service held for the church's decommissioning, she thought his sermon was 'so nicely put over' that 'we could feel it was only the bricks and mortar to give up'. And yet among the riders attached to the sale of Zion is a veto against the building being used for the sale of alcohol or for the purposes of gambling, or 'any other illegal or immoral purpose'. Any direct reference to be made to the 'Baptist Chapel' is also forbidden. As Spurgeon had admitted, Baptists were bound to be fond of places with 'hallowed associations', though not 'superstitiously'. Not merely bricks and mortar, then.

I'd like to see a plaque on Zion's walls. I feel tender towards those who refused to conform and walked up Shrewton's High Street in the opposite direction to St Mary's, cocking a snook, as I imagine it, at squire and parson. They didn't see themselves as victims, or as 'Hodge', the stereotype of the sullen or clodhopping yokel, habitually effaced in the census under the generic label 'Ag. Lab.'. I know it is a fantasy and that makes it all the more compelling. What I want is that moment of rebellion without the reaction that sets in, without the new authority the church represented and the discipline that hedged about their community. What matters to me is social justice; what mattered to them, ultimately, was salvation. The misery and poverty which the congregation suffered on earth is easier for me to appreciate than the joy they may have felt about the prospect of heaven. I want a place of hope in this life rather than the next.

Evangelical religion had long set young men against their fathers and fathers against their sons. For William Swan, London bricklayer and a Strict Baptist of the 1840s, finding faith meant a war with his father, who said he was 'getting righteous overmuch'. When Swan wrote an account of his life, describing the series of insecure jobs that meant near starvation levels of poverty ('we could feed the children', he writes plainly when life was kinder to them), the constant moving for work, the illnesses and sufferings he and his wife endured, what concerned him most was the state of his soul and that question which Christian asked himself at the beginning of *Pilgrim's Progress*, 'What must I do to be saved?' Here was a shabby workman walking down Cheapside, a man barely spoken to by his betters except to give him orders, engaged in a cosmic struggle within himself, depressed by never having funds, tormented by his own failings, his need for strong drink and his longing to let off steam in swearing or womanizing. Such a figure struck others as laughable. Astonishingly impudent, too, that he should hope to make up his own mind without the bullying of priests and the say-so of university men. There was plenty to pillory and caricature in Victorian Nonconformity. The bleak acceptance of misery, the handwringing insistence on repentance, the unctuousness and bigotry of those convinced they were saved: all these rightly received a lashing from the pens of Dickens and others. And yet what comes through Swan's journal and those of his peers is still impressive: the 'inwardly strong' life, the conviction that getting on in the world was not what mattered most; that every human being was capable of 'heartwork', and of fellowship with others. For these working men and women the question about one's soul gave them the self-respect to write themselves into history, but it also meant caring about something beyond the petty limits of the self.

Even Shrewton's Zion at the turn of the twentieth century, purged and stringent, was remembered as a companionable, joyful place. Albert Marrett, a teenager at the time, recalled the pleasurable fug from the coal-burning stove on freezing nights, the music made by the village fiddlers (no brass was allowed), Sarah Miles on harmonium, Fred Dewey on the cello and his father on the double bass, or 'Grandfather', and all the 'grand old tunes' rendered 'with spirit':

> 'Called to be Saints', in some lowly sphere,
> Unwritten large on the roll of fame,
> With few to notice, and less to cheer,
> Possessing withal, God's mystic name.

Again that sense of hidden specialness, of being 'elect', which gave purpose to the lives of villagers: Stephen Kyte, butcher's assistant, 'who mastered the "A.B.C.", in order to read the Bible' – 'writing he never mastered' – or Fred Maidment in Chitterne, nearly seventy-five years a preacher, tall and jovial, known as the 'Bishop' of Salisbury Plain, who handed out his loaves with a scriptural comment: 'Lovely day, Martha, Praise the Lord'; 'Filthy day, Martha, work of the devil.' Such upright lives are easy to sentimentalize or to satirize.

There are still Baptists on the Plain. The nearest chapel is at Tilshead, where the Lollards once protested. Their online mission statement is uncompromising: 'We believe the Bible to be totally reliable and true, written by men inspired by God,' it begins. The Baptists believe they have nothing to fear from time passing. They have built their houses on rock and not, like the rest of us, on sand. But must all community be founded upon exclusion, the warm inclusiveness of fellowship always need the shunning of outsiders? Must it always depend on the building of walls?

PART TWO

Tall Stories

3 The Road to Netherne

Two brothers – there are always two – and another road, but not a turnpike or a track in sight. This road belongs to no one, though the squabbling has been going on for centuries; and while they travel it, they traverse a highway that takes them beyond country, town and parish. This is a road before roads, a roadstead, once so called, whose course was known first by word of mouth and then learnt only by making the voyage. It is not a place but a passage and a way of fathoming the world, of measuring its scope by looking at the sky, by charting winds, currents and tides.

When shall we say it was and where? Sometime in the 1800s, perhaps, while the Lights are making their way across the chalk downs to Portsea Island, these brothers head out in the opposite direction, west towards Plymouth, in a two-masted wooden vessel, packed to the gunwales, low in the water. They are greedy and eager. They have listened since boyhood to fathers and uncles, learnt to knot and lash ropes, heave wet canvas and load goods till their muscles ached. They speak the argot of the amphibious, the strange lingo of their kind, formal and salty. They belong to that confederacy for whom to live is to set sail.

The history of an island is the history of its waters, but their own southern coast is no longer enough for them. The maritime world grows ever larger, adding new seas and new shores, an expanding immensity, inhuman and everyday. The sea is no respecter of persons. It churns and boils, drowns and spews back; it does not want to be crossed. But it is also their workplace and their daily bread. Their seas are commercial, a continual marketplace for trading in quintals and puncheons, barrels and tuns. They do not sail to fight but to get on in the world without let or hindrance of customs and nations, and despite the interference of wars or politicians. Mariners turned merchants, they hope to become planters and landlords on the other side of the ocean. Englishmen who have slipped the net of home, they may end up foreigners or come back to be gentlemen if they can.

This road, which is not a road, has many ports of call: the Dorset harbour where they set sail, a place so swathed in the smell of whale oil in summer that a breakfast egg tastes of fish; the rocky, fog-bound North Atlantic promontory where they build wharves and wooden houses, and find wives among the settlers; and a distant bay of turquoise waters, bathed in heat, fringed with greenery, where the worst of their catch is delivered to feed people who are themselves mere merchandise, sold as stock. The brothers think themselves captains and masters but they too will be scuppered by the winds of trade, their descendants thrown overboard. Long after the brothers have gone down to Davy Jones's locker, a little girl with an itchy scalp sits silent and listless on the floor of the workhouse in an elegant town, derelict among the beached-up children who do nothing but scratch and stare. Her mind is as wild as a storm but for now she battens down the hatches. She has a long road ahead.

A journey begins in history and ends in memory, but not all memories can be borne across the generations. Like loose cargo they threaten to spill their contents, capsizing the future, and can only be salvaged as stories, tall tales and old yarns, the threads that keep tethered the freight of the past.

★

As a child I never felt anyone was missing. The family was horizontal, not vertical, a thickly wooded present rather than a sparse past. The family was my mother's family, the Smiths, her parents and their ten children who were all married with children of their own, and mostly living within reach of our own home. We were sufficient unto ourselves in our urban village not much more than a mile's span. Family was everywhere, unavoidable, bumped into on the street or at the shops, calling out as they rode home from work. An uncle, a conductor on the buses out to the seafront, let us off the fares; an aunt was cashier in the sleazy cinema next to our branch of the Carnegie Library: there was no shortage of family, more than enough to go round.

My mother's parents – my 'Nanny' and 'Grampy' – were not individuals but a relationship. Their Christian names were irrelevant. They were 'Mother' and 'Father' to each other, and even my mother had to think twice before she could confirm that her dad was known, very occasionally, by his second name of 'George'. Utterly familiar, they were also remote figures. I was one of a tribe of grandchildren who came and went in their house, played outside in their backyard, or fidgeted indoors while the grown-ups talked and laughed. Our illnesses mattered, and making sure that we survived, but otherwise, unless we were troublesome, we were a herd – 'the kids'. Before my teenage years I seldom held a conversation alone with either grandparent, and then only a few awkward sentences. I never stayed overnight in their house: why would I want to when my own was just up the road? I never went upstairs. Most of their house was out of bounds to me. Yet I must have been in the front room, a sanctum kept for visitors, bespeaking my grandfather's status as a tradesman, for I remember the gleaming lacquered piano with its lid shut, and that I lifted the heavy receiver of the black Bakelite telephone, cradling it against my ear, listening in awe to the dialling tone as if to the distant sea.

My mother's father died when I was eleven but until then I saw him at least once a week, most weeks, when we congregated noisily on a Saturday afternoon. He has left only one abiding image in my mind. Shrouded in smoke, he sits detached from us all in a corner of the room, a short, tubby man, sleeveless pullover over an open shirt, his shirtsleeves held up by rubber rings, fag-ends mounting in the ashtray balanced on the arm of his chair. He says little during our conflabs, waiting for everyone to leave so he can watch the wrestling on the television in peace. Every now and then he coughs into a handkerchief or taps his watch, half jokingly, willing his family to go. Men were expected to have moods in those days. They threw their weight about and 'didn't know their own strength'. Grampy, I was told, had a temper, but I never saw him angry. A toothless lion, he seemed to me. He might give me sixpence for an ice cream along with a bristly kiss goodbye or he might not.

My grandparents had emerged from the past without origin. Born in that antediluvian world 'before the war' – before the Blitz, before the Somme, before Mafeking had fallen – they were Victorians, their ten children – ten children! – already in my fifties childhood a sign of a distant era, an age gone by. Mum never knew her own grandparents; there were no keepsakes or mementoes, no family graves to visit. The missing did not bother us. On the contrary, it meant that there was no one to contradict my grandparents if they spoke about their pasts. They were the authors of their own lives. And they had plenty of stories to tell.

Secrets and lies are a staple ingredient of family history. Every family has its skeletons in the closet, its black sheep, the children born the wrong side of the blanket, the fortune swindled, the prison sentence hidden. The stories of poorer people and migrants are especially likely to unravel or be full of loose ends: disappearing husbands and wives, children left behind or brought up by relatives, relationships that were never officially registered, trails that go cold. As a 'family detective' the family historian expects to track down the facts about a person, follow the plot of a life and unveil the truth behind the family myths. In the record offices in Britain I got used to hearing other researchers relaying their family legends. In the cloakrooms or lobbies, over paper cups of vile instant coffee from the machines, another fevered searcher, high on an archive hit, would buttonhole me like the Ancient Mariner, and I would listen, slightly glazed, to yet another astonishing revelation that meant so much to the teller and next to nothing to me.

There was nothing unusual in the tissue of fabrications which passed for memories in my family. 'Nan' was an orphan whose parentage was obscure and my grandfather was fond of telling his children he had married beneath him. He had met his wife and 'got her into trouble' when she had been working as a maid in his family's large house in Carshalton, Surrey, south of London. The Smiths lived near Epsom, famous for its races, where a rich titled relation – 'Sir Somebody or other', my mother was told – kept stables, spelt his name 'Smythe' and lived in grand style. Certainly, my grandfather's sisters, Nance and Lottie, as my mother remembered them, always seemed such ladies on the rare sightings she had of them. According to one family legend, my grandfather's father disinherited him when he married the servant and ran away to join the navy. Other fragments filtered through and were added to family lore over time: my grandfather's mother, possibly Welsh, had died when he was young; she had come from a 'good' family. There were even tales, told tongue-in-cheek but relished all the same, of my grandfather being related to the Prince of Wales. But something had gone awry. My great-grandfather had married again and there was talk that his second wife had killed herself, a dark undercurrent which brought its own frisson of doleful pleasure.

It was difficult to believe my grandfather was a scion of the gentry and that he had fallen quite so far as to land up with ten children in a scruffy terraced street in Portsmouth. I imagined that his story would turn out to be far more humdrum, one of those childhoods spent in a dull suburban villa, perhaps, dogged by that kind of penny-pinching shabby gentility the English excel at, keeping up appearances. The fear of 'coming down in the world' so mesmerized and appalled the English middle classes that it often needed to be dressed up as disinheritance. If my grandfather told a romantic version of his past, picturing himself as one who had forsworn wealth and connection for love, he obviously did not want to be just like the rest, a silly young man getting his girl pregnant. He wanted to be an individual, *sui generis*. The maid seduced by the son of the house who was then 'cut off' – this was the stuff of Victorian melodrama, sensation novels or of the films he might have seen on the silent screen. With its victims and villains, its exaggerating of emotion, melodrama lends intensity and a vivid psychological landscape to what otherwise might seem mere ordinary suffering. His story also raised him up at his wife's expense. As it turned out, very little in it was true, except that my grandmother was pregnant when she married, and that he joined the navy.

Sigmund Freud once suggested that a 'family romance', replacing one's biological parents in imagination with more glamorous ones, is a common enough, harmless fantasy. He maintained that the longing to have a different father, usually 'of higher social standing', harked back to early life when father and mother were indeed an emperor and empress to the little child, before he comes to realize they have feet of clay. At first believing utterly in his parents, he (and it is always a 'he') grows disappointed and feels himself slighted, giving himself a different lineage by way of compensation. At best such fantasies help the individual become 'liberated' from the authority of his parents: a liberation that 'is quite essential', he writes, in one of his breath-taking generalizations, because 'the whole progress of society rests upon the opposition between successive generations.' Yet how much of an inner life would Freud's little Viennese 'phantasy-builders' and my grandfather growing up in the 1900s share? Freud was not writing of those whose parentage really was dubious or unknown to them, nor of the large numbers of people who felt slighted as adults because they had grown up in a society where they *were* deemed 'low'.

Genealogy has long fostered grandiloquent forms of family romance and been a source of reassurance to antiquarians, cranks and snobs. 'Old' families anxious to establish their pedigrees, their title to land which was originally stolen or requisitioned, hang family trees and portraits on their walls, nurturing dynastic fantasies that reach back to royalty or even to Jesus Christ, although their 'right' to bear arms and their heraldic shields were awarded them as followers of some warlord or a scheming monarch shoring up his faction in the court. In the seventeenth century, when King James I, uneasy and unpopular, wanted to relegate the old, much-loved monarch, Elizabeth, and promote his own importance, he displayed an elaborate genealogy at the Palace of Whitehall, tracing his lineage back to Brute, the mythical first king of the Britons (it was concocted by Thomas Lyte, one of my forebears, perhaps). More humble aspirants elevate themselves through family hearsay, believing there was once a family pile or manor in the past, or a lost connection to wealth or grandeur. If the creation of a nation rests on its 'foundation myths', family legends too, handed down the generations, are also the stuff, like dreams, of which we make our selves.

Tracking my mother's ancestors, I did not want to discount these old tales as the antithesis of truth; I was a Freudian in this much at least. Who does not want to have led an interesting life? Those who feel they do not have much history to speak of often talk themselves up. But these tall stories are emotional truths as revealing as the census. The facts of a life, however shocking, may convey very little; they are flat and drained, the feeling has haemorrhaged from them. Fabrications are a different matter. Such stories carry something of the emotional undertow, the backwash of what 'the facts' meant in a life.

Who were my grandfather's parents? I had one piece of evidence to start from, a photograph of his sister Lottie's wedding, which surfaced after his death and seemed at first to point to their gentility. My great-grandfather, bald and bespectacled, is the short man behind the bride in her Edwardian lace. Lottie is marrying the upstanding man in uniform, and the strong-faced woman to his right, I imagined, must be her mother, though little of her expression is reflected in her daughter's sweet, if melancholy, smile. My grandfather is the dapper fellow on the far left with the Chaplinesque moustache, sporting his watch-chain; and next to him, her face partially obscured by a crease in the photograph, is my grandmother – the earliest picture of her since there are none of her as a child. But what was the maid doing at a grand family wedding if the story my grandfather told was true? Despite my great-grandfather's stiff collar, the men are in lounge suits, not top hats and tails, and one of the ladies is bareheaded. Their clothes are their 'Sunday best' rather than upper-class dress clothes. The leafy garden with its spreading trees, which I had taken to be the grounds of the house, began to dwindle before my eyes. More likely, it was the churchyard.

I am not writing a thriller. I soon found out that my great-grandmother had been dead three years when this photograph was taken. But the basic information about her life was as dramatic as the story my grandfather had told. She was born Sarah Hill, a workhouse orphan, the lowest of the low, and she had died, aged fifty-three, in another public institution, Netherne County Asylum, not far from Carshalton in Surrey where my grandfather's family were living. Her death certificate gave the cause of death as 'exhaustion after sixteen days of "mania"'. My grandfather's tall stories of a lost patrimony had masked the loss of his mother. His inheritance, if it included the legacy of madness, was not one he would have wished to pass on to his children.

'Very sad,' my mother said thoughtfully, when she learnt of her grandmother's fate, 'poor lady'. But I felt a less honourable emotion, a ripple of excitement. 'Born in the workhouse; died in the mad-house' – what could be more exciting? Family historians always want to find someone made singular, if only by their suffering, and unless I was careful, I would find myself back in the heightened realm of melodrama or wandering the wild reaches of the Gothic novel. From the birth, marriage and death certificates I could see that my great-grandmother Sarah Hill had been shunted over 300 miles across Britain, in a series of displacements, but there was little glamour here; hers was the pedestrian life of a servant, forced to make her own way in the world. She was a nobody who had left nothing behind except her children, and rather than honouring her memory my grandfather had all but obliterated it. I would never see her photograph or know what kind of mother she had been. All I could hope to discover were a few of the staging posts in the road that led her to Netherne, a handful of the facts of a life to serve as anchors for the family romance.

'Miss Nobody'

Where does Sarah's story begin? Perhaps it begins with her mother, Mary Ann Hill, who was also a servant. Both belonged to that vast population, all over the British Isles, of mostly unmarried women who for centuries worked in domestic jobs. Their story starts in a place once 'little more than a good farming village', barely a market town, under the brow of the Malvern Hills dotted with sheep, a place which was utterly transformed by a kind of fairy tale, the belief that it had a healing spring. But the story could equally begin a generation earlier, with Mary Ann's mother, another traveller, born on a faraway shore, on another continent. 'We think back through our mothers if we are women,' wrote the novelist Virginia Woolf, reaching for an umbilical connection to her own mother, who died when she was thirteen. I don't think she had fish in mind.

When I found that Sarah Hill's grandmother Maria Hosier was born on the other side of the Atlantic, in St John's, Newfoundland, it made no sense to me. I was still thinking of rural migrants like the Dowdeswells and the Lights, travelling on country roads in search of work, or making their way to the cities. The Hosiers were Dorset people, and in the Dorset History Centre in Dorchester a wall of books on Newfoundland broadened my horizons. If you sail due west from England's southern shores, Newfoundland is the first landfall. The Hosiers, from nearby Corfe Castle, became innkeepers and brewers, and then sailmakers in Poole, a large natural harbour on the Dorset coast. From sailmaking it was a natural step into being 'sailers', as the word was first spelt, commanding ships or serving as agents ('servants') for merchants. Poole and St John's became close cousins because of the fishing trade. Not just any fishing trade, but the biggest catch of all, cod, which made up much of the European diet, fed the Royal Navy and swarmed in vast shoals on the Grand Banks, or shallows, off North America's most easterly promontory of land. Sarah Hill's forebears joined the 'cod rush' of the eighteenth century.

Ever since 1497, when Giovanni Caboto, anglicized as 'John Cabot' for Tudor propaganda purposes, claimed this 'New-found-land' for England, the island had been a base for an international fishery. Basques, Spanish and Portuguese, who, like the Italians, were the main consumers of salt cod, fished there, as did the French and British, disputing the colonization of the island, fighting or taking the indigenous peoples as slaves (the last surviving member of the Beothuk tribe, Shanawdithit, died at St John's in 1829). From the seventeenth century a handful of English and Irish became residents. Even today in Petty Harbour, which owes its name to the French *petit*, fifth-generation Newfoundlanders speak with a southern Irish brogue. In 1699 William III acknowledged existing property in Newfoundland and allowed settlements, provided that the settlers did not interfere with English fishermen going back and forth. Those who cleared the land were planters; they built wharves and stages, setting up 'flakes', or racks for curing, and bartered their fish in exchange for goods from England, 'everything from beaver hats to strong beer in bottles'. Some fished solely for particular merchant houses, 'drawing on the credit of the cod they hoped to catch', borrowing to set themselves up with boats, fishing gear and even the salt necessary to cure fish.

Sarah Hill's great-grandfather, Maria's father, John Hosier, and his older brother Giles, worked for the merchant house of Jeffrey and Street, shipbuilders and one of the most substantial traders with Newfoundland. The Hosiers followed their father and uncle, who had been sailing the Atlantic since the mid-eighteenth century. In the 1780s, when Jeffrey and Street owned fifteen vessels, Giles became their agent in Bonavista, Newfoundland. In the following decade, after the partnership had dissolved, Jeffrey built a further ten ships, operating a dozen or so at a time, with the Hosiers often at the helm. Trade with Newfoundland depended on the cycle of winds which blew in a triangle and was part of a three-leg journey. One version consisted in bringing back dried or salted cod and salmon, selling it to the ports of the Catholic countries in Europe and, in return, the ships from the Mediterranean brought into England a veritable cornucopia of dried and fresh fruits, wine, oil and, most crucially, salt which could be shipped back to Newfoundland for the curing process. Poole harbour in rural Dorset became a giant entrepôt into which these goods flooded. Newfoundland salt cod was also crucial to the slave trade. In another very lucrative trade triangle, salt fish was shipped to the owners of

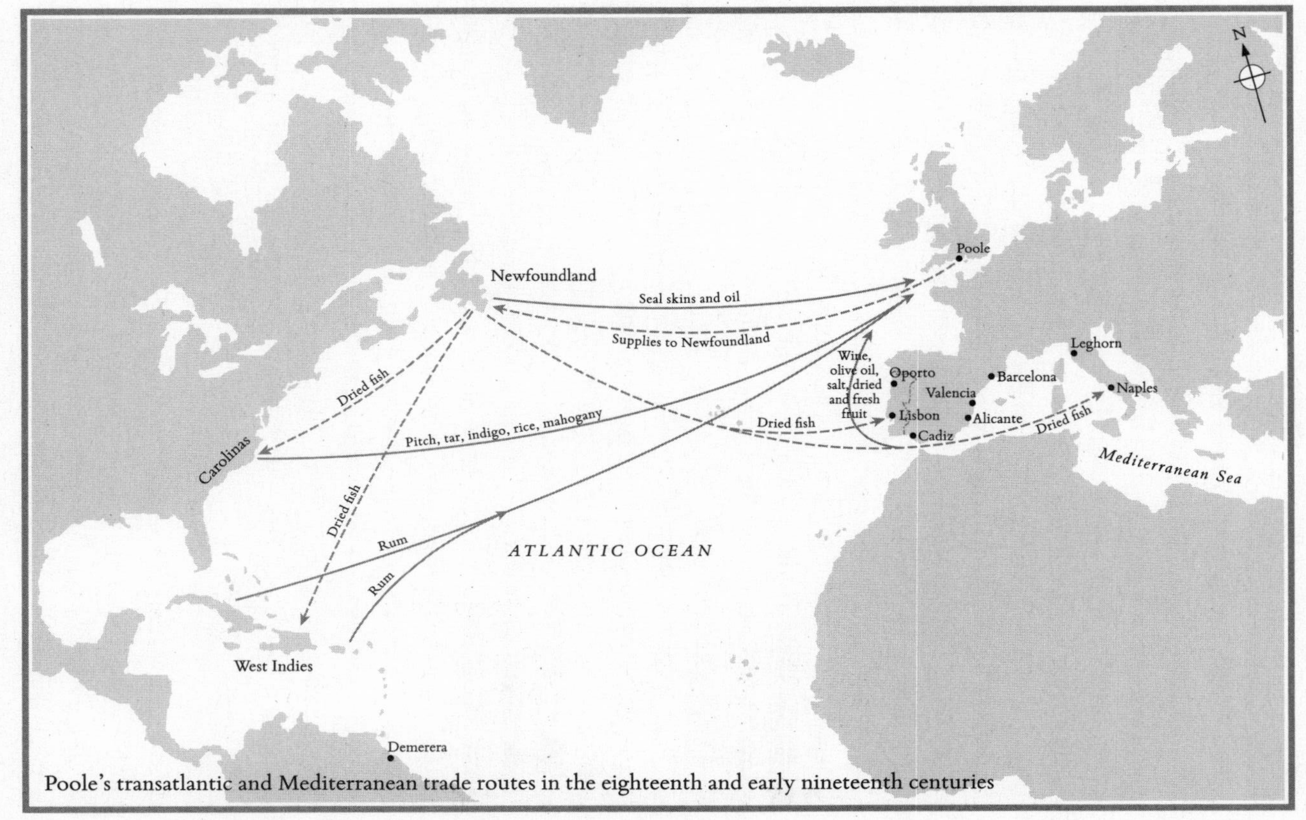

Poole's transatlantic and Mediterranean trade routes in the eighteenth and early nineteenth centuries

the rice fields in the Carolinas, or to the sugar plantations of the West Indies, where it was the staple diet of slaves. Only the rejects, the smallest, badly split cod, were sold here, known commercially as the 'West India cure'. Since Bristol and Liverpool merchants monopolized the importing of sugar and cotton, the Poole vessels brought back tar and indigo from the Carolinas, and rum from the Indies, distilled from sugar cane. Rum punch and rum toddies were popular with the burgeoning middle classes while rum and water – 'grog' – replaced brandy or beer as the navy's ration after the British conquest of Jamaica. Jeffrey and Street were not directly involved in slaving, their own ships never went south down the Atlantic seaboard, but it is a moot point. They were part of the maritime marketplace where the exchange of goods depended on slavery: their cargo included tar and indigo, as well as coffee, and at the height of their trade, about 1786, they exported around 50,000 quintals of salt codfish, slightly less than 10 per cent of the entire total exports from Newfoundland.

These were the wild, freebooting days of trade. Uninsured, lightweight two-masted schooners, heavily freighted, and without proper tools of navigation, plied the ocean in often perilous trips from Poole to Trinity Bay. Even when the seas around Newfoundland were free of ice, thick fogs, sudden squalls and violent weather were among the hazards faced by mariners. Even ships at anchor might be thrown against the wharves and broken into pieces by tremendous storms. The shortest return journeys took only nine days but a voyage could take up to a month or even longer against prevailing westerlies. Trade was a gamble. European prices fluctuated wildly and were intensely vulnerable to the sequence of wars, as was the shipping: Spanish, French and American privateers captured dozens of Poole ships and imprisoned the men. Not the least of the risks was impressment. Hardy and skilled merchant crews were considered 'naturally fair game' by the Royal Navy on the hunt for men. In 1770 the captain of the *Two Brothers* from Poole lost fifty of his men to the navy when a man-of-war stopped him in the Atlantic. Merchants sank everything they had in their cargo, and it could literally sink. But there were huge profits to be made.

Thomas Street and John Jeffrey were among the heirs to the enormous estate valued at £150,000 left by the head of one of Poole's richest families, the Whites, Quaker merchants whose headquarters were at Trinity, the most northerly port engaging in the Grand Banks fishery, and who carried on extensive trade with Barbados. Street, who commanded ships and acted as one of White's agents, was a 'frontier entrepreneur'. Like Jeffrey, White's nephew, Street made his own considerable fortune managing the trade in Newfoundland while John Jeffrey looked after their affairs in Poole. Such men became merchant princes, and like Isaac and Benjamin Lester, for whom the earlier generation of Hosiers had worked, ran several establishments, bought property, land and businesses, on both sides of the Atlantic, and built themselves fine residences (the fireplace in Lester's dining room in his mansion house in Poole was decorated with marble fillets of dried cod). The next step in their advancement into the landed classes was political power: Benjamin Lester was Member of Parliament for Poole and its mayor; Street was also sheriff and mayor; while Jeffrey, Lester's rival, was also MP for Poole, for thirteen years, resigning to become consul-general in Lisbon, a key import centre for cod. This was a ruthlessly commercial age. Jeffrey was a 'free-trader', against all regulations and restrictions, especially those new laws which stipulated employers should pay fishermen half their wages in advance. Like other merchants he took on poorhouse boys, as young as ten years old, apprenticed to avoid 'charges on the parish' and bound to serve until they were twenty-one. Jeffrey docked the cost of clothing and other 'necessaries' from their wages in advance, amounting to a third of what they might earn (other merchants kept back two pounds to pay for a passage home). The merchant houses also operated a 'truck system' whereby their men were paid in vouchers for goods that could only be bought in the company store. There were plenty of fishermen, it was said, who 'never saw money from their birth to their grave and were in debt to the merchants all their lives long'.

In these days, before the end of the French wars, many believed the sea to belong to no one and to have no nationality (pirates militantly asserted this to be the case). International law had barely begun to annexe it. Merchants and traders were deemed 'citizens of the North Atlantic' and might spend decades crossing the ocean; Benjamin Lester spent nearly forty years in transit. John Hosier, Sarah Hill's great-grandfather, was another constant comer and goer, 'a peripatetic, renaissance man: businessman, schoolmaster, seaman'. In 1789, barely eighteen, he bought John Jeffrey's share of the company, the same year that Giles, his older brother, married Grace Newell, the daughter of a sea captain, from one of the most prominent of the settler families. Giles also settled in Newfoundland, joining the many emigrant families from Poole. A man of 'refined tastes and superior attainments', he built 'a lordly home in good English style' in Bonavista. His younger brother was equally well educated, and married another local girl, Sarah Fitzpatrick. Her name suggests Irish ancestry: Roman Catholics were the overwhelming presence in St John's and Trinity Bay, despite government support given to the Church of England, and there were few priests to discourage cross-faith unions. After their two boys died as infants, John and Sarah returned to Poole with their daughter, Maria, but Sarah died there in 1810, aged thirty-three. John and Giles were never to join the ranks of the merchant princes. John had bought into the business as the trade was beginning to decline and the tides were about to turn on Poole and its merchants.

In 1776, posing an inquiry into 'the nature and causes of the wealth of nations', the Scottish moral philosopher Adam Smith gave the cod fishery as evidence that an economy would flourish if individuals were left to do business in an untrammelled market. He cited the colonies in New England, and the 'most perfect freedom' of trade between them and the British West Indies, where merchants were growing rich thanks to cod and other goods. Smith recognized that the division of labour condemned some men to mind-numbing, degrading work but also imagined that wealth would trickle down, benefiting society as a whole, a process whereby the labourers themselves grew more comfortable and well remunerated. In fact the markets proved unpredictable, never free from political upheavals, and run on shaky credit. In the Newfoundland trade, payments were mostly remitted in products, not cash; merchants sold to agents at inflated prices, attempting to recover their wage obligations; planters or independent fishermen were in hock to the merchants; and the crew, most vulnerable of all, were 'hands', whose labour was a commodity, bought and sold under pressure to reduce the costs of production and increase profits. Slavery was the extreme example of the brutal rapacity of a political economy which needed a constant traffic in humans as well as goods. In 1782, when the American colonists gained independence from the mother country, the British kept Newfoundland and granted New England fishing rights on the Grand Banks but the American trade with the British West Indies, supplying salt fish to the slaves, was halted. In the post-war years the old merchant families of Massachusetts – the 'codfish aristocracy' – recovered, moving their money into industry, but during the artificially created famine, 15,000 slaves in Jamaica had starved to death from the lack of protein in their diet.

The heyday for Poole merchant houses ended with the victory at Waterloo. After the defeat of Napoleon, unbridled American competition halved the price of cod and the Newfoundland trade began to founder. Those loaded with debt and with insufficient capital, whose business was already damaged by the ravages of privateers, needed only a bad fishing season or two to find bankruptcy looming. But the Hosiers had already suffered a reversal of fortunes. In 1812, the year of Trafalgar, Giles's eldest son, nineteen-year-old William, was lost at sea with all the firm's uninsured goods. Giles died the same year, 'of a broken heart', it was said, leaving his wife adrift with four daughters. John Hosier, widowed with little Maria, decided to stay in England, remarried, and in his forties set up a school in Poole in Cinnamon Lane (the name redolent of the spices stored on the quayside). A master mariner, 'Captain' John Hosier taught reading, writing, arithmetic and navigation, and became the first honorary member of the Amity Lodge of masons at the Lion and Lamb inn in Poole (he was also a member of the Masonic Benevolent Lodge in St John's, Newfoundland). After John's death in 1833, his second family left the town. Maria's half-brothers were all to be mariners but not merchants, settling in Liverpool. Poole harbour became a backwater, though still a haven for those other free-traders, the smugglers, until it was resurrected, fittingly enough, as a millionaire's playground in our own day.

The maritime world in which my ancestor Maria Hosier, Sarah Hill's grandmother, grew up was a place where families spanned an ocean, children were moved about like cargo, men disappeared for months or could be lost at sea, and a family's fortunes could plummet overnight. Women, blown hither and thither and caught up in the circulation of commodities, usually had only themselves to bring to market. Like a latter-day Moll Flanders, Maria Hosier learnt early how to adapt and survive. In 1816, barely eighteen and pregnant, she was married to Jehudi Witt, another mariner (both his names were common among Dutch Jewish traders). The wedding took place in St James's, Poole, in the presence of no fewer than six witnesses, as if making sure that Jehudi did the right thing. Maria, the daughter of an educated man, wrote her name in the register. Perhaps the marriage was only ever to legalize the child, for both she and Jehudi married again, without, apparently, cutting the first wedding knot. Maria took up with a coachman, Richard Hill, twenty years her senior, and by the early 1830s they were living in Cheltenham, a town in Gloucestershire, with two children and another, Mary Ann, on the way. Maria left her other daughter, Susanna Maria Witt, to grow up with Jehudi and his second wife. He settled down as a retired 'master mariner', tucked into the village of Sopley, close to the New Forest and the Hampshire coast. Or perhaps he did not retire. The village was a favourite haunt for smugglers.

*

Maria Hill, as she now called herself, was probably following the money. Cheltenham was certainly awash with it. She arrived in the town in the golden age of Regency pleasure-seeking. A few plump pigeons pecking at mineral salts had launched Cheltenham spa on the road to celebrity and it became that other kind of English town which grew not, like Birmingham or Manchester, to generate the wealth of the country but to spend it. Those who now had the leisure and the funds were visiting 'resorts' for a few weeks each summer and establishing the habit of 'holidays for health'. Since the 1700s 'taking the waters' at other inland spas such as Bath, Clifton and Tunbridge Wells had become popular with the gentry and the more prosperous middling sort, but Cheltenham, being a one-eyed country place with only a high street and a scattering of inns, took a while to attract the *bon ton*. It was expensive and uncomfortable. Then in 1788, on advice from his doctors, George III visited with Queen Charlotte, firmly putting the town on the map. 'All the fashions,' declared the *Morning Post* instantly, 'are completely Cheltenhamised.'

The spa needed a makeover. Three separate private Acts of Parliament soon dispensed with the common fields that were prime real estate and the 'coarse' old buildings like the Corn Market which were in the way of progress, so that landowners, entrepreneurs and speculators could create what today's tourist industry would call 'the Cheltenham experience'. Scores of houses were built to accommodate the wealthy: elegant crescents, terraces and leafy squares, like those in the new Lansdown and Pittville estates. New springs and wells were conveniently found in the town to cope with the influx of visitors; pump rooms and gardens opened; a theatrical architecture of walks, promenades and assembly rooms allowed one to circulate, to gossip at the evening tea-tables, to see and be seen at the cotillion balls. The *Cheltenham Chronicle* and the aptly named journal the *Looker-On* listed all the luminaries in town and ranked them like so many goods for sale: '4 Dukes, 3 Duchesses, 6 Marquises . . .' were typically among the visitors in 1823, down to a clutch of 'Honorables'. But Cheltenham insisted it was not a vulgar new Ranelagh or Vauxhall. Its delights were not for hoi polloi. The rules for the assembly rooms in 1826 ensured that 'no clerk, hired or otherwise, in this town or neighbourhood; no person concerned in retail trade, no theatrical or other performers by profession, be admitted'. Among the patrons were 'the first personages of the country, in station, affluence and respectibility [*sic*]' – the Duke of Wellington's visits always put the town in a flutter – so naturally the ten acres of the Montpellier Promenade, with its hothouses and Chinese pagoda, and the gardens of the Rotunda were fiercely policed: 'no unprivileged footstep is suffered to intrude upon the circle of their pleasures'. A rash of houses and apartments for rental, new hotels and lodging houses were filled with a slew of lords and ladies, foreign nobility on their uppers, gamblers and ne'er-do-wells, old seadogs and retired warriors who talked incessantly of 'old Boney', and a stream of arrivals who had acquired their wealth 'in the East'. They joined the more familiar spa clientele of doctors and solicitors, only too happy to cater to the 'widows wanting husbands, old men wanting health, and misses wanting partners'.

The Hills found work servicing the rich. The town had little industry and was surrounded by farmland. They joined the throngs of country girls and boys escaping rural poverty, along with the migrants up from London and elsewhere, who housed, fed, watered and dressed Regency Cheltenham, or ferried its inhabitants round the town. During the boom there was work in the building trade and plenty of jobs for tailors, milliners and dressmakers, wig-makers, the makers of lace, boots and buckles, as well as for all manner of craftsmen needed to fashion the accoutrements of a plush lifestyle – everything from coach-makers to picture-framers and upholsterers. Much work was seasonal. But the largest employer in the town was service. Richard Hill, Maria's 'husband', was a footman, though a less employable proposition as he entered his sixties; their sons, Richard and William, were shop boys learning something of the burgeoning retail trade. The town floated on a froth of wealth and luxury, but while her ladyship might be thrilled to find the embargo lifted on Italian straw after Napoleon's defeat, such changes, like the vagaries of fashion, could ruin livelihoods. The hat-maker who earned as much as 10s 6d during the wars found herself working for half as much, though still for the same twelve- to fourteen-hour day. Maria Hill was also an outworker. In her forties and fifties she made stays. Apart from paying for her own candles to work by, she would have needed to buy or borrow the money for her materials from a middleman who passed on her finished goods to a shop man. Both raked up their cut and left her, and all those who were to form the basis of the 'sweated trades' in the nineteenth century, with 'particularly hard work and miserable wages'.

Not everyone was prepared to goggle or grovel. William Cobbett, the radical journalist and Hampshire farmer, loathed Cheltenham, finding its idleness and gaiety an insult to human decency in the days when farm workers and their families were half starved and being thrown on the parish. 'A nasty, ill-looking place' he called it in 1826, inhabited by 'East India plunderers, West India floggers', its 'white tenements' (the stuccoed buildings) full of 'vermin', pension-holders, bankers and monied parasites feeding off the proceeds of war, land enclosures, and the fruits of those taxes which had impoverished the villagers. He lambasted the denizens of the town – 'the lame and lazy, the gourmandising and guzzling, the bilious and the nervous' and they never forgave him. His effigy was later burnt in the High Street. Other outspoken opponents of luxury and mindless consumerism were the Nonconformist clerics, chief among them Francis Close, 'the Pope' of Cheltenham. Deeply Tory, Close pitted himself against the pro-Reform, Liberal elements in the town, enlisting the support of a core of Anglo-Indian families and servicemen in the struggle to keep the town 'True Blue'.

The working people of Cheltenham led a busy, insecure existence among the 'fashionable butterflies and evangelical beetles'. Like so many other English towns, Cheltenham in the nineteenth century grew by class segregation. Artisanal housing was built in the 1820s and 1830s for the likes of the Hills on the fields and marshes to the north-west of the centre, where the gallows had once stood and bodies had hung on gibbets. Two new churches, St Peter's and St Paul's, aimed to exert a civilizing influence. One measure of the gulf between rich and poor, however, was the building of a brand-new workhouse in St Paul's, opened in 1841; three-quarters of its population came from the surrounding district (which is still the poorest area of the town today). The Hills's lives went from bad to worse. In 1842 Richard Hill and his son Richard, now doing labouring jobs, were sentenced at the Gloucestershire Assizes, the father for receiving stolen goods, probably from his son, since Richard junior was had up for housebreaking. Both were imprisoned for three months and Richard junior, aged fifteen, was whipped. The following year, after 'stealing a bag of beef and bread from a young woman's arm', his second offence of larceny, he was transported for seven years. He left the hulks in Sheerness, Kent, in May 1843 to board the *Asiatic*, and after a voyage of four months joined the convict gangs in Van Diemen's Land, the place which has been deemed 'the very quintessence of punishment'.

Having lost her sixteen-year-old son, it seems that her husband also disappeared, and Maria Hosier/Witt/Hill had to scramble to survive again. She took work as a semptress, or seamstress, and married Robert Jackson, a shoemaker, sharing lodgings with a hairdresser and his family on Sun Street, off the High Street in St Paul's, a thriving area for tradesmen: their neighbours included a baker, a butcher, a milkman, a brewer and a coal dealer. Maria gave herself as a widow on the marriage licence, though as far as I can tell she never married Richard Hill and her first husband, Jehudi, was alive and well in Hampshire.

Cheltenham's Imperial Spa was demolished in 1837 and the fad for drinking English medicinal waters was on the way out even before the Continental spas offered competition. By mid-century Cheltenham's glory days were over, but the town's population had swelled from a meagre 3,000 at the turn of the century to ten times that number. Service was still the largest employer for women and some work could be found at the colleges and private schools which offered education at reasonable prices to the better off, and to that core of Anglo-Indian and service families, many of whom had retired on their pensions to the town. Fanny Meredith, who married Maria's son William Hill, was a Cheltenham parlourmaid to a typically nomadic naval family, the Adamses, whose children had been born in Malta, Corfu and Ireland. Maria's daughter, Mary Ann, however, joined the swathes of 'general' servants, or maids-of-all-work, who made up the majority of female domestics. Even within these ranks, domestic service varied hugely, depending on one's place of employment and the generosity of the people in charge; an educational institution, a household, a shop, lodging house or hostelry – all had their pros and cons. At the furthest end of the spectrum, out-of-work servants were among the droves of women who turned to prostitution when they were down on their luck as an alternative to destitution or the workhouse. Most were not organized within a brothel or even attached to a beer house, but working in pairs or as loners trying to survive and hoping to return to 'respectable' employment. Accosted by the night watch, they frequently refused to cooperate with the law, giving their names as 'Miss Nobody'.

I do not know where Mary Ann Hill was working, but she was pregnant at twenty and gave birth in her mother's house (the only other option for confinement was the workhouse). She could not sign her name to register the birth, a measure of how far from the prosperous and educated Hosier world they had come. The baby was deluged with family names, 'Maria Hosier Jackson Hill', compensating, perhaps, for her fatherlessness. Mary Ann's mother and new stepfather had also gone down in the world as they got older, as was common among the poorer sort. Maria Jackson, now in her sixties, worked alongside her husband as a 'boot closer', typical piecework for women, finishing off the bootmaker's articles. The Jacksons were in more crowded lodgings, at 12 St Paul's Street South, with a room or two in a house on four floors, shared with four other households. Little Maria joined them, making a total of twelve adults, five children and two babies. The baby's mother, meanwhile, went back to work.

Seven years after Maria was born, Mary Ann was pregnant again and this time could not turn to her ageing mother. In the parlance of the Poor Law, a 'bastard' was first the mother's responsibility, then her parents', but if no support was possible and no man could be brought to book, a woman could ask for relief from the board of guardians who managed the local workhouse. Cheltenham, with its large population of servants, had far more unmarried mothers than many towns. The workhouse guardians did not offer 'relief' in the form of cash payments or even food and clothing to unmarried mothers, as some places did. It also did not distinguish, as other workhouses did, between those who ought to be given a dole – 'the deserving' – and those who were 'depraved' and 'fit only for the workhouse'. It cut through these niceties and 'offered' them all the 'House'.

Mary Ann waited till she was seven months gone, knocking on the workhouse door when her pregnancy would properly show, though it was a standard procedure for a porter at the workhouse gate to push women hard in the stomach to test for imposters. The receiving officer, who admitted her, noted in his register that she was 'in the family way', and pinned the number 77 to her clothes. The master of the workhouse kept minimal records and did not bother much about address, religion or occupation. How much the paupers would eat, however, and therefore what they would cost the parish they belonged to, was carefully annotated. New arrivals were immediately classified for dietary purposes. Mary Ann was deemed among the 'able-bodied' rather than 'sick' paupers and therefore officially subject to the full rigour of the workhouse regime, including a first nine days 'gruel' diet and a 'low standard diet' for the next fourteen days, aimed at driving as many applicants as possible back on to the streets. She survived to give birth to my mother's grandmother, Sarah Hill, on 3 April 1858. Where other unions disguised the place of birth or put only the name of the street, there was no such leniency in Cheltenham. Sarah's birth certificate baldly states 'workhouse' .

Mary Ann Hill may have been a lazy, stupid woman, or merely foolish and put-upon in an age when servants were sexually vulnerable. She may even have wanted and enjoyed her brief pleasures. But hers was a society where a woman was defined in relation to her man, and the men in Mary Ann's story abscond from it. Pregnant women needed to be at the end of their resources – 'isolated, rejected and desperate' – to end up in the crowded and filthy workhouse labour wards. If the guardians took issue with their residency or settlement in the local area, they risked being carted hundreds of miles back to their place of birth, a haggling which went on, with often dire consequences, into the twentieth century. Those who entered the workhouse were left in no doubt as to their 'shameful' condition. Few now put their 'fallen women' in 'canary' wards, but Cheltenham had a separate exercise yard for 'lewd women'. In 1851 the central agency of the Poor Law Board ruled that the unmarried mother, rather than scrub floors or make beds like the other female 'inmates', should pick oakum, that is, spend hours teasing pieces of old tarred rope apart with her fingers – one of those grindingly repetitive, demoralizing workhouse jobs that mimicked useful work. She alone was usually excluded from attending church 'outside' on Sundays.

In May, a month after Mary Ann gave birth, she and Sarah left. They were back again in July – 'no work', the register notes. Mother and child were out again in November, but who would employ a worn-out woman with a seven-month-old baby? When Mary Ann took Sarah back again to the workhouse after a mere ten days, she was now officially registered as 'destitute', and this time they stayed. Against the rules, Cheltenham kept all the persons of one sex, of all conditions and ages, in one ward. In November there were ninety-two women, fifty-seven girls and six other babies in the 'house. Without a dispensary or separate infirmary the inmates relied on the calls of a doctor, whose fees were subject to the scrutiny of the workhouse officials and guardians, keen to save money. Otherwise the needy were tended by a nurse and her pauper assistants, usually the elderly, semi-abled or 'imbecile'. Mary Ann was still classed as 'able-bodied' when she died, aged twenty-seven, on 30 December, nine months after giving birth. She was buried four days later, without a marker, in Cheltenham's New Burial Ground in what would have been the paupers' plot. But she had not given up entirely. She had managed to give Sarah at least a chance of life.

The 'House

Sarah Hill was to spend the next eight years of her life in the workhouse. I can't imagine it. Or rather, I do not want to. I do not mean the workhouse itself, though that was bad enough. The place I have in mind, or rather from which I squirm away, is not a place at all but an existence, the state, or states of being, in which a sense of self develops from infancy, an inner world of feeling and thought. How could it have felt for Sarah to be an infant and to become a child, in Cheltenham workhouse? To wake, alone, unmothered, in the dark and for this incomprehensible absence to become familiar, even an expectation? The child psychologist and psychoanalyst D. W. Winnicott calls such excessive maternal deprivation a 'primitive agony', as if the infant undergoes a kind of psychic death, which is blankly registered but remains unassimilated. 'In psychology,' Winnicott writes, 'it must be said that the infant falls to pieces unless held together, and physical care is psychological care at these stages,' adding that 'the early stages are never truly abandoned'. When I think about the end of Sarah's life, I am returned to its beginning.

Yet the workhouse baby that survived would have known some care. Sarah may have found some passing comfort and gentleness from other women, perhaps a newcomer whose pity had not dried up, and who was not too exhausted by illness or worry. Did anyone have room for her in their affections and did that affection stay within bounds? As she grew she might make friends among the other orphans, but whatever attachments she formed to others could not be relied upon: a person might be gone or dead next day. If her inner life was precarious, Sarah's outward existence was rigidly organized around the workhouse routine, regimented by the bells for rising, breakfast and prayers, dinner and supper, for taking exercise, for sleep and for beginning the round again. The atmosphere would have remained familiar. Laced with the smells of 'sour potato and stale urine', punctuated by the 'intermittent groans, oaths and screams from the idiots, the howling of babies', and the descant of keys clinking on the belts of those in charge, the workhouse was what she knew as home.

Sarah was there at the worst of times. Until the last quarter of the century, the workhouse did little more than warehouse orphans until they were old enough to be apprenticed or put into service. In the late 1850s, when the well-meaning ladies of the Workhouse Visiting Society first made their way into the wards, they found children and toddlers sitting 'close-packed against a wall . . . dull and stupefied on nursery floors'. This was a world without toys, picture-books or personal possessions, where the offer of erecting a swing outside for exercise was turned down, lest the children, getting hungrier, would want more feeding and also wear out their shoes; where in 1859, in one ward, 'the sole amusement for fifteen children under five years old was found to be the trunk of one doll', and in another, 'thirty or forty infants under five' had nothing to play with at all. Visitors took toys with them: the official authorization allowing their purchase waited until 1891 but it did not make it mandatory. Pauper children, or 'juvenile paupers', as they were officially dubbed – seemed prematurely aged, 'stunted little creatures, neither child-like nor human-like'. Listless and lethargic, with idiotic smiles on their faces, aimed at pleasing, they looked 'vacant' or 'mournful'. Cruelties abounded in these institutions: forcing children to eat at a trough on their knees, without knife or fork; severe beatings; regular confinement in darkened rooms as punishment. Even under the milder regimes, where children were allowed out on accompanied walks, they looked like social misfits and were treated like pariahs. In 1859 one workhouse officer, sadly observing long lines of older boys and girls clumping along in their prisoner-like uniform and ill-fitting boots, wrote that their appearance 'verges on the repulsive'. Long-term inmates got used to being unentitled, like the hapless pauper girls invited to a Sunday-school party, who stood by while the village children helped themselves to cake: 'We did not know *we* were to have any,' one said. When Dickens's Oliver Twist famously asks for more, he is instantly marked out as special since his appetite for food – and life – is not yet suppressed. Much more typical was the boy found lolling against a wall in the children's ward, staring into space. Asked what his aims in life were, he replied, 'To get to the men's side.'

Sarah's infancy in that wretched place was not an accident or an unlucky 'fate'. Cheltenham workhouse was never intended as an asylum for unmarried mothers, an orphanage or a hospital for foundlings. It was not designed to meet the needs of children; it was not designed to meet needs at all. It was built primarily as a 'deterrent', as an economic measure aimed at saving money. The Poor Law Amendment Act of 1834 was in part a reaction to the growth of population and the escalating poor rate. It also responded to a demand for social discipline, a crackdown on increasing numbers of agricultural labourers without work, fuelled by the alarm at continuing rural unrest in the wake of the 'Swing' riots in 1830–31. The Act, which was to blight so many lives, was the result of a rushed commission whose mind was already made up. Only 3,000 of the designated 15,000 parishes were investigated, and about 20 per cent of England and Wales, concentrating on the hardest-hit areas of the rural south. The commissioners argued that the most pressing 'evil' was 'outdoor relief' – payments in cash or kind – to 'able-bodied' men without work, who were to be brought under the roof of a workhouse instead, and thereby chastened and improved. Destitution only should be relieved, since poverty, 'the state of one who, in order to obtain a mere subsistence, is forced to have recourse to labour', was a natural and, some would say, desirable condition among the labouring classes. The 'surplus population' of the countryside would thus be forced to shift to the industrial districts, and those who applied for relief there could be sent back, according to the settlement laws, to their local workhouse, thus saving urban ratepayers from being inundated. The indigent were to be divided into the 'deserving poor', and the 'undeserving pauper' whose dire straits, the commission insisted, arose solely from moral delinquency: 'fraud, indolence or improvidence'. Yet from the beginning it was women who always constituted the majority of those who received relief of any kind and whose specific difficulties were barely recognized by the commission. While unruly labourers, crafty cadgers and work-shy desperadoes haunted the imagination of the authorities, it was the 'deserving' – widows and deserted women with children, the sick, the 'feeble-minded' and elderly – who predominated in the workhouse. In Cheltenham, as elsewhere, the most vulnerable experienced the conditions designed to repress and reform.

Like the whipping of vagabonds and the 'badging' of the poor, punishment for poverty was nothing new. Under the 'old' Poor Law, parish relief administered in the village had offered charity in return for deference. But parish relief had been managed by local people according to their customary notions of mutual aid and some obligation to protect the poor. The New Poor Law after 1834 replaced local overseers with an impersonal bureaucracy and a national system of 'union' workhouses whose catchment area was several parishes. Those in need were now obliged to travel to a strange town and to put their case before strangers, the first of many blows to their self-respect. The rituals of humiliation continued on entering the workhouse: the classifying and numbering, the stripping and bathing in front of staff, the shaving of heads, the replacing of one's own clothes with a second-hand uniform and boots. Workhouse architecture, with its forbidding prison aspect, high walls and locked gates, was deliberately designed to frighten and repel all but the most wretched from entering (who by official definition had fallen so low as to lose all their rights). Poverty, viewed as 'moral contagion', led to the principle of no visitors and of separating parents and children, husbands and wives, and even forcing elderly couples apart. The unvarying diet in which 'deviant extras, like fresh vegetables or even salt' must be removed, and the strict timetable of mind-numbing work, even for the elderly, was meant to produce docile, tractable 'inmates'. Those who were subjected to its miseries knew that the pauper was now little better than a convict, though the food was better in the penitentiaries.

In Cheltenham the ratepayers moved swiftly and 'without too much argument', building a new 'union' workhouse which could accommodate 220 inmates. It opened in 1841 and was full from the outset. They appointed a board of guardians from among those ratepayers whose property was not less than £40 rateable value a year, mainly the local gentlemen, professional men and superior tradesmen. In the 'hungry forties', a period of extreme distress and low earnings, the *Cheltenham Examiner* cheerfully welcomed the removal of 'out relief' because giving doles 'took away from the poor their reliance on their own exertion' (this in a town where fortunes had been frittered away at the gaming tables). Emigration was also encouraged by the New Poor Law as a way in which a parish could be rid of its 'surplus poor'. In the spring of 1850 Cheltenham offloaded 240 paupers to Quebec, but a year later the workhouse was packed with 525 people, nearly double its planned capacity, of whom those over sixty made up nearly a quarter. No doubt many of the emigrants were glad to have the fresh start, but these schemes were only ever short-term measures. The Cheltenham guardians laid on a little tea party to bid farewell to the 'pauper emigrants', which the *Cheltenham Examiner* thought showed their 'human side'.

That human side was little in evidence when it came to the so-called 'infant paupers' in their workhouse. When the new medical officer, Mr Alfred Fleischmann, a young man in his twenties, was appointed in Sarah's last year there, he launched a series of complaints: the workhouse school, with its 'foetid atmosphere' and 'filthy' lavatories, was horribly overcrowded and the children had no hope of improving in a place 'where the means of recreation and physical training would be monotonous for the discipline of a prison'. The children needed baths, vermin abounded, some infants suffered from skin disease and those with infectious illnesses ought to be quarantined. Children going into service, Fleischmann urged, should be 'in a fit state' and supplied with 'clean and decent clothing' – which speaks volumes about former practices. He could not 'cry peace', he wrote, while children and the sick were 'unfairly dealt with'. Fleischmann sent a copy of his report to the Poor Law Board in London, and when the Board duly sought the guardians' view of the master and matron, Mr and Mrs Gunton, the guardians asked for three months' grace to consider matters. In November the guardians postponed again and meanwhile purchased a bath for the girls and a tub or trough for the boys. After more heated exchanges, Fleischmann resigned but his successor, a Mr Digby, then took up the cudgels. The meat for the inmates 'was not only too fat, but literally unfit for humans and kept too long'; the wines and spirits were 'undrinkable' because not properly sealed. Digby suggested that the suppliers tampered with them (the inmates received 'table beer'), but the guardians refused to believe ill of their fellow tradesmen and pointed the finger at the workhouse staff instead. There were not enough beds in the male ward so singles were used as doubles, and the stonebreakers' yard, where men sledgehammered rubble for road building in the pouring rain and freezing cold, had no winter shelter. Finally a Poor Law inspector arrived who suggested building a new workhouse altogether on an enlarged site – an absurdity immediately rebutted by the board of guardians, who stoutly recalled their 'duty towards the ratepayers', including, of course, themselves. There was, however, much agreement that 'it will be absolutely necessary to remove the children to a separate establishment', allowing them better care and providing room for proper hospital accommodation. With a loan to be spread over twenty years, the cost of building would be £5,000 or £6,000, adding about a halfpenny in the pound to the rates. It was all talk. It took *fourteen* years before a local property was acquired to serve as a children's home.

Fleischmann wrote furiously to the Poor Law Board that the Cheltenham workhouse was 'regulated and dependent upon the political prejudices and ignorance of the elected guardians' who were 'unfitted for their post'. It was a place 'of disorganisation, tyranny and petty terrorism'. He or Digby probably penned the anonymous letter to the *Daily Telegraph* which called all the officials and the inspector 'hopeless', and the workhouse a place of 'hopeless misery'. But such complaints were not unusual. The workhouse was far from the uniform, morally regenerating regime that Edwin Chadwick and the other Poor Law commissioners had originally intended. Individual unions varied widely, had much more autonomy, and there was endless scope for passing the buck. The parishes that initially paid for pauper maintenance were unevenly represented and unfairly rated, while the guardians were far from representative of their community, and boards were frequently divided on political lines. National government, made up of the landed classes and property owners, had offloaded the whole business to a central agency, the Poor Law Board (from 1871 the Local Government Board), then left it underfunded and with few powers. The Board could advise but not compel, and in the provinces 'the men in London' were usually resented as interfering.

What actually went on in the workhouse was hidden from most eyes, including those of the guardians, who did not live there. The master and matron, generally husband and wife, like the Guntons in Sarah's time, could rule their tinpot empire as they saw fit, with pauper underlings given extra rations or alcohol for helping and a pauper pecking order, though such privileges and distinctions were officially illegal. According to Fleischmann, the pauper nurses at Cheltenham were 'dense, ignorant, unutterably stupid' with 'a stolid, hopeless, careless manner of performing their duties' – people reduced to the half-life of pauperdom, in other words. The government paid workhouse doctors and teachers not much above a pittance, and the 'miserly nature' of the system 'almost enjoined neglect'. In an age which frowned upon public expenditure, the Poor Law Board expected the guardians to buy workhouse supplies from tradesmen as cheaply as possible, and favouritism was inevitable. Fraud was rife. After the Guntons left, the new master and matron, William Welch and his wife, the fragrantly named Hyacinth, ran their own racket, selling off lard, bones and rags from the workhouse, entertaining their own guests on workhouse food and making a nice little earner by failing to keep a record of the money or effects of deceased paupers. They frequently disappeared from duty. After four years of their fraudulence and 'constant bullying', an official inquiry finally got rid of the pair of them.

By mid-century a mountain of paperwork shored up the system and helped to normalize it. One pamphlet printed in 1858 gives an idea of the veritable landslide of forms that issued from the central Board. Like the increased emphasis on statistical returns, the form-filling was an attempt to standardize and rationalize a national system which was almost impossible to control. Most communication involved copious exchanges of correspondence, often over minor issues and in intense detail, which at least made the Board look as if it was doing something, while action proceeded at a snail's pace. As in Cheltenham, a board of guardians could keep finagling over the finer points of detail for months and for most of them London was a long way away. The outpouring of printed matter, ledgers and registers is certainly testimony to the flourishing of Victorian printers and to the makers of paper and ink. Evidence, too, of the skills of Victorian clerks, those aspirant young men, stooped over high desks, painstakingly transcribing in immaculate copperplate handwriting the 'bastard ceremonial English' (Edward Thompson's splendid phrase), in which the Board's missives were sent to the unions. This monument to nineteenth-century bureaucracy, a labyrinth of letters, forms, annual returns and reports, makes up nearly 17,000 bound volumes in Britain's National Archives. By contrast the workhouses themselves left relatively few records; often only the top-down account of the guardians' minute books survives. Pottering around the local records offices I heard many explanations for this dearth, apart from the problem of storage. One theory had it that the workhouses, like other corrupt regimes, destroyed incriminating documents. Another, less conspiratorial, holds that many records,

Order for Messrs. Knight & Compy., *from the*

August, 1858.

FORMS REQUIRED BY THE OVERSEERS AND COLLECTORS.

SUPER ROYAL, RATE BOOKS. Schedule A. Form 1.

Quantities wanted: Leather Circuit Binding | Cloth Circuit Binding | Half-bound.

Fine Paper, with BLUE CROSS Lines, **13 inches** wide, by 6½ deep, 14 Lines in a Page.
Octavo for 100 Names, „ 150, „ 200, „ 260, „ 320, „ 430, „ 570, „ 650, „ 800, „ 1330, „ 1600, „ 2000, „ 2400, „ 2650.

Superfine thick Paper, with BLUE CROSS Lines, **13 inches** wide, by 6½ deep, 10 Lines in a Page.
Octavo for 100 Names, „ 150, „ 200, „ 260, „ 320, „ 430, „ 570, „ 650, „ 800, „ 1330, „ 1600, „ 2000, „ 2400, „ 2650.

Superfine Paper, ruled faint BLUE and RED Lines, 15 Lines on a Page, **13 inches** by 6½.
OCTAVO.
4 Sheets for 100 Names.
6 „ 150 „
8 „ 200 „
10 „ 260 „
12 „ 320 „
16 „ 430 „
20 „ 570 „
1 Quire 650 „
1¼ „ 800 „
2 „ 1400 „
2½ „ 1750 „
3 „ 2100 „
4 „ 2850 „

Quantities wanted.

SUPER ROYAL, with BLUE CROSS Lines, **13 inches** wide, by 13 inches deep, 30 Lines in a Page.
QUARTO. Half-bound.
1 Quire for 1300 Names; 1½ „ 2000; 2 „ 2650; 2½ „ 3300; 3 „ 4000; 3½ „ 4650; 4 „ 5300; 4½ „ 6000; 5 „ 6650; 5½ „ 7300; 6 „ 8000.

Quantities wanted.

Superfine SUPER ROYAL, with BLUE CROSS Lines, **13 inches** wide, by 13 inches deep, 22 Lines in a Page.
QUARTO. Half-bound.
For 1300 Names; „ 2000; „ 2650; „ 3300; „ 4000; „ 4650; „ 5300; „ 6000; „ 6650; „ 7300; „ 8000.

Quantities wanted.

SUPERFINE PAPER, ruled faint BLUE and RED Lines, 36 Lines on a Page, **15 inches** by 13.
QUARTO. Half-bound.
1 Quire for 1675 Names; 1½ „ 2500; 2 „ 3300; 2½ „ 4250; 3 „ 5000; 3½ „ 6000; 4 „ 6800; 5 „ 8600; 6 „ 10300.

SUPER ROYAL, with BLUE CROSS Lines, **13 inches** wide, by 20 deep, 45 Lines in a Page.
FOLIO. Half-bound.
2 Quires for 4300 Names; 3 „ 6400; 4 „ 8600; 5 „ 10700; 6 „ 15000.

Superfine SUPER ROYAL, with BLUE CROSS Lines, **13 inches** wide, by 20 deep, 35 Lines in a Page.
FOLIO. Half-bound.
For 4000 Names; „ 6000; „ 8000; „ 10000; „ 12000.

RATE RECEIPT CHECK BOOKS. Form 4.
Books of 50 each; „ 100; „ 150; „ 200; „ 250; „ 300.
Books of 400 each; „ 500; „ 600; „ 700; „ 800; „ 1000.

GENERAL RECEIPT CHECK BOOKS. Form 5.
Books of 200 each.

Quantities wanted. | No. in List.

2 Book of Receipts and Payments, 1 qr. / „ 2 qrs. / „ 3 qrs. } Usual Paper and Binding.
...... Ditto, superfine, and whole calf binding extra strong.
3 Balance Sheet of Receipts and Payments.
4 & 5 *see above.*
6 Terrier of Lands, Tenements etc., book.
...... Ditto, in sheets.
7 Inventory of Funds, etc., book.
...... Ditto, in sheets.
6, 7 Terrier and Inventory together, book.
8 Collecting and Deposit Book, 1 qr. / „ „ 2 qrs. / „ „ 3 qrs.
8* Ditto, small size, 1 qr. / „ „ 2 qrs. / „ „ 3 qrs. } 9½ by 6½
9 Collector's Monthly Statement, in sheets.
Ditto ditto books, of 1 quire.
10 Ditto Unpaid Rates Statement, in shts.
Ditto ditto books, of 1 quire.
10 a Overseer's Notice of Deposit of Books.

FORMS FOR THE CLERK.

Sch. B.
...... Minute Book, fcp., superfine thick paper.
...... Ditto, glazed.
...... Minute Book, demy, superfine thick do.
...... Ditto, glazed.
...... Minute Book, demy, with Outline of business, printed to order.
11 The General Ledger, 5 qrs. / „ 6 qrs. / „ 7 qrs.
11* Rough General Ledger, 8 qrs.
12 The Parochial Ledger, 5 qrs. / „ 6 qrs. / „ 7 qrs. } See *Note* at foot.
12* Rough Parochial Ledger, 3 qrs.
12 a The Non-Settled Poor Ledger, 5 qrs.
11 } 12 } The General, Parochial, and Non-Settled Poor Account Ledger, in One, 5 qrs. / „ „ 6 qrs. / „ „ 7 qrs. / „ „ 10 qrs.
13† Relief Order Book, 3 qrs. / „ 5 qrs.
14 Order Check Book.
15 Pauper Classification Book, 3 qrs. / „ „ 5 qrs.
16 Statistical Statement, in sheets.
17 Financial Statement, in sheets.
17 a Ditto, in books of 2 qrs.
18 Annual Abstract, Parishes, in sheets.
18 a Ditto, in books of 1 qr.
19 Parochial List of In-door and Out-door Poor, with Statement of Account appended, in sheets.
19* Parochial List of In-door and Out-door Poor, without Statement.
19 a Parochial List of In-door, separate.
19a* Parochial List of In-door Poor, separate, without Statement of Account.
19 b Ditto, Out door, ditto.
19 bb Ditto, Statement of Account, separate.
19 c Clerk's Notice of Audit, for Workhouse Doors.
19 d Half-Yearly Statement of Expenditure.
19 e **New Weekly Return.** Form B.
Ditto, in books for 2 years.

Quantities wanted. | No. in List.

FORMS FOR THE MASTER OF THE WORKHOUSE.

Sch. C.
20 Inventory Book.
21 Admission & Discharge Book, 4to., 3 qrs. / „ „ 5 qrs.
22 } 23 } In-door Relief List & Abstract, 4to., 3 qrs. / „ „ 5 qrs.
22 } 23 } In-door Relief List & Abstract, folio, 3 qrs. / „ „ 5 qrs.
24 Master's Day Book.
25 } 26 } Provision Consumption Book, for 1 year.
...... Ditto, with Articles printed according to Dietary, in books for 1 year.
...... Ditto, large form, with 7 Columns for each Meal, for half-year.
...... Ditto, with Articles printed according to Dietary.
27 } 28 } 29 } The Provision Receipt and Consumption Book, for 1 year.
...... Ditto, with the Articles printed in.
...... Ditto, post folio, with Articles printed, plain.
...... Ditto, in books for 1 yr.
30 Clothing Materials Receipt and Conversion Book.
31 Clothing Receipt and Expenditure Book.
32 Clothing Register Book.

FORMS FOR THE RELIEVING OFFICER.

Sch. D.
33† Application and Report Book, in leather, 1 qr. / „ 1½ qrs. / „ 2 qrs. / „ 3 qrs.
...... In cloth, 1 qr. / „ 1½ qrs. / „ 2 qrs. / „ 3 qrs.
34† Out door Relief List, in leather, 1 qr. / „ 1½ qrs. / „ 2 qrs. / „ 3 qrs.
...... in cloth, 1 qr. / „ 1½ qrs. / „ 2 qrs. / „ 3 qrs.

Mr. HOTSON'S Forms of OUT-DOOR RELIEF LIST, with separate Columns for Money and Kind.—30 lines on a page, 18 in. by 15 in.
34 A 1 qr. or 24 each, long and short leaves.
...... 2 „ or 48 „ „
...... 3 „ or 72 „ „
...... 4 „ or 96 „ „
...... Ditto, ditto, **smaller Form,** 20 lines on a page, 18 inches by 10½ inches.
34 Aa 1 qr. or 24 each, long and short leaves.
...... 2 „ or 48 „ „
...... 3 „ or 72 „ „
...... 4 „ or 96 „ „
34 b Rough Out-List, for the Pocket, 10 in. by 8 in. Books of 1 quire. / „ 2 quires. / „ 3 quires.
35 Abstract of the Out-door Relief List.
36 Out-door Receipt and Expenditure Book, imperial 4to., with Summary.
36 a Ditto, foolscap ditto ditto.
36 Aa Ditto, *Mr. Hotson's Form* ditto
36 B Summary of Receipts and Expenditure, books of 1 quire.

Quantities wanted. | No. in List.

Other Books and Forms.

FORMS FOR THE MEDICAL OFFICERS.

37 Register of Sickness and Mortality.
37 a Ditto, foolscap size.
38 District Medical Relief Book. Form P.
38 a Ditto, foolscap size. Form P.
38 b Ditto, in sheets, large size. Form P.
38 c Index to ditto.
39 Medical Relief Book for Workhouse. Q.
39 c Index to ditto.
40 Medical Officer's Certificate.
41 Medical Officer's Order for Sick Diet.
42 List of Aged, Infirm, and Permanently Sick and Disabled Poor.
42 a Ditto, in books.
43 Medical Certificate, Cause of Death.
44 Medical Officer's Quarterly Return, In-door or Out-door.
45 Medical Tickets. Form L.
46 Med. Officer's Qtly. Return of Lunatics, (**New Form,** on Thin Paper).
46* Statement of extra Medical Fees due to Medical Officer.

FORMS FOR THE PARISH OFFICERS.

Sch. A.
1 to 10 *see above.*
47 Notice to Medical Officer to attend a Case of urgent Necessity by Churchwardens or Overseers.
48 Instructions to Parish Officers.
49 Notice of having called for Poor Rate.
52 Circular to Parish Officers (Parochial Assessments), 22 June 1837.

FORMS FOR THE MASTER OF THE WORKHOUSE.

Sch. C.
20 to 32 *see above.*
53 Register of Births. Form S.
54 Register of Deaths. Form T.
55 In-door Labour Book.
56 Out-door Labour Book.
57 Visiting Committee's Book.
58 Chaplain's Report Book.
58 a Ditto, with printed Heading.
59 Pauper's Service Book.
60 Leave of Absence Book.
61 Book for entering Articles required in Workhouse.
62 Weekly Report Book for the Master.
63 Book for keeping an Account of the Bread baked in the Workhouse—for 2 years.
64 Porter's Book, 5 qrs., rough calf.
64 a Ditto, 2 quires, half-basil.
65 Pauper Offence Book. Form O.
66 Medical Relief Book for the Workhouse. Form Q.
67 Index to ditto.
68 Report and Journal of the Master of the Workhouse. Form U.
69 Casual Pauper's Examination Book.
70 Book for entry of Relief Tickets.
71 Vagrant's Admission and Discharge Book.
72 Pauper Clothing Deposit Book.
72 a Sick Diet Register.
73 Spirituous Liquor Clauses, ss. 92 and 93 Poor Law Act, sheets.
73 a Ditto ditto, boards.
74 Table of Hours of Rising, sheets.
74 a Ditto ditto, boards.
75 Dietary Tables, printed to pattern.
76 Regulations respecting Disorderly and Refractory Paupers, sheets.
76 a Ditto ditto, boards.

* *Note*—The General Ledger and the Parochial Ledger may also be had printed on Medium Paper, so as to admit of Two Half-Years being entered on one opening.

† The Books Nos. 13, 33, 34, and 34 A, are also kept with the additional Column for Number of Pauper.

Part of a publisher's list of books and forms used for workhouse and parish business, 1858 especially the registers of inmates, were removed to prevent the disgrace of having been a pauper from being known by others.

At the beginning, the New Poor Law met with violent opposition and condemnation, especially in Wales, and also in the industrial north where anti-Poor Law riots fuelled the growth of Chartism, and where it took decades to impose workhouses on the community. Collective protest inevitably dwindled into individual outbursts as it became a familiar, if loathsome, feature of the social landscape. Scandals flared up, like that at Andover in 1845, where inmates were found hungrily gnawing the meat on the rotten bones meant for crushing, but hundreds of less sensational, routine abuses, like those at Cheltenham, went unchecked for years. Of course the workhouse had its share of dangerous characters. Sometimes the inmates threw tables and chairs about and attacked each other; disobedient children tried to escape, like William Bunce at Cheltenham (a 'Class 3' pauper, aged between nine and sixteen or nineteen), who ran away from the garden. Others made a sadder protest, like John Turner, who 'destroyed himself by cutting his throat'. He belonged to Class 2: 'Old and Infirm'. A few brave souls wrote to the authorities, though they feared retaliation from the workhouse staff. One woman at Bethnal Green workhouse in London stumped up the courage to write because she was worried about the children, not herself:

> February 13, 1857
>
> Gentlemen
>
> it is right you do cum and see oure children bad for munths with hich [itch] and gets wors the Master nor gardans [guardians] wont see to it and if we giv oure names we shall get loked up Haste to see all . . . soon as you can
>
> A Mother

My great-grandmother Sarah Hill spent nine years in a vermin-ridden, crowded ward of eighty or ninety women and children, of all ages and all conditions. Her main preparation for life was scrubbing, bed-making, washing and ironing, and working in the kitchen. What Sarah cost the parish of St Mary's was meticulously clocked up on the parish roll by the vestry every six months; what the workhouse cost her, and others like her, is incalculable. But perhaps she was lucky after all. Thirteen girls her age were drafted out to work at the silk mills in nearby Overbury. Orphans were often dispatched to the silk mills, where the work was considered lighter and healthier than in other textile mills, but where discipline could be very harsh and the machinery just as hazardous to life and limb. Others still were forcibly emigrated to Canada to work on farms or as servants. Many never survived the workhouse at all. In the year she left, the fifty deaths there had included nine children all under the age of eleven. Seven of them never reached their third birthday. William Smith lasted eighteen days.

I wonder, though, if she could bear to go. Sarah had spent nearly a decade growing up in the workhouse. She may have made friends, however temporary. The 'house had been her mother and father, abusive, arbitrary, but familiar; the relentless, soul-destroying routine and the stodgy food all she had ever known. And now a woman appeared, who said she was her grandmother, and took her to another country where they spoke another language. Sarah's last charge on the parish – breakfast on Wednesday, 17 April 1867 – was duly recorded on the day she left, two weeks after her ninth birthday.

'Alsatia'

When Maria Jackson's third 'husband', Robert, died in Cheltenham in 1864, Sarah's grandmother faced penury. Nearing seventy with one granddaughter, Sarah's half-sister Maria, on her hands already, she too would be heading for the workhouse. In the workhouse little Sarah had been fed and had a roof over her head. Whether from sentiment or pragmatism, or because she had no choice, Sarah's grandmother now claimed her and took both of Mary Ann's girls across the Gloucestershire border into Wales where her son had made good as a journeyman poulterer and set up in business. From William Hill's point of view, his ageing mother would not be much of a drain on his resources. His niece Maria, now sixteen, would be a useful pair of hands until she married, and Sarah would soon learn to pull her weight.

William and his wife, Fanny, had moved to Haverfordwest. At the end of the eighteenth century, with its Regency terraces and assembly rooms, it had been thought 'the handsomest, the largest and the genteelest town in South Wales' – the 'Bath of the west' – and was still a prosperous county town. They set up shop on Prendergast Hill, just outside the centre, on the road that ran towards Cardigan and Fishguard, Pembrokeshire's main port. At the bottom of the hill was a bridge that crossed to Haverfordwest's busy quayside. Butchering and selling meat was a specialized and very competitive business – pork butchers had separate premises from poulterers – but in Prendergast there would be far less competition. Like many newcomers, they settled in the cheapest, scruffiest and roughest district, which saw a lot of human traffic. According to the authorities, the area had been 'infested with vagrants' (the Irish were especially liable to be described as if they were vermin) during the terrible poverty of the 1840s and a parish constable was drafted in to clear the lodging houses. Prendergast was where the navvies found their lodgings when they arrived to build the railway in the 1850s, adjourning to the Bull after the frequent punch-ups and making their peace by sharing the same mug of ale. During the mass exodus from the land as farmers shrank their workforce, agricultural labourers passed through on the tramp for work to the industrial areas of South Wales. The politer classes deemed Prendergast 'quite an Alsatia', that being the word to signal a place outside the law, a wild frontier offering refuge to all manner of criminals and migrants. An ancient village and a separate parish until 1835, Prendergast had resented its incorporation into the county town. Throughout the century it continued to affront propriety with an annual election of a mock mayor. That honour was given to the man most inebriated on the day, a latter-day Lord of Misrule, who toured his demesne with a sword, nodding benignly at the villagers in a send-up of municipal pomp. Prendergast kept its sense of difference and, like other districts segregated by class, was proud of its clannishness, its 'reputation for being separatist'.

What could Sarah have made of it all? Nine years old, never out in the world, and now suddenly transplanted. Those first months must have seen terrors in equal measure to delights. She had never had her own clothes or possessions, lived in a house or been up a flight of stairs, let alone run errands amid the bustle of a market. After the confinement of the workhouse, she saw fields stretching out behind the houses to the hills, as well as rivers and bridges, pavements and shops; after the ward's troubled human sounds, there was the absolute darkness and the silence of the countryside at night. The smells and sounds of the local tanneries and paper mills, where most of Prendergast now worked, were utterly alien, but she had never encountered farm animals either, seen fish for sale in baskets or tasted toffee like that made locally. One lady, observing girls Sarah's age taken into service from the workhouse, commented that, despite their different characters, they all had 'a downcast frightened look' and were 'like little machines'. But Sarah was not a lonely skivvy. She had gained a family: an uncle and aunt, her half-sister Maria, and seven cousins, four of whom were close to her own age. After nearly ten years in Prendergast, William was doing well and the Hills could afford a housemaid and a nurse for their children. Sarah joined a busy household with surely some of the comforts of a home. And while Prendergast may have been tough and hard-working, there was plenty of cakes and ale. Children especially enjoyed the Portfield fair, with its races and donkey rides, which took place on the common just at the bottom of the hill, while the whole of Haverfordwest was *en fête* during the annual May fair, with its sideshows and sports. Villagers cheerfully made fools of themselves, climbing the greasy pole, or emerging sticky from their bouts in the treacle tart match, a contest peculiar to the town.

Sarah had come to a place with a divided identity. If Prendergast was at Haverfordwest's edge, the county town was itself a kind of border where Welsh and English mixed. Haverfordwest was English-speaking, in that southern part of Pembrokeshire known as 'Little England beyond Wales'. The Normans with their English followers had built their castles here and carved out a territory, isolating the region from the rest of Welsh-speaking Wales (the Tudor king Henry VII was born in Pembroke Castle). In 'Harford', which the Welsh corrupted into Hwlffordd, the locals called themselves 'Honey Harfats' and their English had developed in isolation for nearly 500 years. The Welsh fishwomen in their beaver hats, flannel aprons and shawls, laying out their wares, would be incomprehensible to Sarah, but so was much of the English dialect there, the locals dubbing her 'kift' if she was clumsy, or threatening to 'lam' (thrash) her if she misbehaved. Language was a social marker. English was the language of commerce and business. Haverfordwest's local press, the *Pembrokeshire Herald*, the earliest local paper, set up in 1844, and the *Haverfordwest and Milford Haven Telegraph*, ten years later, were English papers. While the anglicized middle classes associated Welsh with rural backwardness, to Welsh speakers mid-century it was the language of the working man and woman, of their heritage and history, and above all, of religion. To be Welsh was to be Nonconformist, and Nonconformists had their own press in Welsh. In the 1850s, when Dissenters in England, like the Baptists of Shrewton and Lake Lane, constituted about half the church-going population, 87 per cent of attenders in Wales were chapel. Only 9 per cent attended Anglican churches.

In Haverfordwest the Hills were Church of England, out of sync with the rest of the country. The rector of St David's, Prendergast, was a force for improvement, complaining to the borough council about broken guttering and the filthy pools of water in the main street. He also cleared away the rustic music-making in church which struck many Anglican clergymen as vulgar. Out went the village choir and band with its impressive range of instruments, including the clarinet, cornet, concertina and violin, with the shoemaker, Mr Griffiths, playing the double bass and a Mr Vaughan on 'the serpent'; in came the organ and a surpliced choir, standing apart in their own stalls. Their white shirts annoyed the churchwardens and led to whispers that the new rector was 'High'. The Reverend Francis Foster, a man of means, restored the church, built himself a new vicarage, and set up the Working Men's Association 'to raise the intellectual and social life of the labouring classes', hoping no doubt also to dampen the appeal of chapel and radicalism (no Father Dolling, he). Foster baptized and buried the Hills, though he could hardly have suspected, as he watched Maria's coffin being lowered into the ground, that the old lady had been a bigamist living in sin with two 'husbands'; that she had left her only legitimate daughter behind while another daughter died in the workhouse, and her bastard son was transported to the Antipodes. Gravestones tell their own tall stories. Hers elevated her to 'Maria Fitzhozier Jackson', that 'Fitz' suggesting a royal lineage, and a last sigh after the lost Hosier fortunes.

Like many Victorian families, the Hills were well acquainted with death. Sarah lost her grandmother, her only connection with her past, only a year after their arrival, then her cousin John Henry, her contemporary, died when he was thirteen, suffering from a brain 'effusion' or haemorrhage. Her half-sister, Maria, was also soon gone. Married at eighteen to a farm labourer, William Davies, she bore four children before she too died, aged twenty-six, of 'catarrh' (probably bronchitis or pneumonia). Sarah's uncle and aunt, William and Fanny, could afford to put up memorials and they added the names of their own children who had died in infancy to the headstone for John Henry, evidence, were it needed, that those deaths in Victorian families were no less painful for being frequent: their first child, 'William Giles Jackson Hill', eighteen months; their second, Sarah Ann, who died of hydrocephalus, or 'water on the brain', at three; and the three-month-old baby, Arthur Thomas ('decline from birth'). 'The Lord gave and the Lord hath taken away,' the stonemason carved. A second Sarah Ann and Arthur Thomas grew up alongside Sarah. Inside Prendergast church, a tablet addressed the passer-by, unusual in its lack of religious exhortation or consolation,

> Pause, mortal, pause, whose eyes this marble view,
> Learn to be wise, nor fleeting hopes pursue;
> Life is an evening breeze, a murm'ring breath,
> That blows till sunset, then grows calm in death.

Sarah would need no reminder of transience. She had moved on again by the time her aunt Fanny, the only mother she had ever known, died in 1887.

When the census for 1881 was taken, Sarah was working as a servant sixty miles to the south-east of Haverfordwest, in Bridgend, Glamorganshire. As she was in her mid-twenties, it was unlikely to have been her first place. Servants were often migrants, taking jobs for a year or two at most, and often for far less time. They moved on frequently in their search for better conditions or a more generous employer. 'Brecknock Villa', Park Street, belonged to a colliery owner and local magistrate, John Davies, who was born in Haverfordwest, so perhaps Sarah's situation had come via local connections. The two servants, Sarah and Anne Hewitt, looked after their employer, his wife, Elizabeth, and the daughters at home, Miss Florence Kate and Miss Agnes Augusta, both in their twenties. It was a modest household, but compared to Haverfordwest in agricultural Pembrokeshire, Bridgend was forward-facing. A lively market town, benefiting from the boom economy created by coal, it was an important railway junction for the coal trains from the mining valleys to the north of the town and for the ports on the nearby coast. Since the first half of the nineteenth century thousands of people from the rural counties of Wales, and those contiguous in England, had poured into the mining districts with their 'Klondike-like settlements'. Two of Sarah's cousins, William James Hill and his brother Edward, had also recently left Haverfordwest. They were part of the new wave of migrants who 'swept into the coalfield' in the last part of the century, marriageable young men who arrived in their droves, joining industrial communities that became increasingly radicalized and anglicized. William and Edward were miners living with their families in Aberdare, close to Merthyr Tydfil, about fifteen miles from Sarah.

From the age of nine until her mid-twenties, Sarah, though English-speaking, belonged to Wales, as did her family. Her cousins were settled in Pembrokeshire, running the poultry business or in the coal-mining valleys of the south. Yet in a few years she had left the country entirely and travelled over 300 miles across England to Beddington, a village in Surrey, south of London, where she married Arthur Smith. Another break, another dislocation. The records yield no obvious connections: no kin, not one of her employers or their family move to Surrey, nor does anyone in her future husband's family have obvious links with Wales. But the enormous distance is probably an illusion, the effect of having no other record until her wedding. Most likely she travelled in short stages. However Sarah got there, her past went with her. The curate Charles Watson noted punctiliously on the marriage lines that 'the woman did not know her father's name'. The man she married led a wayfaring life. He was a 'carman', or farm carter, lending his cart and his muscle whenever it was needed, moving goods from place to place. Somewhere their roads had crossed.

In the 1800s, it is said, only one in three people in England and Wales lived in a town. By 1900 roughly three-quarters of the population lived in urban districts. The Smiths, like thousands of others, found themselves living in between, in 'hybrid communities', not quite country or town, as the London suburbs edged deeper into Surrey. Beddington and Carshalton, where the Smiths settled, were close to the River Wandle and the Epsom road. As it flowed north from the Surrey hills into south London, the Wandle was intensely industrialized, its water power driving innumerable tanneries, factories and workshops, which poured their effluent into its waters. In the 1870s the art critic and social thinker John Ruskin, who knew that part of the country in his childhood, had lamented the impact of industrialism and the pollution of the river at the Carshalton source. There had been 'no lovelier piece of lowland scenery in South England', he wrote, but – his moral outrage was vented indiscriminately – it was 'defiled' by 'reckless, indolent, animal neglect': 'the human wretches of the place cast their street and house foulness; heaps of dust and slime, and broken sherds of old metal, and rags of putrid clothes.' The Smiths rented a four-room cottage on Mill Lane, Carshalton, close to the river, a halfway house in an urbanizing world. Sarah was forty when William George, my grandfather, was born in 1895, the third and last of their children. Arthur supplemented farm work with a job as a bricklayer's labourer. Mechanization was changing many aspects of farm work, and farm carters like Arthur, once important and trusted figures, were being replaced by commercial carriers.

My grandfather's fabrications about his childhood, his hints that he grew up in a big house, that there were connections to wealth and a lost inheritance, were now wearing thin. He was born into a family on the edge of rural poverty and came from a long line of farm workers, landless labourers struggling to survive. There was no mansion with servants for him to seduce; not even a shabby-genteel villa, but a run-down cottage in a rural slum. There were no well-heeled relatives with stables in Epsom. My grandfather's paternal grandmother, Charlotte, was living close by when his parents married, but she was far from being a lady. She was a widow who took in washing to make ends meet. And when my grandfather's mother, Sarah, went into the asylum in 1911, my grandfather had a job working as a milk boy, carting the urns around Carshalton. But I took no pleasure in cutting his tall stories down to size.

★

Family history can only take in stretches of the road. The journey metaphor, so often used to 'chart' the 'course' of a life in memoir and biography, falters and peters out. The past is formless until historians and storytellers shape it to their own ends, but family history, with its stops and starts, its uncertainties and gaps, can never be a seamless narrative. Perhaps its interminable proliferations bring it closer to the texture of life as it is lived in the present, less a tightly woven fabric than a series of loose ends; less a clear-cut channel through time than a space into which doors open and close. Contingency only hardens into inevitability in retrospect; endings dictate beginnings. It was never certain that Sarah would end her days in Netherne. Yet however much I might want to, I could not avoid her last way station. A death in an asylum was a death in extremity. If it was not Gothic, the stuff of sensational fiction, neither was it merely prosaic.

There were no Epsom stables in my grandfather's life, but there was an 'Epsom cluster' only a few miles away, Britain's largest group of asylums, four of them built during his childhood on a 1,000-acre plot to the west of Epsom: the Manor (1899), Horton (1903), Long Grove (1906), and an 'epileptic colony', St Ebba's (1904); West Park, the fifth, opened in 1924. By 1914 London had eleven but Surrey had fourteen major asylums, more than any other county, mostly to house the patients from the metropolis (Yorkshire came a close second, with thirteen large asylums accommodating people from the industrial towns). Netherne, opening in 1909, was built to take the overflow when yet another nearby asylum, Brookwood, exceeded its statutory maximum of 2,000. Occupying what was once a farming estate five miles south of Croydon, Netherne was a world unto itself, high on a leafy hill, with its own water tower, farm, workshops, laundry and church. It was built in the 'simplified Queen Anne' style, and the accommodation was initially thought by outside inspectors to be 'somewhat lavish'.

Sarah was admitted to Netherne on 9 June 1911, her first and only admission. Public asylums like Netherne were Poor Law institutions and it was necessary to be registered by the local relieving officer as a pauper. The Epsom Union workhouse was the first stop for many of those who arrived at Netherne, local people like Kate Reigate, with nothing apart from 'sad case' by her name; John Russell of Chessington, a labourer in his mid-forties, styled 'village idiot'; and John Peters, categorized as 'immoral' and 'admitted at his own request'. All were removed from the workhouse wards by an order from the magistrate to Netherne not long after its opening. Carshalton, where the Smiths lived, fell into the Epsom Union but Sarah was not in the workhouse. She was still at home when her husband filled in the census form in March 1911, two months before she was committed. There was no sign of her in the Brookwood Asylum records either, so I knew she had not been transferred. Under the column in Netherne's register which commented on her condition – whether 'Recovered, Relieved, Not Improved, Died' – it merely read 'Died'. The register of deaths confirmed the information on her death certificate: she died on 18 June from 'exhaustion' after sixteen days of mania. Seven days were unaccounted for but were most likely spent at home until the family called in a doctor. I would learn nothing more except that she was 'buried by friends', a phrase that included family, though not at Netherne. There were no other medical notes for Sarah. The patient 'case books', or case files, for Netherne's early period have not survived (and only a small sample, about 10 per cent of case files from the Epsom cluster asylums, were kept).

There were more questions than answers. 'Mania' is deemed a 'mood disorder', generally characterized as a state of wild, feverish elation, a hyperactive state of restlessness and often irritability, which leads to sleeplessness. But in the nineteenth century 'mania' was an umbrella term. More than 80 per cent of admissions were for mania; today it would be less than 5 per cent. Under its rubric sheltered many conditions which would now be diagnosed differently, including many organic illnesses. In the days before antibiotics, patients became delirious from high fever, while other acute medical illnesses – brain damage, cancer – might exhibit 'psychiatric' symptoms; some patients might be suicidal, others senile or epileptic; still others would now be labelled 'schizophrenic' or 'psychotic'. I could see from the register that patients at Netherne also died of exhaustion from 'melancholia', but the idea of linking alternating and recurring 'phases' of excitement and stupor was not to take hold in Britain until after the First World War when an English translation of Emil Kraepelin's theory of 'manic depression' was more widely available. Sarah was fifty-three. She may well have been in an asylum earlier in her life elsewhere in the country or have periodically suffered from depression without it being seen as anything other than the utter weariness of a working woman. Alternatively, while 'puerperal disorders' following childbirth had long been seen as a kind of 'temporary insanity', menopause with its storm of hormonal changes was less examined. In fact nothing about Sarah's mania or her death 'from exhaustion' could be taken for granted. If she died of heart failure after a fortnight's frenetic activity and no sleep, she was also likely to be near starvation. Those who were raving were hard to feed, words pouring out of their mouths so that they could take nothing in. Might Sarah have survived in a private asylum in her own comfortable, quiet room with the special care of the best doctors, or 'alienists'? As with her sojourn in the workhouse as a child, the adult Sarah had arrived in a public institution at perhaps the worst time in its history.

During the course of the nineteenth century the humanitarian ideals that had led to the creation of public asylums were overwhelmed by the sheer numbers of pauper lunatics. The early county asylums in the 1820s, housing on average 115 inmates, were designed with an initial emphasis on a 'moral therapy', the belief being that the mad could be restored to reason via a calm and careful regime, though none could be as intimate as the influential Retreat, a small Quaker asylum in York which promoted the use of moral treatment and where the front door stood open. In the 1870s, when around 120 new county asylums were built, the average number of inmates in each was already around 500. Resembling the great Victorian show houses of the aristocracy, asylums were self-sufficient colonies. While their gardens, informal parks, and grand terraces with spectacular views across the countryside, were intended to have therapeutic effects, the popular 'historical' styles used by architects helped soften their appearance and differentiate them from prisons or the workhouses. But as England's population doubled, the number of its certified lunatics increased more than fivefold, with the largest increases among the poorest. 'Custodial realities' overtook 'rehabilitative good intentions'. Institutionalization – prisons, schools, workhouses, asylums – became the state's answer to solving the problems created by demographic changes and urbanization, the insecurities and displacements of an industrial society. At best the asylum continued to offer protection for vulnerable individuals – the 'imbeciles', epileptics and 'weak-minded', as well as the insane – and those 'misfits' who might otherwise be persecuted, abandoned or even exhibited in shows and circuses. It also protected families from its violent or abusive members. The Lunacy Act of 1890 tightened the law and made improper confinement harder, requiring two medical certificates for the detention of any person, but it was now harder for the temporarily or partially disturbed to find institutional care or for any sufferer to come and go. Many patients became institutionalized and the asylum became associated with long-term detention behind locked gates. Ostracized and excluded, pauper lunatics existed outside the life of the community in vast warehouses holding up to 2,000 people. In addition, the asylum's often remote location made it difficult and expensive for relatives to visit. As psychiatry's dreams of curing mad people faded, a new pessimism set in and the quality of care declined. The asylum was increasingly perceived as a 'dustbin for hopeless cases' (in my youth the local mental hospital was still known as 'the loony bin'). Whatever the facts, committal in the popular imagination seemed tantamount to incarceration. In reality it was less a case of the wrongful confinement of the sane as 'the wrongful confinement of the recoverable in categories and institutions dedicated to the "incurable"'.

By the turn of the twentieth century, when Sarah Smith became an inmate, public asylums were full to bursting. Most pauper lunatics lived in wards with fifty or even a hundred others eating communally and sleeping in beds a few inches apart, under a strictly authoritarian regime which used all manner of physical restraints. The most 'refractory', as they were termed, were banished to the 'back wards', synonymous with misery and squalor, where 'the vast mass of human hopelessness became apparent . . . the chronics, the incurables, the intractables', unseen by the visitors who trod only the gleaming floors of the admissions ward or sat in the sunlit day rooms with their homely pot plants and pictures. The census of 1911 gives 950 'lunatics' at Netherne, so it too was running close to capacity. It also functioned according to the Victorian habits of rigid hierarchy, classification and segregation, relying heavily on the unpaid labour of its inmates, who made their clothes in the laundry and worked the farm, making a profit on its produce, and on the strong arms of living-in attendants, working from six in the morning till seven thirty at night and subject to a curfew. A medical officer in the asylum earned £300 and the superintendent, at the top of the pyramid, £800 a year; attendants were on £35 a year – less than a pound a week, on a level with the poorest of farm labourers. The arrival of war brought some 'easing of the aloofness' between the ranks, if only for the duration; half the staff joined up, including the medical superintendent, Sidney Nelson Crowther, who had signed Sarah's death certificate, and who volunteered immediately. But it also revealed to the public the life led by the majority of the inmates pre-war. Carefully rechristened as a 'War Mental Hospital' to avoid any taint of the public lunatic asylum, Netherne took seventy-five military casualties. The authorities, relatives and public campaigners alike were anxious that shell-shocked or neurasthenic servicemen should be given special treatment. Even those certified as lunatics should 'not in any way be graded with pauper lunatics, or, indeed, even with ordinary lunatics'. As 'service patients' they should get 'comforts and privileges' such as nightshirts, individual toothbrushes and towels (toilet paper had only been issued as a matter of course to the pauper lunatics in London asylums from 1913 and not all toilets had even 'dwarf doors'). The servicemen were allowed to wear a lounge suit or even their own clothes, though the paupers at Netherne, as elsewhere, had to wait till 1923 for this token of self-esteem. Service patients who died were not meant to be buried in the same cemetery as the pauper lunatics, as if their degradation and ignominy would spread like a stain, even after death.

My grandfather was sixteen when his mother went into the asylum. Though the family would surely have told themselves it was 'for the best', no one would be in any doubt about the stigma. Sarah's death so soon at Netherne could only add to the horror of the family's experience, the awful, visceral wretchedness of seeing one's mother break down and be taken away to an asylum, and the guilt too that accompanied relief at her absence. How did they mourn her loss in the midst of such complicated emotions? When Sarah disappeared into Netherne, she disappeared from the family annals. My grandfather never mentioned her to his children; not one of his five daughters was given her name. It was as though she simply could not be remembered.

What had I hoped for? Did I really need Sarah's case history, with its questionable assumptions and outmoded categories, to know her life had been hard? In the nineteenth century, poverty was considered to be one of the chief causes of madness, while recent studies draw attention to the effects of migration on Victorian workers, as mentally destabilized by constant relocations as migrants are today. Yet despite more than a century of psychiatry, psychoanalysis, new surgical procedures and drug treatments, madness in its motley guises is still the 'mystery of mysteries'. Psychiatrists and medical specialists hold opposing views about the aetiology of mental disturbances. Some place manic-depressive illness among 'the most biological conditions'; others suspect it to be largely a construct of psychiatric science, pandering to the pharmaceutical companies; still others prioritize the dire social or familial conditions which can unhinge any life, as the more progressive doctors realized when faced with neurasthenic men from the Western Front who had no former history of nervous illness. What research has repeatedly shown, however, is that, as the writer and doctor Jonathan Miller puts it, 'the destiny of people who are assigned the role of mental patient depends on the degree to which those around them recognise and respect how normal they are, rather than how ill they are'. In other words, Sarah's 'destiny' as a pauperized patient in a public asylum was not fate.

Sarah ended her life as she began it, a pauper inmate of a Poor Law institution. She was again put in uniform, her things taken from her and her old identity hung up with her everyday clothes in the cupboard; again she found herself in a crowded women's ward, strictly segregated from the men's. Just as in the workhouse, she would have been put to cleaning and cooking, if she had been capable of it, but Sarah was now done with housework. This was her last resort. If she let loose a torrent of words, I hope she finally had her say, and that someone was listening. All I can be sure of is that she spent the last days of her life in an Alsatia of her own.

Spade Labour

The Smiths had been farm workers for generations. In the hard years of the 1830s, Richard Smith, Arthur's grandfather, had come from Peasemore in Berkshire to Cobham in Surrey, where he married Mary Ann Carpenter in 1839 at St Andrew's church. Four years earlier, Arthur's other grandparents, James Honnor and Eliza Raffel, were also married there. The Honnors had migrated further across county borders, from Bedfordshire to Hertfordshire, then into Surrey via the Oxfordshire border. All were among the landless labourers, who in the wake of enclosures, new farming practices, depression in agriculture, and finally suburbanization, found their world increasingly marginalized as England became the world's first truly urban and industrial nation. In the 1900s farm labourers still made up 80 per cent of the agricultural workforce, but in the counties close to London they were hard to find. While the Edwardian years saw a celebration and idealization of the arts of 'the folk' and of the village, farm labourers and their families, especially in the southern counties, were barely surviving. As a survey of 'the rural labour problem' found, thousands of agricultural workers were earning far less than a pound a week, dependent upon weekly and even daily hiring, their families cooped up in damp and dark cottages often with 'a rat as part tenant'; bread was the mainstay of their diet, and, thanks to women's ingenuity and constant work, all sorts of 'shifts' and 'contrivances' made it just possible for the family to be fed and clothed. There was as yet no minimum wage for a farm worker. 'I couldn't tell you how we do live,' one woman replied in puzzlement to the interviewer, when asked about her struggle through the days, 'I don't know how we manage; *the thing is to get it past*.' Not surprisingly, the rising generation in the village went on leaving when they could – girls to go into service or shop work and boys like my grandfather taking farm jobs temporarily 'as a prelude to adventure in the towns or in the colonies'.

In Surrey arable farming dwindled, but the need to feed the metropolis grew. Market gardening, supplying flowers, fruit and vegetables to the expanding surburbs and towns, all increased, as did the fastest-growing product – milk. Arthur Smith's father, George, had been a stockman, working with cattle, a job which was usually better paid and more secure than general farm work. Five of his eight sons, including Arthur, were all initially 'cowmen' but only three stayed in dairying (my grandfather's cousin Tom was quaintly listed in 1911 as a 'cowboy'). The other brothers joined the exodus from the land, trying their luck as general labourers or navvies. Arthur's progress, if that is the word, from cowman to carter to bricklayer's labourer was typical, though it hardly made him any richer. In 1911, now approaching fifty, he took work from the council, mending roads, another farm worker turned pick-and-shovel labourer.

What was a boy like my grandfather with few prospects and an elementary education to do? When war came in 1914 he had little to lose. His mother was dead and both his sisters had left. Nance had gone to Portsmouth with her sailor husband and Lottie married Stewart Gibson, a clerk soon to join the army, at the end of August (his father was a poor relation of a very well-connected military family with wealth and position in Australia – more stories of lost fortunes, perhaps?). A month later, Arthur Smith married again, to Mary Moore, Nance's mother-in-law. She is probably the strong-faced woman to his left in the photograph of Lottie's wedding whom I first mistook for Sarah. A few weeks after his father's second marriage, my grandfather volunteered for the navy, signing a twelve-year contract. He was taken on as a 'Stoker Second Class' and was going to have to do a lot of shovelling. Not cow muck or asphalt, but coal.

The navy that both my grandfathers joined in the 1910s was being dragged into the twentieth century. Since the introduction of steam, when skilled engineers were not seen as officer material because they were not 'gentlemen', the stoker was looked upon 'as a distinctly lower order of life', paid less even than the regular seaman. Forbidden to appear on deck in their dirty clothes or overalls, treated like the ship's navvies, only the stokers prevented the seamen from being the lowest rung of the ship's ladder. But stokers did not join the navy as boys. Many were men already used to a working life, and in the 1900s some had a background of trade unionism. They were not willing to be treated as fags. Class tension in the hidebound navy came to a head in 1906 when the stokers in Portsmouth barracks rioted, having been ordered by a gunnery officer to go 'on the knee' (to kneel humiliatingly). The stokers' protest was deemed 'the most serious naval riot since the Mutinies at the Nore and Spithead in 1797' and rallied support for reform to the lower deck, where, among other grievances, basic pay had remained static since 1853.

Like Vulcan in the underworld, surely the first of the Smiths, the stoker fed the ship's fires down in the cramped engine spaces, stripped to the waist in an inferno of heat, protecting his eyes from the blinding glare of the furnaces as best he could with blue-tinted glasses. It was hard manual labour, four hours' shovelling coal at a stretch, though it also took skill to spread the fire-bed evenly and manage the oil-sprayers. Stokers earned respect through their sheer toughness. Despite the claim that they were illiterate giants, more brawn than brain, my grandfather, only five foot two and with a chest measurement of thirty-five inches (according to his record), was far from a hulking, barrel-chested specimen. Stoking was a dirty job and a dangerous one. During bombardment or a collision the stoker was confined in a broiling, claustrophobic stokehold or boiler room, surrounded by oil tanks amid 250 pounds of pressure steam, waiting 'to be blowed sky-high at any minute'. The crucial, filthy and frequent duty of 'coaling' a ship, however, was shared and the main occasion when the navy hierarchy was temporarily relaxed. Seamen and officers worked as equals, loading from the collier, hoisting two-ton bags, sacking the coal and pouring it down the chutes while black grit silted every crevice and smothered every surface on deck. The crew put on old clothes and silly outfits to lighten the task, and the ship's band played jaunty tunes as their instruments clogged with dust. As everyone became 'black', the lowest common denominator, rank was effaced. Meanwhile, the stoker perched down in the ship's bunkers, waiting to sort the coal, which came tumbling down the hatch in its hundredweights and might bury him alive or trap him in the dark. Coal dust sat on the lungs for days, though in later life few men made the connection between the 'chestiness' they suffered and their stoker years.

Unlike my dad's reprobate father, who left the navy under a cloud, my mother's father, by all accounts, loved the life. His naval record is glowing, his conduct 'very good' as he was promoted to 'Stoker First Class', then 'Leading Stoker'. Those who got on in the navy were generally 'amenable' to the order and discipline (also unlike my Light grandfather), but not cowed by it, able to assert themselves and keep their spirits up. Hence the dry comment made by one memoirist that good conduct badges were awarded for years of 'undetected crime'. My grandfather was lucky. Both engine rooms were flooded with freezing water when his ship, the battleship *King Edward VII*, was mined off Cape Wrath, on the northern coast of Scotland in January 1916. The ship capsized but all the crew were rescued. For the rest of the war he saw service on the *Canterbury*, one of the light cruisers which took part in the Battle of Jutland the following May, the war's biggest naval engagement, when twenty-five ships were sunk and 6,000 British sailors died. *Canterbury* and its men were unscathed. After the armistice his ship was sent to Russia as part of the British campaign to stop the rise of Bolshevism, going to the aid of the White Russian navy. To some sailors, worn out, expecting to be demobbed and now fighting their former allies, the hostilities were 'incomprehensible, even undesirable': 'Why are we firing at them? They were our friends during the war! Why are we out here?' Food was in short supply. In Sebastopol the men and the officers ran a black market, selling ship's goods at inflated prices to the locals; in Odessa, where my grandfather arrived in March 1919, people were dying of starvation on the streets. A month later he was invalided out with neurasthenia, or 'war weariness', adding the Silver Badge for his honourable discharge to his trio of medals, usually awarded together, the Service Medal, the Victory Medal and the 1914–15 Star – 'Pip, Squeak and Wilfred', as they were dubbed by the men, after a cartoon strip in the *Daily Mirror* which became a huge craze in the 1920s (the adventures of a dog, a penguin and a rabbit).

Not much is written about the navy and neurasthenia. Fewer sailors seem to have suffered from the shell-shock and the 'hysterical' disorders which afflicted the men in the trenches. Obviously, the relatively low numbers were partly due to the infrequency of naval battles but it was also attributed to the conditions of a sea fight where there was far less chance of facing death or injury alone – no 'going over the top'. Seamen, even the wounded, remained in the thick of it among their comrades and in the event of battle sailors were also more likely to die than remain concussed. Naval neurasthenics, 95 per cent of whom were diagnosed with anxiety and exhaustion, were treated in general medical wards, usually with sedatives for insomnia, while 'acute mental cases' were sent to the three large naval hospitals. 'Nerves' affected officers and men alike. Many of the long afloat suffered palpitations, headaches and 'terrifying dreams', as well as feelings of suffocation. After three months' convalescence my grandfather went home, though my grandmother told stories of his being 'too long in the water' and 'never the same again'. Expectations are also a form of inheritance: did memories of his mother plague him while he was in hospital, a fear of total breakdown, or of being put in a place like Netherne?

My grandparents had married not long after Jutland in July 1916. He was twenty-one, she nineteen and pregnant, but there was no seduction story since they had been courting at least two years since Lottie's wedding. Richard George, known as 'John', was born in Portsmouth five months later, and William, my uncle Bill, the outcome of another leave, in the summer of 1918. When my grandfather returned, he was a man with no job; any sense of achievement or authority he had in the navy was gone. Soon there was another baby, a girl, Winifred, a name very much in vogue at the time. He went back to square one, starting work as a general labourer. Eventually, though it took most of his life, he set up in a small way as a builder and decorator, 'W. G. Smith and Son'. He was 'brainy', my mother maintained, 'and a hard worker – I'll give him that'. After several years, thanks to his efforts, and the builder he worked for, the family moved from a two-up, two-down tenement to rent a four-bedroomed terraced house. My grandmother thought it a palace: it even had its own porch and gate. In exchange my grandfather worked for free as a watchman at his landlord's cloth factory at the back of the house. As a treat he sometimes took my mother on his rounds of the empty building, an eerie companionship she long remembered.

What kind of father could this man be, with his lost mother and his frightening secret, his own youth spent in learning subordination and

William George Smith (*middle of the front row*) with his mates in naval training, 1915

the pleasures of male camaraderie in his long, exciting and exhausting war? Moody, morose, used to giving his orders at home; like so many working men of his generation, a hard drinker and a chain-smoker. I see him again in the fug from his Players, still impenetrable, still 'Grampy' to me, the toothless lion. Then there is that young man in the photographs that came to light after he died, fooling around with his mates in the navy. My mother, the ninth child, born when he was thirty-seven, could hardly believe that he had once been so carefree.

*

Netherne, like so many of Britain's Victorian asylums, is long gone. It closed in 1993 in the wake of the 1990 Act which underwrote 'de-institutionalization'. Netherne Hospital (the 'Mental' was dropped in 1935) saw many changes as 'inmates' became patients. First, occupational therapy, and then more satisfying work, was on offer, for the patients' benefit rather than the asylum's profit; vouchers could be spent in the new canteen. The status and pay of attendants – now 'male nurses' – was gradually upgraded, their hours reduced, and they became unionized. A wireless was installed in some wards; there were dances and entertainments, and eventually a hairdresser, a library, a choir and an orchestra, an art studio where art therapy was pioneered. Patients played each other in inter-ward tennis, cricket and football. Of course there were still the 'back wards' and Netherne had its share of difficult 'incidents', like the man who hanged himself out near the cricket pavilion in front of the male wards. A new generation of psychiatrists experimented with advanced forms of treatment: the first use of ammonium chloride in electroconvulsive treatment was at Netherne in 1940 (the actress Vivien Leigh was 'shocked' there after a breakdown in 1953) and in 1942 fifty people received prefrontal leucotomies (lobotomies). Tranquillizers like Largactil, introduced in the 1950s, meant the fences were taken down around the airing grounds and patients could wander the gardens, even go on trips to the coast; the food could be more various since nearly everyone could have a knife and fork. It was not long before 'the chemical cosh' – antipsychotic drugs and mood-stabilizers like lithium – made it possible for the government to open the gates of the mental hospital altogether. For better, and for worse, patients were released into 'care in the community'. A hundred years on, heavily sedated, Sarah might have found herself back home.

In 1995 the developers M. J. Gleeson moved in, converting the old women's block into luxury flats, demolishing the main corridor to create an Italian garden fringed with poplars (elsewhere the hallways still sport the Arts and Crafts green tiles, familiar in many English institutions). The water tower which serviced the community now has four duplexes and a penthouse at the top. Netherne's church, St Luke's, houses the swimming pool, and its stained-glass windows can be enjoyed as residents work up a sweat at the gym. When I visited the village of 'Netherne on the Hill' – 'A Village Come to Life', the welcome sign says – I was told that the new estate has its problems due to its isolation and the mix of million-pound mansions with social housing. Netherne kids are suspected of being a bit 'wild' and the residents are as cut off as the inmates used to be but without the self-sufficiency of the asylum. 'You have to live in your car,' one told me, though the views are appreciated.

The dead have caused problems too. About 1,300 people were buried at Netherne on the edge of a farmer's field. Gleeson let the cemetery alone so that it could 'return to nature', or so the developers claimed. But graves aren't so easily forgotten. In 2010 a history enthusiast began the first rumblings of scandal, discovering that there were war dead buried there. Badgers were rooting about, dislodging the remains and turning up bone fragments among the five-foot-high nettles. A woman looking for the grave of her great-aunt, an epileptic, classified as 'an idiot' in 1915, added her voice, and after a campaign of two and a half years the site was finally cleared, though there are no headstones. I never found where Sarah was buried, though I knew it was not at Netherne. But I was relieved not to find another pauper grave like the one into which her mother disappeared from the Cheltenham workhouse, or rather, to fail to find it.

Sarah Smith's story is 'history from below' but not if that phrase implies a perspective removed from the larger sweep of power. The salted codfish eaten by slaves, the boom and bust of a small town on the Dorset coast, the spa town demanding fresh supplies of migrant labour, then shuffling them off when the fashions changed, the servant girl and her bastard, and the institutions they found themselves in, were subject to a political economy whose blind faith in the operations of a free market left little safety net for its human casualties. On the other side of the Atlantic, Sarah's Hosier forebears, adrift after the collapse of their enterprises, found a haven by turning to Methodism rather than to the market. While Sarah's great-grandfather John Hosier returned to Poole, his brother's widow, Grace, made the Hosier mansion into a lodging house for the early preachers who braved the bleak climate. Two of her daughters married clergymen. As Sarah's grandmother Maria (who ended her days Mrs 'Fitzhosier' Jackson) began her chequered career in Cheltenham, Maria's cousin Jane left Newfoundland with her Wesleyan husband to return to his native Scotland. Their son Thomas Barr went to Oxford University before taking holy orders, while his contemporary, Maria's son Richard, joined the forced labour in Van Diemen's Land building Britain's colonies. The old Hosier home in Bonavista is now the site of the United Church manse.

There is no 'closure' in family history, only the reverberation of a life. Inheritance, psychological, emotional, material, is one name for those reverberations. For a while the ghosts of Mary Ann Hill and her mother, Maria Hosier, glimmered in their namesakes, Mary Ann Davies, the youngest daughter of Sarah's half-sister, and Anna Maria Hill, William and Fanny's eldest, both Sarah's cousins. I lost track of Mary Ann but Anna Maria stayed in Pembrokeshire all her life, marrying a Welsh-speaker. One of her seven daughters, Edith, took the world in her stride, emigrating with her family to Western Australia in 1923, settling in the small wheat-belt town of Kondinin. (Did she know that her grandfather's brother had once made a similar voyage in a convict ship?) Newfoundland to Poole to Cheltenham to Wales and to Australia: I was no longer surprised by these journeys of the labouring classes, nor that a maternal line should stretch halfway around the globe.

What else was passed on? I wonder now if my grandfather first heard hints of lost fortunes and better times from his mother. Perhaps little Sarah, travelling to Wales with that strange lady called her grandmother, kept them close like jewels all those years, those stories of her family who once lived in a big house with servants of their own, far, far away. Fairy tales they must have seemed to her, who had never known riches or seen the sea.

4 Albion Street

She grows up steeped in sound. At night she lies listening to the others snuffling in the fuggy room; a donkey snorts outside and the man next door knocks over a bucket, as he always does, cursing. From the pub on the corner comes a splatter of laughter, fiddle and pipe; the swell of a chorus – 'We'll rant and we'll roar!' – laughter again and broken glass. Somewhere, the muffled drum of the patrol out for the liberty men, and a distant foghorn, drifting in the dark. She wakes to the clatter of the neighbours, feet on wooden stairs, and the frantic, summoning pulse of seagulls.

Hers is a dead-end street, blocked off by the synagogue. Sometimes she ducks down a passage between the courts into White's Row, where the women are no better than they should be, and runs to Queen Street, holding her nose at the slaughterhouse next to the chapel. Past the chandler's display of rope and cordage, the banks and the pawnshops, the outfitters where the officers are kitted up, past Levy's jewellers, dodging the crowd of hawkers and loiterers outside the dockyard gates, on she runs, faster, faster, till she reaches the Hard, where the men hoist timber and heave sacks of coal to a chorus of shouts and hooters. Boys mudlark for pennies thrown by the ferry passengers; a fresh tub of oysters glistens with salt; ships' brasses catch the sun. The sea out on the Solent is calm. The air smells of tar and the ripe slurry of cabbage stalks and bruised fruit. Filling her lungs with the mixture, she turns again, and runs home up Kent Street, squeezing between the barrows and crates, jumping over a stream of beer, swilling out from the Beehive and foaming in sour golden pools. In Albion Street she draws breath, dawdling. Inside the house her father sits hunched over his stitching and shaping; her mother moves in the shadows, a baby in the crook of her arm.

When shall we say it was and where? First, they built in wood, sinking piles down into the seabed, then in stone; they sent men armed in boats to fight the men on the opposite coast; then they took to sailing and trading longer distances, with a battery of guns on their ships. A jumble of wharves and storehouses, the jetties become docks, until the people overflow the town walls, putting up their shacks beyond the reach of the magistrate. It could be any sailor town but it is England, the south coast, where the sea washes in and out of their lives, carrying away its cargo of men, and, sometimes, when the tide turns, casts them back on shore again like netted fish, gasping for air.

If geography is history, where does it begin? Like the next hill on a long walk, origins have a habit of receding as they are approached. Before the men dredge and drain, and the women fetch and carry; before they cut down trees for planking or hammer rings for anchorage; before they venture out beyond their own creeks and gullies, the mist blurs sea and sky, and a few shapeless figures, the colour of the marsh, sift salt pans and shiver with fever. There are no moats or dams, only restless pebble bars, shifting in the tides; morasses and lakes, which will surface in future street names or under floorboards, until the past flows over the land and swamps its features, and the land and sea make a new alignment. People come with their stories to give it form. They make their own kind of time and call it history, human syncopation, an offbeat accompaniment to the stealth of the glacier and the planet's revolution in space.

★

If my family had a foundation then it was my maternal grandmother's life story: from orphan to mother of ten. Her life spanned the twentieth century, her body had borne it, and her ten children were its fruit. Generation was the antidote to loss, and family the sovereign good, a protection and a panacea against all ills. She was born in Portsmouth but both her parents had died young. Her father was a stevedore, she said, unloading at the docks, killed when he struck his head open on the side of a ship. Then, a few weeks later, so the story went, in a dramatic and uncanny echo, her mother had hit her head on the kitchen range and died. My grandmother's maiden name, whose spelling she was unsure of, was the source of endless speculation: Heffren or Heffron. It sounded foreign; French perhaps. Was she Jewish? 'Hebron' was also canvassed amid jokes about long noses which no longer seem funny. Her father's name was possibly Edward, possibly Eduard. Her mother's name had evaporated and seemed lost to time.

I don't think family history mattered to the family much. What mattered was the living not the dead, their daily doings, the currency of family life, pregnancies, errant husbands, sick children, and where the money was coming from. No one had turned yet to family history as a source of personal, private truth, instead patching together an archive which was publicly aired at gatherings, mostly stories of the immediate past, and in particular, of the last war. These were stories fondly repeated over the years, 'embroidered' with new embellishments, threads in the fabric of a continuously unfolding, unfinished saga, epic in reach, domestic and local in detail: each Saturday tea or pub evening would bring another episode of 'the Family'. No one needed to know 'the facts' of my grandmother's childhood. The stories were preferable. Of course the facts would be about pain or separation and, though the word was not used then, trauma. The past was violent and it wrenched children from parents, parents from each other; it blew up houses and took men off to war. Like the soldiers' farewells in the pub sing-songs, where my grandmother sat nursing a port and lemon all evening, '*Goodbye Dolly, I must leave you*', '*Goodbye-ee, Goodbye-ee, wipe the tear, baby dear, from your eye-ee*', '*Wish me luck as you wave me goodbye*', the twentieth century rang with the sound of parting.

My grandmother's tales were in the same key. I often heard how, in the city's orphanage, she and her little brother, Ted, were only able to glimpse each other and wave when the girls and boys filed out separately in long crocodiles, holding hands in pairs for windswept walks across Southsea Common. At twelve or thirteen, she said, she had gone out to service, ending up as a kitchen-maid in the house where she met my grandfather while her brother disappeared into the services. The vision of my grandmother's desperate times in an institution remained with me. Those two small children signalling to each other across an endless stretch of grass, frozen in time like the figures on Keats's 'Grecian Urn', forever pictured in my mind in the pursuit, not of beauty, but of mothering.

My 'nan', my mother's mother, was always old to me, never known without her white hair and the NHS spectacles which became fashionable in the 1960s as 'granny glasses'. I can't say that I loved her; the idea, at the time, would have seemed irrelevant, pointless, like asking if you loved weather. She was a general property, always in the midst of the tribe. She *was* the family, its Alpha and Omega; her survival had meant our survival. She had even lent a hand when I was born at home, ticking off the midwife, Nurse Quartly, whose name, like her crime, had been kept fresh in the family annals – a woman silly enough to ask my grandmother, 'Are you sure you know what to do, dear?' My mother and aunts relied on their mother for physic and advice; she dosed their children with gripe water or rosehip syrup, and my particular favourite, an Oxo cube crumbled into a mug of boiling water, for extra nourishment. Panicking, my mother rushed round to her when she found my scalp crawling with head lice caught at school. Nan smartly washed my hair with vinegar as I kept my eyes tight shut. She was not to me a soft, twinkly kind of granny, whose lap a child might climb into, lisping confidences, hoping for a cuddle. I have only one intimate memory of the two of us. On occasion she took me into the darkened front bedroom on the ground floor of their house (who slept there? I have no idea) and wound up the jewellery box on her dressing table so that I could watch the tiny ballerina in a pink tutu circle endlessly, arms above her head, to the jerky, sweet tune.

Family historians need to be hard-hearted. History's romancers, they are also its killjoys. Many years after her mother's death, my mother began the search for her ancestors and what she found soon put paid to any wild fancy. Lilian Heffren, my grandmother, was the child of Edwin James Heffren, neither Frenchman nor Jew, and Flora Murphy. Both, like her, were born locally, in Portsea, in the city of Portsmouth where we lived, close to the harbour and the docks. Lilian's birth certificate showed her father as a labourer, though he and Flora seem not to have married. Edwin's death record was missing but Flora died of heart disease at the age of fifty-two. In 1908, three months after her mother died, my grandmother had gone, not into an orphanage as she always said, but into what was still the Portsmouth Union Workhouse. She was ten, 'admitted by aunt', according to the register. At first she only spent two weeks there. But the workhouse records for children are incomplete. She and her brother were certainly inmates together, in their separate wards, in 1911. Lilian was there training as a domestic, like every other older girl. Her brother was destined for the navy.

An average, unglamorous story of poverty, then, which my grandmother, or others close to her, had dressed up a little in the finery of melodrama. Being an orphan has a more appealing sound to it, like something out of a novel. It certainly carried less of a stigma than a history as a workhouse pauper. She may have spent months, even years, in the workhouse: I would never know. Weeks can feel like years to a child, especially to one who does not know when she is likely to leave. Add to that the misery and shame of knowing that no one had wanted you or taken you in. Or she may have exaggerated. Perhaps her experience did not seem terrible enough to warrant sympathy in a world where such childhoods were two a penny. She was probably illegitimate, from a pauper family, and her mother was a Murphy to boot. In the poorest dockside districts like Portsea, as in Liverpool or London, the Irish were considered the lowest of the low. And they didn't come more Irish than 'Murphy', the commonest of Irish surnames. Was this, like the workhouse, a part of the past which my grandmother wished to forget? Or had she not known any of it?

Portsea, where my nan was born in 1897, still had an unsavoury reputation when I was growing up in the 1960s, a rough, tough, hard-drinking area full of squaddies and sailors on furlough. No 'decent' girl, I was told, would walk down Queen Street past the barracks on a Saturday night. Only a mile or so from where I lived, I hardly ever went there, except to take a trip or two on the ferry from Portsmouth harbour across to Gosport, an equally foreign place. Like other Portsmuthians, I took the presence of the navy for granted and was excited when a fleet was in: the matelots with their red pom-poms, the Russians with their incomprehensible hatbands and flowing ribbons, or the crew-cut, loud-voiced 'Yanks', all the men on a spree who thronged the shops and the funfair at Clarence Pier. Sailors struck me as friendly and cheerful, far less martial and bloodthirsty than soldiers, in part because of their familiarity – my mother's father, and several uncles and aunts, had been in the navy during the war; my uncle Bill had made a life there, becoming a chief petty officer, though that meant little to me. But the dockyard behind its forbidding brick wall, marines standing sentry at the entrance, was both humdrum and hidden. Every day the 'dockies', as we called them, poured out of the gates on their bikes, my father sometimes one of them, and pedalled home for their tea. What had this to do with the thrilling tales of weather-beaten sea dogs of old, pitted against the elements on ocean-going voyages, or men in tricorn hats engaged in spectacular naval battles? Or with girls like me? One of the hit songs of the day, 'Sailor, stop your roaming', which I sang in our pub sing-songs, reminded me of my place: waiting with the womenfolk back home. Exotic destinations were for us merely words to conjure with:

> As you sail across the sea, I will send my love to guide you:
> From Peru to Amsterdam, Honolulu or Siam.

The records showed that my grandmother came from the heart of Portsmouth's maritime world. She was the fourth generation of women born in Portsea, a connection stretching back to the Napoleonic era, like the songs I had sung unthinkingly in the school playground: 'Boney was a warrior, ra, ra, ra!' In the censuses seamen and seamen's wives abounded but further details were sparse or inconsistent. Men disappeared altogether for a decade or two; marriages were frequently delayed or, like Edwin and Flora, my grandmother's parents, were made in name but not on paper; children were baptized in batches when the men were home, and deaths could seemingly sink without trace. Women were the anchors in this community where their husbands, lovers and sons might be off for weeks, months, even years at a time, and where some never came back. Forget any notion of 'the Angel in the House', that mid-Victorian paragon of femininity, cosseted and confined. These nineteenth-century women had to wear the trousers. Without their men they got on or they went under.

The ship and the shore are usually treated as worlds apart, but every seaman has family somewhere. In seafaring families not everyone went to sea and even the sailors who were lifelong bachelors had relatives who lived in their home town, trying out other trades. Despite all the comings and goings, I found Murphys and Heffrens who went on being born, getting married and dying in the same streets from the early decades of the nineteenth century well into the twentieth. Flora Murphy, for instance, my great-grandmother, set up house in Albion Street, Portsea, in the 1880s with her first husband, John Miller, a carpenter in the dockyard and the son of a seaman. They lived a few doors down from where Flora had spent her childhood and where her mother, Lydia, and Lydia's mother, Elizabeth, had lived, more than half a century earlier. No point in looking for an ancestral home, however. Albion Street, as I soon discovered on my first walk around Portsea, no longer existed. References to the street or immediate area were few, and none complimentary: 'An evil spot,' wrote one of Portsmouth's chroniclers, wholeheartedly convinced that the bulldozers had signalled 'the march of progress'.

Unlike my other grandparents, my nan had been a constant presence in my growing up; if not intimate, the connection was live; umbilical if not visceral. She *was* my mother's origin and my mother loved and cherished her memory. Pursuing a family history beyond a simple catalogue of names is always evidence of separation, of severing ties at least to the extent of holding one's relations at arm's length. The family member who wants to make a private gift of a family tree to a close circle of relatives soon becomes the historian who estranges her antecedents by locating them 'in history'. I found that family history, which humanizes those who might otherwise be mere faces in a crowd, also defamiliarized those closest to me, giving their lives a larger pattern than they had when they were lived. They became both more and less themselves. I consoled myself by thinking that this is what history does to us too. As we grow older we see not how unique our lives have been, but how representative we were and are; that we are part of the figure in the carpet woven by events, by chance and accident, and by the play of forces more powerful than us.

I was born in Portsmouth too (that made me the sixth generation) and for eighteen years I rarely went beyond the bounds of the city. As a child much of what I knew in the 1950s and early 1960s was of a piece with my grandmother's world at the turn of the century. We warmed ourselves by coal fires, heard the strangulated cry of the rag-and-bone man in the street – 'Ra-a-a-g-nbown!' – as he came round with his horse and cart; we took a jug to the corner shop to buy a pint of vinegar, saved old woollens to sell for a few pence at the local dealers – the list might go on. I too grew up in streets full of Victorian terraced houses and knew a life that revolved around the pub, the football and the Sunday dinner. This was my customary life, the one I distanced myself from by leaving home to go to university. Is the family historian looking for 'roots' or 'home'? Unearthing our roots leaves them exposed. How hard it is, perhaps impossible, to disentangle that skein of feelings: the loss of childhood which comes to us all, the shifts in a culture which can leave us stranded, the growing old that is itself a loss or letting go. Sometimes I wondered what family history was, if not extended mourning.

Easy to find survivals of my grandmother's past in my childhood, but what did I really know of *her* childhood, let alone that of her parents and grandparents? I knew that far from being a lonely orphan my grandmother had been surrounded by a bevy of half-siblings, aunts, uncles and cousins, some living within a stone's throw. True Victorians, these were large families, often ten or twelve children in each generation. All this family had not kept her from the workhouse and, at the very least, I wanted to know why.

Ship to Shore

Towns grow up for all kinds of reasons and Portsmouth was born of the sea. But since the Romans first sited a fort in the third century overlooking its harbour, it was also the child of war. The city likes to think that Richard the Lionheart provided its coat of arms, drawn from the Crusades and consisting of a Moorish crescent moon below an eight-point star, which still graces municipal lamp posts, buses and the shirts of the football team. Richard certainly granted the town its first charter in 1194, when, like other Norman and Plantagenet lords, he used the place as an assembly point for his troops, his mercenaries alarming the local inhabitants. Portsmouth took firmer shape as a naval base under the Tudors, who replaced the earlier wooden fortifications with stone, and when Henry VIII oversaw the building of the country's first dry dock. With occasional doldrums of peace, war nourished the growing town: wars with the Dutch, the French and Spanish, with America, and from 1793 with revolutionary and Napoleonic France – the 'Great War', as it was called before the next 'Great War' came along in 1914. With war came booty and commerce, prizes and profits, more docks, more muscle, more ships and men to sail them. Deep waters at all states of the tide gave Portsmouth harbour ample room for any fleet. With a generous offshore anchorage out in the Solent at Spithead, it was also conveniently shielded by the bulk of the Isle of Wight. By 1800 Portsmouth was the chief naval station in Europe and, therefore, the guidebooks boasted, 'the world'.

Portsmouth, a garrison township, lay in the south-west corner of an island off an island. Portsea Island was both highly defended and awash with foreigners. Though never on the scale of a Liverpool or Bristol, its commercial port saw ships from the Atlantic colonies – Bermuda, Barbados and the Leeward Islands – bringing tobacco, sugar and fruit; and from the Baltic powers and Muscovy, with cargoes of tar, timber, flax for canvas, and hemp for rigging; the navy also bought in 'train oil' from the Newfoundland whalers, used as a lubricant. The Royal African Company had links with the port, as did the Arab traders of the Levant. All manner of officials, passengers and servants joined ship or visited the town; men like Andrew Lindgren, a Swedish ore merchant, whose son became the local agent for the East India Company, which had its biggest depot outside London in the town. A large Jewish community of traders arrived from Eastern Europe and sold 'slops', or second-hand clothing, and anything from gingerbread to jewellery to the sailors, as well as offering loans or goods on account. The navy itself was a hive of foreigners, buzzing with a babel of languages – 'Irish, Welsh, Dutch, Portuguese, Spanish, French, Swedish, Italian and all the provincial dialects which prevail between Lands-end and John O'Groats', according to Robert Hay, writing in 1803. Americans, some captured from the privateers; Africans, including liberated or escaped slaves; 'Lascars', 'mulattos' and even 'Johnny Crapaud' could all be shipmates, like the French who served on board *Victory* at Trafalgar (there were also, it was said, sixteen Britishers on the French flagship). Not only foreign sailors but foreign soldiers, like the Hessian and Hanoverian battalions, were billeted in the town. Prisoners of war from France, America and the West Indies were a frequent sight, as were the least fortunate transients, the transports following in the wake of the 'First Fleet' which sailed to Botany Bay in 1787. About 28,000 of them embarked from

Portsmouth in the first half of the nineteenth century. Portsmouth deems itself 'the Mother of Australia'.

'War is the harvest of Portsmouth,' wrote Sir Frederick Eden in 1795, investigating poverty there, 'and peace, which is so ardently wished for in most other parts of England, is dreaded here.' Rumour had it that in peacetime 'long grass grows upon the streets', but in wartime Portsmouth was a mad scramble of activity. 'People seem always in a hurry,' wrote one excited tourist guide, 'so that the inn and taverns are perpetually crowded'; after a frantic victualling and restocking, all the shops were emptied: 'not a loaf, nor a bit of meat, not even a carrot nor a cabage [*sic*] remained'. Prices went through the roof. What with visitors come to see the fleet; migrants arriving from the villages and looking for work; wives looking for their sailor husbands; pedlars and street-sellers, beggars and cadgers, and the crowd of individuals, from thieves to thespians, hoping to improve their fortunes, the town attracted scores of outsiders. But what was a town, especially a sailor town, if not a mongrel place, made by incomers?

Not surprisingly, few people can trace their ancestors living continuously on the island much before the 1800s. All I could be sure of was that the Heffrens (or Heffrons, Heffrins, Hefferns, depending on the scribe) were definitely not Hampshire men and that the Murphys were from Ireland (the census does not give a village or town). A Dennis 'Hefferon', a waterman, married Hannah Hoar in 1809, over in Gosport on the other side of Portsmouth harbour, and in 1813 my direct ancestor George Heffron (my grandmother's great-grandfather) and another new arrival, Sarah Wareham, were wed. Sarah had come from a poor family in rural Hampshire and was clearly marked as a 'bastard' by the vicar on the Ringwood parish register. George, her husband, given as a labourer, died before the 1841 census might tell me his birthplace, as did Dennis Heffren. He was probably George's older brother since George and Sarah called their first son Dennis; the story always seems to start with brothers leaving home. Heffren is possibly Irish: one website deems it an abbreviation of 'Heffernan', from County Mayo, or from Dublin, Cork or Waterford, all common sea-routes to Portsmouth.

Like the Heffrens, the Murphys were Protestants, perhaps among those who came over after the Union of 1800. Anthony Murphy and Margaret (Fitzpatrick) called their first-born girl 'Rosina', which sounds like a nod back to the old country, and the name was given to the first girl child in each generation. The rest of their children had staunchly loyalist names: Elizabeth, Charlotte, George, Edward, William. It may have been expedient. Catholics were not welcome in Portsmouth, which had been for Parliament in the Civil War and was still a very Protestant town with only a tiny Catholic chapel. Catholics were especially suspect during the French wars. Anthony and Margaret already had six children before they tied the knot in 1816 – a delay in which poverty, absences at sea or disinclination may have played their part. In the next generation, my grandmother's grandfather William Murphy married Lydia Nobes, whose mother, Elizabeth, was also Irish (her father, John, eluded me in the records). In 1843 they married in a registry office, a new option, but this may have had less to do with religion than with Lydia being five months pregnant – also to become a tradition on my mother's side.

Most of the Irish who came to Portsmouth in the early nineteenth century were either soldiers or sailors. To judge by their memoirs, there were plenty of boys who 'ran away to sea with Crusoe', simply seeking novelty and diversion, or to escape poverty. But Waterford, Dublin and Cork also 'supplied' the navy with men; large numbers of poor Irish were sold by 'crimps' to the press gangs or the privateers. In 1792 the navy had around 16,500 men. In 1809–10 numbers peaked at 140,000. Somewhere between a half and a third of these men were 'pressed'. Critics, including some in the Admiralty, loathed this system but saw no other workable way of addressing 'the manning problem'. The more radical made bitter comments on the fact that while 'Rule Britannia' celebrated an ideal of liberty, the authorities did little better than kidnap British men into legalized slavery. Of course, only the lower orders were subject to impressment.

Those most vulnerable to the Impress Service were those known as 'the common pool' of seafarers: fishermen, whalers, men in the merchant shipping, returning on the slave ships, or in the coasting trades. Also fair game were the numbers of men who plied their own craft, as in Portsmouth, where two-oared rowboats and low-sided wherries delivered local produce, took sailors, family and friends to the ships, or workers across the harbour to the various naval establishments. William Hutchins, another of my direct ancestors, whose daughter Mary Ann was to marry George Heffren junior, was a waterman from Longfleet, near Poole in Dorset. He and his wife, Martha, another Irish immigrant, also arrived on Portsea Island during the 1800s. In March 1803, when the brief peace between Britain and France was on the verge of collapse, invasion fears were again rife. The watermen in Portsmouth were so much in 'terror of a press gang', it was claimed, that no boat could be found to cross the harbour to Gosport. Every single vessel 'of every description' was searched, 'and the men, even boys, taken out'. In theory some labourers and dockyard men in the town were protected, like those bricklayers and carpenters who had built the splendid new naval hospital at Haslar, the biggest brick building and the largest hospital in Europe, which was to treat the injured of Trafalgar, Corunna and Waterloo. But a 'hot press' or 'sweep' made mincemeat of many such guarantees. Desertion rates in Nelson's navy were very high, so even Haslar was cannily positioned, surrounded by the waters of Gosport creek. Seamen rarely knew how to swim.

'The navy' was not the one I knew, where men were uniformed, housed on shore in barracks and served continuously, or for a minimum of twelve years. *That* navy, which both my grandfathers joined, was a creation of the second half of the nineteenth century. In previous times men were generally mustered for wars and expeditions on a hire-and-discharge basis. For the majority of men on the lower decks, the distinction between a merchant seaman and a naval rating was 'virtually meaningless' until around the time of the Crimean War, with the establishment of a regular standing navy. Among those men who chose to 'follow the sea', as the phrase was, 'mariners', more latterly known as 'sailors', had flexible allegiances. They would readily serve under foreign captains on merchant ships, or on board an American vessel, where conditions were believed to be better, rewards more reliable and flogging less frequent. Seafaring was temporary, irregular work. Sailors were taken on only for the duration of a voyage and between commissions there might be weeks before a ship found its crew. They were paid off only at the end of a trip – if they were paid at all and not immediately 'turned over' to another ship. Often, especially in wartime, they were given only a day or two's shore leave. Those out of work took to humping loads in the port, wheeling barrows, shifting cargoes or carrying sacks of coal on their backs up the long ladders from the ship's holds, or doing spadework, paid petty sums by the day. Few men, of whatever stripe, were useful on board ship after the age of forty. Horatio Nelson, who argued for annuities to reward service and prevent desertion, thought a seaman finished 'from *old* age' at forty-five.

Sailors and dockyard men were far from being separate species. Sailors who learnt skills on ship during wartime could move into the dockyard, building or refitting ships laid up 'in ordinary', during the peace. As a young man in his twenties, Flora's grandfather Anthony Murphy is listed as a dockyard labourer but his death certificate has him as a 'superannuated rigger', a pensioned worker. He would most likely have learnt the ropes at sea; no mere metaphor for sailors, when a warship might have about forty miles of rope of different sizes, 1,000 pulley blocks and about an acre's worth of sails to manipulate. In the dockyard, the rigger also 'walked' the ships in and out of the docks and basins by means of a network of hawsers and ropes lashed to capstans. Anthony's second son, George, was a seaman, a rigger, like his father, who came ashore in his forties to refit ships in the dockyard; in turn, George's son Arthur followed the same pattern; Arthur's son Fred was a fourth-generation rigger just before the First World War, while his brothers were 'dockies' in skilled, industrial jobs – William a brass moulder, Tom an iron driller, and fifteen-year-old Edward had his foot in the door as a dockyard messenger boy.

Though far less thrilling to us than the navy, the dockyard was the star attraction in the war years, the powerhouse fuelling Britain's imperial expansion. Visitors flocked to this place of marvels, puffing their chests with patriotic pride. The scale and the noise of the operation astonished them. Superlatives abounded – the 'largest naval arsenal in the world'; the largest rope-house known, with cables needing 100 men to work on them. They gasped at the 'vast size of the bellows' in the forge, a 'Cyclopean' cave, where gigantic anchors were cast – 'truly grand and awful'. Ships were leviathans, depicted in contemporary illustrations of their launches looming over a shoal of tiny people. The dockyard was a factory before the factories, highly organized and specialized, the largest industrial undertaking in the country, employing very nearly 4,000 by 1814 and never falling much below 1,500 even at its nadir in the 1830s. A typical Manchester cotton mill, on the other hand, rarely took on more than 300. In 1803 Marc Brunel's steam-driven pulley-block machines were the first instance in Britain, and indeed the world, of machine tools being used for mass production (they made craftsmen who had previously worked by hand redundant). The Industrial Revolution, it has been argued, took place in the naval dockyards well before the age of steam and iron. But the colossal feats of mechanical and marine engineering, the skilled workmanship of 'artificers', rested on the Herculean labour of those men who reclaimed land from the sea, working the pumps, dredging and shifting tons of mud and spoil, loading, carrying and laying the timbers and blocks of granite and Portland stone for docks and basins the size of inverted churches. In Portsea the Admiralty and the town's building contractors could also exploit the free labour of the convicts housed in the hulks. They offered townsfolk and visitors another amusing or edifying spectacle.

In the first couple of decades of the century, my ancestors the Heffrens, Nobes and Hutchins, seamen, watermen and labourers, all lived close to the Point, the area for disembarking and arrival, near Portsmouth High Street, and hard by the old poorhouse. The Murphys, though, were in Portsea, the 'upstart district' to the north, where shipwrights and dockyard labourers had been allowed to build on the common fields near their place of work. During the war years, 'the two towns', as they were called, of Portsmouth and Portsea were volatile, sometimes violent, places. The 1790s saw the mutinies at Spithead, numerous disputes in the dockyard over new ways of working, spontaneous protests, and bread riots, in which even some troops, expected to buy their own food, participated. The dockyard, in response, turned to self-help and set up its own cooperative mill and bake house. Portsea Island had supporters of the French Revolution among its advanced Whigs or liberals, and radical artisans who communicated with the London Corresponding Society, whose members were opposed to the wars altogether and wanted parliamentary reform. In 1796 Kyd Wake, a bookbinder in Gosport, was one of many to fall foul of the harsh censorship laws during Pitt's repressive government. He was sentenced to five years' hard labour and the pillory, simply for saying 'No George, no war', and subsequently died in prison.

With so many men periodically absent on service, out of work or disabled, Portsea's women kept the households going. Their options were limited. They could serve beer or provisions, help out as general servants, pilot the 'bumboats' – 'floating chandler's shops' notorious for charging extortionate prices for their goods – but the majority of them sewed, mended or washed. Sailors were natty dressers and liked to be well turned out (reminding me of the tongue-twister 'Silly Susie sits sewing shirts for sailors', which encouraged us to mild obscenities in my childhood). Since the dockyard and navy were a wholly male workforce, and large numbers of women were relying on irregular and scant payments from their absent men, female labour came extremely cheap. So much so that over the course of the nineteenth century the navy created its other in a dual economy – the clothing industry – which grew in Portsea Island at a rate unknown anywhere else in the south of England. Elizabeth Nobes, Lydia's mother, worked as a needlewoman but at the bottom of the heap were elderly washerwomen, among them Sarah Heffren (the parish bastard from Ringwood), listed in her seventies as a 'pauper laundress'. In the 1930s my grandmother kept the family's head above water taking in sailors' washing. My oldest auntie, Winnie, remembered her with an old tub and a piece of old sacking tied round her waist as her apron, no doubt looking much like her ancestor.

Not quite the bottom of the heap, perhaps. In wartime especially, the navy turned a blind eye to the crowds of young women and girls trafficked from vessel to vessel, a sop to penned-up crews, who might be liable otherwise to desert, or be driven, it was feared, to 'unclean' acts. A sailor might choose a 'wife' from the waterman or bumboat woman for a shilling or so a piece. Up to 400 women were on board ship at a time, according to one shocked Irish seaman in Portsmouth in 1809, while there might be 500 men on the lower decks. The fate of many of those caricatured as brawling 'Spithead Nymphs' out to rob honest 'Jack' of his pay, and whose 'bad characters' the age's double standard so often condemned, can be found in the 'muster book' of the old Portsmouth poorhouse. The word 'venereal' is appended to several sad entries, including that of 'Harriet Hutson', age not known, 'very bad'; Jane Clark, aged nineteen, 'in a most deplorable state'; or Charlott (*sic*) Williams, equally so, admitted 23 August 1808 only to die a month later. 'Miss Nobodies', and whatever their histories or their moral condition, like so many men in the services, they were expendable. They died in the sickroom, which was also the laying-in room, and where female paupers spent hours picking oakum. About a quarter of the inmates were women aged between sixteen and twenty-five.

Thanks to the dockyard, Portsea Island was 'proletarianized early' and it stayed a very working-class place. Working people, apprentices, soldiers and sailors crowded into the theatres, crammed into the galleries or perched on the stone steps. During a performance of Sheridan's *The School for Scandal* a couple of seamen shimmied down from the gods to drink the wine from the stage to much hilarity, though the same uproarious gatherings fell silent and rapt when Anne Holbrook performed her 'monody' on the death of Lord Nelson. The unruly energies of the place certainly disturbed Jane Austen, whose brother Charles had been at the Naval Academy in Portsmouth – 'a sink of vice and abomination', according to Lord St Vincent, the reforming First Lord of the Admiralty. In Austen's *Mansfield Park* (1814) Henry Crawford, the flirtatious Londoner, has been to see the dockyard 'again and again', and Fanny Price's Portsmouth home thrums with news of the navy and of its doings. But it also teeters on the brink of squalor and is a picture of domestic disorder.

On one of my many visits to Portsmouth Museum I bought a cheery greeting card, a reproduction of a popular engraving, *Portsmouth Point* by Thomas Rowlandson, circa 1811. It shows wildly carousing sailors cavorting with their 'Portsmouth Polls' on the promontory, where sailors 'wet their whistles' before making their way back to their ships. The area was known as 'Spice Island', as much an ironic reference to its noxious smells as to any Caribbean trade. Studded with beer shops and brothels, it lay just outside the garrison town and its jurisdiction, not far from where my ancestors lived, and was once as notorious as the old Point at Port Royal, Jamaica. As one officer's son put it: 'if that was Sodom, this is Gomorrah.' Here is the familiar image of the sailor and of Portsmouth: rowdy, footloose and fun-loving, but loyal and patriotic at heart. But what of the pig-faced grotesque cowering on the far left and the bare-breasted Amazon who cudgels him, the dog-faced porter behind them wheeling the kitbags, or the sot to the far right, reduced to hugging a stray? This half-circle of tumbling, degraded figures contrasts with the upright officer in the centre of the scene, making a manly leg, clearly their moral as well as physical superior. Off to the right another officer is saying goodbye to his wife in a proper show of domestic affection. In these counter-revolutionary decades, paternalist tales of quaint and childish seamen, drunken innocents at best, brutish savages at worst, incapable of the finer feelings, were reassuring to the status quo. Contempt for the 'swinish multitude', in Edmund Burke's phrase, fear and distrust of the common people and their families, lurked behind the romance of jolly Jack Tar.

Portsmouth Common

Apart from George and Sarah Heffren, first-generation arrivals who stayed in the garrison town, all my ancestors were living in Portsea by the 1830s. The half-dozen streets where they lived were soon to be deemed 'slums', a new word for dwellings frequently likened to those of animals: 'warrens', 'rookeries', 'dens'. Portsea had gone rapidly downhill. After Napoleon's defeat the Admiralty was keen 'to get rid of the men as quickly as possible in the interests of economy': around 200,000 common soldiers and sailors were demobbed, with little chance of returning to their old lives at a time when the economy was retracting. The workforce at the dockyard fell by 1,500; wages were at rock bottom and hours drastically cut back. Discharged men drifted round the town or stayed near the docks and harbour, hoping to be taken on. Widows – and all those women who had no idea if their menfolk would return – were equally badly off. The poorhouse in Portsea was full, with upwards of 600 people. Three thousand

Thomas Rowlandson, *Portsmouth Point*, *c.*1811

were on 'out relief' and lodging houses were packed. In 1822, surveying the 'hellish assemblage' of Portsmouth, Portsea and Gosport, which he blamed for sucking all the young men from the villages, William Cobbett saw 'an absolute tumbling down taking place'.

Portsea, or Portsmouth Common, as it had first been called, had mushroomed during the eighteenth century and the boom conditions of the French wars. The township had its ornaments: a graceful church, St George's, in an elegant square, built by a company of shipwrights, and a number of superior businesses along the broad stretch of Queen Street (a nod to Anne, who had originally granted the permission to build). It had its tranche of officers, lawyers, surgeons and an architect or two, but the most fashionable streets were in Portsmouth. Guidebooks might be at pains to emphasize the 'elegant assembly room at the Crown' and the 'very commodious' coffee house on Portsmouth High Street, but other observers noted that some quarters were filthy and squalid, and the children 'indigent', especially in Portsea, 'the Wapping of Portsmouth'. Many of Portsea's earliest streets, like Butcher Street and Kent Street (1697), were crammed from the start with inns, shops, workmen's cottages and lodging houses. Few Portsea houses had double frontages, and any larger residences for Admiralty officials were inside the dockyard walls. Some of the better houses, with one room on several storeys and the occasional bow-window, were inhabited by service personnel, tradesmen and skilled artisans. Charles Dickens was born in such a house in 1812, his father a clerk in the Naval Pay Office. These were palatial compared to the squat two-storey weatherboarded cottages in which the majority of people lived, where the front door opened from the street straight into a twelve-foot room; above, a single tiny bedroom, and outside, a handkerchief of backyard. Some of the smallest terraced properties in Britain were built here in the 1800s.

Homely drawings or sepia photographs of wooden cottages with their low eaves and clapboard fronts may look pleasingly rustic to our eyes, especially without their unsightly occupants. But they were deathtraps. Cholera first arrived in 1832. Portsea Island was low-lying, 'aguish', and short on fresh water; some older houses had been built on stilts, since the buildings were prone to flooding. The

Houses in Kent Street, Portsea (Portsmouth Museums)

workmen's dwellings, mainly constructed, like HMS *Victory*, of oak from the New Forest, were as damp and leaky as Nelson's flagship. The more prosperous Hampshire merchants and the gentry had long avoided the townships, favouring a 'bucolic and prestigious setting' over the 'unhealthy confines' of Portsmouth and Portsea, where the inhabitants were effectively kettled, walled in behind fortifications and moats. As the housing stock in Portsea deteriorated, builders and developers abandoned a sinking ship. The new development of Southsea, the third of the 'towns' on the island, to the east of Portsmouth, offered a berth to the higher ranks of army and navy and a small professional elite. Southsea became a polite ghetto dominated by the service families, many born in foreign parts, a high-end version of a motley crew, where only the servants were likely to be local. By the late 1840s its denizens were among Britain's wealthiest inhabitants, with a large number of unmarried ladies under thirty, living on unearned income from Papa's investments (family historians are well placed to investigate their sources). From their smart white-stuccoed terraces and crescents adorned with Italianate balconies, or their picturesquely rustic villas, officers' wives and clergymen's daughters could now wind their way down the artificially curvy lanes – 'The Vale', 'The Thicket' or 'The Grove' – to the seafront. Fresh migrants of the poorer sort, meanwhile, made do with brand-new cheap and nasty housing in Landport, the fourth 'town', next to Portsea, where my father's forebears, the Baptist bricklayers, settled.

In Portsea even the tiny wooden houses were preferable to shared rooms in the crowded courts that had been hurriedly erected as 'infilling' on the garden plots of other houses. Set back from the side streets and entered via a dark low tunnel, up to twelve multi-occupied houses huddled together with an outdoor pump and a dry privy between them. Map-makers, defeated by the cramped topography, often ignored such dwellings, thus adding to the idea of their 'impenetrability'. Local churchmen, as I found, might record the street but not the court in their parish registers. Cranley's Court off Butcher Street, where Anthony and Margaret Murphy lived, was noted in the census but not in the baptism records. Havant Street, the address frequently given for the Hutchinses, William, Martha and Mary Ann, hid Wodger's, Woodger's or Widger's Court, next to 'Dedicotts' Court, the latter perhaps a corruption of the Romany *diddecai* or *diddikai*, for 'gypsy' or 'Jew'. The widowed Elizabeth Nobes and her daughters, meanwhile, colonized Albion Street. The oldest, Mrs Elizabeth Lavender, lived first at number 4½, so styled because the house was shared with a bricklayer and his family, and then at number 3 for the next thirty years. The youngest, my grandmother's grandmother Lydia Nobes, first started married life with William Murphy, a shoemaker, and their baby Rosina, in King's Bench Alley, a dark and narrow strip of tenements running along the back of Albion Street, before it too became their home. Lavenders and Murphys grew up together.

For those who lived there, Portsea was full of familiar faces and a network of kith and kin, far from the impersonality which contemporary commentators deplored as one consequence of city life. Most of the Dickensian-sounding courts and alleys – Frett's, Wigg's, Grubb's – were called after their owners, frequently local tradesmen with shops close by, chancing their arm by venturing into property, or consolidating a slow climb to respectability on the backs of their tenants. John Treadgold, whose name turned out to be a portent, was typical. The son of a cabinetmaker, he opened an ironmongery on Bishop Street in 1820 (not a salubrious address, the road, then as now, only thirteen feet wide) but was soon selling everything from chisels and coat hooks to iron railings and downpipes. By 1845 he owned ten tenement-type dwellings in Treadgold's Court, four houses in Albion Street and a store in King's Bench Alley. His son William became more of a man of means, supplying the contractors for the dockyard. In 1871 his Albion Street houses, each bringing in rent of up to £6 a year, cost him only 14 shillings in rates – a mammoth profit. He added a stable and slaughterhouse, and three houses in White's Row, to his portfolio. Until they became rich enough to absent themselves, landlords were on the doorstep in more ways than one.

Much of the 'tumbling down' that Cobbett saw happening in Portsea took place all over Britain in the early decades of the nineteenth century. Budding towns were straining to accommodate an ever-increasing population and a workforce of rural migrants. New building happened piecemeal, almost overnight. The market ruled unchallenged, with no regulations or restrictions on shape or size. If investors had thought it worthwhile, Portsea's streets might have been wider, but a get-rich-quick mentality had prevailed. Paving and other amenities were in the hands of house owners or developers; often the clay dug out for foundations was unceremoniously dumped in a pile outside the houses. On Portsea Island, as elsewhere, local government had barely changed from medieval times. Abattoirs spilling offal and blood into open drains shared with dwellings; backyard agriculture that allowed hens, rabbits and pigs the run of the house and street; decomposing vegetables, rotting fish, rat infestations: these were some of the least objectionable 'nuisances'. After 1835, when a new borough council, elected by the ratepayers, replaced the old corporation, the state of Portsea's streets was still the responsibility of a board of independent 'Improvement Commissioners'. These worthies, who drew on levies from the ratepayers, were lackadaisical if not downright corrupt. Money for 'macadamizing' or repairs was spent only on the principal thoroughfares: Queen Street 'predictably had twenty-four repairs' while Albion Street and White's Row had none. In 1843 Andrew Nance, posting master, owner of several of the best inns in Portsmouth and also a local councillor, was handed the contract for 'scavenging' – collecting rubbish – and 'watering', or cleaning the streets from water-carts, over the summer. He proceeded to do nothing much for five years. No one would cough up the money to flush out the defensive moats, foul open sewers, nominally the property of the military authorities. Public wells were contaminated, while buckets from the water carriers at a halfpence for two pails were actually beyond the pockets of the poorest. 'We get water where we can,' said one resident, 'we frequently have to steal it.' The Nuisance Removal Act of 1846 made little difference. Fines of up to £2 were brandished at repeat offenders, but 'the Board's minutes', writes one local historian wearily, 'provide no evidence that any serious attempt was made to enforce penalties'.

After 1815 the dockyard economy was stagnant for nearly three decades. But while many 'hired men', including the labourers, were dismissed, the yard always retained a nucleus of highly skilled 'established' men, like shipwrights, who might be on the books for life. Compared to factory workers and others, their jobs were unusually secure. The dockyard looked after and policed its own and 'the People of the Yard', with their own culture and organizations, formed a world unto themselves. Provided they kept their noses clean, they were eligible after twenty years for a pension, still a rarity for working men. After 1859 other benefits included paid holidays, paid sick leave and free medical attention; 'first-class labourers' also received pensions. In the hungry forties, political radicalism was thin on the ground. Disputes and grievances were handled internally, usually via petition. Trade unions developed late and strikes were infrequent. The second generation of Murphy boys, William's older brothers, were among the favoured few and not likely to rock the boat. Tom was a 'caulker', a crucial and well-paid job, sealing up the gaps between the ship's planks, or seams, with oakum and tar (the sticky, smelly substance which waterproofed everything and gave 'Jack' his soubriquet); he stayed on till his pension. His brother George, rigger on land and sea, also appears, aged eighty-four, in the 1891 census as a 'shipwright pensioner'.

A naval base, with shipbuilding at its heart, was not a place for the entrepreneurial. Before 1835 the unreformed borough was in the pocket of the Admiralty, with two MPs in their gift. Jealous of their territory, the Admiralty vetoed much commercial enterprise, handing out 'a fat wad of contracts' to those they favoured. The civil port continued to come second to the needs of the armed forces, and 'far-reaching schemes' to construct a large commercial docks were frustrated. Nearby Southampton, though smaller, soon had far more ships, merchants and civilian passengers. The Portsmouth dockyard made money for its contractors but followed the policy of self-sufficiency, with its own 'plant' on site, generating little capital. Since local industry could not possibly compete with the great iron, steel and engineering districts for supply contracts, there was little opportunity for local men to become rich industrialists or even for smaller firms to flourish. Tourism got off to a poor start too. The seedy reputation of a naval and dockyard town made Portsmouth a less-favoured spot for the new sea-bathing fad in those post-war decades when Brighton, further along the south coast, turned itself into London's 'greatest sanitarium'.

During the 'Great Slump' or the 'Long Peace' (1814–64), as the navy calls it, sailor volunteers most often came from the southern counties or from navy or dockyard families, men like John Ball, an Irishman, the son of a seaman, who married the Murphys' oldest girl, Rosina. Four of their six sons joined the navy (William, Charles and Edwin, all serving until their pensions). Tom Murphy's son Walter became a seaman caulker like his father before 'retiring' to the dockyard, while five of the six boys born to Tom's brother George and his wife, Mary Ann, with twenty years between them, also enlisted, as the old full-rigged wooden ships gave way to steam. The decades after Trafalgar were nostalgic for 'Jack Tar', and the glory days of the war were celebrated in ballads and popular entertainments. By mid-century a plethora of nautically themed objects, from Staffordshire earthenware jugs and figurines, commemorative fans, mugs and tea sets to trident-and-anchor windows, had made their way into British homes. Nelson's Column was erected in London's completed Trafalgar Square in the mid-1840s, and in 1848 Queen Victoria belatedly recognized the men who had served between 1793 and 1815, awarding them the new General Service Medal. But in the nation's premier naval base the nation's heroes and their families were living in conditions far less than glorious.

In the summer of 1848, 'King Cholera' returned to Britain and killed 20,000 people nationwide. Upwards of a thousand of them were on Portsea Island. The first case of cholera on the island appeared in Fountain Street, Portsea, and soon spread – Albion Street, Hawke Street and Kent Street were among the affected. The worst dwellings, makeshift hovels entered via a foot-wide tunnel, had no drainage or sanitation at all, though Henry Carter, a local surgeon for Portsea, reported that 'some of the houses are, however, kept as clean as existing circumstances will permit' by 'the industrious'. Even the better streets were narrow and airless and often covered with 'foetid mud and water, green and rank'. Fifteen people died in the fifteen small houses of Nance's Row alone (named for Andrew Nance, the man who had not watered the streets), where in each four-roomed 'cottage', nine or ten people had only a foul, open drain at the back of their houses, their only way of disposing of waste water, which sluiced back into their kitchens. The government set up a cohort of medical officers to encourage town councils to adopt the new Public Health Act. In his report of 1850 Dr Robert Rawlinson noted that despite the great lengths gone to 'cleanse the surface' of the townships and remove 'superficial filth' in preparation for his inspection, the cholera had not been fooled. The island of Portsea 'was one huge cesspool', daily permitting 30,000 gallons of urine to penetrate the soil, making its way 'with a host of other abominations' into the well water. Permanent drainage, sewerage and a good water supply were urgently needed. Among the cholera deaths in July 1849 was Anthony Ball, Rosina's second son, named for his grandfather. At twenty-one, he was a 'cordwainer', a shoemaker, like his uncle William. In the dilapidated dwellings of Crown Street, Portsmouth town, where Sarah Heffren was living, fifteen to twenty deaths occurred, mostly elderly people and paupers. She must have been a tough old bird, surviving to die a natural death aged eighty-one.

The cholera epidemics were a testament to a poorly nourished urban population living in foul conditions, to the relative helplessness of medical science, but also to the heartless laissez-faire attitude on the part of the governing classes, whose anxieties about the poorer sort had more to do with keeping public order than alleviating distress. Across Britain the arguments and proposals concerning 'the Sanitation Idea' in the middle of the century witnessed the birth throes of the novel concept of public health clashing headlong with a political economy and an industrialized society which upheld private property as its foundation. Intervention by government in such matters smacked of Continental despotism. On Portsea Island, as elsewhere, bitter debates between the 'Sanitizers', who wanted improvements, and the 'Muckabites' went on for years, but despite appeals to conscience, or to the costs ultimately incurred by a diseased population, the 'dirty party', in favour of doing nothing, won the day. In 1854 the idea of having a Board of Health was dropped; it took almost another decade before the town council took limited charge and slowly began building some sewers. But not in the worst districts of Portsea. Piped clean water 'for all' in the 1870s was only for those who could afford it. Many Portsea residents were still using communal standpipes and polluted wells, or buying water from the carts as the twentieth century dawned (beer, of course, was safer to drink, which suited the brewers fine).

Portsea Island bore the brunt of government indifference towards servicemen and their families. When ships went down, sailors' dependants relied mainly on subscription funds or collections. Sailors mustered a few shillings by auctioning their mates' kit for money to send to the widows. Many were likely to need parish funds while the families of absent or discharged servicemen added to the strain on resources. The poor rate was steep, nearly three times that which obtained in other Hampshire parishes, but Admiralty and military buildings were as yet unrated. This rankled deeply with the ratepayers, especially those slum landlords under pressure to improve their properties. Putting in drains and sewers would not only cost them but make the property more valuable, and thereby increase the rates they paid. Within five years the spacious new Portsmouth Union Workhouse, built in 1846, and the biggest in the county, was reaching its capacity of 1,200 (Cheltenham's was 220). William Heffren, Sarah and George's son, was one of the mariners washed up there mid-century, a young man in his twenties, with nothing to tide him over. William

– though 'Bill' or 'Will' is more likely and less estranging – left to marry a seaman's widow with the fetching name of Maria Kneebone (she was also a seaman's daughter). He died of bronchitis in his mid-forties, having joined the ranks, inevitably, of general labourers.

The greatest influx of people into Portsea and Landport was not during the French wars but in the 1850s, when in theory the town's economy took a turn for the better as the navy's gradual acceptance of steam led to new workshops, foundries, and a steam basin in the dockyard. The colonial wars with Burma and India, and the Crimean War, stepped up the need for ships and brought in another wave of servicemen. But what did that mean on the ground? After the cholera, Henry Slight, a Portsmouth doctor, published a series of newspaper articles revealing the level of overcrowding in the town. In one long, low room of a Portsea tenement in Cut Throat Alley, sixty people, sailors' wives among them, too poor to pay for any other accommodation, slept in beds that were almost touching. Newcomers crowded into the districts close to the docks and harbour, including the 'common women' whom the council blamed for adding to the town's problems, pushing the rates up still higher. Among the 'painted ladies' in Prospect Row, hard by the fortifications in the garrison town, were surely the eleven women, all unmarried and apparently unemployed, who lodged next door to James Addison, a licensed victualler at number 22, close to Sarah Heffren in Crown Street (Sarah had given birth to three sons in Prospect Row). Nineteen-year-old Emma Strong was a village girl from Lovedean in Hampshire, but Ann Harding, aged twenty-two, was born in South Wales, and Caroline Carey, now twenty-three, had started life in the 'East Indies'.

Every town has its Rawlinson report, its grim accounts of filthy streets and wretched, overcrowded hovels. Why dwell on such details? In Britain most of us doing family history will find that our ancestors were poor by our standards; their lives were harder, shorter; they lived in accommodation we could hardly stomach, on streets whose stench would make us gag; their diseases were more terrible and unchecked; their morality wayward and improvised; their accidents crippling. They coped; they put up with it; they died of it. From the perspective of much of the documentation of the period, my ancestors were merely part of what one local historian of Portsmouth calls 'the perennial inescapable problem of poverty'. But much of it *was* escapable. Why go back to the past only to feel washed by an amorphous pity? Anger is more bracing.

Nor is this merely a matter of hindsight. Voices *were* raised; other views *were* put. Listen only to the mounting fury of the first Medical Officer of Health for Portsmouth Borough, taken on in 1873 *after* the Public Health Act was at last adopted, a growing crescendo fuelled by exasperation and disbelief. George Turner was a young man in his first job. Born in Portsea, he knew it well. For several years he wrote increasingly irate annual reports: in his first year, nearly twenty-five years after Rawlinson, still only a third of the 19,000 houses in the borough were connected to sewers; 'liquid portions', Turner's vivid phrase, still escaped from drains on to kitchen floors. His requests for an infectious diseases hospital fell on deaf ears, though scarlet fever had killed around 408 people in 1875–6 (starting in Bishop Street, Portsea); the new by-laws concerning common lodging houses were 'almost universally infringed' by landlords – people were still sleeping in damp, filthy basements; yards were not paved, and so on – and year after year his request for a public mortuary 'at small cost' was ignored. Turner found himself performing post-mortems in sight of the prisoners at the police station, or *in situ* with the curious crowding in. He was driven to expostulate:

> I have seen bodies which the sorrowing relations were obliged to keep in the room in which they ate and slept . . . Fancy what this implies in a small house let to more than one family in summer time!

But the council would rather not imagine. Instead they wanted Turner 'confined to narrower limits' of comment. Before he left in 1880, he tried again – 'for the sixth time, Gentlemen, I formally call your attention to . . .' – raising once more the need for a hospital for fever cases, as yet unbuilt, even though the borough had been in possession of a site for seven years; he again urged compliance with lodging-house regulations, a measure 'most unwelcome to many members of the Authority' who were themselves landlords. How relieved they must have been when he resigned.

Ebbs and Flows

No place is a backwater completely sequestered from the currents of national history, but Portsea Island was peculiarly subject to the vicissitudes of foreign policy, its population periodically swelled by servicemen, and its fortunes tied to those of the navy and the dockyard. Yet war was hardly an unmixed blessing for working people and although in boom years the dockyard might employ up to half of the island's industrial workers, most of the inhabitants had to find other work. Survival was what mattered, whatever a far-off government might decree. History writing is always a matter of perspective: how near we are, how far, when we try to imagine past lives. National events shatter the lives of one generation but not the next; family life has its own pace, its own ups and downs; women and men punctuate their lives differently; children create their own worlds. Historical chronology that seems so hard and fast – 'the march of time', as the newsreels in the wartime cinemas used to call it – cannot capture the time of childhood or old age, or those times out of time, like falling in love or mourning, when time is less a narrative than a space, porous, saturated, diaphanous. The experience of time passing, the time *inside* our minds and memories, is another dimension, different again as we ourselves age. Family history is never just a case of scuttling backwards and forwards from present to past. Its time travellers move between all these dimensions.

Taking the long view over the generations, I can see that the Heffrens kept afloat by adapting. The second George Heffren, born 1820, my grandmother's grandfather, probably began life as a sailor but became a 'corn meter', or measurer, whose task it was to weigh corn before it was discharged from shipping or for local milling. In the 1860s he moved from measuring corn to measuring coal, the ubiquitous fuel for everything from fireplaces to steamships, and he also worked, since coal was largely a seasonal business, as a house agent, finding tenants for landlords and perhaps collecting rent. George then started his own business as a coal merchant, supplementing that work with selling and delivering milk. William Murphy, my grandmother's other grandfather, on the other hand, stuck at the same trade of shoemaking for over thirty years. After agricultural work and the building trades, shoemaking and tailoring were the largest single artisan trades in the early decades of the century, and the army and navy were a ready market. A few of the swankier military and naval outfitters had done well out of the French wars, among them the grandfather of the novelist George Meredith, who owned a shop on Portsmouth High Street. He was said to have clothed Nelson for Trafalgar and the infamous Captain Bligh. Most others were much smaller fry. Mass production of shoes in other towns saw shoemaking in Portsea – like tailoring – rapidly becoming sweated labour. Middlemen passed on materials to those 'jobbing' on pieces at home or in 'dishonourable', ununionized workshops crowded with impoverished, half-starved assistants (the eponymous tailor hero of Charles Kingsley's *Alton Locke*, published in 1850, turns to radical politics after his exploitation in one such garret, dubbed by his workmates 'the Consumptive Hospital'). William Murphy rose to journeyman, though not master. In the 1870s, as befitted the widow of a small tradesman, Lydia was able to open a grocery store. After nearly half a century of labour, this shop, a pokey, backstreet affair, not a grand emporium, was a fragile advance towards security. Such small businesses were as close to a move from rags to riches as the Heffrens and Murphys were to get. Neither business survived far into the 1900s.

When my great-grandmother Flora was born in Albion Street in 1856, hers was the second generation of Murphys native to Portsea. No longer foreigners or settlers, they were locals. When her grandfather Anthony Murphy died in 1858, the last direct link to the old country was severed. There would be nobody left in the immediate family with an Irish accent. As William and Lydia's seventh child, Flora was born at a bad time in the family's affairs: six children at home and none yet earning, five more to come. Her one-year-old older brother Edward had died in 1852, of dehydration from diarrhoea, and her younger brother David was to die aged thirteen of 'haemoptysis' – spitting up blood, a sign of lung disease. Inadequately fed and clothed, surrounded by dirt and disease, children in Portsea dropped like flies. If they were not picked off by whooping cough, measles, smallpox, scarlet fever, diphtheria, typhus, tuberculosis or other maladies, children faced the hazards of spoiled and adulterated food, accidents indoors, and in the unlit streets, where they risked being killed or maimed as they played almost under the horses' hooves. It seems a miracle that she survived. Too old for the new elementary state school which began in Kent Street in 1873, Flora could at least write her name, so may have scraped up a few days' learning from the Sunday schools or a 'ragged school' – Portsmouth's first Free Ragged School, set up the year Flora was born, was in Richmond Place, Portsea. Even closer was the charity-led Beneficial School in Kent Street, but she is not on the register. 'The Benny' had been known to turn away a mother and her sons whose clothes 'were scarcely secured to their persons'. I imagine her as one of those small children, as seen now in the streets of Mumbai or the favelas of Brazil, bright and lively, faces flecked with dirt, running errands, learning to scavenge and do small jobs in the street economy; perhaps to beg or steal.

Yet childhood is lived closer to the present; self-consciousness comes with difference, anger with comparison and knowledge. Portsea's memoirists look back with affection on their childhoods in some of the worst places imaginable, recall their impromptu pleasures, playing hopscotch on filthy roads, leapfrogging bollards, jumping wooden cable drums and logs, or 'mudlarking' in the smelly mud of the harbour, picking up coins thrown by passers-by (my mother remembered my uncles doing the same in the 1930s, shrieking with delight at being hosed down in the backyard as they handed over the much-needed pennies and sixpences to my nan). The street and the court offered endless excitements, from street vendors to street music, and Flora would have found her diversions in those games whose astonishing staying power suggest the resilience of childhood confederacies. In the 1860s, Portsea 'street arabs' irritated their neighbours by knocking on their doors then scarpering, just as I did 100 years later – a game still called 'gingerbread', though no one knows why. Generations of girls before me formed a narrow arch with one hand up against a brick wall, catching others in their grip as they sang, 'The big ship sailed on the Alley, Alley Oh!', with no idea it referred to the Atlantic, and wagging our fingers in admonitory fashion when 'The Captain said, This will never, never do, never, never do'. Apparently they did this in Liverpool, Glasgow and – because of the ship canal – Manchester. Port towns held plenty of thrills for the young, not least the marches and parades with their brass bands, or the coming and going of the fleet, accompanied by glimpses of the Queen, which brought huge crowds and all the fun of the fair. Perhaps Flora saw the famous waxworks in Portsea's St George's Square of 'Androcles and the Lion' with 'moving effects', which made such an impression on other children.

Flora's world would revolve around street and home, but the rhythm of men and women's lives in Portsea was often out of kilter. The skilled dockyard men had something like an industrial day, keeping regular hours and returning for their dinners. Shoemakers like her father worked all hours indoors or at a workshop. Like other Portsea women, sailors' wives and mothers juggled their own jobs with looking after children but had to cope with the irregular absences of their menfolk, and their unexpected arrivals. Even when welcome, this could put a strain on relations when women were used to ruling the roost. Local girls who married men in the services frequently left with them, as did all Flora's older sisters, Rosina, Lydia and Eleanor. Rosina's husband, Johannes Braun, from Berlin, a cook in the Royal Navy, was probably a shipmate of Eleanor's husband, Abraham Bricknell, a steward, since both women went with them to Birkenhead near Liverpool. Lydia married David Carver, one of scores of pauper lads drafted straight into the navy as a 'boy first class'. The Carver children had ended up in the Guildford Union when their father, Absalom, was transported for sheep-stealing, and David's record gives his parents as dead. David's mother had certainly died in the workhouse, but his father returned from Van Diemen's Land after serving his fifteen years, went back to his Surrey village, married again and lived to eighty, working as a labourer in a market garden. Did he ever see David again? Unlikely. David Carver had left for service on HMS *Spiteful* in Port Royal, Jamaica, and then died or disappeared not long after his father's return, leaving his wife, Lydia, with a small child. In due course, Flora's sister Lydia remarried and went to Hull with her second husband, Charles Jeffery, a shipyard labourer. Her daughter, little Eliza, was to be brought up by her Murphy grandparents in Portsea. Unlikely, too, that Eliza ever saw her mother again or knew of her eight half-siblings in Yorkshire. Children were often the flotsam and jetsam of maritime marriages.

Does every place have an emotional topography, peaks of intense feeling and level plains of calm? If so, the wharf at the Hard, 'a sort of inland quarter-deck' and the main embarkation point in town, was the storm centre of Portsea. In March 1854, before the Baltic fleet set sail for the Crimea, when according to *The Times* 'the whole world was moving again towards Portsmouth', boatmen loaded 'swarms of sea-boats and luggers' to go out to the ships, each crammed with forty or fifty women and children bearing packages and messages for their menfolk. Sightseers pushed their way through huddles of crying mothers and sisters, wives and sweethearts. They returned to weep again as the vessels that took out the hale and hearty came back with the sick and wounded; eighty ships landed nearly 10,000 casualties of war during 1855. Peacetime brought other catastrophes for Portsea's women: shipwrecks like that of the sailing ship *Eurydice* in 1878, which went down with 320 crew, many of them Portsmuthians. New ship designs brought new disasters: Flora's cousin Walter Murphy served on the iron-clad *Thunderer*, whose boiler blew up as it left Portsmouth harbour in 1876, killing forty-five men. Ten times as many were drowned when HMS *Captain* capsized on its maiden voyage, thanks to its being badly built and top heavy, its guns experimentally sited in a turret overhead. A 'sad little card' was sold, price twopence, to help the dependants of the crew, which included thirty widows in one Portsea street alone. The ramming of the battleship *Victoria* by *Camperdown* near Tripoli, during manoeuvres in 1893, was a national sensation. Because experienced officers had given and followed patently dangerous commands, 358 men died. In three weeks £50,000 (about £5 million in today's money) was raised for the families, but in Portsea the campaigning local priest, Father Dolling, set up his own relief fund, not trusting the authorities to handle 'the Patriotic Fund' fairly. In St Agatha's, Dolling told his congregation that the men were especially heroic:

> To die in the midst of battle, that were easy, but to die by the mistake of one man, to die by a little fault in the machinery, to go down in a calm sea under the blue sky, to stand in order in your place without

> murmuring, as orderly as if you were in the barrack square, that was splendid, that was sublime.

He knew, however, that on most other occasions there was 'literally no provision' for sailors' families. (Death and poverty continued to unite Portsea's women: a single street saw forty women made widows after the battle of Jutland in 1916.)

For much of the nineteenth century the Royal Navy's role as the supreme maritime power was as 'the shield of empire', protecting British interests, delivering troops and transports safely, keeping the seas open for commerce. Having been the leading slave traders of their day, British anti-slavery patrols after abolition in 1807 turned to suppressing the continuing slave trade 'with astonishing speed and remarkable zeal', a humanitarian crusade of many decades which shored up the British sense of national and moral superiority, and laid the ground for partition and colonial rule. A posting to the West Africa station was bad news. With the navy's highest mortality rate, it had a bleak reputation as 'the White Man's Graveyard'. Seamen found themselves scattered ever further across the globe, keeping 'the watchful eye and strong arm of England', in Lord Palmerston's famous words of 1850, as they policed 'Pax Britannica', acting as bullyboys if necessary by means of 'gunboat diplomacy', and bombardment, of the kind which enforced the opium trade to China. An impressive fleet was concentrated in the Mediterranean – the 'British Lake' – with bases stretching from Gibraltar to Egypt, where, as one historian puts it, 'war-driven commercialism' was creating a new 'emporium for British industrial output'. In the 1860s Flora's oldest cousin, William Ball – her aunt Rosina's son – was 'Captain of the Forecastle' on HMS *Renown*, sailing to Portugal and Ireland and then calling at Malta and Sardinia, until stationed near Beirut. His younger brother Edwin, who joined at eighteen, another 'boy first class', was meanwhile in the North Atlantic on *Diadem*, a thirty-two-gun wooden screw frigate, one of the gunboats ordered to American waters during the Trent crisis when Britain almost came to blows with the Union during the American Civil War. William Lavender, Flora's cousin on her mother's side, who grew up in Albion Street, was an ordinary seaman on HMS *Newport*, commissioned to survey the Gulf of Suez, when in

1869 it became the first ship to sail through the Suez Canal. The night before the opening ceremony, without lights and in darkness, its captain sneaked the ship ahead of the French imperial yacht and a mass of waiting vessels, an act of bravado and a show of British seamanship which earned him a reprimand and an unofficial vote of thanks from the Admiralty. The Suez Canal made the Mediterranean the centre of the British Empire. In the 1870s William was stationed at Ras Gharib, on the African side of the Red Sea where the rich oilfields were later to supply the navy as it moved from coal to oil.

The seaman's life in the Royal Navy was improving, if slowly. Uniform was at last issued in 1857, though surgeons had been asking for it on the grounds of hygiene for at least 100 years; and the old hire-and-discharge system disappeared with the establishment of the navy as a long-service career. From 1873 continuous service for ten years became compulsory. Flogging was suspended after 1879, though not actually abolished until after the Second World War, and boys under eighteen could still receive up to twenty-four 'cuts on the bare breech' with a birch. Rations were larger and better, especially with tinned foods. Leave increased, becoming a right rather than a privilege after 1890. Barracks on shore replaced the rotting hulks, while Agnes Weston's Sailors' Rests, or temperance hostels, offered an alternative to the pub and a decent meal, though some felt it came with too large a serving of humble pie. More and better training was provided, and men were paid monthly rather than at the end of a voyage. Those who put in twenty years were now eligible for a small pension, so might even come ashore at thirty-eight. The merchant and the royal navies became more distinct as men enlisted long term and no longer belonged to the old 'pool', fluctuating between them. After the Mercantile Marine Act of 1850, examinations were compulsory for new masters or mates on commercial shipping. Among those who gained his Certificates of Competency was another of Flora's cousins, William Murphy, one of George and Mary Ann's six sons, five of whom went to sea. Like many sailors he married late, a local woman from Devonport, Plymouth's equivalent of Portsea, and as a master mariner worked with the Royal Naval Ordnance Depot, shipping ammunition out to troops in the build-up of armaments towards the end of the century.

Not one Heffren or Murphy joined the army and not one of Flora's generation of girls married a soldier. Although soldiers and marines flooded into Portsea to embark on troopships, and thousands were stationed there, Portsmouth with its garrison church remained the army's stamping ground while Portsea belonged to the navy and the docks. Men returned from far-flung places with news, stories and souvenirs; fleet reviews and battleship launches reached a frenzy of patriotic fervour as ships grew ever more mighty in the race to retain naval supremacy, their names brazenly asserting brute force – *Colossus*, *Caesar*, *Powerful*, *Terrible*, *Formidable* – though, incongruously, each was still a 'she'. Docks of gargantuan size gave birth to monsters whose speed of building was matched only by 'the rapidity of obsolescence' that left even the giant *Dreadnought*, laid down and launched at Portsmouth in 1906, soon surpassed. But whatever the level of their patriotic feeling, the majority of men who served the Empire and who died for it, whether from wounds or from tropical diseases, or from the tuberculosis that developed in the damp conditions of iron-clad ships, disappeared into an anonymous watery grave, without having had a say in the running of their country. The franchise was property-based, requiring a householder or lodger to pay rent of £10 a year or more. Most of the working people of Portsea and Landport were disqualified. In the 1870s, 38 Albion Street, home to Flora's family, was at the top end of the slum houses, its rent assessed at a maximum of £9 a year, but lodgings in White's Row fetched in a third as much. Even after the reforms of 1884, 40 per cent of British adult males and, of course, all women were without the vote.

As the sailor's latest incarnation, the 'Blue Jacket', became 'the idol of late Victorian England, the hero of the cigarette packet, the music hall, and the popular song'. If he was now a species of public servant, he was never quite a fully paid-up member of the uniformed working class (and he had no trade union). Nor was Portsea Island with its floating population ever quite amenable to the discipline imposed elsewhere on industrial workers. Sailors and soldiers on leave were always a wild card, a rogue element, ebbing and flowing, turning the world upside down in their wake, in a brief respite from the rigid hierarchy of the Victorian Royal Navy. However bright and breezy my naval ancestors may have been, they were usually at the bottom of the ship's ladder. There was little chance of promotion in a navy that was 'more stodgily class-bound' even than in Nelson's day, its officers acting like 'members of some semi-aristocratic yacht club, electing and re-electing each other over and over again'. Among the lowest of the low was George Pink Murphy, the oldest of George and Mary Ann's six sons, working as a sickbay steward. One committee on nursing staff in 1898 deemed his ilk men who had been 'failures elsewhere'. They were paid a lower rate, a mere 1s 4d a day, 3d less even than an able seaman, which was hardly likely to raise esteem. Nonetheless, George Pink's son, George Richard Murphy, followed suit, the fourth generation to go to sea; he ended his days as a hospital porter at Haslar, the naval hospital. Seafaring was still a young man's life – Flora's cousin William Lavender returned to tailoring after his stint – but many sailors could never become landlubbers. Flora's uncle George senior was a boatman in his seventies (while her aunt Mary Ann took in washing), as was another of their sons, Edward, working as a licensed waterman. Edward had joined the Royal Navy in the 1860s as a cabin boy. His mother told the inquest on his death that she thought it was 'our Ted playing a joke' when she found him unconscious outside their house. He had mysteriously died from 'syncope', or fainting, passing out because he had tied his comforter too tight on a cold Boxing Day.

In 1875 the fortifications, walls and moats around Portsea and Portsmouth had come down. By the end of the century, the townships had merged into the great conglomerate borough generally known as Portsmouth, or, as the locals and generations of service people and football fans were to nickname it, 'Pompey'. Rows and rows of criss-crossing terraces spread all over the island, including some better housing for the better-paid artisans, office workers, petty officers and NCOs, though much of it indistinguishable to the outsider, leaving the older slums untouched. Southsea drew in its skirts, keeping a social distance from the rest of the population (an attitude heralded in the naming of the railway station with its imaginary boundary between 'Portsmouth and Southsea'). Visitors who strolled along the prom would tour the ships in the harbour but steer clear of

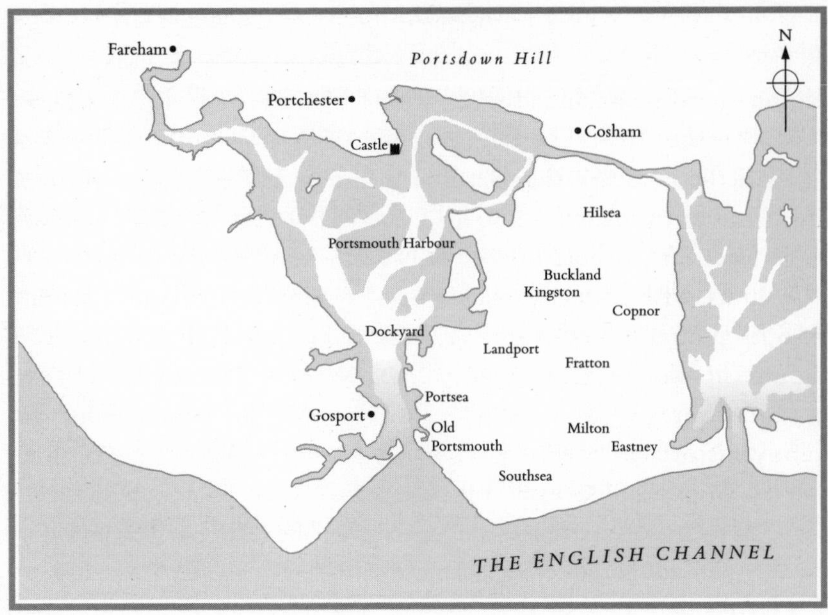

Map of Portsea Island with local districts

Portsea's 'dirty old backstreets'. Falling hook, line and sinker for the romance, they forgot that sailors ever went home or had families locally. In 1884 the young Beatrix Potter thought the seamen 'swarming' up and down the ropes and hanging on 'like monkeys' all very jolly: 'What funny people they are, like children, tumbling over one another singing.' 'I would think,' she added in her innocence, 'sailors never have sorrows.' But on Southsea pleasure beach, on the esplanade between the two amusement piers, the town put up granite memorials to the seamen who died overseas. 'A strange fancy,' one holidaymaker thought, 'to mix up boats and bathing machines, restaurants and lollypops with seaside tombstones.' Peiho, Lucknow, Jeddah, Sierra Leone, the names engraved on those obelisks and columns, some all but weathered away, fascinated me when I was a child. I could not fathom their meaning nor gauge the dark undertow they brought home from the saltwater empires of the past.

Beached Up

No one need be excluded from family history – the man sleeping rough on the street, the felon on his way to the hulks, the madwoman, the swindler, the so-called failure – but if some descendants are tempted to disown or to whitewash the more disreputable of their forebears, others find equally alluring the dark glamour of 'the slums' with its ready-made cast of victims and villains. I found no outstanding successes among the Murphys and Heffrens. Equally significant was the absence of criminal records. No one likes to be thought average – the ordinary are always other people – but as family historians reveal the varieties of work, the chequered life stories, hopes and dreams of individuals across the generations, they can begin to disaggregate 'the poor'. 'Poverty', with its bleak power to efface and homogenize, can be seen not as an identity but as a condition.

When my mother first found her grandmother Flora in Albion Street in 1881, she was relieved and impressed by what she saw as the Murphys' respectability: 'a good variety of employment', she wrote in the margins of her notes, 'obviously a resourceful family of trades people'. She was right. They were a hard-working family and with only five of Lydia's eleven children left at home, all adults, they were at the peak of their family prosperity, running a grocer's at 25 Kent Street, where they had moved, just round the corner from Albion Street. Lydia had her son William as an assistant; Alfred and George were both shopmen, working in a china and glass warehouse; Flora was a sewing machinist at home; while the youngest son, Tom, at eighteen was styled slightly grandly as 'paraffin oil merchant', selling the cheap and dangerous fuel used for lamps and heaters. (Gas came to Portsea Island in 1821, but most of Portsea went on using lamps and candles until after the First World War.) A shop was a step towards respectability for the Murphys, as it was – and is – for generations of immigrants willing to work all hours. A few doors down at 33 Kent Street, Luigi Deluchi, originally from Genoa, and his wife, Jane, ran a fried-fish shop and an ice-cream parlour. They lodged with her parents, as did eleven other Italians and two children, Fortunato and Raffaella – the largest group of Italians on the island. Surprisingly, all the adults were listed in the census as 'organ grinders'.

But the Murphy family's hold on security was tenuous. Kent Street was a busy thoroughfare where every other house doubled as a shop. Grocers needed little capital and were two a penny: next door at number 26, Mrs Mary Barr kept a fruit and veg shop, and on the other side of the Murphys, Edward Triggs at 24 ran a general grocer's (number 27 is a butcher's). In retail, as in every kind of work, there was a sliding scale. Employing family labour was one way of saving money but was also a sign that a shop was at the lower end of the spectrum. Shops like the Murphys', run from home, were more like stalls than plate-glass affairs, where owners put their wares out daily on display and their clientele were their neighbours. A shop was an advance on hawking goods but anyone could be a shop-hand. It needed no industrial qualifications, nor was it a training for much else. Within ten years William Murphy was a messenger, and then a warder at Holloway, the women's prison in London (the prison service was another route to respectability). George and Tom were lodging on the Strand, Tom still a shopman, while his brother was a cook.

Now getting on for thirty, Flora, the only daughter at home, was an 'outworker', making shirts as her grandmother Elizabeth had done, but by machine. In Elizabeth's day, Thomas Hood's immensely popular ballad 'The Song of the Shirt' had drawn the public's attention to the miserable conditions in which women plied needle and thread – 'It is not linen you're wearing out/ But human creatures' lives!' – but shirt-making by modern machine was no better. Machines were usually paid for by instalments set against wages; as they required less skill, they were further casualizing the work. Women were paid variable rates depending on age, availability and productivity. On Portsea Island there was no huge market for finished articles as in London's West End, but with so few other outlets – no textile industry or potteries – there was no end of cheap female labour. A few local men cashed in, especially in the corset industry, and canny businessmen avoided the overheads of premises by 'putting out' materials to women who worked at home. Nor was it likely that outworkers would ever organize themselves into trade unions as factory girls were beginning to do. Women could keep an eye on little children or babies when they worked at home and they need not disoblige their husbands or neglect household chores (it just meant doing two jobs). Although the working conditions were often as injurious to their health as industrial labour, no one suggested sewing was 'unwomanly'. Shut up at home, their machines going full pelt day and night, women like Flora slaved away in their 'sweatshop with a staff of one' to help put bread on the table.

According to Father Dolling, who knew the district intimately in the 1890s, 'the wages of the majority of people in regular employment were so small they lived in continuous poverty; the larger part had no settled wages at all, many of them being hawkers, greengrocers with a capital of five shillings, old pensioners past work with a shilling to eighteen pence a day, sailors' wives with three or four children living upon £2 a month, and soldiers' wives married "off the strength" with no pay at all'. The poorest bought minuscule amounts of food as they needed it – tea and sugar by the ounce or the halfpennyworth – and relied on the local stall and shopkeepers for reduced goods like 'pecked' fruit and broken biscuits or to give credit if need be. Those women seeking outwork needed their local contacts with the dealers. Labourers needed to be known as good workers if they were to be picked by the foreman when they arrived at the crack of dawn to stamp their feet at the dockyard gates or outside the builders' yards. News of jobs would be passed on in the pub or from mates, so those who stayed local always had the edge. Many jobs were seasonal and, like coal-heaving and carting, involved heavy manual labour, which left older men out in the cold; ex-sailors were preferred for some dockyard tasks. Accidents at work or a week's illness could be devastating. Those who had the wherewithal might live off the proceeds from pawning furniture or clothing. Sunday clothes were regularly 'popped' on a Monday morning and out of hock on Saturday night, and women were adept at haggling with the pawnbroker. But the pawnbroker needed to know you to trust you, as did the landlord if rent fell into arrears. Neighbourhood and family were the only safety net and people feared falling on hard times elsewhere. The right to relief outside one's own parish depended on continuous residence, usually up to five years, and on no claim being made, otherwise newcomers faced the prospect of being shunted back to where they came from. Rents too high for working-class wages, the need to be on the spot for irregular employment, and not only attachments to friends and family, conspired to keep Portsea residents trapped in poverty, or, as the topography of class put it, 'submerged'.

Young men, like George and Tom Murphy, might leave town but those with families, the elderly or the more vulnerable could hardly take the risk. They *did* move but only within their own neck of the woods. Those streets and courts that all looked the same to the outsider had their own individual character and reputation, their 'degrees of slumminess'. Landlords judged their rents nicely: houses in varying stages of dilapidation; tenements and lodging houses where a floor of the house, a room, half-room, even a quarter-room, might be let from week to week or by the night if need be. People moved as incomes changed, houses became uninhabitable or families expanded and shrank. The nastiest, cheapest lodgings were kept for those starting out or with the fewest encumbrances. Anthony and Margaret Murphy's rooms at Cranley's Court, off Butcher Street, were home to the second and third generation. When George and Mary Ann Murphy rented a house in Union Street, once they had two adult children bringing in a wage, their son Arthur took over Cranley's Court. Similarly, the second generation of Heffrens, another George and Mary Ann, moved into 4 Widger's Court, off Havant Street. My great-grandfather Edwin Heffren was born there in 1849; his older brother George William, a two-year-old, died there the following March, of smallpox. When they left the court, the Heffrens took 17 Hawke Street throughout the 1860s and 1870s, a house later lived in by Arthur Murphy and his clan. Perhaps the two sides of my mother's family knew each other, not unlikely given the tight networks of families in Portsea. Arthur watched his oldest seaman son, Arthur Aylwin, die of tuberculosis in Hawke Street in 1911, while Butcher Street was a Murphy home until 1947 when Tom Murphy, one of Flora's younger brothers, died there. When a home came courtesy of friends or family connections, it had to be a movable feast. Flora Murphy/Miller lived in four different houses in Albion Street.

Even the skilled workers in the naval dockyard could no longer take their jobs for granted. Each technological advance brought its own wave of redundancies. The steamships and iron-clads increased the numbers of engineering workers and metalworkers but sailmakers, sawyers and rope-makers were all 'decimated by these developments'. When the sawyers went on strike in 1859, the Admiralty discharged them out of hand. There were always retrenchments in peacetime, but during the vast excavations and building of the 'Great Extension' of the dockyard from the late 1860s, costs were cut by employing 800 or so convicts as labourers, depriving local men of wages. In 1868 the town was shocked when 1,500 men were dismissed; a year later the Admiralty kindly supplied the troopships to encourage them to go to Canada. History repeated itself when in 1887 1,000 men were dumped, mostly shipwrights, prized workers who might have thought themselves untouchable. Eight hundred and fifty people were given free passage to Buenos Aires under the Argentine Republic scheme but were soon disillusioned on arrival. They found families living mostly in tents, sick from contaminated water and lacking medicine (the Irish colony experiment at La Viticola left more than 100 dead, most of them children buried in unknown graves).

The navy was always an escape route of sorts for eager, unlettered young men, but for those who stayed there was little work beyond supplying the inhabitants with whatever goods they needed. Shipbuilding and the clothing industry were the big employers. Brewing made the brewers rich – and financed their political ambitions – but created few jobs. Fred Murphy, the only one of George and Mary Ann Murphy's six boys who did not join the navy, got out via the police (he needed to be over five foot eight, so in working-class terms he was a giant among men; my nan too was 'big-boned'). Initially Fred was billeted with six other young constables in Surrey, on the edge of London. They were all migrants from different English counties, the sons of agricultural labourers and carpenters, except for Thomas Irwin from Ireland and Fred himself. In the 1880s Fred wound up in the East End, in 'H' Division of the Metropolitan Police, at Leman Street, Whitechapel, during the Ripper murders, and then in Shoreditch, the roughest spot on the map, though a Portsea man ought to be tough enough to cope with 'darkest London'. A policeman was no better paid than a seaman, but his wages increased with experience and there was a better chance of promotion; the injured received gratuities and the Metropolitan Police pension, however small, was higher than that of other police forces or the railway workers. But men needed to knuckle under to severe discipline, as well as suffering isolation or downright hostility from their peers. They might be pounding a beat of up to twenty miles, mostly at night without break-times, and in all weathers. Exhaustion, alcoholism, injury and suicide took their toll on the force. Fred got his pension but he did not live long to enjoy it. He died at home, aged forty-six, from 'fifteen hours' epilepsy'. He might just as well have been a sailor, like his older brother, George Pink Murphy, a naval pensioner, who had died six years earlier, also in his mid-forties, also of epilepsy after 'three days' fits'. Their mother, Mary Ann, who had found their brother Ted choked by his scarf, signed their death certificates too.

And what a backward place my home town was! Compared to other ports where commercial docks and large-scale industry produced those self-made men who offset their often ill-gotten gains with generous donations for the public good, the town was a cul-de-sac for the inquiring mind. The Hampshire Library (1805), the most notable of the subscription libraries, with 12,000 volumes, was way beyond the pockets of most people, with its membership costing around a guinea a year. When it ran into debt, 'municipal indifference' saw the whole collection sold off cheap to Wolverhampton in 1873. The Portsmouth and Portsea Literary and Philosophical Society, begun in 1818, only found a building in 1831 and, though it built up an impressive book stock and museum, was sold to the Freemasons in 1860. Its library and collection were offered to the town on condition that they adopt the Public Libraries Act, but the council 'declined to bear the burden'. A Mechanics Institute, catering especially for the working man, was founded in 1825, with its own 'Athenaeum', a library, reading room and lecture series, in Bishop's

Street, Portsea, but this closed around 1870, not helped by the attitude of the skilled artisans in the dockyard, who had their own reading rooms and newpapers on site. At public meetings they voted in majorities against free libraries for the working classes, apparently not keen on adult education for the masses. The 1880s, we are assured, saw 'the enormous growth of civic pride'. Certainly the corporation spent the vast sum of nearly £150,000 on a new town hall in Landport, but no one stepped forward to found a university, a museum or an art gallery as they did in Newcastle or Liverpool. A public reading room opened in 1883, but the first branch libraries a decade or so later were in rooms above police stations, hardly inviting to the wider populace. 'Portsmouth,' wrote William Tarring, a local man born in 1840 looking back from the vantage point of his eighties, 'was never celebrated for its literary excellence.' In 1925 an inquiry found Portsmouth had one of the worst library provisions in the country compared to towns of similar size. It became 'notorious for its meagre service'. Between the wars the council spent 'a derisory amount' on museums and even now barely has an art gallery worth the name.

Naturally, women were not expected to 'get on'. The most respectable gave up work and attended to their menfolk, like the wives of the Baptist Lights. But elementary education opened a door for intelligent poor girls and a handful squeezed through it. Eliza Jane and Emily Kate Murphy, George and Mary Ann's daughters (and sisters of all those seafaring brothers), were unique among Flora's cousins. They became elementary-school teachers, which also meant staying single throughout their twenties. Eliza had a few years working in Devon, but as the only unmarried daughter, she came home in her forties to live with her ageing parents. (Emily) Kate, fifteen years her junior, found a school in Folkestone in Kent. She married George Chapman, a solicitor's clerk – a late marriage, which meant only three children, and a house with a servant. While Kate was leading her respectable Pooterish life in a seaside villa, her husband now a tax collector for the Inland Revenue, Eliza had drawn the short straw. Eliza's homecoming was followed by a series of losses: her brother Ted, the waterman, and Fred, the policeman, then both her parents died and she was left to shift for herself. She did not manage. In 1911 she was an inmate of

Portsmouth Lunatic Asylum, 'lunatic' at fifty, according to the census record. Eventually she died there aged eighty-five, with 'spinster school mistress' the epitaph on her death certificate.

Family history has its own mythologies, not least about the family itself. Even though family stories reveal time and again that the membrane of family can stretch only so far before it tears, the idea of the family as sufficient unto itself remains a powerful and appealing fantasy. Flora's mother, Lydia, did well from her shop, leaving a legacy of £90 when she died in 1887. She left the money, as was conventional, to her oldest son, William. Much good it did him: he seems to have squandered it, abandoning his London family and ending his days a painter in the dockyard. Alfred took over selling paraffin but he died in 1899. Flora had meanwhile been working as a barmaid, and in 1883 had had a child, Rosina, whom she sent to live with her childless sister, Rosina Braun, who was living near the docks in Southwark, London (when Aunt Rosina died, little 'Rose' lived with her aunt Eleanor). Three years later she found some security, marrying John Henry Miller, a dockyard carpenter and joiner, the son of a seaman (with a typically fluid history). But when John died in 1895 of tuberculosis, aged thirty-eight, he left Flora with four children and no pension. She would not be able to find the rent for their house in Albion Street of nearly twelve shillings a month (£7 a year). There was no child support. Her parents were dead, as were his; her sisters far away; her brothers gone or with children of their own. So despite the family's brief advance – but who is 'the family'? – Flora and her four young children went to the workhouse a few months after her husband's death. They stayed a year.

Flora's only realistic option was to find another man. Edwin Heffren, the man she set up with, was also in the workhouse in the autumn of 1895, and while they were unlikely to have met there, both knew what it was to hit rock bottom. At first glance I thought my great-grandfather sounded a dodgy character, a fly-by-night with a whole raft of jobs. Working first as a clerk for a telephone company, he is missing from two censuses, most probably on merchant ships, then resurfaces further down the social scale as a railway porter and a dockyard labourer. Perhaps he was a bad lot. When his father, the coal merchant and dairyman George Heffren, died and left £205, no mean sum, Edwin's brother Arthur took over the business. Edwin's mother must not have thought her other sons much of an investment either. On her death she bequeathed the remaining sum of £128 to her daughter, Mary Ann, who was married to Thomas Augustus Holmes, a pawnshop manager in Queen Street. Edwin went into the workhouse not long after she died, William was at sea, and Alfred was to wear out the pavements, having sunk to the desperate ranks of the 'sandwichman', wearing placards to advertise someone else's goods. They were often men who had fallen from the more genteel positions of shopman, servant or clerk, and were deemed the 'bearers of the most pathetic insignia of poverty and failure'.

Moral judgement rushes in when evidence is scarce. Edwin's flurry of jobs need not mean that he was a wastrel. In London in the 1850s Henry Mayhew called the dockyard labourers 'this most wretched class . . . mere brute force with brute appetites', but he immediately contradicted himself by insisting that 'the human locomotive' could be fashioned from 'anyone who wants a loaf and is willing to work for it'. He found 'decayed and bankrupt master-butchers, master-bakers, publicans, grocers, old soldiers, old sailors . . . clerks' reduced to labouring in a market flooded with 'casual' labour. Far from being 'shiftless', a skiver or shirker, Edwin might have pulled out all the stops, taking any job he could. He and Flora moved to another Portsea tenement where my grandmother Lilian and her brother, Ted, were born. On one occasion, Edwin admitted himself to the Portsea Union for four nights, a common strategy when relief would only be given to a family if the man entered the workhouse. It was also a way of saving money and food so that mother and children could survive and stay together.

These then were the poorer sort whom generations of social investigators, politicians, moral improvers and slum journalists sought to divvy up and set against each other, singling out a 'vitiated' or pathological poor who were a class or even a race apart: the undeserving as opposed to the deserving, the 'dangerous' classes, the 'lumpenproletariat', or, to use another popular term, the 'residuum', a Victorian euphemism for excrement or human waste. But family history shows such divisions were far from cut and dried. The paupers and the hard-working families, the 'rough' and the 'respectable', were often the same families, indeed, the same people: the clerk turned dockyard labourer; the elementary-school teacher become a pauper lunatic, sister to the taxman's wife. Take another of Flora's cousins, another Fred, son of her uncle Tom, who grows to lower-middle-class prosperity in the 1880s as a master baker, employing two assistants with premises in the flourishing Lake Road. He and his wife, Clarissa, can afford a nursemaid for their eight children, and Milly Ross, a local girl, 'does' for them. But the wheel of fortune turns. In her mid-forties Clarissa dies from septicaemia and pneumonia two months after their twelfth, Edith Kate, is born. How can Fred earn and bring up the children? They divide their forces. Fred's oldest girls, Clara and Alice, in their twenties, take over the business, turn it into a general grocer's and look after the eight still at home. Meanwhile, he starts up again on his own as a grocer in Portsea. When Clara marries, the others strike out for London, where the oldest son has made his way into the Inland Revenue as a 'second division clerk'. Alice keeps house for him and six siblings in a Camberwell ménage, one of those suburban houses full of the 'odd women' who so fascinated the novelist George Gissing (Madeleine is a typist and shorthand writer, Blanche works in a drapery, Jessie teaches), a household at least as adventurous as their more famous Edwardian contemporaries, the Stephen siblings in Bloomsbury. In Portsmouth their father has gone on working but has moved into digs, lodging in one room. He keeps his pride and his children their independence, but Fred Murphy must spend his last years in the workhouse, where he dies from a fall in 1917.

Or take Flora's cousin, on her mother's side, Harriett Lavender, an Albion Street girl. She starts off a tailoress, following her father's line of work, and marries a blacksmith, both honourable trades. As Mrs Jim Langston she goes back to his dockside home in Rotherhithe; there are seven children and Jim builds barges, but during the depression of the 1880s, as shipbuilding declines on the Thames and affects all the river trade, he joins the 'casuals' – the word wrongly implying some kind of choice – among the dock labourers. Down they go, down, down, to the industrial marshlands of Canning Town, Jim now the inevitable 'general labourer', and as the new century dawns he finds work in his sixties as an elderly servant in a coffee house at Silvertown, near the river as always. Harriett survives by charring until she lands in the West Ham Union Workhouse, widowed, pauperized, like those other old women whose list of occupations conjures the dazzlingly ingenious ways in which they had worn themselves out for a pittance: Rose Taylor, seventy-eight, of Bermondsey, 'artificial flower-maker', or Jane Jelly, aged ninety-one, 'formerly a shirt-ironer' who came from Norfolk all those years ago, and the scores of domestic servants. But even Harriett, with her hard-working man and long marriage, was better off than her sister, Lydia. Lydia married Michael Worthington, a shipmate of their brother, William, and was left widowed in her twenties with two small sons. Her second husband, a merchant seaman, disappears and Lydia becomes another inmate of the Portsmouth Lunatic Asylum – 'formerly charwoman' – two husbands gone, but also, the census notes, two children dead. One of her surviving sons is a coal porter with seven daughters to feed; another, widowed, lives in one room in Bishop Street, Portsea, caring for his own little boy. Lydia died in the asylum of tuberculosis in 1914.

And what had happened to 'Phyllis White', 'formerly an actress', married, three children, two dead, place of birth 'N.K.' (not known), to bring her to the Portsmouth asylum in her fifties? Or in Emily Barnes's life – born in Bermuda, her husband a shipwright, now nearly seventy, no occupation, four children still living? Emily came from Ireland Island, the island at the north-west of Bermuda, where the Admiralty used local labour – free and enslaved – to build a crucial naval base until they ran out of men and had to ship out Irish and British convicts in the 1820s to work on the dockyard. Another history of Britain's navy and of the casualties of its imperial ambitions awaits its historians, down among the women in the madhouses.

I am filled with sadness when I trace the contours of these lives, because they ended in degrading circumstances in public institutions. Always that feeling, did it all come to this? All the efforts and struggles and days and nights, the worries about money, the children, the ageing parents, finding work, keeping on – why did it all end this way? But we cannot know the quality of the life, nor ultimately judge its meaning. The ending is not the most important part of a life.

In my ancestors' Portsea, those best off were the penny-capitalists, the grocers and bakers, the shopkeeper gently milking her neighbours or the pawnbroker, part 'housewives saviour', part loan-shark, but there was not much ballast if the tide turned. Lives could easily founder. Edwin Heffren died a casual's death in North Shields, near Newcastle upon Tyne, 350 miles away in the north-east of Britain. Employed by a contractor to work as an 'outside waiter' on HMS *Lancaster*, he slipped on a worn landing step at the New Quay, turning a complete somersault to hit his head, surviving for eighteen hours with a fractured skull. At the inquest, one of the blue jackets who rescued him was sure there was no 'smell of any drink about him' and Mr Herbert Black, his employer, testified that he 'was a very steady man'. So not a rascal after all. He was buried locally in a pauper's grave. Flora would not have made the funeral. Family legend raised his standing after death – and who can blame them? – calling him a 'stevedore', one of the hereditary elite among dockyard workers, the highly skilled master of the loading gang. But perhaps he himself had told Flora that. Better than admitting to waiting at tables.

My great-grandmother Flora now had only her oldest son, John Miller, to lean on. He too was a dockyard labourer. When she died four years after Edwin, John and his sister, also Flora, both in their early twenties, were left with their two younger sisters and the Heffren children. Their grandparents were all dead, their mother's sisters still far away, and if Edwin's sister, their aunt Mary Ann Holmes, tucked up in her pawnshop, knew that they faced destitution, she had six of her own to worry about. The year 1908 was a bad one. Carrie and Maud Miller, at nearly sixteen and fourteen, were just old enough to find some work, but in the next eighteen months, at different times, first Lily, my grandmother, aged ten, then seven-year-old Ted, and finally the oldest, Flora, spent time in the workhouse. Admitting children briefly – 'respite relief' – was another emergency measure for families. I do not know how often they went to and fro – the records are patchy – but my grandmother and her brother were back in what was now 'the Parish of Portsmouth Children's Home' when the census was taken in 1911. This was the history, a family history of being paupers, that my grandmother never told.

*

When she died in 1907, aged fifty-two, of a weak heart, my great-grandmother Flora had given birth to seven children, six after the age of thirty. She had given up her first child, both her husbands were dead and her children were left destitute. A misery tale, if ever there was one, but I have learnt that what seems like fate is often only what survives as documents, the story given us from above. Here are some salient facts to play with. For most of her life Flora was surrounded by family in Albion Street; at home, she helped her mother and managed to get respectable work, sewing shirts. Her first child was being looked after, the only child in her sister's home, and Flora found a husband, a proper skilled man working in the dockyard. There were ten years with John and they had their own house, not a one- or two-room lodging, or a bed rented by the week. Some of her neighbours, to be sure, were not all they should be (the girls at number 8 with their seaman 'visitors' prompted the census enumerator to write 'questionable' in the column under 'profession or occupation'), but she was in no position to cast the first stone. There were plenty in worse straits: sailor's wives, like Alice McCarthy at number 27, fifty-six soon, with no man at home; or Ellen Collins a few doors down, a washerwoman in her forties. Did Flora count her blessings?

Spool back and pause the reel. Let us leave her for a while in 1890. Let's not treat death as destiny. Let us imagine a different story: a measure of happiness, a steady husband, two healthy children, little John and Flora, a house to herself. If a man in a frock coat had come to the door, she may have felt insulted, like the woman who ticked off the well-meaning journalist, poised with his notebook and his assumptions: 'Call me poor?' she said. 'I have got a half a loaf of bread in the house, and a little milk.' She knew how well off she was.

*

If anywhere can claim to be my ancestral home it is the workhouse. Somebody in every generation fetched up there: on my mother's maternal side, my grandmother and her brother, their mother, Flora, with the Miller children and their father, Edwin; Edwin Heffren's uncle, William, the mariner who married Maria Kneebone, and in that first generation who came to Portsmouth in the 1800s, Edwin's grandfather, William Hutchins, the waterman from Dorset, who spent his old age there until he died aged eighty-one in 1871. On the paternal side, my mother's other grandmother, Sarah Hill, was born there; Sarah's mother died there. And those are only the relatives I found. The experience of the workhouse was etched into family history and memory as well as threaded deep into the social fabric of Victorian Britain. Whatever relief it offered, however much it could be used temporarily to provide a bed for the night, or a square meal, the 'house cast a shadow, looming large over the lives not only of inmates (the word that says it all) but of millions who never entered its portals. In the 1890s the workhouses were still known as 'Bastilles'.

In the 1860s, in William Hutchins's time, the sick wards were crowded with patients lying on the floor, and the 'matron' of the hospital and her assistant were both eighty-two years old (both widows and former paupers). By the end of the century those over sixty made up nearly half of all the persons relieved by the parish and half of these were in the workhouse. Dying in the workhouse was far from a remote possibility for the elderly and it was not only the ignominy of a parish burial and pauper grave that they dreaded. The Anatomy Act of 1832 allowed for the unclaimed body of a pauper to be sent to a medical school or hospital for dissection, so that, in the words of the historian Ruth Richardson, 'what had for years been a feared and hated punishment for murder became one for poverty'. William Hutchins might well have fallen prey to the knife-happy Dr Thomas Oliver in the Portsea Union, who treated the pauper dead as his private laboratory, cutting up their bodies on the quiet, without writing reports or seeking permission from the relatives, even when they too were in the workhouse. As the scandal surfaced, the body of George Eyers, for instance, who died of 'cirrhosis exhaustion' (liver disease) was examined: 'in addition to the post-mortem this corpse had both arms cut off, one thumb and some fingers cut off, one leg cut off at the knee joint, and the other at the middle of the thigh, the tongue and the windpipe were taken away . . . the underjaw having been taken off by sawing.' A man of six feet one in life, Eyers was buried in a five-foot coffin. Old people and the mad were especially liable to Oliver's post-mortem butchery. Despite complaints from the workhouse guardians, the Local Government Board did 'not think that the proceedings of Dr Oliver have been such as to require that he should resign his office'. The good doctor was only pressured into resigning once he was discovered filching drugs from the dispensary for his private practice. 'Rattle his bones over the stones,' children would chant behind the workhouse cart heading for the pauper pit, 'it's only a pauper whom nobody owns.'

My father's ancestors William and Charles Light, Baptists and builders, were among the guardians of Portsmouth workhouse. Both took a turn as chairman of the board in the last decades of the century. William Light was still a guardian when Flora and her four children, and also Edwin Heffren, were admitted. The Lights helped shut down Dr Oliver's activities and inaugurated 'breastplates' on coffins where names had formerly been scrawled in chalk, and a proper burial service with four inmates to follow the funeral procession. They also ruled that 'parents be allowed to see their children every alternate Thursday for one hour in the chapel after service'. One hour a fortnight! They moved for 'a few easy chairs' to be provided for the patients, flowers in the hospital wards, and an annual treat for children, but made no bones about arresting Caroline Jacobs 'for absconding with clothes belonging to the Guardians' (how desperate she must have been to want to flog that miserable uniform). In 1881 separate wards for 'casuals' were added. This was followed by separate lunatic wards for those not removed to the new borough asylum, and a new laundry block in which women like Flora could do the heavy work which was meant to deter all but the most deserving (the so-called labour test), not only by scrubbing workhouse floors but by turning out sparkling linen, a favourite metaphor for moral cleansing, which much appealed to the Victorian middle classes. Those inmates who had special duties as nurses now had weekly stipends from three shillings to one and nine, but, even so, the *British Medical Journal*, in its survey of workhouses in 1894, reported that the hospital accommodation was 'far removed from what would now be considered good sick wards for acute cases'. The long crusade against giving any support, or 'out relief', even to widows with children, had crowded the building with around 1,700 people when the Millers arrived. The workhouse was a small township in itself but with a high turnover of people who came and went.

There was no official order compelling the removal of children from the workhouse environment until 1913, and as short-term admissions – children of the 'in and outs' – my grandmother Lilian and her brother, Ted, were retained in the wards. In the 1900s children over the age of eight were now sent to the local elementary schools. Unclaimed orphans would be boarded out in an early version of fostering, though some boys were forcibly emigrated, like thirteen-year-old George Light (no relation, I think), sent to Ontario, Canada, to work as a farm labourer. The rules were strict for those little ones, like Ted, who stayed in the workhouse school, the day topped and tailed with prayers; and 'disorderly' children, who refused to wash or work, or who tried pathetically to 'climb over the fence', would be put on bread and water. The most refractory, especially those who swore or disturbed Divine Service, might get solitary confinement for up to eight hours, but no girls could officially be beaten and no child put in a dark room or confined at night. The workhouse gave my grandmother Lilian, and thousands more like her, a roof over her head, a decent meal, a clean bed and medical attention. It trained her to be a domestic servant. But why were there so many children living in poverty?

In the 1880s, and again after the Boer War, mass joblessness was making it hard for social investigators and fact-gathering agencies to maintain that 'pauperism' was a matter of choice. A new term, 'unemployment', suggested poverty might be the result of trade cycles, economic recession or slump; low income not simply a matter of improvidence but of other factors such as old age, childbirth, illness, irregular wages. Rowntree's study of poverty in the 1900s revealed that nearly three-quarters of inadequate family incomes were actually from full-time earnings: 'the poor' were not separate and different from the working class; poverty was a phase through which many individuals passed. The old Poor Law was clearly out of its depth faced with the crises in an industrial and urban economy. A new Royal Commission was set up, investigating 200 unions from 1905 to 1909, but the commissioners ultimately failed to agree on their main recommendations, publishing two reports. The *Majority Report* wanted a reorganization which would give charitable assistance and voluntary action a much more prominent role. One of its key members was Octavia Hill, who led the Charity Organization Society, keen believers that outdoor relief should be a rare privilege, given only to persons of 'good character' and in exceptional circumstances – the COS was popularly known among the poor as 'Cringe or Starve'. The *Minority Report*, whose writers included the Fabian socialists Sidney and Beatrice Webb, argued that poverty arose primarily from the organization of the economy. They recommended repealing the Poor Laws and establishing separate local authority committees to deal with different constituencies and separate types of poverty – an education committee, health committee, and pensions for the elderly – with unemployment requiring a government Ministry of Labour.

But neither camp abandoned the idea of a 'residuum', 'a deadweight', as the *Majority Report* put it, of 'useless and costly inefficients'. Part of 'the unemployable', the *Minority Report* chimed in, was 'in bulk, almost homogenous in its worthlessness'. Both echoed the 'Darwinesque' language of Charles Booth (one of the commissioners in 1905) in his study of London labour, who had deemed the unemployed 'a selection of the unfit', adding that 'on the whole, those most in want are the most unfit'. Most offensive to Booth were the 'loafers', and those whose ideal was 'to work when they like and play when they like'. 'They cannot stand the regularity and dullness of civilised existence,' Booth wrote, almost prompting me to feel sorry for him, so joyless is his vision of a good society. Almost. Like other social investigators and commentators, he thought the majority of my ancestors, especially the casual labourers and any who had yet to submit entirely to the discipline of an industrial world, needed to be removed from the labour market altogether. Far better, were it possible, to dispatch them to 'labour farms' or penal colonies.

Neither report was adopted but, under the Liberal government, welfare reforms went forward in a piecemeal fashion, intended, in part, to keep socialism and workers' agitation at bay. As hospital facilities were expanded, medical provision for the elderly, the sick and the mentally ill undermined some of the workhouse assumptions, bringing in free dispensaries and free treatment, though the new old-age pension, enacted in 1909, was not initially to be given to those who had claimed poor relief in the last two years. The Local Government Act of 1929 finally brought the workhouse system to an end, with the local authorities taking over its many functions in providing social services. As was common across the country, the workhouse in Portsmouth became a hospital – my nan was to die in St Mary's, the building where she had first gone as an orphan – and in due course the former paupers of the Portsmouth Lunatic Asylum found themselves in 'The City Mental Hospital' and then St James's. No one seems to have noticed the Freudian slip when 'Asylum Road' was turned into 'Locksway Road'.

Salvage

'The urban past has never had a very secure future,' wrote the urban historian H. J. Dyos. Every city is made up of disappearances. In Portsmouth, as elsewhere typically, throughout the century, as the old thoroughfares hardened into streets, much of the nomenclature that had once pointed to the lives and work of labouring people underwent the usual deodorizing to make the map more polite, or was replaced by references to town luminaries, or at least its landlords (Kent Street, once the Old Rope Walk, was a nod to the Kent family, local farmers dabbling in politics). The central market, once called 'Bloody Row' for its number of slaughterhouses, was sanitized as 'Charlotte Street' after George III's wife; the Devil's Acre became 'the Common Hard' by the harbour; the graphic Deadman's Lane was by 1850 St Mary's Road, now directing mourners towards the life to come rather than marking the corpse's transit to the burial ground. Pubs were made to stand up straight and salute: in Hawke Street, the familiar 'George' (1784) became the more respectful King George; the 'Sir John Barleycorn' (first listed in 1823), that mascot of the ploughmen, who is no sir at all but a scion of the drink, was renamed mid-century 'The Royal Standard'; in Clock Street, 'The Vine', which dated back to 1733, became 'The Benbow' after 1888. In 1896 the first clearance of brothels and beer houses firmly obliterated the memory of Smiths Lane, once Ankersmiths Lane, under Victory

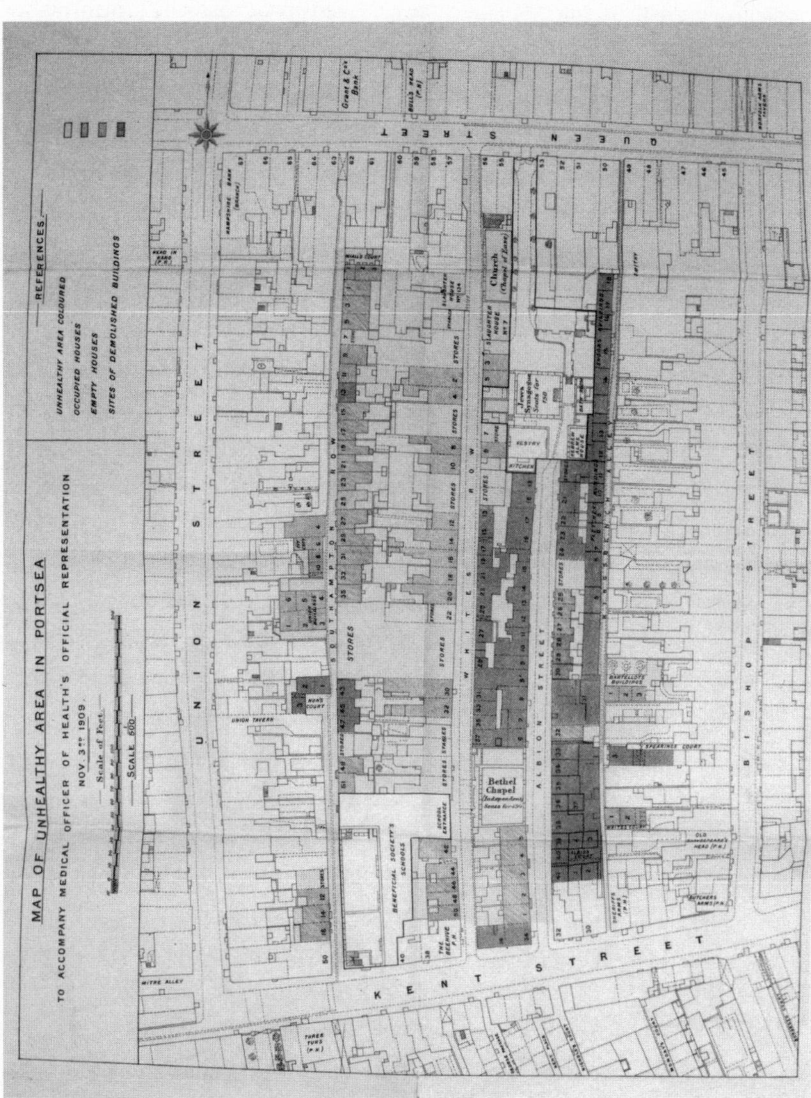

The Albion Street district, marked out for clearance in 1909
(Portsmouth Museums)

Road. Chapel Row, where George Turner, the campaigning medical officer was born, was later elevated to Admiralty Road.

Albion Street, White's Row and King's Bench Alley were part of an 'insanitary area' wiped off the map in 1911–12, the largest clearance to date. The district had never been 'improved', though a few houses here and there had been demolished. Many houses were dilapidated and empty; others were lived in at a reduced rent, the rooms riddled with damp, the walls so infested that the wallpaper appeared to be moving. Before they demolished White's Row they set the houses alight to get rid of the bugs and the vermin. Only seven of the thirty-two occupied houses in Albion Street had a wash house; eleven shared the water closets with others, and another eleven had no water for flushing. Several were used 'for immoral purposes'. Where 200 dwellings had stood, forty-three two-storey 'model' houses were built, each with three bedrooms, a bath and an outside lavatory (though the council had ended up cutting costs and adopting 'a cheaper scheme' than originally intended). The nest of courts and alleys was replaced with one tree-lined road named after Admiral the Honourable Sir Assheton Gore Curzon-Howe, commander-in-chief in Portsmouth, flying his flag from HMS *Victory*. Although the medical officer who had urged demolition pointed out that the old slums had been 'very profitable investments' despite their total neglect, he advised the council to keep hold of the land in order 'to control the class of tenants in the new houses'. Council housing, in other words, was not rehousing intended for the poorest sort but a dehousing that simply moved the problem on. 'Of course, the former dwellers did not inhabit these nice new houses,' as the pastor of Kent Street Baptist church observed. 'They were just driven into the other wretched holes and corners,' adding, 'nothing more seems to have been done for many years.'

Nearly 1,000 dwellings were demolished between 1896 and 1933, though many courts and alleys, like Hope Place where my father grew up, lingered on. A substantial number of streets in Portsea and Landport were flattened during the Blitz, but a 'vigorous programme of slum clearance' in the aftermath of the war razed more houses than were destroyed by German bombing. In Portsea the corporation went overboard, replacing the terraced rows with blocks of high-density flats named after admirals: among them, on Bishop Street, Lestock House and Barham, both to be demolished in 2004 (and replaced with terraced housing), Rooke and Kempenfelt; on Hanover Street, Calder House; on Britain Street, Raleigh and Grenville; and on Hawke Street, Codrington and Craddock faced Benbow and Frobisher. In 2007 a new complex of private flats was built off Queen Street, dubbed, with a singular lack of imagination, the 'Admiralty Quarter', but by then most of Portsea's residents had been moved on. 'A considerable overspill population has been accommodated on estates outside the City boundaries,' write two local historians, sympathetically recording memories of 'old' Portsea.

What does home mean in the memory? When the industrial slums first began to appear, John Ruskin and others saw in them the great blight on nature, the uglification of England, and mourned the destruction of rural values (though many from the villages had escaped rural poverty and the paternalistic grip of the farmer or 'the big house'). No one would want to keep their verminous Portsea lodgings, surely? In January 1930 Mrs Jones, an elderly lady living alone in three cramped rooms in Margery's Court, off Butcher Street, was one of many interviewed prior to demolition. Despite the dirt and the damp in these back-to-backs, the lack of ventilation, and sharing an outside toilet entered from the street, as well as paying nearly five shillings' rent a week for the privilege, she was 'not anxious to obtain a better house . . . wants to remain in Portsea'. The owner, who lived comfortably distant in South Wales, and acted through her daughter, a Mrs Kenwood of Southsea, also had a number of houses in Hawke Street for which she charged ten shillings a week. At number 30, Mr and Mrs Warlow, with their five children and cat, had four rooms on three floors, the biggest barely more than nine feet by nine, the walls and ceilings brown with age, no fireplaces, no place for refuse, sharing two toilets between four houses. Unlike Mrs Jones, the Warlows were 'anxious to leave', noted the inspector, but 'want to stay in Portsea'. So the refrain went on – decent housing but staying local – but it was wishful thinking.

If the history of a family is in part the history of a place, Portsea's history can be viewed from many angles: a history of wilful neglect by national and local government; a story charting the milestones on the road to urban improvement, thanks to the sporadic boosts to the dockyard economy and the efforts of the medical officers of health. It paints a picture of a narrow, in-turned tribe, prone to drunkenness, flag waving and violence amid the squalid playground of the navy and the emergence of a close-knit, hard-working community forging a pride in itself out of suffering and generosity. The reports on health and housing expose appalling conditions and invite our sympathy, but the testimonies of the residents themselves resist their victimization, insisting on a way of life they often reckoned better than that of their 'betters': communal values over individual possessiveness, work as a means to relish life's pleasures rather than a means to accumulate.

Those born, like my nan, at the turn of the century were shrewd rather than sentimental when they looked back, remembering which prostitutes they could trust to mind their kids, that their doors were never locked because there was nothing to steal and, the locals recalled, 'half your home was in their home anyway', that regular punch-ups were a bitter fact of life and some men drank away the housekeeping in the pubs and came home, fists flailing. But 'you could always turn to somebody if you wanted something', the people were friendly and the shops were on your doorstep. At least one little girl thought 'Portsea was lovely, especially when the sun shone through Queen Street which then was a mass of people hustling and bustling. Civilians and Navy going backwards and forwards.' These places were as deeply missed as any village green or blue remembered hill.

*

Lydia Murphy's house in Albion Street, where her daughter Flora was born, was cleared in 1911. St John's View, where Flora's daughter Lilian, my grandmother, was born; Chatham Row, where Flora died; and Nutfield Place, where my grandparents first lived and my mother was born in 1932, all in Portsea, have also all gone. In 1941 the Luftwaffe raids destroyed my mother's subsequent childhood home, the house in St Mary's Road, which her mother had thought 'a palace'. Then in 1970 my grandparents' house in Longs Road off Lake

Road, where I held the Bakelite telephone to my ear and watched the clockwork ballet dancer pirouette, came under a compulsory purchase order. Despite an uproar of protests from the inhabitants, that whole area, where my father too had grown up, was razed by eager planners. 'It was slaughter really,' my mother recalled, as if the houses were the people. My nan, now widowed, had to move on again. When I think of working-class conservatism, the desire to hold on and to defend, the resentment and pride that manifests itself in a variety of forms, emotional, social and political, I think too of this history of dispossession, eviction and displacement.

There were survivals. If we had been a religious family we might have found solace in St Mary's, the 'mother church' of Portsea Island where Anthony and Margaret Murphy were wed in 1816 and countless Murphys baptized, and where my older sister, Sandra, also got married in 1972, the last of the big weddings in our family (but she had been to teacher-training college and was marrying an Oxford graduate, the first sign of our diaspora). More important to us as children was the free education of the elementary and junior schools, and the Kingston recreation ground made over in 1891 to the residents of Fratton from the thirteen-acre workhouse farm which once fed the inmates. Next to it, Fratton Park, from 1898 home to a football pitch and later a stadium. And in a city which did little to encourage autodidacts, we owed much to Andrew Carnegie, the Scottish philanthropist, whose random gift to Portsmouth in 1906 of a local free library just happened to be near us (and to my mother, always hungry for books, who regularly took us there).

Easy to imagine, because our terraced houses looked similar, with their doors on to the street and back gardens where nothing much grew, that our past was seamless. Especially in the shape-shifting world of childhood play, bounded in one direction by St Mary's churchyard, where the winos sat swigging Emva Cream sherry, holding court on a wooden seat that encircled a huge horse chestnut, and by 'the rec' on St Mary's Road, where I picnicked on sugar sandwiches and swooped on to the swings and roundabouts. I kept away from the far side of the ground where, beyond the railway line, I could see the cliff of flint walls which made up the grim perimeter of the prison, another Victorian legacy. And across the road, on the northern edge of the rec, its *ultima Thule*, was the cemetery, but I was afraid of ghosts so never once went in. No one I knew was buried there.

★

My grandmother Lilian must have known a great deal about her family, I now realize, but I think that the past was no use to her in its original form. She told some fine tales about her half-sisters, the Miller girls – Carrie, who had gone on the stage; Maud, who married well and went north – but the 1911 census was disillusioning: both half-sisters were in service and Carrie was working in Carshalton, Surrey, as a cook. My grandmother had probably joined her there as a maid where she met my grandfather. While my grandfather was at sea as a stoker during the war, Lilian returned to Portsmouth and moved in with Flora Miller, her other half-sister (what became of Rosina/Rose Miller I do not know). John Miller, my nan's half-brother, had died of bronchitis in 1915, aged thirty. He was buried in a pauper grave in St Mary's Cemetery in the same pauper plot, though not the same grave, as their mother. Flora Miller the younger called her own little girls Flora and 'Lilian Flora'. My grandmother's mother had never actually been missing, though she had been missed.

As so often, the family history was hidden in plain sight. In the late 1930s my nan took my mother to visit 'Uncle' Tom and Auntie Em. Tom Murphy, Flora's brother, was my grandmother's uncle, the paraffin seller, waiter on the Strand, merchant seaman, painter, and now crane driver in the dockyard. My mum, the child of a sprawling, noisy family, loved the little wooden house in Butcher Street with its one tiny room over the other, 'Blackie', the dubiously named cat asleep in the bow-window seat, and Em in rustling alpaca dresses, a tiny Victorian sprite. Upstairs, lying in state in his bedcap, puffing on his pipe, was 'Uncle Tom', who had 'sailed the seven seas' – an old sea dog, with ships in bottles lining the windowsills. She was slightly afraid of him. Tom would have known about Flora and Edwin and that there were still Murphys galore in Portsea. His cousin Arthur, one of George Murphy's nautical brood, lived till he was ninety-three ('Pensioned Inspector of Riggers H. M. Dockyard', his death certificate proudly reads). Arthur might even have remembered his Irish grandfather Anthony, from the very first generation, who died when he was eight. 'Would have', 'could have': the syntax of lost connections, wistful and useless – except to remind us that history bides its time. My nan never told her schoolgirl daughter about the family, and the little girl would never have asked. The house, though, stayed in my mother's memory. Such a strange and wonderful place, like a doll's house, she thought, this tiny house of the past, that had such people in it.

Stories could always be salvaged. In the 1970s, once the council had taken away my grandmother's home, she became a lodger, first with her oldest daughter, and then sharing with a pal from one of her clubs, ignoring the 'awful' kitchen for the sake of the company. On my returns from college, I went on paying calls, though with increasing ill-grace. I was probably only interested in my own doings, but in the midst of my clock-watching she suddenly told a story that clung to my memory like a burr. She used to visit her father-in-law, she said, when he was locked up in St James's. 'Stark naked' she found him, crying, 'Take me home, Lily, take me home!'

Had she really visited him in the mental hospital? Arthur Smith had moved to Portsmouth but his records were still embargoed. His death certificate of 1932 says he died in St Mary's, as she well knew, since she was the one who registered his death. While I was wrinkling my nose at the brown tea stains on my grandmother's cups which the myopia of age had missed, was she spinning me a yarn? All the time I sat there, kidding myself that I was humouring her, was she humouring me? Every generation of her family had been in institutions, and as a child, with her hair close-cropped in the workhouse, she would have heard tell of the lunatics housed in their own wards. Did she know about her husband's mother locked up in Netherne? I imagine my grandparents, when they first met, exchanging family histories in fragments. Whether they told each other about the workhouse or the lunatic asylum, their romances about the past gave each a protective colouring.

'Take me home, Lily, take me home!' I was back in the world of Victorian melodrama or the shilling-shocker – heightened feelings, the scenes of abandonment, but also of the cry of pain, of the child who wants to go home. Perhaps my grandmother had twisted the story, turned my grandfather's mad mother into a helpless man, a small gesture of revenge against the world's bullies. But she too had been abandoned, institutionalized and confined; it did not matter for how long. She too had lost a mother and home. There was an element of triumph: she had lost her childhood but she hadn't lost her sanity. She had lived to tell the tale. And if her stories were a way of getting listened to and of being respected, they were also a reparation, a way of generating life through art and talk, and of making something other than homes and children. 'She always had a fertile mind,' my mother said.

Lilian Heffren before her marriage, *c.*1915

Postscript

My father always hated his first name, the source of much bullying at school. Prompted by a sadistic master who had mimicked his lisp, the boys would chorus: '*Thid*-ney, *Thid*-ney.' Dad re-baptized himself when he met my mother at a demob dance in 1949. She too hated 'Sidney', and asked for a middle name instead. He swiftly jettisoned his inheritance of 'Herbert' and 'Henry', plucking 'Robert' out of the air (in the 1940s it had a hint of Hollywood to it, with Robert Donat, Robert Mitchum, Robert Montgomery, Robert Taylor all on the screen). Thus he became 'Rob' to his in-laws and new workmates, 'Sid' to his siblings and old pals, and as children we got used to his dual identity. The curse of his Christian name faded as time went on but it was never quite shaken off. 'Mr S. H. H. Light' survived for official purposes and in hospital, during his last illness, he was back to suffering that babyish 'Sidney', wincing as he bantered with the nurses. He never corrected them, not wanting to make a fuss.

My father is the person I have most missed while I have been writing this book. Proud of being a 'freeborn Englishman', he would have enjoyed knowing that there was a direct line back to Isaac Light in 1688 and that his serendipitous 'Robert' was a family name after all. But Isaac Light was a newcomer to Shrewton when he married Elizabeth Philips. During the English Civil War many people were on the move and record-keeping was patchy. Civil registration took over from the church, and villages were meant to appoint a secular 'Register' to replace the parish priest. Only one Isaac Light was officially registered in Wiltshire in the last years of the Protectorate. His father, probably, Nathaniell Leight or Lyte (spellings wander too), brought him for baptism in 1656 in Yatton Keynell, a village to the north of the county. Light is a medieval name but it could equally well be Norman French. The seventeenth-century writer and antiquarian John Aubrey claimed his lineage in Wiltshire from one

William le Lyte (Aubrey's grandfather was called Isaac Lyte). But even if, as is most likely, my ancestors were not robber barons but serfs, the soil they tilled was not 'England' but Saxon Wessex. Magna Carta, which limited the powers of the king, was not the work of Englishmen.

Penhale Road Infant School

I wish I could have told my father about the Lights nearer to home. How could he not have known? Every time he and my mother went to buy their fruit and vegetables at the Charlotte Street market, St Agatha's, 'the cathedral of the car parks', loomed over them. The Baptist William Light's name was on a board inside, but not being church-goers they never went in. They might so easily have spotted the plaque outside on a wall at St Mary's Hospital, designating what was once the casuals' ward of the workhouse. It lists the guardians, including both William and Charles Light, but my parents had other things to think about as my father went for his radiotherapy. Most startling was finding that W. R. and C. Light had built Penhale Road Infant and Junior Schools in 1886 in Fratton, the schools my sister, brother and I attended from the ages of four to eleven. But would it have made any difference to us had we known? Beyond a vague thrill of pride or the occasional playground joke, it was not a live connection. These Lights were not 'ours'.

Family historians are always stumbling over uncanny coincidences. Magical thinking is part of our stock in trade. The place once unbeknownst to us, or which we passed heedlessly every day, suddenly becomes luminous with significance, uniting disparate people and random moments, making them radiate and rhyme. Since family history moves in a psychological dimension, it is always plangent, resonating with loss, and coincidences are like ley lines mysteriously transforming the map of time. Such discoveries find pattern and meaning in what otherwise threatens to be mere accident, but they also seem to offer evidence of commonality. Family history knows that everyone – and everything – is ultimately, and intimately, connected. And there is truth in this. Though my scapegrace grandfather parted company from his religious relatives, in my mind, at least, the Lights will always be building Zion, the mud-walled chapel and the school, and last but not least, the Troxy cinema, where I sat enraptured in the 1960s, watching Stewart Granger as 'Scaramouche' as he swashbuckled his way across the balconies of the Opéra Français.

*

There is a 'Light' section in Kingston Cemetery, across the road from St Mary's Hospital (another thing my father did not know). In the mid-nineteenth century, when the government intervened in the public health crisis, they passed Burial Acts which established a national system of public cemeteries funded by the rates. Parishes set up their own Burial Boards and William Light was one of Portsmouth's founding members. William's grave is near the entrance to the cemetery, the headstone just another mouldy epitaph in a row of crumbling stones and the grave unkempt. I do not believe the decay would have mattered to him. He would surely have agreed with his friend the Baptist minister Reverend Joseph, who reminded the mourners at William's funeral 'how vain were all earthly positions and distinctions'. I prefer the version I got from my parents: 'You can't take it with you when you go.' Or as my nan would have put it, even more pithily, 'There are no pockets in a shroud.'

Kingston Cemetery buries about 400 people a year; a smaller ground at nearby Milton can take 200, and Portsmouth has one public crematorium. This for a city of more than 200,000 with an outlying district of thousands more. The island is still the only place in England with a greater density of population than London, the UK's most crowded city. In June 2008 it was a fortnight's wait for my father's funeral because of the backlog; eighteen months later, the delay was extended to nearly three weeks for my brother's wife, Anita, who was foolish enough to die on New Year's Day, in the middle of a bureaucratic break, and a peak period for deaths. Her body would have stayed at the funeral directors for yet another fortnight, making it an unconscionable five weeks if we hadn't taken the unpopular ten o'clock slot to cremate her body. We know the crematorium well. My mother's father, my 'grampy', who died in 1967, was the first of the Smiths to be cremated. Since then our visits have been so frequent that we used to make jokes, as we stood about in the draughty cloisters, looking at the flowers, about taking out shares. That joke rings hollow now as the running of public cemeteries and crematoria is increasingly 'outsourced' by the local authorities. Soon the graveyards may be privatized. As the costs of funerals increase and government funds to help the needy are cut or capped, 'funeral poverty' is on the rise. The wheel has come full circle since Victorian times and Britain is in the midst of another burial crisis.

I sometimes wish I had somewhere to mourn my father but graves can also be a reprimand, as if the dead can be hurt or affronted by the weeds that will inevitably grow there. Millions of people have never had a place to mourn, although until I found Evelyn's grave I had not considered that common or public graves still existed. In Britain 'public health' burials (the latest euphemism) are still contracted to firms of undertakers and paid for by the local authorities. Those who die destitute, unnamed or unclaimed go on sharing graves. In the USA, Hart's Island has its 'Potter's Field' run by the New York City Department of Correction where more than a million are buried,

1,500 a year, roughly half of them infants and stillborn babies whose mothers do not always know what a 'City Burial' is. Prison inmates from Rikers Island dig, and re-dig, the trenches for burial. If we could relinquish 'owning' a plot, there would be no more pauper graves or 'potter's fields', the name which bears the stigma of blood money, those pieces of silver Judas flung back at the Pharisees, when he threw Christ's ransom at their feet. Cemeteries would turn back to woodlands again.

I now know that nothing about a graveyard can be taken at face value. The idea of personal memorialization in a church or churchyard was virtually unknown before the seventeenth century for those below the watermark of wealth; their bones were consigned to a charnel house or mass grave. Those who could afford it might have Masses said for the dead by priests, but the belief in purgatory meant that all prayers for the dead uttered by descendants could also atone for a person's sins and affect the fate of the soul. After the Reformation, Protestantism stressed the individual life whose virtues and acts needed to be weighed in the balance. The fate of the soul after death was in the hands of God alone. Gravestones gradually sported fewer death's heads or didactic 'vanities', becoming less a general warning to all of the Great Leveller than an account of a life and, increasingly, a display of familial affections and ties. Memorials for individuals made the idea of 'visiting' a graveyard feasible, while landscaping and funerary art addressed the sensibility of the mourner, evoking that now familiar and domestic image of sleep. The cemetery became a dormitory with its inhabitants lying down, eyes closed, their heads on imaginary pillows, the headstone as a bedstead. Family history is always the history of bereavement, but in death, as in life, no man is an island. The coffin, as opposed to a winding sheet or shroud, the idea of an individual plot, its shape and depth, the placing of the grave, the layout of the cemetery: all aspects of burial and remembrance are signs of social activity, of laws and regulations, attitudes towards the body, religious beliefs, and assumptions about the social order.

An early view of ghosts saw them as the unnamed. 'Conjuring' meant having the courage to face them and call them by their names in order to lay them to rest. All historians are resurrectionists, but perhaps family historians only want to give their ancestors a proper burial. Sometimes all we can hope to find is a name. When I first visited Evelyn's grave I thought I would write a book called 'A History of Absences', in which I would move around the missing people, feeling the shape of the hollow in time that they had left, like a tongue probing a cavity. But there are so many kinds of absence from the historical record, a whole spectrum of disappearances, from those airbrushed out of the records for political or ideological reasons, those who did not fit the official categories, to those we do not see because we are blindsided by our own ignorance. Then there are others obscured by the legends and myths, the make-believe in which their descendants have dressed them, turning our ancestors into heroes or villains, martyrs or victims, an amplification which makes us feel we matter.

Absence and disappearance are weak words for what, like death, is formative. Absences ripple through time like a stone skimming the surface of water, shaping events, reverberating into the future. What's missing is where another story begins, and if absences are gaps, they can also be portals through which we glimpse what went before and try to catch the shimmer of what is to come. Evelyn's grave was not an empty space but 'a fair field full of folk', not a dead end but a place from which to start.

*

I remember exactly when the idea for this book seeded itself. It began with a vision. I was on a train between London and Newcastle, glancing out of the window across the wide, open fields of Lincolnshire. The fields were empty, not even a solitary farmer on a tractor, and suddenly I had a sense of how crowded and peopled those acres would have been in earlier centuries, and all at once a swarm of ghosts, nameless, their faces blurred with time, filled my mind. Now, as I shut up my A3 lever-arch files crammed with birth, marriage and death certificates, I feel a wrench and think of all those who did not make it into these chapters, the airlessness of the past stifling them again. A delusion of grandeur, no doubt: the historian or author as a godlike figure, selecting *this*, not *that* fact, *this*, not *that* life. Yet history writing is always the chance to change the terms in which some are remembered and others forgotten. I comfort myself with the thought that people might not mind being forgotten if they are forgotten in the right way.

What have I learnt? Has it changed me? Doing family history I found that I stood, a tiny figure, on a jetty or a pier, and stretching far to the horizon before me was the prospect of an infinite past, like an ever-moving sea, rolling towards me and receding. I understand more now why my family seemed to come from nowhere and had nothing. I thought I might find an ancestral place, but what I found was movement. I am as English as they come, the descendant of migrants from all over the southern counties, Ireland too, and beyond. I have learnt whom I come from. Farm workers and lace-makers, carters and caulkers; women who made needles and plied them; saddlers and stay-makers; old ladies who washed sailors' rig-outs, young ones who sorted paper and rags; bricklayers and builders, and so many servants; those who sailed to sea, who fed the engines and the men; shopkeepers and milk boys; paraffin sellers, barmaids, watermen, lifters and loaders and porters, and people who made everything from shirts to churches, and the roads they walked away on. Their history is local, national and global as they went about their world, finding work, dreaming their dreams. Southern England was hard hit: enclosures of land, workhouses and the pauperization of the labourers drove many out on to the road, and this too is our island story, the other face of the Industrial Revolution, which produced losers as well as winners in a modernizing capitalist economy. A 'free' market always has it costs.

What are places if not the people who made them? My immediate forebears did not come from Portsmouth; it came from them. I also hail from that island city which was once four 'towns', once a garrison, once a few hovels on some salt flats, but I have learnt that the search for origins is as vertiginous a freefall as the address I used to scribble as a girl when I still thought I was the centre of all things: '11 Liverpool Road, Fratton, Portsmouth, Hants, England, United Kingdom, Europe, the World, the Galaxy, the Universe, Outer Space'.

Notes

Historians usually give chapter and verse for every document consulted, but the dozens of people I've tracked for this book would necessitate an avalanche of references were I to annotate every census, baptism, marriage or burial record. I have confined myself to summarizing some of that information in family trees, making it clear where records can be found, while referencing in detail only the least accessible or most important of the materials. I've also tried to indicate here or in the main body of the book where records don't exist or where I was simply stumped. Where I have dealt with a topic in detail, I give a selection of the books I consulted, a mix of specialist volumes and those for the general reader who may wish to pursue a particular area. I hope this book encourages others to write their family history as a public history.

Abbreviations

AL	Angus Library, Regent's Park College, Oxford
DHC	Dorset History Centre
GRO	Gloucester Record Office
HTSC	*Hampshire Telegraph and Sussex Chronicle*
IWM	Imperial War Museum
MERL	Museum of English Rural Life, Reading
PA	Pembrokeshire Archives
PCC	Portsmouth City Council
PCRO	Portsmouth City Record Office
PP	Portsmouth Papers
SHC	Surrey History Centre
TNA	The National Archives

VCH *Victoria County History*
WCRO Warwick Record Office
WEA Workers' Educational Association
WSA Wiltshire and Swindon Archives

The place of publication for all works is London unless otherwise stated.

Preface

xxvii **'What's the point of forgetting/ if it ends in dying?':** Joseph Brodsky, 'Song', *So Forth* (Hamish Hamilton, 1996).

Part One: Missing Persons

1. Evelyn's Grave

12 **Brandwood End Cemetery:** Barrie Simpson's short history of Brandwood End Cemetery can be found via the Friends of the Cemetery at www.fbec.co.uk.

15 **'guinea graves':** Sylvia Barnard, *To Prove I'm Not Forgot: Living and Dying in a Victorian City* (Manchester University Press, Manchester, 1990), p. 37.

15 **'gardenesque' style of John Claudius Loudon:** a way of planting, introducing exotic plants especially, which revealed the deliberate formality and art of the design.

TIME-TRAVELLING

21 **They have come from Syresham:** the Whitlocks can be tracked back to Anthony Whitlock, born 1645 in Paulerspury, Northamptonshire, one of the most important local centres of pillow lacemaking.

CAKE-TOWN

22 **Alcester:** I drew on G. Edward Saville (ed.), *Alcester: A History*

(Brewin Books, Studley, 1986), which mentions 'Dowdeswells', pp. 74–5; and Saville, *Alcester in Camera* (Quotes, Buckingham, 1992). John G. Rollins, *Needlemaking* (Shire, Oxford, 1981) also gives a detailed description and history of needle-making in the Redditch district.

24 **'encouraged her nobles to install foreign craftsmen':** Rollins, *Needlemaking*, p. 12.

26 **nail-making was the largest employer of women:** for the Birmingham metal trades, see Ivy Pinchbeck, *Women Workers and the Industrial Revolution 1750–1850* (Virago, 1981); also Raphael Samuel, 'The Workshop of the World: Steam Power and Hand Technology in Mid-Victorian Britain', *History Workshop Journal*, 3 (1977).

27 **'The effects of early work, particularly in forges':** quoted in Pinchbeck, *Women Workers*, p. 273.

27 **over 50 million needles *a week* . . . 1,000 million a year:** Asa Briggs, *Victorian Things* (Batsford, 1988), p. 209.

27–8 **Samuel Dowdeswell, Charles's father, hailed from Gloucestershire:** thanks to Gareth Dowdeswell for information on the family in earlier centuries.

28 **he acquired a piece of freehold land:** WCRO/DR58/71, 20 June 1833. Thanks to Dale Gatherum-Goss, another Dowdeswell descendant, for this.

29 **the 'Old Bear Society':** Saville, *Alcester*, p. 158.

29 **Russen supplied special brass tokens . . . tried to convert another public house:** Alcester and District Local History Society, *Index* (Spring 1990), (Summer 1997).

29 **Bowen's drapery stores:** Saville, *Alcester*, p. 196.

29 **he left his wife nearly £700:** England and Wales, National Probate Calendar (Index of Wills and Administrations 1861–1941), p. 248. This is available through most family history websites.

29 **worth about six times as much today:** according to TNA website.

30 **William Allwood went bankrupt in 1912 . . . the guiding light and captain of the local cricket team:** Saville, *Alcester*, pp. 72, 162.

30 **in 1926 Charles Henry became a postman:** POST 58/123, British Postal Museum and Archive, also via www.ancestry.com.

LONGITUDE AND LATITUDE

32 **hand-lacemaking was in decline:** Pinchbeck, *Women Workers*, pp. 203–9; Bridget Hill, *Women Alone: Spinsters in England 1660–1850* (Yale University Press, New Haven, 2001), p. 31, and for other cottage industries, such as gloving.

34 **George Lionel Dashwood JP . . . with 'considerable pleasure grounds':** *VCH: Hertford*, Vol. 2 (1908), ed. William Page, pp. 264–73.

34 **First a porter at Bradford station:** 23 June 1870, Midland Railway Staff Register, Class no. 491, piece no. 1032, from www.ancestry.com.

35 **'a sacrifice to their own notions . . .':** *Daily Chronicle*, March/April 1898, quoted in Alan Ereira, *The People's England* (Routledge and Kegan Paul, 1981), p. 218.

35 **'vast and hopeless':** F. B. Smith, *The People's Health 1830–1910* (Weidenfeld and Nicolson, 1990), p. 291.

36 **In 1824 there was not a single railwayman:** Frank McKenna, 'Victorian Railway Workers', *History Workshop Journal*, 1 (1976), and for other details here.

36 **The police also offered country boys:** for the local force, see Saville, *Alcester*, p. 137; Carolyn Steedman's *Policing the Victorian Community* (Routledge and Kegan Paul, 1984) gives the bigger picture.

37 **a 'loyal servitude':** the phrase used by Michael Reynolds in his *Engine-Driving Life* (1881), quoted in McKenna, 'Victorian Railway Workers', 37.

37 **an eye not only on goods traffic:** J. R. Whitbread's *The Railway Policeman: The Story of the Constable on the Track* (Harrap, 1961) is the only work I could find solely devoted to this subject.

SETTLERS

39 **King's Norton:** for the parish, its industrial history and the growth of Cotteridge, I have relied on *VCH: Worcester*, Vol. 3 (1913), ed. J. W. Willis-Bund; and George Demidowicz and Stephen Price, *King's Norton: A History* (Phillimore, Chichester, 2009). Two books

of photographs were also helpful: Wendy Norton, *King's Norton: Past and Present* (Sutton, Stroud, 2004) and Pauline Caswell, *King's Norton* (Chalford Publishing, Stroud, 1997). I turned to Asa Briggs's *History of Birmingham*, Vol. 2, *Borough and City, 1865–1938* (Oxford University Press, Oxford, 1952) for the wider history.

39 **Birmingham grew at a phenomenal rate:** Demidowicz and Price, *King's Norton*, p. 107, and for the details in this paragraph.

41 **'thin red line' . . . 'the outposts of the enemy':** John A. Bridges, *Idylls of a Lost Village* (Macmillan, 1889), pp. 4–5.

41 **'like two opposing armies holding high ground':** Demidowicz and Price, *King's Norton*, p. 154.

41 **Frances Road at the turn of the century:** I am grateful to have found Janet Lovesey's initial transcription for the road of the census of 1901, and also for personal information about the road where she still lives: www.lovesy.org.uk (accessed 26 December 2009).

43 **the 'sweated trades' at home:** Carl Chinn, *Homes for People: Council Housing and Urban Renewal in Birmingham 1849–1999* (Brewin Books, Studley, 2004), p. 21.

45–6 **an average wage of eighteen shillings . . . rents at five shillings (25p) . . . a soup kitchen:** 'Cotteridge and Its Churches before 1911', a memoir by F. E. Hopkins at www.cotteridge.com/historical/long-history (accessed 7 November 2011).

47 **paper sorters were engaged in another kind of recycling:** Demidowicz and Price, *King's Norton*, p. 190.

48 **'the nerve centre':** 'A History of Cotteridge', a memoir by N. J. Staley (1983), and for details of the Picturedrome and the redoubtable Sergeant Dawns, www.cotteridge.com/historical/long-history (accessed 7 November 2011).

HAPPY VALLEY

51 **Dr Lillias Hamilton . . . 'exceptionally full with students':** D. M. Garstang, 'Studley College', *Agricultural Progress*, Vol. XXVIII: FR/WAR5/8/7, Studley papers held at MERL.

51 **photograph of sixteen-year-old Annie Webb:** Carol Twinch, *Women on the Land* (Butterworth Press, Cambridge, 1990), p. 22.

51 **the Forage Corps:** all the records for the Women's Forage Corps, including Medal Index Cards (Record Series WO372), were transferred to TNA, but there are no registers or separate Series of Records of Service for its members. It is possible that they were among the many records severely damaged in a German air raid in September 1940. The Imperial War Museum has a leaflet and a few badges, very few photographs and one interview with a member who worked in the office as a clerical assistant for the Corps.

52 **more than 600,000 horses:** Gill Clarke, *The Women's Land Army: A Portrait* (Sansom, 2008), p. 27.

53 **the recruiting leaflet for the Forage Corps:** IWM: LAND6/14.

53 **guarding forage dumps:** Caroline Dakers, *The Countryside at War 1914–1918* (Constable, 1987), p. 151.

53 **Some women were based:** Twinch, *Women on the Land*, p. 21. Evelyn Whitlock is not among those who received a medal for serving abroad.

54 **a 'gipsy life':** *Land and Water Extra*, Women in the War edition (April 1919). A copy can be found online at www.scarletfinders.co.uk.

54 **'You are doing a man's work . . .':** *The Handbook of the Women's Land Army*, IWM, quoted in Dakers, *The Countryside at War*, p. 150, and for other details here.

55 **'most of whom were drawn . . .':** *Land and Water Extra* (April 1919).

55 **Gladys Wiles:** 'Life on a Hay Baler', *Landswoman* (April 1918), 88.

55 **The Forage Corps was disbanded:** *The Times*, Wednesday, 31 December 1919. The article also mentions their hardships during the influenza epidemic, and a memorial in York Minster is dedicated to eighteen women of the Corps who died at this time.

57 **'archive fever':** Carolyn Steedman explores this experience as part of the nature of history writing in *Dust* (Manchester University Press, Manchester, 2001).

57 **'recovered from ordinary oblivion' . . . the 'dumb effect of events':** Christopher Bollas, 'The Functions of History', in *Cracking Up: The Work of Unconscious Experience* (Routledge, 1995), pp. 133, 141.

58 **By 1926 Birmingham council had built more municipal houses:** for these details, see Briggs, *History of Birmingham*, Vol. 2.

59 **My father was born:** Cleeve Road does not exist in the April and Autumn volumes of the electoral rolls for 1926; my father was born in late September that year but his birth was registered in mid-November, probably about a month after the houses were built.

60 **he might have taken home as much as eighteen shillings (90p):** R. W. Postgate, *The Builders' History* (Labour Publishing Company, 1923), Appendix 1, 'Wages in the Building Trade'.

61–2 **associated with silicosis . . . tuberculosis . . . killed twice as many people:** H. P. Newsholme, the Medical Officer of Health in Birmingham, 1930 report (printed Birmingham, Templar, 1931), 78, 10.

61–2 **was noted as early as the 1840s:** H. J. Dyos and M. Wolff, *The Victorian City: Images and Realities* (Routledge and Kegan Paul, 1973), Vol. 2, p. 643.

63 **'voluntary segregation' . . . 'practised benevolently' . . . 'granted concessions':** G. B. Dixon, 'Pulmonary Tuberculosis in Childhood', *British Medical Journal*, 25 April 1931, 697.

63 **a 'decent' funeral:** Julie Marie Strange, *Death, Grief and Poverty in Britain* (Cambridge University Press, Cambridge, 2005), p. 156.

2. *Hope Place*

69 **In feudal times:** David Rollison, 'Exploding England: The Dialectics of Mobility and Settlement in Early Modern England', *Social History*, 24:1 (January 1999).

69 **tramping artisans would call at inns:** Eric Hobsbawm, 'The Tramping Artisan', in *Labouring Men: Studies in the History of Labour* (Weidenfeld and Nicolson, 1968).

71 **350 people . . . taken in 1851:** *VCH: Wiltshire*, Vol. 15, ed. D. A. Crowley (Oxford University Press, Oxford, 1995).

SHERIFFS AND MAIDENS

My discussion of the overseers and how they implemented the 'Old Poor Law' before 1834 owes much to recent scholarship, in particular: Steve Hindle, *On the Parish? The Micro-Politics of Poor Relief in Rural England c. 1550–1750* (Clarendon, Oxford, 2004); Steven King, *Poverty and Welfare in*

England 1700–1850 (Manchester University Press, Manchester, 2000). For details about Poor Law relief in Wiltshire parishes and a close study of how the Poor Law was administered in a rural parish in the Cheese Country, see F. H. Hinton, 'Notes on the Administration of the Relief of the Poor in Lacock, 1583–1834', *Wiltshire Archaeological and Natural History Magazine*, 49 (1940), 166–218. For Wiltshire agriculture, see J. H. Bettey, *Rural Life in Wessex* (Sutton, 1987), and Avice R. Wilson's sympathetic account: *Forgotten Labour: The Wiltshire Agricultural Worker and His Environment, 4500 BC–AD 1950* (Hobnob Press, Salisbury, 2007), which points the reader to more specialist volumes. More generally, K. D. M. Snell, *Annals of the Labouring Poor: Social Change and Agrarian England, 1600–1900* (Cambridge University Press, Cambridge, 1985); Barry Reay, *Rural Englands: Labouring Lives in the Nineteenth Century* (Palgrave, Basingstoke, 2004).

74 **'cob' walls:** Sue Robinson's *Chitterne: A Wiltshire Village* (Hobnob Press, Salisbury, 2007), p. 113, has the eighteenth-century instructions for building a cob wall – a mortar that can include sheep's wool and has to be trodden in bare feet.

75 **Shrewton was one of several tiny hamlets:** *VCH: Wiltshire*, Vol. 15, pp. 242–52.

75 **Isaac Light:** he appears to have been baptized in Yatton Keynell, to the north of Wiltshire, by Nathaniel and Mary Light in 1656. The Philipses are in the earliest Shrewton records: Elizabeth Philips's grandmother Agnes was baptized by her father, William, in 1582.

75 **John Hillman . . . Richard Bygge:** Shrewton Parish registers, WSA/1336/1-5.

76 **churchwardens' accounts:** interleaved at the back of the accounts of the Shrewton Overseers of the Poor: WSA/1336/36.

77 **The novelist Thomas Hardy:** Michael Millgate, *Thomas Hardy: A Biography* (Random House, New York, 1982), p. 420.

77 **Shrewton has only one surviving volume:** WSA/1336/36. Maddington has an earlier set of records, but the Lights were living in Shrewton in this period.

77 **'poor in infrastructure':** Wilson, *Forgotten Labour*, p. 180, and for other details in this paragraph.

78 **with less than a quarter of the land unenclosed:** Thomas Davis,

General View of the Agriculture of Wiltshire (Board of Agriculture, 1811), p. 39.

78 **By 1803 nearly a quarter of Wiltshire's population:** King, *Poverty and Welfare*, p. 141.

78 **'penumbral poor':** Hindle, *On the Parish?*, p. 4.

78 **men like Thomas Munday:** J. B. Hamilton, 'Some Wiltshire Village Wills 1589–1856 of the Munday, Best and Small Families of Shrewton and Wylye' (private publication, 2008).

79 **'an economy of makeshifts':** the phrase is Olwen Hufton's, from *The Poor of Eighteenth-Century France 1750–1789* (Clarendon, Oxford, 1974), and has been much taken up by historians of the poor.

80 **'The fox had access to the hen house at will':** Wilson, *Forgotten Labour*, p. 141.

80 **Wiltshire was at the bottom:** Bettey, *Rural Life*, p. 67.

81 **Thomas Harper:** Militia Database compiled at the WSA, 906/W/270.

82 **nearly 400 inhabitants by 1811:** *VCH: Wiltshire*, Vol. 15, p. 244. There was a steep increase from 269 inhabitants in 1801 to 399 ten years later.

82 **John Skinner DD:** *VCH: Wiltshire*, Vol. 15, p. 251.

82 **'Careless indolence':** Eric J. Evans, 'Some Reasons for the Growth of English Rural Anti-Clericalism, *c.* 1750–*c.* 1830', *Past and Present*, 66:1 (1975), 99, and for Cruickshank's cartoon.

82 **By the 1830s half the parishes:** Wilson, *Forgotten Labour*, pp. 226–7.

82 **John Elderton, the vicar of Aldbourne:** Mary Ransome (ed.), *Wiltshire Returns to the Bishop's Visitation Queries, 1783* (Wiltshire Record Society, Devizes, 1972), pp. 20–21.

83 **a clergyman magistrate on the bench:** Evans, 'Some Reasons'; and Harry Hopkins, *The Long Affray: The Poaching Wars in Britain* (Secker and Warburg, 1985).

83 **Bunyan's phrase:** *A Few Sighs from Hell* (1658), quoted in Christopher Hill, *John Bunyan and His England 1628–88*, ed. Anne Laurence et al. (Hambledon, 1990), p. 6.

BUILDING ZION

The Strict Baptist History Society gives useful advice for those looking for family members. Three volumes published by the Baptist Historical Society open up the wider field: B. R. White, *The English Baptists of the Seventeenth Century* (1996); R. Brown, *The English Baptists of the Eighteenth Century* (1986) and J. H. Y. Briggs, *The English Baptists of the Nineteenth Century* (1994). For Nonconformist history in Wiltshire, see Marjorie Reeves, 'Protestant Nonconformity', in *VCH: Wiltshire*, Vol. 3, ed. R. B. Pugh and E. Crittall (Oxford University Press, Oxford, 1956), pp. 99–149; and 'Salisbury: Protestant Nonconformity', in *VCH: Wiltshire*, Vol. 6, ed. R. B. Pugh and E. Crittall (Oxford University Press, Oxford, 1962), pp. 156–61. I am also grateful to Karen Smith's unpublished D.Phil., 'The Community and the Believers: A Study of Calvinistic Baptist Spirituality in Some Towns and Villages of Hampshire and the Borders of Wiltshire *c.*1730–1830', Cardiff University, 1986. Baptist records – circular letters, handbooks and magazines – are all to be found in the Angus Library, Oxford; these give lists of churches, ministers and figures for attendance. Marjorie Reeves's family history, *Sheep Bell and Ploughshare* (Paladin, 1978), is an evocative account of the Baptist tradition and social life in the villages close to Salisbury Plain.

The story of the Sunday schools has generally had an urban slant and many village schools, like Shrewton, have disappeared from official histories. I have found nothing to match T. W. Laqueur's moving and convincing *Religion and Respectability: Sunday Schools and Working-Class Culture, 1780–1850* (Yale University Press, New Haven, 1976); his arguments are discussed in K. D. M. Snell and Paul S. Ell, *Rival Jerusalems: The Geography of Victorian Religion* (Cambridge University Press, Cambridge, 2000). I also drew on J. H. Y. Briggs, *The Sunday School Movement* (Paternoster, 2007); and for an initial engagement with the evangelical 'frame of mind' in poetry and prose, Donald Davie, *A Gathered Church: The Literature of the Dissenting Interest 1700–1930* (Routledge and Kegan Paul, 1978).

83 **William Hewett:** WSA/D1/2/29 Meeting House certificates.

83 **tiny pocket-size leather-bound books:** WSA/1112/141; 'Mr Light' was almost certainly Robert Light, repairer of church walls and senior village bricklayer. There are no registers of Baptist church members at this time.

84 **'amidst great opposition':** the story of the forming of the church is told in the *Baptist Magazine* (June 1812), 269–70: AL26/A7.

84 **the Particular Baptists at Brown Street in Salisbury:** *VCH: Wiltshire*, Vol. 6, pp. 156–61; also, for John Saffery: M. E. Reeves, 'Note Written for the Biographical Dictionary of the Earlier Evangelical Movement', AL/ R18/4.

84 **Wastfield's journal:** printed as Appendix A in Deryck W. Lovegrove, *Established Church, Sectarian People* (Cambridge University Press, Cambridge, 2003), which looks closely at itinerant preachers.

85 **Richard Parsons:** Reeves, *VCH: Wiltshire*, Vol. 3, p. 138.

85 **nearly 1,200 premises:** J. Chandler and D. Parker, *The Church in Wiltshire* (Hobnob Press, Salisbury, 2006), p. 141 ; and John Chandler (ed.), *Wiltshire Dissenters' Meeting House Certificates and Registrations 1689–1852* (Wiltshire Record Society, Devizes, 1985).

85–6 **'speech- and thought-sharing' . . . In the fifteenth century the Lollards':** Wilson, *Forgotten Labour*, pp. 228, 114–15.

86 **'absolute separation from the Church of England . . .':** White, *The English Baptists*, p. 48.

87 **Thomas Shergold:** TNA/RG4/Piece 1433/Folio 19 for Brown Street chapel, Salisbury.

87 **In January 1837 Thomas Light:** TNA/RG4/Piece 1433/Folios 65 and 67.

87 **In 1798 there were sixteen Baptist chapels:** Reeves, *VCH: Wiltshire*, Vol. 3, p. 137.

87 **letter of 'dismission':** WSA/3319/87.

87 **'from a very early age to evangelise':** obituary of Charles Light, AL: *Baptist Union Handbook* (1889–90), p. 149.

87 **In 1838 he had his own house licensed:** Meeting House certificate 1521, WSA/D1/9/2/1; the other names on the certificate are John Feltham, George Windsor and James Kellow; the latter was the owner of 'Bethesda Buildings', cottages next to the chapel. There is still a wall plaque inside Zion chapel to Abraham and Hannah Windsor and their daughter Hannah. (Personal communication: Georgina von Etzdorf.)

87 **a large second meeting in Shrewton:** WSA/33319/87.

87 **'healthy enthusiasm' . . . 'called out':** Smith, 'The Community and the Believers', p. 98.

88 **'By his Almighty operations . . .':** The Eastern Association Circular Letter of 1780, quoted in Lovegrove, *Established Church*, p. 193.

88 **the private efforts at schooling:** *VCH: Wiltshire*, Vol. 15, p. 252.

89 **'flowing with cheerfulness':** Watts, quoted in F. J. Harvey Darton, *Children's Books in England* (Cambridge University Press, Cambridge, 1932), p. 109; see also Laqueur, *Religion and Respectability*, pp. 11–15, which I draw on in this paragraph.

89 **'familiarly about Jesus Christ, as if he were a labourer . . .':** Alun Howkins, *Reshaping Rural England: A Social History 1850–1925* (Routledge, 1992), pp. 182–3.

90 **'affectionately' . . . 'the support of such publications . . .':** Circular Letter of the several Baptist churches belonging to the Bristol Association, no. xxvi (May 1849), 13.

90 **Upavon's 'Cave of Adullam':** for this and other details of chapels, see Chandler and Parker, *The Church in Wiltshire*.

91 **From John Bunyan to James Hogg:** for a very helpful discussion of the dynamics of the Calvinist inner life, see the introduction to John Bunyan, *Grace Abounding, and Other Spiritual Autobiographies*, ed. John Stachniewski (Oxford University Press, Oxford, 1998).

91 **'non-conformity loosened tongues . . .':** Reeves, *Sheep Bell and Ploughshare*, p. 65.

91 **Large numbers of villagers gave notice to marry:** marriage notice book, WSA/F26: Salisbury Registration District Amesbury Sub-District, from 23 September 1839 – 22 May 1878. From 1837 a licensed chapel could be used for marriage provided a civil registrar completed the legal formalities.

91 **in parts of Wiltshire Anglicans . . . 'the State Church':** Chandler and Parker, *The Church in Wiltshire*, pp. 146–7.

91 **On Census Sunday in March 1851:** *VCH: Wiltshire*, Vol. 15, p. 252; the details of occupations are from the marriage notice book: WSA/F26.

91 **'with a somewhat extensive business':** obituary, *Baptist Union Handbook* (1889–90), p. 149.

91 **In 1854 he was fined £3:** WSA/A1/260 Wiltshire Minor Offences.

92 **as a trustee:** Kellow's will, WSA/776/840.

92 **In the early 1860s a schism broke off:** *VCH: Wiltshire*, Vol. 15, p. 252. Zion's church book makes no mention of this.

92 **the Wickhams:** thanks to their descendant Charles Bailey of Tucson, Arizona, for this information via the web.

92–3 **entered village lore . . . 'If that's the sort of people . . .':** Personal communication: Sue Robinson.

93 **Henry Light's ministry began:** the *Baptist Union Handbook* for 1873 dates Henry Light's ministry from 1858 and ceases to mention him after 1877, the year before Charles's retirement.

93 **'dismissed' . . . to form a congregation at Chitterne:** WSA/3319/87; no church book survives for Chitterne's early chapel.

93 **Charles was alive, though ill:** *Baptist Union Handbook* (1889–90), p. 149.

93 **'the new book was accepted . . .':** 24 January 1883, WSA/3319/87.

LIGHT AND SON

The social history of the British building trade or construction industry, especially from the point of view of the workers, is sparse. I have drawn on R. W. Postgate's *The Builders' History* (Labour Publishing Company, 1923), which is largely a history of trade union activity, and found especially useful Richard Price's *Masters, Unions and Men: Work Control in Building and the Rise of Labour 1830–1914* (Cambridge University Press, Cambridge, 1980). By contrast, there is an enormous amount of literature on Victorian Nonconformity. David W. Bebbington's *Victorian Nonconformity* (Cascade, Eugene, Oregon, 2011) is an introduction which also gives extensive further reading.

94 **'What with sailors out for prize money . . .':** Alistair Geddes, *Portsmouth during the Great French Wars, 1770–1800*, PP 9 (PCC, 1970), p. 3.

95 **At first it was 'Halfway Houses':** *Pigot and Co's Portsea Directory* (1823–4); the address of 'Esau Light, bricklayer' is given as Lake Lane, 'Southport', 'the first time that name has appeared in print', in the 1830 edition. By the 1841 census it is 'Landport'.

95 **Nearly 4,000 dwellings:** C. W. Chalklin, *The Provincial Towns of Georgian England, a Study of the Building Process, 1740–1820* (Edward Arnold, 1974), p. 126. Chalklin looks at Portsea in detail.

95 **'generally taken' . . . 'as soon as the foundations are laid':** *HTSC*, 26 September 1808.

95 **anyone with £100 to risk:** Chalklin, *The Provincial Towns*, p. 124.

95 **single heads of 'the brocoli':** *Hunt and Co's Hampshire Directory* (1852), p. 65.

95 **The links between the Baptists of Shrewton and of Portsea Island:** Smith, 'The Community and the Believers', 78.

96 **In 1813 'missionaries' with ties:** F. Ridoutt, *The Early Baptist History of Portsmouth* (Strict Baptist Society Library, Landport, Portsmouth, 1888).

96 **one of the first four people to be baptized:** ibid., p. 87; AL/CH/POR/LAK: Revd C. S. Hall's *Lake Road Baptist Church Souvenir History* (1970) gives 'seven hundred children' attending Sunday school, but the documents do not distinguish between children and adults at this time. The later religious census for 1851 has a maximum of 450 attending evening services, with about 250 children in the schoolroom 'for want of more room in the Chapel': John A. Vickers (ed.), *The Religious Census of Hampshire 1851* (Hampshire County Council, Winchester, 1993), p. 11.

96 **among the first of the Sunday-school teachers:** Lake Lane Sunday School Teachers Book (1819), PCRO/CHU 86/5/1; Sunday School Teachers Attendance Book (1822), PCRO/CHU/86/5/9. Jane and Robert probably belonged first to the church at Meeting House Alley, which became Kent St chapel, but these records were destroyed in the Blitz.

96 **a collection of £1 12s:** Laqueur, *Religion and Respectability*, p. 172.

96 **'Neat little new private houses . . .':** *Hunt and Co's Hampshire Directory* (1852), p. 65.

97 **that 'leviathan' of builders:** Price's *Masters, Unions and Men*, pp. 23ff., gives a thorough account of the growth of general contracting.

97 **the fourth-largest number of workers:** Price, *Masters, Unions and Men*, p. 19.

97 **Men were putting nearly twice as much money:** R. A. Church, *The Great Victorian Boom, 1850–1873* (Macmillan, 1975), p. 34.

97 **in London, 80 per cent of them:** H. J. Dyos, 'The Speculative Builders and Developers of Victorian London', *Victorian Studies*, 11: Supplement (Summer 1968), 652.

97 **'this most anarchic of industries':** Price, *Masters, Unions and Men*, p. 31.

97 **doing house repairs for the council:** Borough of Portsmouth Council Minutes, 4 February 1856, PCRO/CM1/3.

97 **drifted towards the sea:** Esau's daughter Martha had married a ship's cook; Martha's son Joshua eventually combined both family leanings as a stonemason working in the dockyard in Devonport.

97 **Robert and Elizabeth's twin boys:** TNA/RG4/403.

97 **the Gas Company offices:** obituaries of W. R. Light, *Portsmouth Times*, 25 January 1896; *HTSC*, 25 January 1896.

98 **'the greatest preacher of the Victorian age':** Bebbington, *Victorian Nonconformity*, p. 9. Spurgeon's Metropolitan Tabernacle in south London, purpose-built for him, held up to 6,000 people.

98 **'where diligent young men could catch the eye . . .':** ibid., p. 23.

100 **'a loving and watchful oversight':** Lake Road Chapel Year Book for 1879, PCRO/CHU86/10/5.

100 **'with much sorrow and regret':** for William Robert's activities, see PCRO/CHU86/2/5 and the minutes of deacons' meetings, PCRO/CHU86/1/1-2.

100 **W. R. and C. Light built the new Sunday school:** There is no record of who built the chapel itself, though William Robert Light is one of the signatories on the agreement for its execution, dated 28 September 1864: PCRO/CHU86/10/5.

100 **'from the thraldom of the family pew':** S. G. Green, *The Pastor in the Sunday School* (1884), quoted in J. H. Y. Briggs, *The Sunday School Movement*, p. 56.

100 **this had been allowed in the previous century:** Leonore Davidoff and Catherine Hall, *Family Fortunes: Men and Women of the English Middle Class, 1780–1850* (Hutchinson, 1987), p. 137.

100 **and later their daughters:** *Christian Citizen*, 6:8 (January 1896).

100 **Youth's Temperance Institute:** *Lake Road Baptist Church, Souvenir History, 1820–1970*, PCRO/CH86/10/2.

100 **Maternal and Dorcas Societies:** Lake Road Chapel Year Books for 1876, 1879, PCRO/CHU86/10/5. The first Dorcas Society, founded in 1834 on Douglas, Isle of Man, to provide clothing for the poor, was

named after Tabitha, also called Dorcas, in the Acts of the Apostles, 9:36.

100 **under the pastorate of Reverend T. W. Medhurst:** *Lake Road Baptist Church, Souvenir History, 1820–1970*, PCRO/CH86/10/2.

101 **'a white cap, white cotton gloves . . .':** PCRO/CHU86/4/4.

101 **the membership rolls at Lake Road:** PCRO/CHU86/4/1-2.

102 **'incontestably' the strongest branches:** Postgate, *The Builders' History*, p. 227.

102 **During one dispute locally:** Letters to the Editor, *HTSC*, 1 August 1874.

103 **'individuals might be at liberty . . .':** Bebbington, *Victorian Nonconformity*, p. 45.

103 **At the Association annual dinner:** *HTSC*, 16 January 1875.

103 **Seconding William Robert Light's motions:** *HTSC*, 16 April 1881.

103 **William Robert Light was a director, then its chairman:** *HTSC*, 25 January 1896.

103 **'Romish-Priest architecture':** *Baptist Magazine* (March 1867), 171–2, quoted in Bebbington, *Victorian Nonconformity*, p. 40.

103 **the aid of £4,000 from the Duke of Norfolk:** J. Webb, S. Quail, P. Haskell and R. Riley, *The Spirit of Portsmouth: A History* (Phillimore, Chichester, 2001), p. 116.

104 **leant towards Christian Socialism:** in 1890 Dolling invited Stewart Headlam, an advocate of land reform, free education and free breakfasts in board schools for poorer children, to give a lecture at St Agatha's. Even this much radicalism led many wealthier supporters of St Agatha's mission to cancel their subscriptions: Nigel Yates, *The Anglican Revival in Victorian Portsmouth*, PP 37 (PCC, 1983), p. 11.

104 **'perfect equality' . . . 'one of the most useful, honoured . . .':** Robert R. Dolling, *Ten Years in a Portsmouth Slum* (Swan Sonnenschein, 1896), pp. 131, 166.

104 **'men who meant business . . .' . . . to 'go for' . . . the brothel-keepers included magistrates:** Charles E. Osborne, *The Life of Father Dolling* (Edward Arnold, 1903), pp. 113, 131.

104 **'a touch of Venice':** Revd Fr. J. D. Maunder, *A History of the Furnishings of St Agatha's Church, Portsmouth* (St Agatha's Trust, n.d.).

104 **London Italians . . . £1,200 when William Light died:** Dolling, *Ten Years in a Portsmouth Slum*, pp. 166, 231.

A HOUSE OF MANY MANSIONS

106 **'A most courteous man . . .':** *Portsmouth Times*, 25 January 1896; *HTSC*, 25 January 1896; *Christian Citizen*, 6:9 (February 1896), pasted into the minutes of deacons' meetings, PCRO/CHU86/1/4.

106 **'Builders in the Country':** *HTSC*, 18 July 1891.

107 **general strike:** *HTSC*, 11 March 1893.

107 **'command' . . . 'if necessary, endure their hatred':** Price, *Masters, Unions and Men*, p. 101.

107 **'a £5 note and plenty of cheek':** Raphael Samuel, 'The Workshop of the World: Steam Power and Hand Technology', *History Workshop Journal*, 3 (1977), 29.

107 **'a *Pilgrim's Progress* of our time':** Raphael Samuel, 'A Spiritual Elect?: Robert Tressell and the Early Socialists', in *The Robert Tressell Lectures 1981–88*, ed. David Alfred (WEA, Rochester, 1988), p. 56. Tressell, who died in 1911, could not get his book, originally called 'The Ragged-Arsed Philanthropists', published in his lifetime. An abridged version was published in 1914; the unexpurgated version waited until 1955.

108 **a trustee of Lake Road chapel:** PCRO/CHU86/10/5.

108 **named for membership:** 18 December 1889, PRO CHU86/2/6.

108 **Mrs Bramwell Booth:** *HTSC*, 25 February 1893.

108 **About 90 per cent:** Pamela J. Walker, *Pulling the Devil's Kingdom Down: The Salvation Army in Victorian Britain* (University of California Press, Berkeley, 2001), p. 72.

108 **'expressly to oppose the staid complacency':** ibid., p. 3.

108 **new 'holiness movement':** D. W. Bebbington, *Evangelicalism in Modern Britain* (Routledge, 2002), pp. 152ff.

109 **the estate of £10,000:** all details of inheritances can be found in the England and Wales National Probate Calendar (Index of Wills and Administrations 1861–1941), available through family history websites.

110 **his grandchildren were attending Lake Road:** Attendance register, 1909–13, PCRO/CHU86/5/10. There were also Salvationists in

Benjamin Light's family: information from Hazel Vitler, his granddaughter.

BRICKS AND MORTAR

111 **'I claim for socialism,' said Keir Hardie:** quoted in Bebbington, *Evangelicalism in Modern Britain*, p. 143. Hardie's closest friend, Frank Smith, who joined the socialist movement, had been General Booth's right-hand man in the Salvation Army.

111 **the navy recorded punctiliously:** TNA/ADM/188/1021.

111 **A 'slushy' . . . 'a strong sense of self-worth':** Christopher McKee, *Sober Men and True: Sailor Lives in the Royal Navy 1900–1914* (Harvard, Cambridge, Mass., 2002), p. 104.

112 **'on the batter':** Kevin Brown, *Poxed and Scurvied: The Story of Sickness and Health at Sea* (Seaforth, Barnsley, 2011), p. 184.

112 **Venereal disease was declared a national emergency:** Kevin Brown, *Fighting Fit: Health, Medicine and War in the Twentieth Century* (The History Press, Stroud, 2008), p. 97; M. Harrison's *The Medical War: British Military Medicine in the First World War* (Oxford University Press, Oxford, 2010), pp. 152–70, gives a full account of the problem of VD, but primarily deals with the army and the Western Front.

112 **'dreadnought packages' . . . 'the ignorant class':** TNA/HO45/10893/359931, letter from a chief petty officer on active service, 2 November 1918, quoted in Brown, *Poxed and Scurvied*, p. 186.

112 **'skilled disinfection':** R. Cooter, M. Harrison and S. Sturdy (eds.), *War, Medicine and Modernity* (Phoenix Mill, Gloucester, 1998), p. 178, fn. 70.

113 **free boots from the Brotherhood:** *Arundel Street Memories* (WEA, Portsmouth, 2002), p. 36.

113 **He was buried with his wife:** Kingston Cemetery, Portsmouth, Andrews Plot 96, row 13, grave 59.

113 **seven new picture-houses opened in Portsmouth:** Juliet Gardiner, *The Thirties: An Intimate History* (Harper Press, 2010), p. 667.

113–14 **'a peculiar, crudely festive version . . .':** D. W. Lloyd, *Buildings of Portsmouth and Its Environs* (City of Portsmouth, 1974), p. 112.

116 **the memorial reading desk:** *Christian Citizen*, 11:6 (June 1897), PCRO/CHU/86/10/8.

116 **'did not believe in the special sacredness of places':** PRO/CHU 86/10/6.

117 **Writing to thank the minister:** WSA/3319/101.

117–18 **'getting righteous overmuch' . . . 'inwardly strong':** *The Journals of Two Poor Dissenters 1786–1880*, introduction by John Holloway (Routledge and Kegan Paul, 1970), pp. 4, xiv.

118 **Albert Marrett, a teenager:** *Albert Marrett, Memories 1884–1916*, WSA/3319/96.

118 **Fred Maidment:** Robinson, *Chitterne*, pp. 84–5.

Part Two: Tall Stories

3. The Road to Netherne

For the North Atlantic, Marcus Rediker's *Between the Devil and the Deep Blue Sea: Merchant Seamen, Pirates, and the Anglo-American Maritime World 1700–1750* (Cambridge University Press, Cambridge, 1987) and Peter Earle's *Sailors: English Merchant Seamen 1650–1775* (Methuen, 2007) provide different starting points; John Mack's *The Sea: A Cultural History* (Reaktion, 2013) broadens the horizon for thinking about 'saltwater people'. I relied on Mark Kurlansky's *Cod: A Biography of the Fish That Changed the World* (Vintage, 1999) and on the work of W. Gordon Handcock for migration and the Newfoundland fishery.

129 **Sigmund Freud once suggested:** 'Family Romances' (1908), *Standard Edition of the Complete Works*, Vol. 9 (Hogarth Press, 1959), pp. 234–41.

130 **Thomas Lyte:** H. Tait, *Catalogue of the Waddesdon Bequest* (The British Museum Press, 1986).

'MISS NOBODY'

133 **'little more than a good farming village':** William Winterbotham, remembering Cheltenham in 1773, in Gwen Hart, *A History of Cheltenham* (1965; Alan Sutton, Stroud, 1990), p. 123.

133 **'We think back through our mothers . . .':** Virginia Woolf, *A Room of One's Own* (1929; Penguin, Harmondsworth, 1993), p. 69.

133 **innkeepers and brewers, and then sailmakers:** will of Giles Hosier, dated 22 October 1750, Poole, Dorset: DHC/Cp/W/H; Event Record Number 32. His son William is given as a sailmaker in DHC/Cp/A/S, Event Record Number 25, administration of the will of Elizabeth Stanworth by her daughter Maria Hosier, William's wife, dated 6 April 1762.

133–4 **the 'cod rush' . . . fifth-generation Newfoundlanders:** Kurlansky, *Cod*, pp. 48, 5.

134 **'everything from beaver hats to strong beer in bottles':** A. J. Miller, *The Story of Poole: An Outline History* (English Press, Poole, 1984), p. 38.

134 **'drawing on the credit of the cod . . .':** D. Beamish, J. Dockerill and J. Hillier, *Mansions and Merchants of Poole and Dorset* (Poole Historical Trust, 1976), p. 144.

134 **The Hosiers followed their father and uncle:** the diaries of Isaac and Benjamin Lester, traders and merchants on a very large scale, mention – one can hear the Dorset accent – a Captain 'Joyles Hosier' and his brother William in the 1760s. The entry for 12 September 1774 (DHC/D365) reads, 'Wm Hosier came in today ab[out] his boy', probably young Giles, who would be around thirteen, wanting employment with Lester. Thanks to Professor Gordon Handcock for these references.

134 **Jeffrey and Street owned fifteen vessels:** for these and other details about Jeffrey and Street, I am indebted to Professor Gordon Handcock's unpublished paper, 'A Biographical Profile of 18th and Early 19th Century Merchant Families and Entrepreneurs in Trinity, Trinity Bay' (Memorial University of Newfoundland, 1980), and his entry for 'Thomas Street' in the *Dictionary of Canadian Biography*, Vol. V, *1801–1820* (1983), now available online at www.biographi.ca/en/bio/street_thomas.

134 **part of a three-leg journey:** Cecil N. Cullingford, *A History of Poole* (Phillimore, Chichester, 1998), pp. 122ff.

136 **the Poole vessels brought back tar and indigo . . . 50,000 quintals:** Handcock, 'Thomas Street'.

136 **'naturally fair game' . . . the captain of the *Two Brothers*:** D. Beamish, J. Dockerill and J. Hillier, *The Pride of Poole 1688–1851* (Borough of Poole, 1974), p. 15.

137 **extensive trade with Barbados:** Beamish et al., *Mansions and Merchants*, p. 132.

137 **'frontier entrepreneur':** Handcock, 'Thomas Street'.

137 **the fireplace in Lester's dining room:** Beamish et al., *Mansions and Merchants*, p. 94.

137 **a 'free-trader', against all regulations and restrictions:** Jeffrey's testimony to the House of Commons Report on the State of Trade to Newfoundland, 1793, quoted in Handcock, 'A Biographical Profile', 38ff.

137 **'never saw money from their birth . . .':** Cullingford, *A History of Poole*, p. 127.

138 **'a peripatetic, renaissance man . . .':** Francis I. W. Jones, 'The Newell Family', *Newfoundland Ancestor*, 15 (Summer 1999), 61–5.

138 **'refined tastes and superior attainments' . . . 'a lordly home . . .':** Revd Charles Lench, *The Story of Methodism in Bonavista* (1919; reprinted H. Cuff, Bonavista Region, Newfoundland, 1985), pp. 53–6, for all details of Giles Hosier.

138 **Sarah Fitzpatrick:** Maria's mother or grandmother may have been one of the many Irish servant girls brought to Newfoundland by merchants, their agents, or some of the wealthier planters: W. Gordon Handcock's *So Longe as There Comes Noe Women: Origins of English Settlement in Newfoundland* (Global Heritage Press, Milton, 2003) discusses intermarriage.

138 **Roman Catholics were the overwhelming presence:** David Davis, *Newfoundland Ancestor*, 28:1 (2012).

138 **'most perfect freedom':** Adam Smith, *The Wealth of Nations*, Books IV–V (1796; Penguin Classics, Harmondsworth, 1999), p. 162.

139 **15,000 slaves in Jamaica had starved:** Kurlansky, *Cod*, p. 100, which also refers to Smith.

139 **in his forties set up a school in Poole:** details here from Jones, 'The Newell Family'.

140 **she was married to Jehudi Witt:** the baptism of their daughter, Susanna Maria, in Poole was delayed until she was seventeen in October 1834 (her father is given as 'Judith', a mariner).

140 **both his names were common among Dutch Jewish traders:** Jehudi was born in Sopley, Hampshire, and moved back to be near his parents, David and Hannah Witt, in nearby Minstead, who are listed as of 'independent means' in the 1841 census and not natives of England.

140 **the village of Sopley:** a favourite spot for transatlantic fishermen: Newfoundland's Grand Banks genealogical website, www.ngb.chebucto.org.

141 **'holidays for health':** Christopher Chalklin, *The Rise of the English Town, 1650–1850* (Cambridge University Press, Cambridge, 2001), p. 14.

141 **'All the fashions . . .':** Hart, *A History of Cheltenham*, p. 130, and for the details in the following paragraph.

142 **the embargo lifted on Italian straw . . . 'particularly hard work and miserable wages':** Bridget Hill, *Women Alone: Spinsters in England 1660–1850* (Yale University Press, New Haven, 2001), pp. 33, 4.

143 **'A nasty, ill-looking place':** William Cobbett, *Rural Rides* (1830; Penguin Classics, Harmondsworth, 2001), pp. 370–71.

143 **'fashionable butterflies and evangelical beetles':** *Gentleman's Magazine*, n.d., quoted in Hart, *A History of Cheltenham*, p. 184.

143 **were sentenced at the Gloucestershire Assizes:** GRO/Q/GC5/7; England and Wales Criminal Registers, 1791–1892, HO27/66/322. I found this information initially thanks to Muriel Woodford researching her own family tree online.

143 **'stealing a bag of beef and bread . . .':** Tasmania State Library Archives: CON33/1/42; CON14/1/24, confirming his offence and trial, age, birthplace and the names of the parents of 'Richard Hill the younger' and his sister, 'Marian'. The son of a schoolmaster's daughter, he could read and write.

144 **'the very quintessence of punishment':** Robert Hughes, *The Fatal Shore: A History of the Transportation of Convicts to Australia 1787–1868* (Vintage, 2003), p. 368. Richard was given his freedom on 13 April 1850 and appears not to have married in Tasmania; beyond that the trail goes cold.

144 **married Robert Jackson:** at Cheltenham Register Office on 3 October 1845. I could find no death record for Richard Hill. Jehudi Witt is recorded (with their daughter, Susanna Maria, and his 'wife',

Elizabeth) on the 1851 census for Minstead, Hampshire. He died in 1861. Divorce, of course, was next to impossible for the lower orders.

144–5 **Most were not organized within a brothel . . . 'Miss Nobody':** Hill, *Women Alone*, p. 111.

145 **The workhouse guardians did not offer 'relief':** GRO/GAL/G353117, Christine V. Seal, 'Poor Relief and Welfare: A Comparative Study of the Belper and Cheltenham Poor Law Unions, 1780–1914', Ph.D. thesis (unpublished), Leicester University, December 2009, 21. My discussion is indebted to this work.

145 **a standard procedure:** F. B. Smith, *The People's Health 1830–1910* (Weidenfeld and Nicolson, 1990), p. 50.

146 **The receiving officer ... noted in his register:** GRO/G/CH/60/12, Admission and Discharge Book, March 1857–September 1859. The same book gives the birth of Sarah Hill, Class 9 (Infants), number 245, to Mary Hill.

146 **New arrivals were immediately classified:** 'Class 1: Able-bodied Men; Class 2: Old and Infirm Men; Class 3: Boys from 9 to 13 or 16; Class 4: Boys from 2 to 4; Class 5: Able-bodied Women; Class 6: Old and Infirm Women; Class 7: Girls from 9 to 13 or 16; Class 8: Girls from 2 to 9; and Class 9: Infants', Schedule C, Form 21, front page of Admission and Discharge Book.

146 **a first nine days . . . 'isolated, rejected and desperate' . . . crowded and filthy workhouse labour wards:** Smith, *The People's Health*, pp. 47–55.

146 **they risked being carted hundreds of miles:** GRO/G/CH/124 includes a reverse example, the removal of Christina Macdonald, aged thirty-five, with Alexander, four months, born in Cheltenham: 'admitted June 1st 1894. Child died at Liverpool on its way from Glasgow to Cheltenham'.

146 **'canary' wards:** the practice was banned in 1839, although at Andover workhouse, and no doubt elsewhere, unmarried mothers continued to wear frocks with a yellow stripe down them. Yellow was already the colour of a ship's plague flag. See Norman Longmate, *The Workhouse* (Pimlico, 2003), p. 157.

146 **exercise yard for 'lewd women':** Old Town Survey Map, 1855–7, GRO/PC757 Sheet 28.

146 **In 1851 the central agency of the Poor Law Board:** Pat Thane, 'Women and the Poor Law in Victorian and Edwardian England', *History Workshop Journal*, 6 (Autumn 1978).

147 **In May, a month after Mary Ann gave birth:** the details here are all from GRO/G/CH/60/12, Admission and Discharge Book.

147 **Without a dispensary or separate infirmary:** the former opened in August 1866, the infirmary waited until 1884. See Christine Seal, 'Medical Assistance to the Poor in Nineteenth-century Cheltenham', *Cheltenham Local History Society Journal*, 26 (2010), 45, 47.

147 **usually the elderly, semi-abled or 'imbecile':** Smith, *The People's Health*, p. 388.

147 **she died . . . on 30 December:** GRO/P78/1/INI/67, St Mary's, Cheltenham, 1858–61 Register of Burials. The workhouse did not keep medical notes at that time.

THE 'HOUSE

There has been fierce debate about the nature of the Victorian Poor Law and much written about the workhouse. I draw mostly on David Englander, *Poverty and Poor Law Reform in 19th Century Britain, 1834–1914* (Longman, 1998), which gives an analysis of changing attitudes to poverty throughout the period, an overview of debates about the Poor Law among historians, and some key documents; Peter Wood, *Poverty and the Workhouse in Victorian Britain* (Alan Sutton, Stroud, 1991), includes an assessment of the bureaucracy and administration; and Norman Longmate, *The Workhouse* (Pimlico, 2003), is a detailed and moving account of the human experience.

147–8 **'primitive agony' . . . 'In psychology' . . . :** D. W. Winnicott, *Human Nature* (Free Association, 1998), pp. 117, 158. I am also grateful to Adam Phillips's account, *Winnicott* (Fontana, 1988).

148 **'sour potato and stale urine' . . . 'intermittent groans, oaths . . .':** George Lansbury's account of the Poplar workhouse in London in the mid-1890s, quoted in Smith, *The People's Health*, pp. 399–400.

148 **'close-packed against a wall . . .' . . . 'the sole amusement for fifteen children . . .' . . . 'thirty or forty infants under five':** quotations

taken from the *Journal of the Workhouse Visiting Society* (1859–65), quoted in Longmate, *The Workhouse*, to which I owe the other details in this paragraph.

149 **Dickens's Oliver Twist famously asks for more:** The novel appeared in book form in 1838, though it deals with the parish poorhouse before 1834.

149 **the boy found lolling:** Longmate, *The Workhouse*, p. 167.

149 **Only 3,000 of the designated 15,000 parishes:** Englander, *Poverty and Poor Law Reform*, p. 10, and for other details here.

150 **'the state of one who, in order to obtain . . .':** Report of the Royal Commission on the Poor Laws, 1834, quoted in ibid., *Poverty and Poor Law Reform*, p. 95.

150 **women who always constituted the majority:** Alan Kidd, *State, Society, and the Poor in Nineteenth-Century England* (Macmillan, 1999), p. 37; Thane, 'Women and the Poor Law'.

151 **'deviant extras, like fresh vegetables or even salt':** Englander, *Poverty and Poor Law Reform*, p. 39.

151 **'without too much argument' . . . property was not less than £40:** Seal, 'Poor Relief and Welfare', 75, 69. Seal points out that in the north the qualification was often nearer to £30.

151 **could accommodate 220 inmates:** Heather Atkinson, 'The Workhouse System, 1834–1929: Did It Really Help the Poor?', *Cheltenham Local History Society Journal*, 26 (2010), 1.

151 **'took away from the poor their reliance . . .':** *Cheltenham Examiner*, 25 January 1843.

151 **240 paupers to Quebec:** *Cheltenham Examiner*, 10 April 1850.

151 **525 people . . . nearly a quarter:** Seal, 'Poor Relief and Welfare', 12, 8.

152 **Mr Alfred Fleischmann, a young man in his twenties:** the census shows that he was born in Cheltenham, the son of a London innkeeper, and later had a private practice there.

152 **launched a series of complaints:** GRO/G/CH/8a/13, Board of Guardians' Minute Book, 1 May 1867, which also mentions a report of nine months earlier; 26 June 1867; 4 July 1867.

152 **'was not only too fat, but literally unfit . . .' . . . singles were used as doubles . . . the stonebreakers' yard:** GRO/G/CH/8a/13, 26 September 1867; 19 December 1867; 2 January 1868.

152 **'duty towards the ratepayers' . . . 'it will be absolutely necessary . . .':** GRO/G/CH/8a/13, 6 February 1868.

153 **Fleischmann wrote furiously . . . letter to the *Daily Telegraph*:** TNA/MH12/3926, correspondence files of 14 November 1868; *Daily Telegraph*, 18 May 1868.

153 **underfunded and with few powers:** Wood, *Poverty and the Workhouse*, pp. 81ff.

153 **the pauper nurses at Cheltenham:** Seal, 'Medical Assistance to the Poor', 46.

153 **'miserly nature' . . . 'almost enjoined neglect':** Smith, *The People's Health*, p. 53.

154 **ran their own racket:** GRO/G/CH/8a/17, 17 December 1874.

154 **'constant bullying':** GRO/G/CH/8a/17, 24 September 1874.

154 **'bastard ceremonial English':** E. P. Thompson, *The Making of the English Working Class* (Victor Gollancz, 1965), p. 267.

154 **a labyrinth of letters:** passage through the material has been made far more navigable by the recent National Archives project 'Living the Poor Life', which has digitized and catalogued 105 volumes of the MH12 record series, covering twenty-two Poor Law unions, available through the TNA website. For details: Paul Carter and Natalie Whistance, 'The Poor Law Commission: A New Digital Resource for Nineteenth-Century Domestic Historians', *History Workshop Journal*, 71 (Spring 2011).

156 **Andover in 1845:** Longmate, *The Workhouse*, p. 122.

156 **William Bunce:** GRO/G/CH/60/14, February 1864; John Turner: GRO/G/CH/60/18, 29 September 1870.

156 **One woman at Bethnal Green workhouse:** TNA/MH12/6847, given in full by Englander, *Poverty and Poor Law Reform*, pp. 102–3.

156–7 **meticulously clocked up on the parish roll:** GRO/P78/1/OV2/14.

157 **Thirteen girls her age:** GRO/G/CH/60/15, 29 September 1865.

157 **Orphans were often dispatched to the silk mills:** Tom McCunnie, 'Regulation and the Health of Child Workers in the Mid-Victorian Silk Industry', *Local Population Studies*, 74 (Spring 2005); Jane Humphries, *Childhood and Child Labour in the British Industrial Revolution* (Cambridge University Press, Cambridge, 2011), gives the wider analysis.

157 **the fifty deaths there:** GRO/G/CH/69/4. The workhouse year started on 1 April, and I counted from the end of March 1866 to the end of April 1867.

157 **Sarah's last charge on the parish:** GRO/G/CH/60/16.

'ALSATIA'

158 **'the handsomest, the largest . . .':** Mary Morgan, *Tour to Milford Haven in 1791*, quoted in Dillwyn Miles, *Portrait of Pembrokeshire* (Robert Hale, 1984), p. 108.

158 **'infested with vagrants' . . . a parish constable:** *Pembrokeshire Herald*, 27 November 1846. I'm grateful to Simon Hancock for this reference.

158 **adjourning to the Bull:** Brian John (ed.), *Honey Harfat: A Haverfordwest Miscellany* (Greencroft Books, Newport, Dyfed, 1979), p. 59.

158 **the mass exodus from the land:** D. Gareth Evans, *A History of Wales 1815–1906* (University of Wales Press, Cardiff, 1989), p. 205.

158 **'quite an Alsatia':** Christopher Cobbe-Webbe [John Brown], *Haverfordwest and Its Story* (Llewellyn Brigstocke, Haverfordwest, 1882), p. 127. The term was originally used of Whitefriars in London, which until the end of the seventeenth century was one of the last places of official sanctuary for criminals and debtors. Alsace, ravaged during the Thirty Years War, was perceived as a place of relative independence, outside clear juridical boundaries, hence a 'debatable ground': Eric Partridge, *Dictionary of Historical Slang* (Routledge and Kegan Paul, 1973).

158 **'reputation for being separatist':** J. Ivor John, *A Haverfordwest Childhood 1901–15* (Greencroft Books, Newport, Dyfed, 1983), p. 29.

159 **toffee like that made locally:** toffee-making and sharing was a Christmas tradition in North Wales; in the south it was usually made by housewives and sold from their houses or from market stalls: John, *A Haverfordwest Childhood*, p. 8, gives a Mrs Merriman making toffee in Prendergast Hill.

159 **'a downcast frightened look':** *Journal of the Workhouse Visiting Society* (1859–65), quoted in Longmate, *The Workhouse*, p. 89.

159 **After nearly ten years:** the Hills went first to Pembroke, where

their first two children were born; Anna Maria was the first of their children to be baptized in Prendergast on 4 March 1855: PA/HPR/71/33 Prendergast Baptism registers.

159 **climbing the greasy pole . . . treacle tart match:** Simon Hancock, *A Photographic History of Victorian and Edwardian Haverfordwest 1860–1914* (Haverfordwest Town Museum, 2010), p. 578.

159 **the Welsh corrupted into Hwlffordd:** Miles, *Portrait of Pembrokeshire*, p. 109.

160 **dubbing her 'kift':** I take these examples from John (ed.), *Honey Harfat*, p. 31.

160 **87 per cent of attenders . . . 9 per cent attended Anglican churches:** Evans, *A History of Wales*, p. 219.

160 **complaining to the borough council:** Hancock, *A Photographic History*, p. 578.

160 **Out went the village choir:** W. D. Phillips, *Old Haverfordwest* (Hammond and Co, Haverfordwest, 1926; a reprint of articles in the *Pembroke County Guardian*, 1924–5), p. 42.

160 **'to raise the intellectual and social life . . .':** Hancock, *A Photographic History*, p. 578.

161 **'Maria Fitzhozier Jackson':** Burials Prendergast 15, PA/HPR/71/36; Lower Prendergast Cemetery Catalogue of Headstones with Epitaphs, PA/HDX/1127/2.

161 **Her half-sister, Maria:** 'Maria Hosier Jackson Hill' proved too much for the registrar at her marriage, who dubbed her 'Maria o'Gho Jackson Hill', thinking perhaps of the number of Irish drifting in and out of Prendergast.

161 **Servants were often migrants:** the 'roving disposition' of servants and the consequent myth of the old retainer are discussed in Light, *Mrs Woolf and the Servants* (Fig Tree, 2007).

162 **'Klondike-like settlements' . . . 'swept into the coalfield' . . . radicalized and anglicized:** Evans, *A History of Wales*, pp. 76, 243.

162 **settled in Pembrokeshire, running the poultry business:** *Kelly's Street Directory of South Wales* for 1920 gives Sarah's cousin A. T. Hill as a poulterer in Prendergast; his widow, Margaret, carried on at least until 1928.

163 **In the 1800s, it is said:** David Hey, *Journeys in Family History* (TNA, 2004), p. 57.

163 **'hybrid communities':** Barry Reay, *Rural Englands: Labouring Lives in the Nineteenth Century* (Palgrave, Basingstoke, 2004), p. 16. Reay opens with a discussion of such places.

163 **'no lovelier piece of lowland scenery . . .':** *The Crown of Wild Olive* (1873), quoted in Nicholas Goddard, 'Environmental Conflict in Victorian Croydon', in P. Barnwell and M. Palmer, *Post Medieval Landscapes* (Windgather Press, Macclesfield, 2007), p. 132. The Wandle was officially declared a sewer, but this process has now been reversed and it was recently listed by the Environment Agency as one of the ten most improved rivers in England and Wales: *Guardian*, 30 August 2011.

165 **'simplified Queen Anne' style:** Sarah Rutherford, *The Victorian Asylum* (Shire, Oxford, 2011), p. 21; the architect was G. T. Hine, consulting architect to the Commissioners in Lunacy and involved in the design of about twenty institutions.

165 **'somewhat lavish':** J. C. Welch and G. Frogley, *A Pictorial History of Netherne* (printed at Netherne Hospital, Surrey, 1993). This invaluable booklet has no page numbers and full references for its source material are not given.

165 **Sarah was admitted to Netherne:** Alphabetical Register: SHC/7338/1/4/2.

165 **Kate Reigate . . . John Russell . . . John Peters:** Admission and Discharge Book, Epsom Union: SHC/BG3/36/27.

165 **the Brookwood Asylum records:** Alphabetical Registers: SHC/3043/5/2/2; 3.

166 **The register of deaths:** SHC/7338/1/6/1.

166 **about 10 per cent of case files:** information from SHC.

166 **More than 80 per cent of admissions . . . an English translation of Emil Kraepelin's theory:** David Healy, *Mania: A Short History of Bipolar Disorder* (Johns Hopkins University Press, Baltimore, 2008), pp. 87, 75.

166 **'puerperal disorders':** Hilary Marland, 'Maternity and Madness: Puerperal Insanity in the Nineteenth Century' (2003), www.nursing.manchester.ac.uk/ukchnm/publications/seminarpapers (accessed 17 October 2013).

167 **the influential Retreat, a small Quaker asylum:** Anne Digby, 'Moral Treatment at the Retreat, 1796–1846', in W. F. Bynum, R. Porter and M. Shepherd (eds.), *The Anatomy of Madness*, Vol. II (Tavistock, 1985).

167 **number of inmates in each was already around 500 . . . 'Custodial realities' . . . 'rehabilitative good intentions':** details here from Peter Barham, *Closing the Asylum: The Mental Patient in Modern Society* (Penguin, Harmondsworth, 1997), pp. 67–8.

167 **or even exhibited in shows and circuses:** Harriet Burbidge, for example, whose 'diminutive appearance has led to her being exhibited as a Talking Monkey about the country', was sent to Leicester Lunatic Asylum in the mid-1860s: Peter Bartlett, 'The Asylum, the Workhouse, and the Voice of the Insane Poor in 19th-Century England', *International Journal of Law and Psychiatry*, 21:4 (1998), 427.

168 **'dustbin for hopeless cases':** Roy Porter, *Madness: A Brief History* (Oxford University Press, Oxford, 2002), p. 119.

168 **'the wrongful confinement of the recoverable . . .':** Peter Barham, *Forgotten Lunatics of the Great War* (Yale University Press, New Haven, 2004), p. 41.

168 **'the vast mass of human hopelessness . . .':** D. H. Clark, *The Story of a Mental Hospital, Fulbourn 1858–1983* (Process Press, 1996), quoted in Barham, *Closing the Asylum*, p. 159. Clark is describing the situation that still prevailed in the 1950s and 1960s when he arrived as a reforming medical superintendent.

168–9 **living-in attendants . . . 'easing of the aloofness' . . . Sidney Nelson Crowther:** Welch and Frogley, *A Pictorial History of Netherne*. Crowther had come to Netherne via the navy and Netley, the naval hospital, and was a member of the Medico-Psychological Association, later the Royal College of Psychiatrists. Surprisingly, he joined up as a corporal, haring about as a motorcycle scout in the Royal Engineers. His great escape from the asylum made him an early casualty. He was killed on 18 October 1914, aged thirty-nine: obituary, *British Medical Journal*, 5 December 1914, 1003.

169 **Netherne took seventy-five military casualties:** Barham, *Forgotten Lunatics*, Appendix, p. 372, and for other details concerning service patients.

169 **had to wait till 1923:** Welch and Frogley, *A Pictorial History of Netherne*.

169 **not meant to be buried:** Barham, *Forgotten Lunatics*, p. 57.

170 **poverty was considered to be one of the chief causes:** Bartlett, 'The Asylum, the Workhouse, and the Voice of the Insane Poor', 428, and his *The Poor Law of Lunacy: The Administration of Pauper Lunatics in Mid-Nineteenth-Century Britain* (Leicester University Press, Leicester, 1999).

170 **the effects of migration on Victorian workers:** one example is V. Bhavsar and D. Bhugra, 'Bethlem's Irish: Migration and Distress in Nineteenth Century London', *History of Psychiatry*, 20:2 (2009), 184–98; and for recent workers, D. Bhugra and S. Gupta (eds.), *Migration and Mental Health* (Cambridge University Press, Cambridge, 2011).

170 **'mystery of mysteries':** Porter, *Madness*, p. 1.

170 **'the most biological conditions':** for one discussion, see S. Nassir Ghaemi, MD, MPH, book review strongly criticizing Healy's *Mania* as 'social science dogma', *American Journal of Psychiatry*, 166:4 (April 2009).

170 **'the destiny of people who are assigned . . .':** Jonathan Miller, quoted in Barham, *Closing the Asylum*, p. 151.

SPADE LABOUR

171 **80 per cent of the agricultural workforce:** Alun Howkins, *The Death of Rural England: A Social History of the Countryside since 1900* (Routledge, 2003), p. 18.

171 **the Edwardian years saw a celebration and idealization:** Reay, *Rural Englands*, pp. 172–203, explores this in detail; for 'Old Surrey', see Light, *Mrs Woolf and the Servants*, p. 102.

171 **a survey of 'the rural labour problem':** B. S. Rowntree and M. Kendall, *How the Labourer Lives* (Thomas Nelson, 1913). The details in this paragraph are from here. The investigators deliberately selected families who were 'of good reputation for sobriety, thrift and honesty', and none with abnormally large families, in order to point up the level of deprivation.

171 **There was as yet no minimum wage:** although the farm workers

unions had argued for this since 1912, the Agricultural Wages Board was not set up until 1917. It was abolished by David Cameron's coalition government in June 2013.

171 **'as a prelude to adventure . . .':** Rowntree and Kendall, *How the Labourer Lives*, p. 46.

172 **the fastest-growing product:** Alun Howkins, *Reshaping Rural England: A Social History 1850–1925* (Routledge, 1992), pp. 142–3.

172 **a very well-connected military family:** Stewart Gibson's father was born in Tasmania then came to London and joined the police. A military family, originally from Scotland, the Gibsons had made money as early 'squatters' on land that is now Bendigo, Victoria, and became wealthy settlers in Van Diemen's Land in the 1830s. His great-aunt, Helen Abigail Gibson, was married to William Champ, former commandant of the Port Arthur convict prison in Van Diemen's Land and later – briefly – the first premier of Tasmania, before being a prominent politician in Victoria and inspector-general of penal establishments. Champ, Stewart's great-uncle, was in charge at Port Arthur when Richard Hill junior, Lottie Smith's great-uncle, arrived off the convict ship. I am grateful to Caroline Gibson in Wollongong, Australia, for this information. What did Lottie tell her husband about her mother, I wonder?

172 **not seen as officer material:** J. Winton, 'Life and Education in a Technically Evolving Navy, 1815–1925', in J. R. Hill (ed.), *Oxford Illustrated History of the Royal Navy* (Oxford University Press, Oxford, 1995), p. 275.

172 **'a distinctly lower order of life':** Peter Kemp, *The British Sailor* (Dent, 1970), p. 198.

173 **the stokers in Portsmouth barracks rioted:** I am grateful here to Michael Kimber, 'Stokers' Riots of 1906 and the Portsmouth Naval Barracks', Portsmouth Polytechnic, Diploma in English Local History, 1990–91, PCRO; also Anthony Carew, *The Lower Deck of the Royal Navy 1900–1939: Invergordon in Perspective* (Manchester University Press, Manchester, 1981).

173 **'the most serious naval riot since the Mutinies . . .':** *HTSC*, 10 November 1906.

173 **blue-tinted glasses:** leading stoker Jack Cotterell, in Max Arthur, *Lost Voices of the Royal Navy* (Hodder, 2005), p. 12.

173 **'to be blowed sky-high at any minute':** James Dunn, stoker petty officer, in Christopher McKee, *Sober Men and True: Sailor Lives in the Royal Navy 1900–1945* (Harvard University Press, Harvard, 2002), p. 117.

173–4 **'coaling' a ship ... 'amenable' ... 'undetected crime':** ibid., pp. 121–6, 45–6.

174 **Both engine rooms were flooded:** TNA/ADM 137/3613, *King Edward VII.*

174 **'incomprehensible, even undesirable':** Henry Baynham, *Men from the Dreadnoughts* (Hutchinson, 1976), p. 251.

174 **In Sebastopol ... in Odessa:** C. A. N. Kershaw, 'Reminiscences', Liddell Collection, University of Leeds: RNMN(REC) 058. Kershaw was a paymaster commander on the *Canterbury*.

174–5 **it was also attributed ... 95 per cent:** Thomas Beaton, 'The Psychoses and the Psycho-neuroses', *Journal of the Royal Naval Medical Service*, 6 (January 1920), 19–65. He compares his findings to those of W. H. R. Rivers's work on the 'war neursoses'.

175 **treated in general medical wards:** 'Acute Mental Cases', Hansard, HC (series 5) vol. 84, cols. 1212–14W (20 July 1916).

175 **headaches and 'terrifying dreams':** Thomas Beaton, 'Neurasthenia in the Navy', *Journal of the Royal Naval Medical Service*, 4 (April 1918), 163. Beaton also recommended massage and a 'full and liberal' diet.

176 **It closed in 1993:** the details here are from Welch and Frogley, *A Pictorial History of Netherne.*

177 **the man who hanged himself out near the cricket pavilion:** private information from George Frogley.

177 **the first use of ammonium chloride:** E. C. Dax, 'Convulsion Therapy by Ammonium Chloride', *British Journal of Psychiatry*, 86 (1940), 66–7.

177 **received prefrontal leucotomies:** E. C. Dax and E. J. Radley Smith, 'The Early Effects of Prefrontal Leucotomy on Disturbed Patients with Mental Illness of Long Duration', *British Journal of Psychiatry*, 89 (1943), 182–8. Two of the patients died of cerebral haemorrhage and only two were discharged (one lapsed); of those remaining, two-thirds showed 'some improvement', were less aggressive, and needed far less

supervision by staff; a third showed no change. 'On the whole the patients showed a distinct diminution in energy.' The authors recommended choosing the 'violent, obstructive, resistive and interfering patient' as the best 'type' to operate upon. Cunningham Dax was medical superintendent of Netherne. Dax was also the pioneer of the use of art in the treatment and diagnosis of psychiatric illness.

177 **The water tower . . . has four duplexes:** I am grateful to George Frogley for this and other information in this paragraph.

178 **'return to nature':** and other details here, *Sutton Guardian*, 15 September 2010, 30 September 2010; *Croydon Guardian*, 19 June 2013.

178 **Sarah's Hosier forebears:** Lench, *The Story of Methodism.*

179 **emigrating . . . to Western Australia:** I am grateful to her grandson Brian Rogers in Australia for this information.

4. Albion Street

Until recently naval historians have largely concentrated on ships and warfare, national policy, or the administration and growth of 'the senior service', their accounts leaning heavily towards the glory days of Nelson and Collingwood; less has been written about the later navy or the sailor towns in general, though this is beginning to change. For the social history of the navy, and reforms to it, I drew in particular on Christopher Lloyd, *The British Seaman 1200–1860: A Social Survey* (Paladin, 1970); Michael Lewis, *The Navy in Transition, 1814–1864: A Social History* (Hodder and Stoughton, 1965); and Eugene Rasor, *Reform in the Royal Navy: A Social History of the Lower Deck, 1850–1880* (Archon, 1976); the essays in J. R. Hill (ed.), *Oxford Illustrated History of the Royal Navy* (Oxford University Press, Oxford, 1995), give an overview. Two very different histories, N. A. M. Rodger, *The Wooden World: An Anatomy of the Georgian Navy* (Fontana, 1988), and Roy and Lesley Adkins, *Jack Tar* (Little, Brown, 2008), provided a way into the eighteenth- and early-nineteenth-century navy; by contrast, Isaac Land's *War, Nationalism and the British Sailor 1750–1850* (Palgrave, Basingstoke, 2009) is part of a new wave of 'coastal history', suggesting other approaches. Also helpful was Margarette Lincoln's *Naval Wives and Mistresses* (National Maritime Museum, 2007), though it deals largely with the officer class.

I have relied heavily throughout upon the work of the local historians who produced the Portsmouth Papers, available in the Portsmouth City Record Office, and the collection edited by J. Webb, S. Quail, P. Haskell and R. Riley, *The Spirit of Portsmouth: A History* (Phillimore, Chichester, 2001).

186 **the Portsmouth Union Workhouse:** Creed Registers: PCRO/BG/W2/5 March 1904 –August 1908.

189 **'An evil spot':** William Gates, *Portsmouth in the Past* (Charpentier, Portsmouth, 1926), p. 91.

SHIP TO SHORE

190 **Towns grow up for all kinds of reasons:** Webb et al. (eds.), *The Spirit of Portsmouth*, Chapter 1.

191 **'the world':** *Portsmouth: Ancient History and Modern*, no author, sold by William Matthews, Broad St, Portesmouth [*sic*] (1800), p. 11.

191 **Bermuda, Barbados and the Leeward Islands:** this, and other details in this paragraph, from James H. Thomas, *The Seaborne Trade of Portsmouth 1650–1800*, PP 40 (PCC, 1984); and *Portsmouth and the East India Company, 1700–1815* (Edwin Mellen Press, 1999).

191 **Andrew Lindgren, a Swedish ore merchant . . . Jewish community of traders:** Philip MacDougall, *Settlers, Visitors and Asylum Seekers: Diversity in Portsmouth since the Late 18th Century*, PP 75 (PCC, 2007), p. 3; Aubrey Weinberg, *Portsmouth Jewry*, PP 41 (PCC, 1985).

191 **'Irish, Welsh, Dutch, Portuguese . . . ':** Robert Hay, writing in 1803, quoted in Adkins, *Jack Tar*, p. 11.

191 **Africans, including liberated or escaped slaves:** by the end of the Napoleonic wars roughly a quarter of the Royal Navy was black; see Ira Dye, 'Physical and Social Profiles of Early American Seafarers, 1812–1815', in C. Howell and R. Twomey (eds.), *Jack Tar in History* (Acadiensis Press, Fredericton, 1991).

191 **the French who served:** Lloyd, *The British Seaman*, using *Victory*'s muster book of 1805, gives a crew of 837 of whom 319 were pressed men. The ship's company came from every county in the British Isles but also included forty-eight foreigners: twenty-three gave their

birthplace as America (including some 'Negroes'); two, Africa; one, France; one, Switzerland; and 'a fair number from Holland, Sweden, Denmark and Prussia', p. 112; Paul Brown, *Maritime Portsmouth* (The History Press, 2005), gives four Frenchmen, p. 46.

191 **sixteen Britishers:** Lloyd, *The British Seaman*, p. 241.

191 **About 28,000:** John Winton, *The Naval Heritage of Portsmouth* (Ensign, Southampton, 1989), p. 70.

192 **'War is the harvest . . .':** *The State of the Poor, or An History of the Labouring Classes in England from the Conquest to the Present Period* (London, 1797), Vol. II, p. 228.

192 **'long grass grows upon the streets':** Dr George Pinckard, visiting in 1795, quoted in Margaret J. Hoad (ed.), *Portsmouth as Others Have Seen It*, Part 2, *1790–1900*, PP 20 (PCC, 1973).

192 **'People seem always in a hurry':** P. Barfoot and J. Wilkes, *The Universal British Directory of Trade, Commerce and Manufacture, 1793–1798*, Vol. 4, p. 194.

192 **'not a loaf, nor a bit of meat . . .':** Pinckard, in Hoad (ed.), *Portsmouth as Others Have Seen It*, p. 8.

192 **few people can trace their ancestors:** in addition, neither Portsmouth's nor Portsea's parish registers survive before 1653–4.

192 **not Hampshire men:** HGS index: CD reference for baptisms 1752–1812; marriages from 1660–1753; 1754–1837; marriage for George and Sarah: PCRO/CHU3/1D/12; Dennis and Mary: PCRO/CHU3/1D/29; deaths of George and Dennis: PCRO/CHU2/1D/3. Sarah Wareham's mother died in 1785 giving birth to her and got a parish burial, as did Sarah's grandparents.

192 **one website deems it an abbreviation of 'Heffernan':** www.surnamedb.com/Surname.

193 **already had six children:** all except Rosina, the eldest, who may have come from Ireland with them, baptized at St John's chapel, built in 1788, near the dockyard, Portsea: PCRO/CHU5/1A/5; it was destroyed by incendiary bombs in 1941. Their marriage at St Mary's Portsea: CHU3/1D/12.

193 **John, eluded me in the records:** there are plenty of men called John Nobes or Nobbs, but it is hard to be sure of antecedents (Nobes is a Norfolk surname). There is no record of his marriage, but he is given

as a labourer at Lydia's birth in 1824 in Warblington Street: PCRO/CHU2/1B/2. He died before 1841.

193 **'ran away to sea with Crusoe' . . . 'crimps':** Lloyd, *The British Seaman*, pp. 93, 135; a critical survey of some memoirs can be found in Land, *War, Nationalism and the British Sailor*.

193 **In 1792 the navy had around 16,500 men . . . peaked at 140,000:** Lloyd, *The British Seaman*, pp. 112–13.

193 **between a half and a third of these:** MacDougall, *Settlers*, pp. 2–3. He cites W. E. H. Lecky's estimate of 30 per cent given in *A History of Ireland in the Eighteenth Century* (Longmans, 1892); Lewis, *The Navy in Transition*, gives up to three-quarters, but Lloyd, *The British Seaman*, p. 179, points out the problems of establishing estimates based on recruiting returns since captains sometimes marked pressed men as 'voluntary' in order to claim the head money; he reckons around 50 per cent were pressed men with rather more in the later years of the war.

194 **The watermen in Portsmouth:** *Naval Chronicle*, 9 (1803), 247, cited in Adkins, *Jack Tar*, p. 48.

194 **Desertion rates:** Nelson reckoned that whenever a large convoy of merchant ships was assembled at Portsmouth, and 'our fleet in port', 'not less than 1000 men' deserted; see Adkins, *Jack Tar*, p. 67.

194 **'virtually meaningless':** Lloyd, *The British Seaman*, p. 10.

195 **finished 'from *old* age' at forty-five:** Nelson in 1803, cited in Adkins, *Jack Tar*, p. 67.

195 **came ashore in his forties:** George is away at sea when the census is taken in 1851; when his eighth child, William, is baptized in 1866, he is 'Rigger, D.Y.'. In 1871 the enumerator noted that he was working for the master attendant in the dockyard but was also 'C.S.' and 'R.N.' – continuous service in the Royal Navy was brought in after 1853.

195 **'largest naval arsenal in the world' . . . 'vast size of the bellows' . . . 'truly grand and awful':** Lake Allen, *The History of Portsmouth* (Hatfield and Co., 1817) pp. 162, 166–7.

196 **very nearly 4,000 by 1814 . . . typical Manchester cotton mill:** John Field, *Portsmouth Dockyard and Its Workers 1815–1875*, PP 64 (PCC, 1994), p. 1.

196 **steam-driven pulley-block machines:** Ray Riley, *The Evolution of*

the Docks and Industrial Buildings in Portsmouth Royal Dockyard, PP 44 (PCC, 1985), p. 13.

196 **The Industrial Revolution . . . took place in the naval dockyards:** Ray Riley, *Portsmouth: Ships, Dockyard and Town* (The History Press, Stroud, 2012), p. 13.

196 **the free labour of the convicts:** Margaret Spence, *Hampshire and Australia, 1783–1791: Crime and Transportation*, Hampshire Papers 2 (Hampshire County Council, 1992), p. 9. Twelve hundred convicts from the hulks helped build the first steam basin in 1843: Riley, *The Evolution of the Docks*, p. 15.

196 **mutinies . . . disputes in the dockyard:** details here from Alastair Geddes, *Portsmouth during the Great French Wars 1770–1800*, PP 9 (PCC, 1970).

196 **even some troops:** Clive Emsley, *British Society and the French Wars 1793–1815* (Macmillan, 1979), p. 42. In 1795 the Gloucestershires joined the riots in Portsmouth. They were mostly militiamen, like new recruits, less well disciplined than the hardened regulars.

196 **supporters of the French Revolution:** Geddes, *Portsmouth during the Great French Wars*, pp. 16–17; N. A. M. Rodger, The *Command of the Ocean: A Naval History of Britain 1649–1815* (Penguin, 2005), p. 442.

196–7 **communicated with the London Corresponding Society . . . Kyd Wake:** E. P. Thompson, *The Making of the English Working Class* (Victor Gollancz, 1965), pp. 147, 175.

197 **'bumboats':** the origin of the word is probably from the Low German (*bum* meaning 'tree' and *boot* meaning 'boat').) In Tobias Smollett's 1748 novel *The Adventures of Roderick Random* a bumboat woman conducts business with sailors imprisoned on board a pressing tender moored near the Tower Wharf on the Thames.

197 **'floating chandler's shops':** Henry Baynham, *From the Lower Decks: The Navy 1700–1840* (Arrow, 1972), p. 93.

197 **the navy created its other in a dual economy:** Ray Riley, *The Industries of Portsmouth in the Nineteenth Century*, PP 25 (PCC, 1976).

197 **sailor might choose a 'wife':** Henry Walsh, cited in Adkins, *Jack Tar*, p. 155.

198 **the 'muster book' of the old Portsmouth poorhouse:** PCRO/PL/6/14.

198 **About a quarter of the inmates:** Elizabeth Edwards, 'The Poor of Portsmouth and their Relief, 1820–1850', Diploma in Local History, Portsmouth Polytechnic, 1977: PCRO.

198 **'proletarianized early':** Miles Ogborn, 'Poverty and Prostitution in Nineteenth-Century Portsmouth', Ph.D. thesis (unpublished), Robinson College, Cambridge, 38: PCRO.

198 **During a performance . . . Anne Holbrook:** Paul Ranger, *The Georgian Playhouses of Hampshire 1730–1830*, Hampshire Papers 10 (Hampshire County Council, 1996), p. 9.

198 **'a sink of vice and abomination':** Winton, *The Naval Heritage of Portsmouth*, p. 53.

199 **'if that was Sodom . . . Gomorrah':** C. R. Markham, *Life of Captain Stephen Martin 1666–1740* (Navy Records Society, 1895), p. 210, quoted in Linda Colley, *The Ordeal of Elizabeth Marsh: A Woman in World History* (HarperCollins, 2007), though she does not note that the comment appears in a letter from Stephen Martin's son, Stephen Martin-Leake, who was in the Navy Pay Office, and who does at least add, 'It is by no means so bad as some would make it, though bad enough.'

199 **paternalist tales of quaint and childish seamen:** in his history of the navy in 1965 Professor Michael Lewis described the common sailor affectionately as 'a simple, uninhibited and rather primitive animal, a unique blend of a noble horse and an obstinate mule': *The Navy in Transition*, p. 173.

199 **'swinish multitude':** Edmund Burke's infamous phrase from his *Reflections on the Revolution in France* (1790), which enraged many radicals and provoked a barrage of retorts. Land discusses the strategic way the Spithead strikers stressed their domestic affections as family men in *War, Nationalism and the British Sailor*, pp. 98–9. Adkins, *Jack Tar*, and Lincoln, *Naval Wives and Mistresses*, give much evidence for the attachments and finer feelings of seamen, should anyone need it.

PORTSMOUTH COMMON

199 **'slums':** it was originally a slang word meaning, among other things, a room of low repute. Dickens writes of taking 'a back-slums kind of

walk' in London in 1841, using the word to signify 'low unfrequented parts of town': H. J. Dyos and M. Wolff, *The Victorian City: Images and Realities* (Routledge and Kegan Paul, 1973), Vol. 1, p. 362.

199 **'to get rid of the men as quickly as possible . . .':** Lloyd, *The British Seaman*, p. 243.

199 **200,000 common soldiers and sailors:** Emsley, *British Society and the French Wars*, p. 173.

199 **The workforce at the dockyard:** Field, *Portsmouth Dockyard*, p. 3.

199 **Widows . . . were equally badly off:** Lincoln, *Naval Wives and Mistresses*, gives an outline of the situation and the class bias of many widows' pensions, which favoured 'gentlewomen', pp. 44–7.

199 **The poorhouse in Portsea:** Henry Slight, *Chronicles of Portsmouth* (Lupton Relfe, 1828), p. 230.

201 **William Cobbett:** *Rural Rides* (1830; Penguin Classics, Harmondsworth, 2001), p. 47. At least one man, James Ings, a Portsea butcher and landlord, was spurred to radical politics after the collapse of the rents on his tenements. He was later hanged at Newgate for his part in the Cato Street conspiracy, which failed to assassinate the Cabinet and the Prime Minister, having offered his skill with a knife to cut off the heads of Lords Castlereagh and Sidmouth: Emsley, *British Society and the French Wars*, p. 170.

201 **Portsea, or Portsmouth Common:** a full account of its development can be found in Webb et al. (eds.), *The Spirit of Portsmouth*, to which I owe details in this paragraph.

201 **'elegant assembly room at the Crown' . . . 'very commodious':** *Portsmouth: Ancient History and Modern*, sold by William Matthews, p. 83.

201 **the children 'indigent':** Allen, *The History of Portsmouth*, p. 172.

201 **'the Wapping of Portsmouth':** Markham, *Life of Captain Stephen Martin*, p. 10.

201 **Some of the smallest terraced properties:** C. W. Chalklin, *The Provincial Towns of Georgian England, a Study of the Building Process, 1740–1820* (Edward Arnold, 1974), p. 218.

202 **'bucolic and prestigious setting' . . . 'unhealthy confines':** B. Stapleton and J. H. Thomas (eds.), *The Portsmouth Region* (Sutton, 1989), p. 75.

202 **Southsea became a polite ghetto:** Ray Riley, *The Houses and Inhabitants of Thomas Ellis Owen's Southsea*, PP 32 (PCC, 1980), pp. 15–16.

203 **The widowed Elizabeth Nobes:** Portsmouth Poorhouse Casual Book, PCRO PL5, gives an Elizabeth Nobes two shillings weekly 'outrelief' from 22 June 1826 to 1834, which is probably her; if so, she had three girls under ten. She is definitely a widow in 1841.

204 **John Treadgold:** J. Cramer, 'Messrs. Treadgold of Portsea Town', Dip. Local History, 1982, PCRO, has these details, though it breaks off in 1875 before the Treadgolds, for all their charitable efforts, become slum landlords.

204 **each bringing in rent of up to £6 . . . three houses in White's Row:** Albion Street Rate Book 1871; District G Rate Book 1891: PCRO. Rate assessors could give properties only a gross estimated rental, but it serves as an indicator of income nonetheless: M. J. Daunton, 'House Ownership from Rate Books', *Urban History Yearbook* (Leicester University Press, Leicester, 1976), pp. 21–7.

204 **Portsea's streets might have been wider:** Chalklin, *The Provincial Towns*, p. 128.

204 **clay dug out for foundations:** Sarah E. Peacock, *Borough Government in Portsmouth, 1835–1974*, PP 23 (PCC, 1975), p. 4.

204–5 **'predictably had twenty-four repairs':** Robert Otter, 'Aspects of Environmental Public Health in Portsmouth 1764–1864', Ph.D. thesis (unpublished), Portsmouth University, 1994, 72, and for other details here concerning the ill-named 'Improvement Commissioners': PCRO.

205 **Andrew Nance:** Peacock, *Borough Government in Portsmouth*, p. 6.

205 **a halfpence for two pails:** Robert Rawlinson, *Report to the General Board of Health on the Sewage, Drainage and Water Supply of Portsmouth* (1850), p. 23, PCRO; a bucket was about two gallons.

205 **'We get water where we can':** Webb et al. (eds.), *The Spirit of Portsmouth*, p. 89.

205 **'the Board's minutes', writes one local historian:** Otter, 'Aspects of Environmental Public Health', 86.

205 **'the People of the Yard':** Field, *Portsmouth Dockyard*, explores this world in depth.

206 **'a fat wad of contracts' . . . 'far-reaching schemes':** Webb et al. (eds.), *The Spirit of Portsmouth*, pp. 132, 73.

206 **'greatest sanitarium':** A. L. Wigan, 'Brighton and Its Three Climates' (1845), quoted in Asa Briggs, *Victorian Cities* (Penguin, Harmondsworth, 1990), p. 31. Brighton grew more rapidly than any other town in Britain between 1821 and 1831.

206 **celebrated in ballads and popular entertainments:** Lloyd, *The British Seaman*, p. 225; Lincoln, *Naval Wives and Mistresses*.

207 **Henry Carter, a local surgeon for Portsea:** Rawlinson, *Report to the General Board of Health*, p. 26. I draw on the report here.

208 **the 'Sanitizers' . . . and the 'Muckabites':** Sue Pike, *Thomas Ellis Owen: Shaper of Portsmouth, 'Father of Southsea'* (Tricorn, Portsmouth, 1988), pp. 93–4,100–101. Owen was twice Lord Mayor and an ardent 'Sanitizer'. As well as building much superior housing in Southsea, he designed the new workhouse and prison.

208 **clean water 'for all' . . . communal standpipes:** Webb et al. (eds.), *The Spirit of Portsmouth*, pp. 88–9.

208 **The poor rate was steep:** 6s 8d, mid-century, according to Owen, who launched a blistering attack on the military: Pike, *Thomas Ellis Owen*, p. 97.

209 **The greatest influx of people into Portsea:** Webb et al. (eds.), *The Spirit of Portsmouth*, p. 15.

209 **Henry Slight, a Portsmouth doctor:** J. Noon, *King Cholera Comes to Portsmouth* (Portsmouth Museum Society, 1982), p. 10.

209 **the council blamed for adding to the town's problems:** Pike, *Thomas Ellis Owen*, p. 97.

209 **Among the 'painted ladies' in Prospect Row:** Ray Riley, *Old Portsmouth: A Garrison Town in the Mid-19th Century*, PP 76 (PCC, 2010), pp. 20–21.

210 **'the perennial inescapable problem of poverty':** Webb et al. (eds.), *The Spirit of Portsmouth*, p. 90.

210 **he wrote increasingly irate annual reports:** Reports of the Medical Officer of Health, 1873–1880, PCRO/CCR/V1/1.

210 **How relieved they must have been:** after working in Essex and studying in Cambridge, Turner was a lecturer in Hygiene at Guy's Hospital, London. Aged fifty he went to South Africa and Cape Colony and worked on rinderpest and at the leper asylum at Pretoria for twelve years, where he also studied the disease; he was also active

in politics there, until he caught leprosy and returned to England. In 1913 he was knighted for his work. He died in Devon, remembered as a reclusive, kindly man with bandaged hands: 'Another Father Damien', PCRO/55A/2.

EBBS AND FLOWS

211 **dockyard might employ up to half of the island's industrial workers:** Stapleton and Thomas (eds.), *The Portsmouth Region*, p. 76.

211 **probably began life as a sailor:** a court record for Portsmouth Borough Sessions, 19 October 1838, has a George Heffren of the right age (twenty) acquitted of stealing from a vessel.

212 **shoemaking and tailoring were the largest single artisan trades:** Thompson, *The Making of the English Working Class*, p. 258.

212 **the grandfather of the novelist George Meredith:** Meredith, who was born over the shop, recast his grandfather Melchizidic as 'the Great Mel' in his romance *Evan Harrington* (1861), transposing Portsmouth to 'Lymport'. The novelist tended to deny his origins, and his hero, Evan, tellingly does not want to be known as a tailor. Thanks to Jonathan Wilde for this reference.

212 **Mass production of shoes in other towns:** Riley, *The Industries of Portsmouth*, pp. 12, 14.

213 **Portsmouth's first Free Ragged School . . . Beneficial School:** details here from J. Stanford and A. T. Patterson, *The Condition of the Children of the Poor in Mid-Victorian Portsmouth*, PP 21 (PCC, 1974).

213 **she is not on the register:** PCRO/536A/18/1-3. But in the next generation, her second cousins Tom, Fred and Ted Murphy, her cousin Arthur's sons living in Hawke Street, are. Their years there in the 1890s would have helped them gain their skilled jobs in the dockyard.

213 **'mudlarking' . . . 'gingerbread':** Stanford and Patterson, *The Condition of the Children*; but Anna Davin, *Growing Up Poor: Home, School, Street in London 1870–1914* (Rivers Oram, 1996), gives a much more child-centred view of the possibilities for play in the street and court.

214 **'Androcles and the Lion' with 'moving effects':** William Tarring, born 1840, in *Memories of Portsea* (Portsmouth WEA, Southsea, 2007), p. 49.

214 **their father . . . was transported for sheep-stealing:** Absalom's trial date was 20 October 1840: England and Wales, Criminal Registers, 1791–1892, HO27/62/237. He sailed on the *Asia*, 12 April 1841, and though there is no sailing record of his return, the chances of there being a second Absalom, of the right age in his home village at the right time in the census for 1861 and 1871, are slim: State Library of Queensland, convict transportation registers, HO11/12/305 (153).

214 **David's record:** TNA/ADM/139/199.

215 **'a sort of inland quarter-deck':** Robert R. Dolling, *Ten Years in a Portsmouth Slum* (Swan Sonnenschein, 1896), p. 10.

215 **'swarms of sea-boats and luggers':** details from 'The Journal of "Miss Bird"' (1855), in Margaret J. Hoad and A. T. Patterson, *Portsmouth and the Crimean War* (1855), PP 19 (PCC, 1973), p. 11.

215 **eighty ships landed nearly 10,000 . . . 'sad little card':** Winton, *The Naval Heritage of Portsmouth*, pp. 97, 107. The Crimean War left so many families in dire straits that the government was persuaded to contribute to the poor rates in the garrison and navy towns – though it assessed the value of its own property.

215 **thirty widows in one Portsea street:** Riley, *Portsmouth: Ships, Dockyard and Town*, p. 41.

215 **Dolling told his congregation:** Charles E. Osborne, *The Life of Father Dolling* (Edward Arnold, 1903), pp. 143–4.

216 **'literally no provision':** Dolling, *Ten Years in a Portsmouth Slum*, p. 111.

216 **forty women made widows:** Webb et al. (eds.), *The Spirit of Portsmouth*, p. 80.

216 **'the shield of empire':** A. Lambert, 'The Shield of Empire, 1815–1895', in Hill (ed.), *Oxford Illustrated History of the Royal Navy*, pp. 161–99.

216 **'with astonishing speed and remarkable zeal':** Robert Blyth, 'Britain, the Royal Navy and the Suppression of Slave Trades in the Nineteenth Century', in D. Hamilton and R. Blyth (eds.), *Representing Slavery* (Lund Humphries and National Maritime Museum, 2007), p. 78.

216 **the navy's highest mortality rate:** Christopher Lloyd, *The Navy and the Slave Trade* (Longmans, 1949), Appendix F.

216 **'war-driven commercialism' . . . 'emporium for British industrial output':** Robert Holland, *Blue-Water Empire: The British in the Mediterranean since 1800* (Penguin, 2013), pp. 15–16.

216 **an ordinary seaman on HMS *Newport*:** TNA/ADM 139/849/4900; William Lavender, Continuous Service Number: 4900B. Other details of seamen here are from the 1861 and 1871 censuses.

217 **up to twenty-four 'cuts on the bare breech':** Rasor, *Reform in the Royal Navy*, p. 55.

217 **some felt it came with too large a serving of humble pie:** Weston used to make a number of charitable appeals for 'Poor Jack' which many men found condescending: Henry Baynham, *Men from the Dreadnoughts* (Hutchinson, 1976), pp. 198–9.

218 **'the rapidity of obsolescence':** Riley, *The Evolution of the Docks*, p. 26.

218 **40 per cent of British adult males:** Chris Cook, *The Routledge Companion to Britain in the Nineteenth Century, 1815–1914* (Routledge, 2005), p. 68.

218–19 **'the idol of late Victorian England . . .' . . . 'more stodgily class-bound':** Lewis, *The Navy in Transition*, pp. 188, 25.

219 **'members of some semi-aristocratic yacht club . . .':** Winton, 'Life and Education in a Technically Evolving Navy', p. 273.

219 **men who had been 'failures elsewhere':** TNA/ADM 116/516, quoted in Kevin Brown, *Poxed and Scurvied: The Story of Sickness and Health at Sea* (Seaforth, Barnsley, 2011), p. 175.

219 **His mother told the inquest:** 'Singular Death of a Waterman', *HTSC*, 30 December 1893.

220 **'dirty old backstreets' . . . the young Beatrix Potter . . . one holidaymaker thought:** Hoad (ed.), *Portsmouth as Others Have Seen It*, pp. 18–22. The holidaymaker was Clement Scott, playwright and theatre critic for the *Daily Telegraph*.

BEACHED UP

Although concerned only with the metropolis, the four volumes of Henry Mayhew's *London Labour and the London Poor* (1861) and the seventeen of Charles Booth's monumental study *Life and Labour of the People in London* (1889–1903) are endlessly suggestive to anyone exploring the lives of the

English working classes in the nineteenth century. My sketch of the 'casual' labour market in Portsea owes much to Gareth Stedman Jones, *Outcast London: A Study in the Relationship between Classes in Victorian Society* (Penguin, Harmondsworth, 1976); for more on women's experience, I turned, in particular, to Sally Alexander, *Becoming a Woman: And Other Essays in 19th and 20th Century Feminist History* (Virago, 1994), and Ellen Ross, *Love and Toil: Motherhood in Outcast London 1870–1918* (Oxford University Press, Oxford, 1993). For an overview of the ways in which social investigators have categorized those at the bottom of society, I found helpful John Welshman, *Underclass: A History of the Excluded 1881–2000* (Hambledon Continuum, 2006); D. Englander and R. O'Day (eds.), *Retrieved Riches: Social Investigation in Britain 1840–1914* (Scolar Press, Aldershot, 1995), assesses the work of Charles Booth in particular and explores the intellectual and methodological history of social investigation. Also extremely useful for family historians is Robert Burlison, *Tracing Your Pauper Ancestors* (Pen and Sword, Barnsley, 2009), which gives a sensitive and accessible account of the history of poor relief. There is no volume which concentrates on the poorer sort in Portsea Island in depth.

221 **Gas came to Portsea Island in 1821:** Webb et al. (eds.), *The Spirit of Portsmouth*, p. 89.

222 **the largest group of Italians:** 1881 census for St George, Portsea. I was alerted to the Italian household by MacDougall, *Settlers*, p. 9, though he gives only nine lodgers.

222 **a warder at Holloway, the women's prison:** Thanks here to Caroline Watkins for sharing information online.

222 **Thomas Hood's immensely popular ballad:** it was published anonymously in the Christmas edition of *Punch* in 1843.

223 **'sweatshop with a staff of one':** Michael Collins, *The Likes of Us: A Biography of the White Working Class* (Granta, 2004), p. 62. His great-grandmother Kate Larter was a trouser-maker in Walworth, London.

223 **'the wages of the majority of people . . .':** Dolling, *Ten Years in a Portsmouth Slum*, p. 20. Ellen Ross reckons that in London about £1 a week for a family of five was a poor but subsistence wage, 'the top of the poverty scale', *Love and Toil*, p. xiv.

224 **right to relief outside one's own parish:** for a detailed discussion,

K. D. M. Snell, *Parish and Belonging: Community, Identity and Welfare in England and Wales, 1700–1950* (Cambridge University Press, Cambridge, 2006).

224 **'degrees of slumminess':** Dyos and Wolff, *The Victorian City*, Vol. 1, p. 363.

225 **'decimated by these developments':** Stapleton and Thomas (eds.), *The Portsmouth Region*, p. 76.

225 **800 or so convicts as labourers:** Riley, *The Evolution of the Docks*, p. 23, and for other details here.

225 **Eight hundred and fifty people:** *HTSC*, 9 March 1889; first 350, then 500 followed in the second batch.

225 **the Irish colony experiment:** I learnt of this from Peter Mulvany's website, www.mariner.ie/history/articles/emigration/the-dresden-affair.

226 **A policeman was no better paid:** for details, Haia Shpayer-Makov, *The Making of a Policeman: A Social History of a Labour Force in Metropolitan London, 1829–1914* (Ashgate, Aldershot, 2002); a survey of recruiting in 1874 showed that about a third of the Metropolitan Police came from land jobs and the majority from outside London.

226 **'municipal indifference':** Webb et al. (eds.), *The Spirit of Portsmouth*, pp. 95, 163–4.

226 **'declined to bear the burden':** Peacock, *Borough Government in Portsmouth*, p. 14.

227 **the attitude of the skilled artisans:** Field, *Portsmouth Dockyard*, p. 19.

227 **'the enormous growth of civic pride':** Peacock, *Borough Government in Portsmouth*, p. 15.

227 **'Portsmouth,' wrote William Tarring:** 'An Octogenarian Reverie', PCRO.

227 **'notorious for its meagre service' . . . 'a derisory amount':** Webb et al. (eds.), *The Spirit of Portsmouth*, pp. 166–7. In 1933 it spent a halfpenny a head on museums for its citizens, compared to Leicester's eight pence, Nottingham's seven pence and Plymouth's four pence, all towns of similar size.

228 **leaving a legacy of £90:** England and Wales, National Probate Calendar (Index of Wills and Administrations, 1861–1941), 22 August 1888.

228 **he seems to have squandered it:** both William and Tom disappear

from the 1891 census, probably on merchant ships, or on a spree, and then live together in Butcher Street in 1901; William dies in 1905. The third Murphy son, John, who sets up shop in Chilcomb, a village in Hampshire, also disappears from the records after 1891, with his wife and six children. I assume they emigrated but I could not find where.

228 **with a typically fluid history:** the gist of which is that his father, John Miller senior, had married his mother's sister after she died, so John junior grew up with his aunt, Antoinette Bidgood, then Miller (was she named in the 1790s for the doomed Queen of France?). After John senior's death, John junior lived with Antoinette and her new husband, James Hamilton, an Irishman and a Chelsea Pensioner.

228 **the rent . . . of nearly twelve shillings a month:** PCRO/District G, 1891 Rate Book.

228 **Flora and her four young children went to the workhouse:** PCRO/BGW2/3: Creed Register 1895–1900; BGW2/2 for Edwin Heffren, who was also there in 1893.

228 **George Heffren, died and left £205:** England and Wales, National Probate Calendar (Index of Wills and Administrations, 1861–1941), 29 August 1894.

229 **she bequeathed the remaining sum:** ibid., 25 March 1895.

229 **'bearers of the most pathetic insignia . . .':** Stedman Jones, *Outcast London*, p. 77.

229 **Henry Mayhew called the dockyard labourers:** Mayhew, *London Labour and the London Poor*, Vol. 3, pp. 300–301.

229 **Edwin admitted himself to the Portsea Union for four nights:** PCRO/BG/W2/4. A John Miller of the right age is also admitted for the day, probably Flora's son.

229 **a common strategy when relief would only be given:** Peter Wood, *Poverty and the Workhouse in Victorian Britain* (Alan Sutton, 1991), p. 146.

230 **as shipbuilding declines on the Thames:** Stedman Jones, *Outcast London*, p. 57.

232 **part 'housewives saviour':** Melanie Tebbutt, *Making Ends Meet: Pawnbroking and Working-Class Credit* (Methuen, 1984), is the best way into this subject.

232 **Edwin Heffren died a casual's death:** 'Accident at North Shields', *Shields Daily News*, Thursday, 13 August 1903; 'The Fatal Fall at North Shields', *Shields Daily News*, 14 August 1903. His correct age is given, and that he was 'belonging to Portsmouth'.

232 **He was buried locally:** Register for Burials for Tynemouth, no. 2273, 15 August 1903.

232 **Lily . . . Ted . . . Flora, spent time in the workhouse:** PCRO/BG/W2/5-6.

233 **'Call me poor?' . . . 'I have got a half a loaf . . .':** Andrew Mearns, *The Bitter Cry of Outcast London* (James Clarke and Co, 1883), quoted in Collins, *The Likes of Us*, p. 37.

234 **patients lying on the floor . . . the 'matron' of the hospital:** PCRO/BGM1/4: Letter from Medical Officer, Dr Rapere, 18 October 1861; Census for Portsea Island Union Workhouse 1861.

234 **those over sixty made up nearly half of all the persons relieved:** M. A. Crowther, 'The Later Years of the Workhouse 1890–1929', in P. Thane (ed.), *The Origins of British Social Policy* (Croom Helm, 1978), p. 45.

234 **'what had for years been a feared . . .':** Ruth Richardson, *Death, Dissection and the Destitute* (Phoenix Press, 2001), p. 15. Richardson estimates that in the first century after the Act less than *half a per cent* of bodies for dissection came from anywhere other than institutions which housed the poor (p. 271).

234 **the knife-happy Dr Thomas Oliver in the Portsea Union:** PCRO/BGM1/13: 30 September 1874. This scandal has escaped the notice of local historians, as far as I can tell.

235 **the Local Government Board did 'not think . . .':** PCRO/BGM1/14: 11 November 1874; 17 February 1875.

235 **'Rattle his bones over the stones':** Thomas Noel's poem 'The Pauper's Drive' (1841) is the source of this refrain.

235 **'breastplates' on coffins . . . 'parents be allowed . . .' . . . 'a few easy chairs' . . . flowers . . . 'for absconding . . .':** PCRO/BGM1/12: 30 April 1873; BGM1/14: 10 June 1874; BGM1/13: 9 July 1873; BGM1/12: 28 May 1873.

235 **inmates who had special duties as nurses:** 'Paupers' Wages', *Portsmouth Evening News*, 19 September 1895.

236 **some boys were forcibly emigrated:** PCRO/BG/AY10/1.

236 **The rules were strict:** Workhouse School Regulations, 14 February 1906, PCRO/BG/W7/1,

236 **Rowntree's study of poverty in the 1900s:** B. S. Rowntree, *Poverty: A Study of Town Life* (Macmillan, 1901).

237 **'a deadweight' . . . 'useless and costly inefficients':** Royal Commission on Poor Laws and Relief of Distress, *Majority Report*, Part IX, Section XXXVIII (1909), pp. 643–4.

237 **'the unemployable' . . . 'in bulk, almost homogenous . . .':** Royal Commission on Poor Laws and Relief of Distress, *Minority Report* (1909), quoted in Welshman, *Underclass*, p. 23.

237 **the 'Darwinesque' language of Charles Booth:** Jose Harris, in England and O'Day (eds.), *Retrieved Riches*, argues that Booth used such language 'very loosely and metaphorically', p. 79.

237 **the unemployed 'a selection of the unfit':** Charles Booth, *Life and Labour of the People in London: First Series: Poverty. 1. East, Central and South London* (Macmillan,1904), p. 150.

237 **'to work when they like . . .' . . . 'They cannot stand the regularity . . .':** Booth, quoted in Wood, *Poverty and the Workhouse*, p. 36.

237 **to dispatch them to 'labour farms' or penal colonies:** Stedman Jones, *Outcast London*, gives many examples of such proposals.

SALVAGE

238 **'The urban past has never had a very secure future':** Dyos and Wolff, *The Victorian City*, Vol. 2, p. 893.

238 **as the old thoroughfares hardened into streets:** for a guide to the ghostly missing streets and some of its pubs, see the Portsmouth WEA's *Memories of Portsea*.

238 **the graphic Deadman's Lane was by 1850:** Rosemary Phillips, 'Burial Administration in Portsmouth and Southsea, 1820–1900', 28, PCRO/460A/2.

240 **they set the houses alight to get rid of the bugs:** PCC, *A History of Council Housing in Portsmouth*, p. 14 (accessed May 2013 via www.portsmouth.gov.uk).

240 **Only seven of the thirty-two occupied houses:** A. Mearns Fraser,

Report of the Medical Officer of Health (1908), p. 52, PCRO/CCR/V1/6.

240 **Where 200 dwellings had stood:** S. Quail and J. Stedman, *Images of Portsmouth* (Fisher Nautical, Sussex, 1993), p. 177.

240 **'a cheaper scheme' . . . 'very profitable investments' . . . 'to control the class of tenants in the new houses':** Report of the Medical Officer of Health (1912), p. 81; (1910), p. 79: PCRO/CCR/V1/6.

240 **'Of course, the former dwellers did not inhabit . . .':** F. W. Rumsby, Kent Street Baptist Church, *Souvenir History of the Church* (1948): AL/CH/POR/KEN.

240 **Nearly 1,000 dwellings . . . 'vigorous programme of slum clearance':** Webb et al. (eds.), *The Spirit of Portsmouth*, pp. 129, 171.

241 **'A considerable overspill population . . .':** K. Haines and C. Shilton, *Hard Times, Good Times: Tales of Portsea People* (Milestone, Horndean, 1987), p. 7.

241 **Mrs Jones, an elderly lady living alone:** all the details here are from the Register of Closing Orders, PCRO/DV9B/1.

242 **'half your home . . .' . . . 'you could always turn to somebody . . .' . . . 'Portsea was lovely . . .':** Gwenda Board, Winifred Osborne, May Harris, interviewed in Haines and Shilton, *Hard Times, Good Times*, pp. 47, 45, 78.

Postscript

250 **Kingston Cemetery buries about 400:** www.portsmouth.gov.uk/living (accessed 7 February 2014).

250 **'funeral poverty' is on the rise:** *Guardian*, 24 April 2013.

251 **nothing about a graveyard can be taken at face value:** for an introduction to the study of death and remembrance in the past, I found very helpful Sarah Tarlow, *Bereavement and Commemoration: An Archaeology of Mortality* (Blackwell, Oxford, 1999).

252 **'a fair field full of folk':** William Langland, *The Vision of Piers Plowman*, a late-fourteenth-century poem, 'Prologue', l.17.

Acknowledgements

I am delighted to be able to acknowledge the help of all those across the country who answered enquiries and put me on the right track. I am grateful to the staff at the Birmingham Central Library, at the Museum for English Rural Life at Reading, and at the history centres and record offices of Berkshire, Dorset, Hampshire, Warwickshire and Worcestershire; to Marie Lewis at the Pembrokeshire Archives; Sue South at the National Archives, Kew; Matthew Piggott at the Surrey History Centre; Robert Pearson at the Wiltshire and Swindon Archives; and to Vicky Thorpe at the Gloucester Record Office. A special thanks to the registrars at the Portsmouth Register Office, who bore patiently and courteously with my endless requests and never once failed to find the relevant information. I am indebted to the staff at the Portsmouth City Record Office, especially to John Stedman, editor of the Portsmouth Papers, and to Diana Gregg, 'the human oracle', now sadly – for family historians – retired. I would also like to thank Revd Emma Walsh and Emily Burgoyne at the Angus Library, Regent's College, Oxford; Jane Wickenden at the Institute for Naval Medicine in Gosport; Sally Webb at the Imperial War Museum; Dean Philips at Yardley Wood Library, Birmingham; Eileen Dwane at the State Library of Queensland; Leanne J. Franklin at the State Library of Tasmania; and at the North Tyneside Local Studies Centre, Kevin Dresser, who guided me round the 'Jungle' on Tyneside.

When I began this book in 2008, I was lucky enough to be given a tour of Netherne by George Frogley, who was once the manager of the hospital's print department, and he made it come alive for me. Others were also splendidly free with their time and local knowledge: Simon Hancock, curator of the Haverfordwest's Town Museum; Robert Nisbet; John Chandler; Sue Robinson; Peter Haylor at the Holy Cross Community Centre, Warstock; Christine Pavey of the Hampshire Genealogical Society; and Peter Watkins. Professor Gordon Handcock at Memorial University, Newfoundland, kindly shared much salient information and his own research with me. I would also like to thank Ian Wheeler, Assistant Bereavement Officer at Brandwood End Cemetery; Barrie Simpson of the Friends of Brandwood End Cemetery, Birmingham; Gerry O'Brien, Cemetery Officer of Kingston Cemetery, Portsmouth; David Cufley of the British Brick Society; Viv Head, Chairman of the British Transport Police History Group; Peter Barham; Mark Harrison at the Wellcome Unit for the History of Medicine, Oxford; John Fitzgerald of the Family History Society of Newfoundland and Labrador; Stephen Spencer at the Salvation Army International Heritage Centre; Simon Harmer and Ted Parker of the Salvation Army in Portsmouth; and Hazel Vitler for information on her grandfather, Benjamin Light: my grandfather's cousin. Janet Lovesey's Internet site, exploring Frances Road in 'the Cotteridge', was a boon. Simon Fowler undertook some final research into naval records, the Liddell Collection and the archives of the Poor Law with great efficiency. My brother, Chris Light, stepped in at the eleventh hour to take the photograph of Penhale Road Infant School. I am grateful to everyone.

During a spell lecturing at Newcastle University, I was the fortunate recipient of a research travel grant, which made it possible for me to visit archives around the country. I would like to thank all my colleagues in the School of English, especially Professor Linda Anderson and Professor Jenny Richards, for their support. Special events at Manchester University, at the École des Hautes Études in Paris and at UCL's History Department Neale colloquium advanced the work: my thanks to Professor Jackie Stacey, Professor Laura Lee Downs and Professor Catherine Hall for the invitations and to the attendees. The offer of a visiting fellowship at the Australian National University at Canberra came as a great fillip: thanks to Dr Kynan Gentry and Professor Melanie Nolan. I am also grateful to Professor Laura Marcus and the English Faculty of Oxford University for giving me access to the resources of the university as a visiting member.

Although it has greatly benefited from contact with academic communities, *Common People* was written outside the university and grew as much from life and politics as from research. I particularly want to thank those friends and family who kept me going during the summer and autumn of 2012 when I was being treated for cancer: Lenore and Yasha Abramsky, Sally Alexander, Jane Caplan, Erica Carter, Norma Clarke and Barbara Taylor, Basil Comely, Simon and Cathy Cooke, Alison and Adam Elgar, Mary Grover, Catherine Hall, Marybeth Hamilton, Ken Jones, Cora Kaplan, Andrew Macdonald and Pete Swaab, Dick Newman, Sandra Pidoux, Michael Rossington, Nick Stargardt, Helen Taylor. Without their stimulating talk, their curiosity and care, this book would have taken far longer than it did. Working briefly with new colleagues for the BBC, especially Annabel Hobley, Emma Hindley and Hugo Macgregor, was also a boost. Thanks too to Kate Binnie, yoga teacher extraordinaire. And especially to Kasia Boddy, for being generous and listening, and always willing to go shopping.

David Godwin has been a great ally and lifter of spirits throughout. My editor, Juliet Annan, took to the idea of *Common People* from the first and was warmly encouraging when both it and I languished. It has been a great pleasure working with her and with the team at Fig Tree/Penguin, who made the process of production speedy, smooth and congenial; I am especially grateful to Sophie Missing for her help with the images, to Jeff Edwards for working on the family trees and maps, and to Caroline Pretty for her scrupulous copy-editing. Early versions of parts of this book appeared in the *London Review of Books*, *New Formations*, the *Sarum Chronicle* and the *Revue D'Histoire du XIXe Siècle*. I am grateful to the editors of those journals.

Family history is always a family affair, and I owe thanks to my cousin Marilyn Betts, who began the research into the Smiths, Hosiers and Sarah Hill. My mother, Barbara Light, was the first to unearth her own mother's history and to begin looking for the Lights. This book is dedicated to her and to the memory of my father.

In the closing stages of the book, Sally Alexander read the chapter on Netherne, and Norma Clarke and Cora Kaplan read the complete manuscript: their thoughtful comments spurred me on to the finishing line and I owe them warm thanks. My friend and neighbour Lyndal Roper discussed the book with me as it evolved, closely read various drafts and saw me through the ups and downs of the writing life, or just of life in general. I did not always take her advice, but I know how much better the book is for her contribution. Fran Bennett knows far more about poverty in Britain than I do and I learnt much from our conversations. She found the Dowdeswell graves on a wet afternoon in Alcester and spent many hours at my side on that strange planet known as hospital; a friend in need indeed. My deepest debt is to my husband, John O'Halloran. I won't begin to thank him, because I cannot thank him enough. Only, I mean to say, 'What larks, eh, what larks!'

Alison Light, Oxford, June 2014

Index

Page numbers in *italic* indicate illustrations. These can also be found listed in full after the Contents.

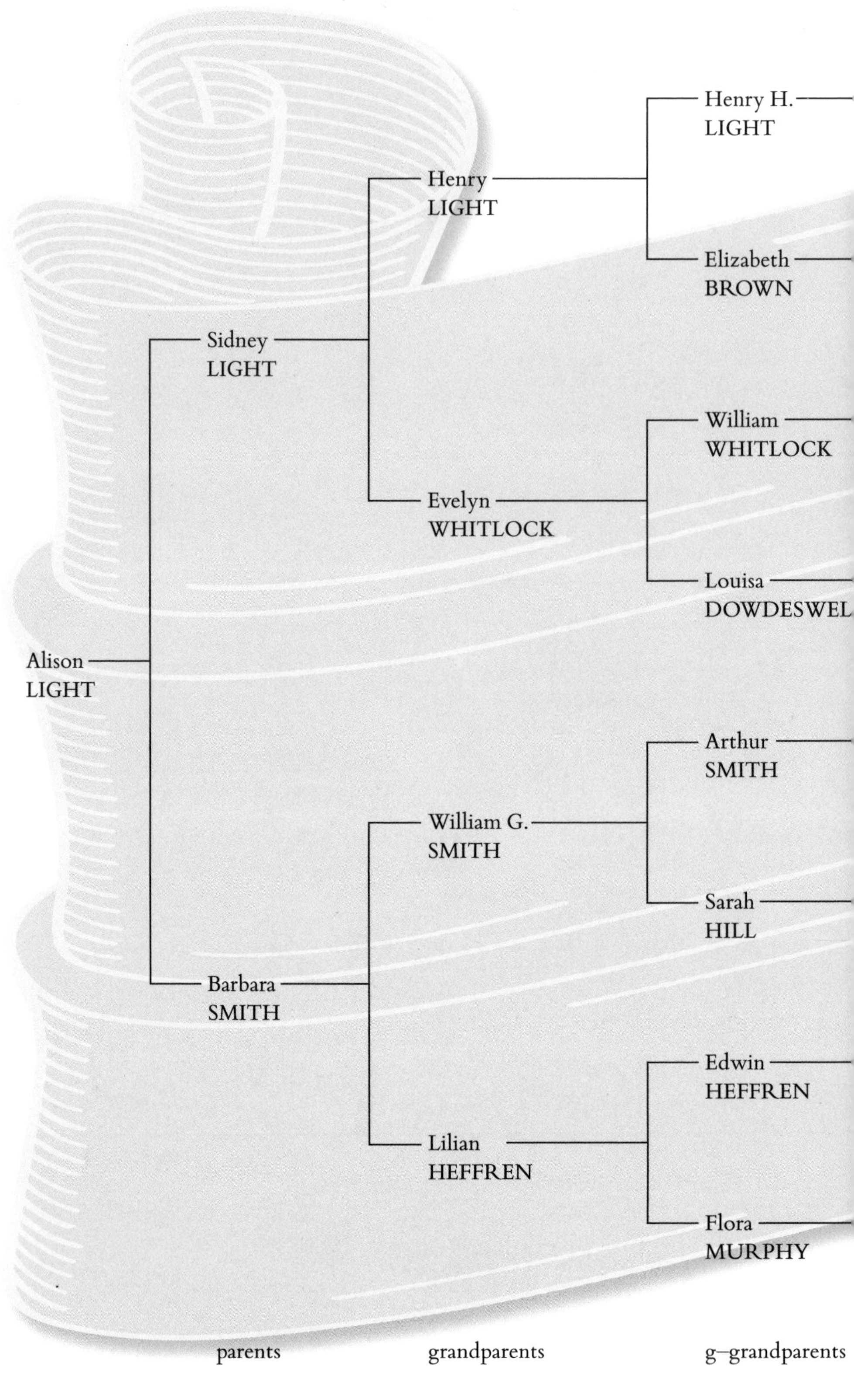
Henry H.
LIGHT
Henry
LIGHT
Elizabeth
BROWN
Sidney
LIGHT
William
WHITLOCK
Evelyn
WHITLOCK
Louisa
DOWDESWEL
Alison
LIGHT
Arthur
SMITH
William G.
SMITH
Sarah
HILL
Barbara
SMITH
Edwin
HEFFREN
Lilian
HEFFREN
Flora
MURPHY
parents
grandparents
g–grandparents